Policy formation in the
European Communities

Policy formation in the European Communities

A bibliographical guide to Community documentation
1958–1978

Michael Hopkins

Mansell

ISBN 0 7201 1597 3

Mansell Publishing, 3 Bloomsbury Place, London WC1A 2QA

Distributed in the United States and Canada by The H. W. Wilson
Company, 950 University Avenue, Bronx New York 10452

First published 1981
© Michael Hopkins, 1981

British Library Cataloguing in Publication Data

Hopkins, Michael, b. 1945
    Policy formation in the European Communities.
    1. European Economic Community countries—Bibliography
    I. Title
    016.382'9142   Z7165.E8

    ISBN 0-7201-1597-3

Typeset by Computacomp (UK) Ltd,
Fort William, Scotland.
Printed and bound in Great Britain

For Eleri, too often left holding the baby

Contents

Introduction

Policy-making in the European Communities is based on an elaborate network of relationships between Community institutions, national governments and other interest groups. In addition to constant interaction between Community institutions whose respective roles are clearly defined in the founding Treaties, this process must involve both formal and informal discussions with national governments and other parties if solutions to policy issues considered within the Community framework are to attract general support. Shared responsibility between Community institutions and extensive consultation with external authorities are characteristics which inevitably lead to the generation of large numbers of documents for circulation within and between institutions and for discussion with national officials. However, despite the fact that such documents constitute an unrivalled source of raw material for those who wish to undertake research into European integration and are equally valuable for the businessman, civil servant or local government officer whose activities are directly affected by Community rules and regulations, the value of this immense corpus of material to outside users is still more potential than real. Problems concerning the use of the documentation are various but stem in the main from the fact that these are essentially working documents designed for internal use. Inadequate publicity and almost non-existent levels of bibliographical control mean that documents receive only a fraction of their potential use outside the organization simply because their existence is not known; the sheer volume of documentation available serves only to multiply difficulties and to discourage use.

It is the purpose of this bibliographical guide to contribute to the better appreciation and more effective exploitation of this rich collection of primary source material by drawing attention to key policy documents prepared by and for the Commission of the European Communities during the period 1958 to 1978. Attention is focused on the Commission in view of its role as the chief policy-making body in the Community institutional structure. The fact that in this structure the power of decision rests with the Council of the European Communities means that whenever the Commission takes a policy initiative it invariably generates a document for transmission to, and ultimate decision by, the Council. Consequently, the documents which form the subject of this book constitute an accurate historical profile of the way in which policy has evolved in each Community sector, highlighting the blueprints which have heralded major leaps forward, the less ambitious but nevertheless important initiatives which have assured steady if slow progress in many fields, and the proposals which have been more significant for the sentiments they express than for their practical impact. Although first and foremost a guide to Commission documents, the opportunity is also taken to illustrate the interdependence of Community institutions in the policy-making process by including reference within the body of individual entries to documentation generated by other Community institutions in response to Commission initiatives, notably the European Parliament and the Economic and Social Committee. Moreover, mindful of the powerful position enjoyed by the Council and of the fact that policy-making cannot easily be separated from law-making in the Community context, reference is also made to the Council response to Commission initiatives and in particular to important pieces of subsequent Community legislation.

Scope

Such is the volume of documentation produced by the Commission during the period from 1958 to 1978, much of it of a technical or ephemeral nature, that a bibliographical guide of this kind must of necessity be highly selective if it is to give due prominence to documents of particular significance. Consequently, a number of guidelines have been established to determine practical parameters for the selection of main entries.

(a) Entries in this guide are reserved primarily for documents rather than publications. Publications are secondary sources of information intended as instruments for making Community activities better known in the outside world. Documents, on the other hand, are primary sources which constitute the authentic record of the work of Community institutions. They are the medium through which the Commission conducts its business; they form the usual mode of communication between officials, Directorates-General and the Commission and other Community institutions. It is common practice for the Commission to give particularly important documents a wider audience by means of publication, usually in the form of Supplements to the *Bulletin of the European Communities* or separate monographs. In such cases, primary reference is made to the original document and the published version is cited in the body of the entry. Very occasionally primary reference is made to the published version when the original document has not been located. For ease of identification, the catalogue numbers allocated to Community publications by the Office for Official Publications of the European Communities and International Standard Book Numbers (ISBNs) where present, are given.

(b) The documents generated by the Commission can be divided into two main categories. Firstly, there are those which have an internal life; their purpose is to facilitate the work of the organization, to act as channels of communication between separate administrative units and generally to ensure that an organization of more than 8000 officials drawn from nine European countries working in six official languages acts as a cohesive and efficient organization. Secondly, there are those documents which have a formal existence outside the Commission in the sense that they are submitted as statements of official Commission policy to other Community institutions. Consequent upon the provisions made in the founding Treaties for shared responsibility between Community institutions for making Community law, the majority of such documents are directed to the Council of the European Communities, the institution which enjoys decision-making powers in this process. Documents falling into the former category are addressed to specific internal audiences, are not generally released for public consumption and are not represented in this guide. Documents in the latter category represent the culmination of the work of the Commission staff and departments; they contain the official Commission viewpoint on matters concerning the functioning of the European Communities; they are generally publicly available and constitute the body of documentation from which entries for this guide are selected.

(c)   Attention is concentrated on those documents submitted to the Council in which the Commission seeks to define policy rather than to make Community law. Any attempt to include the many thousands of specific proposals for legislation upon which the Council has been asked to decide since 1958 would have necessitated a multi-volume publication far exceeding the scope of the present work. This is illustrated by the fact that in the three years from 1976 to 1978 alone, the Commission laid before the Council 649, 747 and 625 drafts and proposals for legislation respectively. Rather, this book is concerned with those broad statements of policy submitted to the Council in the form of communications, reports and memoranda. Even here the large number of documents submitted during the period covered necessitates a high level of selection; in the last three years of the period covered, for instance, the Commission submitted to the Council 174, 197 and 177 communications, memoranda and reports. The documents which are the subject of this guide are those in which overall policy objectives are set, principles established and guidelines for legislative action proposed. They constitute the blueprints upon which Community policy is founded and upon which legislative action programmes are based. Separate chapters for each main policy sector identify the documents which have become important landmarks in the evolution of policy, Commission initiatives whose purpose is further to refine policy, and other documents in which the Commission takes stock of progress in the application of already established policy.

(d)   In view of their positive contribution to the overall definition of policy, this guide also contains entries for reports and studies prepared at the invitation of the Commission by groups of independent experts. During the formative stage of policy development, particularly when the Commission is moving into a new field of interest, it often calls upon such expertise for an objective assessment of the present position in that policy area, or for independent advice on the complexion Community policy should take. At a later stage, independent experts are often used to conduct in-depth surveys and analyses of particular aspects of policy in anticipation of Community action on the matter. Such reports and studies circulate within the Commission in document form. However, important contributions of potential general interest are often published by the Commission, either as separate monographs, usually in one of the *Studies* series, or as Supplements to the *Bulletin of the European Communities*. Wherever possible, primary reference is made to original documents with secondary reference in the body of the entry to published versions. In some cases, reference is made direct to the published version.

(e)   Practical considerations have played a part in determining the scope of this guide. No complete collection of Commission documents exists outside Brussels, where the historic set of documents preserved in the Secretariat-General is closely guarded and the Central Archives not yet open to the general public. Neither is there a compensatory source of bibliographical information on what constitutes a complete collection. There are, to the author's knowledge, no complete numerical lists or comprehensive catalogues which provide an authoritative public record of documents issued during the period covered. This book is based on the substantial, but partial, collection housed in the London Office of the Commission, supplemented by the resources of Directorate-General X (Information) in Brussels and several European Documentation Centres. It represents a personal selection from fugitive documents tracked down in collections in London and Brussels. Despite the lack of a checklist of documents against which to verify its adequacy, it is hoped that the selection of documents listed is reasonably representative of policy formation in the various Community sectors and that it will prove to be a useful initial guide to previously uncharted waters.

Arrangement

By way of introduction, Chapter 1 consists of a documentary description of policy formation in the European Communities and of the consultative and legislative process through which the documents listed in this book must pass before they achieve the status of official Community policy. Chapter 2 is concerned with general developments in the Communities during the 21 years covered by this guide; the opportunity is taken in the introduction to the chapter to mention the general publications programme pursued by the European Communities. Subsequent chapters correspond to the main policy sectors over which the Communities have competence. Each chapter begins with a descriptive essay, which sets out the general policy context in which the documents cited exist. Reference is made to the main Community publications, particularly serial and statistical, from which useful supplementary information may be obtained. It should be noted however that the book makes no reference to non-Community publications. The main body of each chapter consists of a bibliographical record of the evolution of policy in one broad sector, highlighting policy statements, discussion documents and other policy initiatives made by the Commission of the European Communities. Documents are listed in strict chronological order; items for which no precise date of issue is available, including publications, appear at the beginning of the appropriate annual sequence. Entries for series of annual reports are listed according to the date of the first report cited.

Style of entry

Individual entries are composed of up to three separate elements:

(a) A bibliographic description of the document, consisting of its title, document number, date of issue and pagination. Items issued before 1973, when English became an official language of the European Communities, are referred to in their French language form. In most cases, document numbers consist of the prefix COM (Commission) or SEC (Secretariat-General), followed by a date code, running number and the word 'final' to signify the document's finalized version, for example, COM(78)546 final and SEC(78)648 final. However, reports and studies prepared by independent experts often bear Directorate-General rather than Commission document numbers, and consist of the Directorate-General number, running number and date code, for example, doc X/654/78, being the 654th document issued by Directorate-General X (Information) during 1978. In a small number of instances where personal consultation was not possible, date of issue and/or pagination is omitted. Where primary citation is to a publication, the publisher, date of publication, pagination and European Communities catalogue number are given.

(b) Bibliographic references to European Parliament and Economic and Social Committee deliberations on the original Commission documents, the intention of which is to facilitate study of the passage of Commission documents through the legislative process defined in the founding Treaties. Reference is made to the *European Parliament working documents* in which specialized parliamentary committees report their views on Commission proposals to the Parliament as a whole. Information provided consists of the document number, made up of a running number and date code referring to the first of the two calendar years which a parliamentary session normally spans, the date of issue, name of the rapporteur responsible for the report's compilation and its pagination. Reference is also made to the subsequent debate in plenary session as recorded in the pages of the *Debates of the European Parliament*, and to the Resolution, embodying the opinion of the European Parliament, adopted at the end of the debate and published in the *Official journal of the European Communities*. Opinions expressed by the Economic and Social Committee, also published in the *Official journal of the European Communities*, are also cited. This element is not always present in individual entries because some documents are never submitted to the European Parliament and Economic and Social Committee in a formal way, and because it is not the aim of this guide to be a comprehensive guide to the documents of those two consultative institutions.

(c) A descriptive commentary, the purpose of which is twofold. Firstly, it highlights the main topics with which the document is concerned and describes its general arrangement. The intention is not to provide a detailed synopsis of views expressed or arguments advanced; rather, it is to provide sufficient information on scope and contents for judgements to be made as to the virtue of consulting the document itself. Secondly, the commentary places the document in its policy context. Reference is made to the circumstances surrounding its preparation, its general significance and consequences for policy development. Taken as a whole, the commentaries contained in any one chapter constitute an almost continuous narrative, illustrative of the gradual unfolding of policy over a 21 year period. In this connection, reference is regularly made to other sources of information, both published and documentary. Commission documents which fall outside the scope of this guide, but which are relevant to discussion of policy and its implementation are often referred to (by document number alone) in the descriptive commentaries. Similarly, discussion of policy documents and their impact cannot be divorced from consideration of Community legislation. Consequently, important legislative milestones in the evolution of policy, particularly those which are the direct result of legislative proposals appended to policy documents or the practical expression of sentiments advanced in them, are also mentioned. Although this book does not represent a systematic guide to the Regulations, Directives and Decisions of the European Communities, each chapter does contain reference to many major pieces of legislation adopted in that particular policy field. Particular attention is paid to the Resolutions often adopted by the Council after consideration of Commission policy statements, in which the Council establishes broad lines of policy and expresses its political will to make progress, usually on the basis of concrete proposals the Commission is invited to submit in due course. Where appropriate, other Community publications are also mentioned.

Availability

Finally, it should be said that the documents listed in this guide are publicly available, as witnessed by the fact that all but a very few have been personally examined by the author. As mentioned, the most complete but still largely inaccessible collections reside in Brussels. Outside the headquarters of the Commission substantial collections, normally freely available to interested external users, have been accumulated in the Information Offices maintained by the Commission in member countries and in other countries such as the United States of America. The London Office, for instance, has an extensive and well-maintained collection of documents and a small library where they may be consulted along with other Community publications. The documents and publications that form the subject of this guide are also sent on a regular basis to nearly 200 European Documentation Centres established in institutions of higher education all over the world, 45 of which are located in the United Kingdom, in an attempt to stimulate academic research into European integration. Similar collections of documents and publications are distributed to 100 or so Depository Libraries, four of which are in the United Kingdom, established with a view to improving general public access to Community information. Copies of individual documents are often available for retention from the Information Offices situated in member and other countries and may also be obtained direct from Brussels.

Michael Hopkins
The Library
Loughborough University of Technology
Leicestershire
June 1980

Acknowledgements

A book of this kind could not have been completed without the assistance and forebearance of a large number of people. Firstly, I am indebted to those in positions of power who have knowingly or otherwise provided me with the opportunity to undertake this piece of work. Special thanks must go to Professor A. J. Evans, Librarian of Loughborough University of Technology, not only for his interest and encouragement but also for the numerous privileges and practical expressions of support I enjoyed during the book's long and sometimes painful gestation period. Assistance of an equally tangible and vital kind was gratefully received from the British Library Research and Development Department, whose generous travel grant enabled me to spend a fortnight in Brussels and for whom a report was subsequently prepared (*Publications, documents and means for their dissemination in the Commission of the European Communities: report on a study visit to Brussels, November 1979*, British Library Research & Development Report No. 5618, 1981); from Loughborough University, whose generosity also financed a visit to Brussels and from Leicester University, whose research fund financed a number of visits to London at the very outset of the project. Then I am indebted to those who have given me assistance and advice in a professional capacity, particularly those members of the Commission of the European Communities too numerous to name but without whose cooperation this book would not have been possible. However, I must record my thanks to the staff of the London Office of the Commission, particularly its three ex-librarians Valerie Williams, Lolli Duvivier and Emma Harte and to Carlo Pau for his helpfulness and the caring and expert way in which he tends the files upon which so much of this book is based. In Brussels, I must mention Jacqueline Lastenouse, a constant source of inspiration to those involved in European Studies, and Eric Gaskell, Librarian of the Commission, without whose assistance and company my visits to Brussels would have been much less productive and enjoyable. Thanks are also due to my colleague at Loughborough University, Dave Allen, who kindly read part of the typescript and to Mavis Hawkes who typed some of it. Needless to say, none of these people absolve me from any responsibility for the errors and omissions from which this book may suffer. Finally, I am indebted to those in my personal life who have suffered the consequences of this labour of love, particularly my sons Richard and Mark and my wife Eleri.

Abbreviations and acronyms

AASM	Associated African States and Madagascar
ACP	African, Caribbean and Pacific States
Annex OJ	*Debates of the European Parliament.* Published as an *Annex* to the *Official journal of the European Communities*
AUA	Agricultural unit of account
Bull	Bulletin
CAP	Common agricultural policy
Cat	Catalogue number
CC ECSC	Consultative Committee of the European Coal and Steel Community
CCT	Common Customs Tariff
CE	Communautés européennes
CECA	Communauté européenne du charbon et de l'acier
CEDEFOP	European Centre for the Development of Vocational Training
CEE	Communauté économique européenne
CERD	European Research and Development Committee
CIEC	Conference on International Economic Cooperation
COGECA	General Committee for Agricultural Cooperation in the EEC Countries
COM	Commission document
Comm	Commission
COPENUR	Standing Committee on Uranium Enrichment
COREPER	Committee of Permanent Representatives
COST	Coopération Scientifique et Technique
CREST	Scientific and Technical Research Committee
Débs	*Débats du Parlement européen*
DG	Directorate-General
Doc	Document
Doc de séance	*Document de séance du Parlement européen*
EAEC	European Atomic Energy Community
EAGGF	European Agricultural Guidance and Guarantee Fund
EC	European Communities
ECSC	European Coal and Steel Community
EDC	European Documentation Centre

EDF	European Development Fund
EEC	European Economic Community
EFTA	European Free Trade Association
EIB	European Investment Bank
EMS	European Monetary System
EMU	Economic and Monetary Union
EP	European Parliament
ERDF	European Regional Development Fund
ESC	Economic and Social Committee
ESF	European Social Fund
EUA	European Unit of Account
EURATOM	European Atomic Energy Community
FADN	Farm Accountancy Data Network
FEOGA	Le Fonds européen d'orientation et de garantie agricole. *See also* EAGGF
GATT	General Agreement on Tariffs and Trade
GSP	Generalized Scheme of Preferences
HA	High Authority
IEA	International Energy Agency
IGO	Intergovernmental organization
ILO	International Labour Organization
JO	*Journal officiel des Communautés européennes*
JO CECA	*Journal officiel de la Communauté européenne du charbon et de l'acier*
JRC	Joint Research Centre
MCA	Monetary compensatory amount
MOT for res	Motion for a Resolution
N.d.	No date
NGO	Non-governmental organization
NIMEXE	Harmonized Nomenclature for the Foreign Trade Statistics of the European Communities
NUTS	Nomenclature of Statistical Territorial Units
OCT	Overseas countries and territories
OECD	Organization for Economic Co-operation and Development
OJ	*Official journal of the European Communities*
PREST	Working Party on Scientific and Technical Research
SCAD	Central Archives and Documentation Service
SEC	Secretariat-General of the Commission
SOEC	Statistical Office of the European Communities

STABEX	Stabilization of export earnings
Supp	Supplement
UA	Unit of account
UNCTAD	United Nations Conference on Trade and Development
UNIDO	United Nations Industrial Development Organization
VAT	Value added tax
Vol	Volume
Working doc	*European Parliament working document*

CHAPTER I

Policy formation in the European Communities*

The basic framework and broad objectives of the three European Communities are defined in the founding Treaties, namely, the *Treaty establishing the European Coal and Steel Community*, signed by Belgium, France, the Federal Republic of Germany, Italy, Luxembourg and the Netherlands in Paris on 18 April 1951, the *Treaty establishing the European Economic Community*, signed by the same six countries in Rome on 25 March 1957 and the *Treaty establishing the European Atomic Energy Community*, also signed by the Six in Rome on 25 March 1957. These three Treaties embody the fundamental principles upon which subsequent Community action is based and make provision for the creation of institutional machinery to give practical effect to the sentiments they express. Although the basic framework established in the founding Treaties remains intact, amendments have been made in later Treaties. Significant institutional modifications were introduced by the *Treaty establishing a single Council and a single Commission of the European Communities*, popularly known as the 'Merger Treaty', signed in Brussels on 8 April 1965; financial arrangements were amended by the *Treaty amending certain budgetary provisions of the Treaties establishing the European Communities and the Treaty establishing a single Council and a single Commission of the European Communities*, commonly called the 'Budgetary Treaty', signed in Luxembourg on 22 April 1970; membership of the Communities was increased by the *Treaty concerning the accession of the Kingdom of Denmark, Ireland, the Kingdom of Norway and the United Kingdom of Great Britain and Northern Ireland to the European Economic Community and to the European Atomic Energy Community*, signed in Brussels on 22 January 1972; institutional control of Community finances was improved by the *Treaty amending certain financial provisions of the Treaties establishing the European Communities and of the Treaty establishing a single Council and a single Commission of the European Communities*, signed in Brussels on 22 July 1975. Although the European Communities, national governments and commercial publishers have issued a variety of official and unofficial, historic and consolidated texts of these Treaties, most needs will be met perfectly adequately by *Treaties establishing the European Communities: treaties amending these treaties: documents concerning the accession* (cat FX-23-77-962-EN-C.

* A revised and expanded version of an article which first appeared in the *Journal of librarianship*, Vol 6, no 3, July 1974, pp 165–178.

ISBN 92-823-0002-1), a handy pocket compendium of all those Treaties mentioned above, published in its second edition in 1978.

Together these Treaties constitute the primary legislation of the European Communities and provide a legal base for the action subsequently undertaken by Community institutions. However, the founding Treaties are concerned in the main with the definition of general principles, broad objectives and basic institutional machinery. It is left to Community institutions to give practical effect to the commitments entered into by member states and to ensure that the rules and obligations of Community membership are observed. To this end, Community institutions are invested by the Treaties with the power to make Community law. Article 189 of the EEC Treaty and 161 of the EAEC Treaty define the legal instruments at the disposal of Community institutions in the following terms:

> In order to carry out their task the Council and the Commission shall, in accordance with the provisions of this Treaty, make regulations, issue directives, take decisions, make recommendations or deliver opinions.
> A regulation shall have general application. It shall be binding in its entirety and directly applicable in all Member States.
> A directive shall be binding, as to the result to be achieved, upon each Member State to which it is addressed, but shall leave to the national authorities the choice of form and methods.
> A decision shall be binding in its entirety upon those to whom it is addressed.
> Recommendations and opinions shall have no binding force.

Since the authority to make Community law is derived from, and is therefore secondary to the Treaties, the term 'secondary legislation' has come to be used as a general descriptor for these legal instruments. However, such phraseology can be misleading because there is nothing secondary, for instance, about the power of a Regulation over existing national legislation. More confusingly, Article 14 of the ECSC Treaty uses somewhat different terminology to describe the legal instruments available to Community institutions within the ECSC context. However, since the majority of documents referred to in this bibliographical guide fall within the scope of the EEC Treaty, no further mention will be made of ECSC legislation.

The processes through which proposals for legislation must pass before they assume the force of Community law are governed by the provisions of the founding Treaties. Each of the four main Community institutions, the Commission, the European Parliament, the Council and the Court of Justice, is given a part to play in a process which demands constant interaction between institutions and whose inherent checks and balances ensure that no one institution can on its own make Community law. In order to place the documents which form the subject of this bibliographic guide into their proper institutional and legislative context, the remainder of this chapter is devoted to an account of this legislative process, with particular emphasis on the documentation it generates.

Formative stage within the Commission

In its narrowest sense, the Commission of the European Communities is composed of 13 Commissioners nominated by, but pledged to be independent of, national governments, whose task it is to uphold the interests of the Communities in the face of often conflicting national interests. Commissioners are usually eminent persons drawn from the political, diplomatic or academic life of member countries and are appointed for renewable four year terms of office. Although responsibility for all decisions taken by the Commission is collective, its work is divided into a number of separate portfolios, each of which becomes the responsibility of one Commissioner. The Commission proper, under the guidance of its President, is assisted in its work by a European civil service of over 8000 officials organized into departments, or Directorates-General, each of which is further sub-divided into numerous Directorates, Divisions and specialized services.

A principal function of the Commission is to initiate policy. Although the impetus for action can come from elsewhere, say the European Council, only the Commission has the ability to set the legislative process in motion. The Commission uses its power of initiative in two ways. Firstly, it submits to the Council draft proposals for Regulations, Directives and Decisions in pursuit of the goals established in the founding Treaties. Secondly, it presents to the Council more general communications and memoranda in which it presents its views on the development of overall policy strategy in major areas of activity. Documents from this latter category form the subject of this book.

Policy proposals are first formulated within the appropriate Directorate-General, often after lengthy consultation with government officials, other Community institutions and specialized interest groups and after groups of independent experts have undertaken preparatory work on behalf of the Commission. Documents abound at this early stage in policy formulation. Documents take the form of discussion papers, explanatory notes and other background material together with the actual texts of draft legislation or policy statements. At this stage, when proposals are only rough outlines, when internal discussion and external consultation make frequent amendments and modifications necessary, documents are no more than working tools; they do not represent official Commission policy or enter the public domain.

As soon as consultations have been completed and documents cleared with other Directorates-General and with the Legal Service, the texts are submitted by the appropriate Directorate-General to the Secretariat-General for consideration by the Commission proper. To assist in their internal identification and control, documents placed on the Commission's agenda receive a unique document number consisting of the prefix COM (a contraction of Commission), a date code and running number, for example COM(78)675. In the majority of cases, draft proposals for legislation are approved by the Commission by written procedure. Proposals are circulated to individual Commissioners according to a standard procedure and are deemed to have been approved unless reservations have been expressed by an announced date. Contentious or particularly important proposals or memoranda are dealt with by the Commission in oral procedure at one of its regular weekly meetings. Only when the Commission proper has given its formal approval to a proposal does it represent official Commission policy.

Documents which attain this status are dispatched to the Council and to other Community institutions, usually in the form of 'COM finals', so called because their document numbers are followed by the word 'final', reflecting the fact that the text now represents the Commission's formal viewpoint on a particular matter. Other documents of a less formal nature, whose aim is more to provide information, become SEC documents, so called because their document numbers consist of the prefix SEC (a contraction of Secretariat-General), a date code and a running number, for example, SEC(78)642. Such documents do not have the same political or juridical significance as COM documents. They may take the form of progress reports on the implementation of Community policy, factual and statistical reports to assist in the decision-making process or general memoranda in which the Commission sketches the outline of its strategy in a particular policy sector.

As Emile Noël, Secretary-General of the Commission, makes clear in his useful introductory text *The European Community: how it works* (cat CB-28-79-390-EN-C. ISBN 92-825-1015-8) published in 1979, the Commission is also the executive arm of the Communities and the guardian of the Treaties. It enjoys wide executive powers which derive directly from the provisions of the founding Treaties and from powers subsequently conferred on it by the Council of the European Communities. The ECSC Treaty gives to the High Authority, now the Commission, wide-ranging responsibilities to effect and administer a common market for coal and steel; the EAEC Treaty grants to the Commission similar supervisory powers regarding the peaceful use of nuclear energy; the EEC Treaty gives the Commission responsibility for the creation of the customs union and for application of the rules of competition. All three Treaties make the Commission responsible for the administration of Community finances through such funds as the European Social Fund. In addition, the Council has delegated to the Commission wide rule-making powers in connection with the implementation and administration of common policies such as the CAP and transport policy.

Consequently, the Commission has occasion to issue many hundreds of documents relating to the detailed, day-to-day supervision and administration of established policy. These implementing measures, which normally take the form of Commission Regulations and other legislative acts, appear in draft form as 'C' documents, so named because their document numbers begin with the prefix 'C' for Commission. Since these documents concern matters over which the Commission has sole responsibility, they neither pass to other Community institutions for approval nor through the legislative process which is the subject of this chapter. However, many are placed before Management Committees composed of government representatives before their formal enactment and promulgation. 'C' documents are similar to draft Statutory Instruments in the British legislative context; they are concerned with the detailed implementation of policy, are numerous, specific, have an extremely short life and are not represented in this bibliographic guide.

Receipt of proposals by the Council

The Council of the European Communities dominates Community development and dictates the pace and direction of progress. It is both the decision-making institution of the Communities and the institution in which the interests of national governments are represented. It is not in permanent session nor does it have a permanent membership; its composition varies from meeting to meeting according to the matters in hand. The Council has its own Secretariat in Brussels and is assisted in its work by government representatives of ambassadorial rank, called Permanent Representatives, who meet regularly in the Committee of Permanent Representatives (COREPER). Information on the composition of the Council, COREPER, its many subordinate committees and its Secretariat appears in the *Guide to the Council of the European Communities*, a loose-leaf publication issued by the General Secretariat of the Council.

It is to COREPER that Commission communications and legislative proposals are referred for initial consideration. The Committee also decides whether to invite the European Parliament and the Economic and Social Committee to express an opinion on Commission proposals. As soon as consultation takes place, Commission proposals for legislation receive their first formal publication in the *Official journal of the European Communities*, the official gazette of the organization and a principal source of authoritative information on Community affairs. More precisely, Commission proposals are published, albeit without the very useful explanatory memorandum invariably present in the original COM document, in the *Information and notices* section of the *Official journal*, usually referred to as the 'C' series after its French title *Communications et informations*, one of two parts into which the *Official journal* is divided. The *Legislation*, or 'L' series, is referred to later in this chapter. It should also be noted that the *Debates of the European Parliament* are also published as an annex to the *Official journal* and that since 1978, a separate supplement has been produced to the *Official journal* containing invitations to tender for contracts and other official announcements.

Although legislative proposals are published in the *Official journal*, the numerous communications and memoranda submitted by the Commission to the Council, many of which are of primary importance in the development of policy strategy, are not. A relatively small number may subsequently appear as Supplements to the *Bulletin of the European Communities* and a few receive full publication as separate monographs but the vast majority remain in document form, fugitive documents little known and consequently little used outside the organization. Problems are compounded for the external user in that documents are not subject to very satisfactory bibliographical control. Those reference aids such as the *Catalogue des publications 1952–1971*, its annual updates and the monthly lists published in the *Bulletin of the European Communities* are all concerned with publications; individual documents are not listed. Indeed, the only source of information of any note on Commission documents is the *Documentation bulletin*, Series A, published weekly by the Commission's Central Archives and Documentation Service (SCAD), which lists Community documents, legislative acts and periodical articles. However, Series A must be considered as little more than a current awareness tool because it lacks an index to ease retrieval of individual documents. More useful for specific document searches are the irregular series of subject bibliographies and cumulative subject issues, issued in Series B and C.

Consideration by the European Parliament

The European Parliament is a deliberative and consultative body composed, as a result of direct elections held for the first time in 1979, of 410 members organized into a number of party political rather than national groups. Previously, a much smaller assembly consisted of 198 members nominated by national parliaments in member countries. The European Parliament has a number of specific powers. It can dismiss the Commission as a whole; it can, as a result of the 1975 Budgetary Treaty, reject the Community budget as a whole and it has a measure of control over non-obligatory expenditure. However, these somewhat negative powers do not compensate for a lack of the genuine legislative function characteristic of most national parliaments. As we have seen, the Commission has the power of initiative and the Council the power of decision. The founding Treaties require the Council to consult with the European Parliament on most Commission proposals but do not oblige it to take any heed of the Parliament's opinions.

Much of the notable work of the European Parliament is carried out in specialized committees whose membership reflects the party political composition of the assembly as a whole. It is to one of the twelve functional committees that the President of the European Parliament refers Commission proposals for detailed scrutiny as soon as they have been received from the Council. Although in practice, proposals will have already been received direct from the Commission on an informal basis. Copies of Commission proposals are circulated to members of the Parliament in the form of *European Parliament working documents*. These documents consist of the original Commission document, attached to which is a copy of the formal letter of presentation from the President of the Council to the President of the European Parliament, referring to the authority under which consultation is made and any time limits for the presentation of the Parliament's opinion. A title page, bearing a unique document number consisting of a running number and date code, is added before distribution.

Committees of the European Parliament examine Commission proposals in private and no record of proceedings is made public. Members of the Commission are called to give first-hand accounts of their proposals before a rapporteur draws up a report on the committee's deliberations for consideration by the European Parliament in plenary session. This report is also circulated as a publicly available *European Parliament working document*, usually consisting of a Motion for a Resolution of the European Parliament together with an explanatory memorandum. A verbatim record of the subsequent plenary session debate on committee reports is published in the *Debates of the European Parliament*, which since 1968 has been published as an annex to the *Official journal*. The texts of Resolutions adoped at the end of parliamentary debates are published in the Minutes of Proceedings of the European Parliament, published in the 'C' series of the *Official journal*.

Consideration by the Economic and Social Committee

Many legislative proposals and policy documents from the Commission are referred not only to the European Parliament but also to the Economic and Social Committee. This is another consultative institution composed of 144 members appointed by member governments to represent the views and interests of three main groups, employers, employees and general interest groups such as farmers and consumers. Biographical information on individual members of the Committee appears in the *Yearbook* and the annual *Directory* published by the Committee. The role of the Committee is to establish a link between main Community institutions and national interest groups; in common with the European Parliament, the Economic and Social Committee has the task of submitting to the Council opinions on draft legislation and policy memoranda from the Commission, although such opinions are again purely advisory. In matters governed by the ECSC Treaty, the role of the Committee is performed by the Consultative Committee, composed of employees, employers, consumers and other interest groups from the coal and steel industries.

The work of the Economic and Social Committee is organized by the Chairman and Bureau, elected from among the members of the institution for two year terms of office. The Committee is divided into various sections corresponding to the principal fields covered by the founding Treaties. It is to such sections that Commission documents are referred for detailed scrutiny. The full Committee subsequently adopts opinions on Commission documents on the basis of recommendations from the appropriate section. The 100 or so opinions delivered by the Committee each year are first circulated as Committee documents. Although such documents are not confidential, they do not receive widespread distribution outside Community institutions; general public access is provided by their ultimate publication in the 'C' series of the *Official journal*. Particularly important Committee opinions are occasionally published separately as small booklets. In 1978, for instance, the Committee published separately opinions on such matters as monetary disorders, employee participation in companies and youth unemployment. Summaries of the opinions adopted and more general information on the work of the institution appear in the *Bulletin* of the Economic and Social Committee and in its *Annual report*. Useful bibliographical information on Committee opinions appears in *Opinions delivered by the Economic and Social Committee of the European Economic Community*, each issue of which presents, in tabular form, bibliographical details of the opinions adopted during the past three months or so.

Consideration by the Council

Initial consideration of Commission proposals and policy documents takes place in working groups set up by COREPER and then in COREPER itself. It is the task of the Committee, or the Special Committee on Agriculture on agricultural matters, to decide whether to place Commission proposals on the Council's agenda as 'A' items, indicating that they merely require formal approval, or as 'B' items, indicating that further consideration at ministerial level is needed. Although the founding Treaties make provision for decisions to be taken by majority vote, all important issues have been settled on the basis of unanimity since the Luxembourg Compromise in 1966. Consequently, whenever conflicting national interests are involved, the Community decision-making process can involve lengthy, hard-bargaining sessions in which the Commission acts as mediator, constantly amending its proposals in an effort to achieve consensus. In cases of deadlock over major issues, it is usual for matters to be referred to Heads of Government who meet usually three times a year in the European Council.

No record of Council meetings, COREPER deliberations or the meetings of other Council committees and working parties is made public. It is the responsibility of each national government to decide how much to disclose about its own participation in Council affairs. However, leaks to the press are commonplace and the General Secretariat of the Council issues press releases at the end of Council meetings, outlining in general terms the conclusions reached. In the longer term, the annual *Review of the Council's work* provides a useful, if somewhat bald, record of Council decisions.

Also published is the end result of successful discussions in Council, that is, the secondary legislation itself. Regulations, Decisions and Directives are all published in the *Official journal of the European Communities*, the 'L' or Legislation series of which is devoted to Community legislative acts. Published at least daily in a numbered sequence that starts afresh each calendar year, the 'L' series is divided into two main parts. The first contains the texts of Regulations which, according to Article 191 of the EEC Treaty, must be published in the *Official journal* and which 'shall enter into force on the date specified in them or, in the absence thereof, on the twentieth day following their publication'. EEC and Euratom Regulations are individually numbered in an annual sequence which starts afresh at the beginning of each calendar year, except during the period 1958 to 1962 when they were numbered in one continuous sequence regardless of date. Since 1968, Regulations emanating from both the EEC and Euratom have been numbered in one annual sequence common to both Communities, for example, Regulation (EEC) No 734/78 and Regulation (Euratom) No 735/78. In the second part of each issue of the 'L' series appear the texts of those legislative instruments whose publication is not obligatory according to Treaty provisions, that is, Decisions, Directives, Recommendations and Opinions. These too are listed in one sequence, common to both the EEC and Euratom since 1968, which begins anew each year. However, the method of citation is the reverse of that adoped for Regulations, for example, Decision 78/131/EEC and Directive 78/132/Euratom.

In 1978 more than 3000 Regulations appeared in the *Official journal* and over 1000 Directives and Decisions. However, only a fraction were enacted according to the full procedure described in this chapter. The majority were adopted by the Commission in accordance with powers delegated to the Commission by previous Council enactments. In order to distinguish important Council legislation from the mass of technical and administrative legislation adopted by the Commission in connection with the day-to-day management of the customs union, common agricultural policy and other Community sectors, the former are listed in the contents to each issue of the 'L' series in bold type and are asterisked. Separate monthly and annual indexes assist the identification of separate pieces of legislation in the ever expanding pages of the *Official journal*.

Court of Justice

The Court of Justice is composed of nine judges chosen, according to Article 167 of the EEC Treaty, from 'persons whose independence is beyond doubt and who possess the qualifications required for appointment to the highest judicial offices in their respective countries', assisted by four Advocates-General. It is the task of the Court to ensure that Community law is upheld, to review the legality of the acts of Community institutions, member governments and other parties and to act as arbiter in cases of dispute over Community law. Summary details of cases brought before the Court and of its judgements are published in the 'C' series of the *Official journal*. The principal source of information on Court cases is the series of law reports published under the title *Reports of cases before the Court*. A quarterly bulletin called *Information on the Court of Justice of the European Communities* is available free of charge from the Court to members of the legal profession.

CHAPTER 2

General Community development

Descriptive essay

This chapter is not typical of those which it precedes in that it is not concerned with one particular area of policy. It contains references to an assortment of documents concerned with the general development of the European Communities as a whole. There are references to documents representing the early concern with the implementation of transitional arrangements set out in the EEC Treaty for the phased introduction of the EEC (*see* 1 & 4), to documents in which the Commission takes stock of progress so far (*see* 2) and lays plans for its future work programmes (*see* 3). Also included are references to documents of more recent origin in which the future shape of the European Communities is discussed in the context of European Union (*see* 9, 11 & 13). Although this book is concerned with policy formation rather than Community administration, a number of key documents on Community financial and budgetary arrangements are included (*see* 6, 10, 15 & 16), a complex topic simplified in a booklet called *The European Community's budget* (cat CB-NC-79-001-EN-C. ISBN 92-825-0702-5) published as *European documentation* 1/79. Reference is also made in this chapter to the implications of budgetary arrangements for the role of Community institutions, particularly the European Parliament (*see* 7 & 8).

Appreciative of the need to draw public attention to its activities and achievements, the European Community pursues a vigorous publications programme designed to keep the citizens of Europe informed about the broad issues touched upon in this chapter, and abreast of more specific matters relating to the evolution and implementation of policy in sectors covered in other chapters of this book. Undoubtedly, the single most useful source of information on the general trends of Community development over a period of years and on the gradual and often piecemeal implementation of sectoral policy is the *General report on the activities of the European Communities*, presented to the European Parliament by the Commission each February since 1968 in accordance with Article 18 of the Merger Treaty. Preceded by annual reports from each of the three formerly separate Community executives, each *General report* contains an assessment of the state of the Community in the year in question, a review of the work of the Commission and other Community institutions and a detailed description of the year's main events, legislation proposed and adopted and other initiatives in each of the policy sectors over which the Communities have competence. From 1970 to 1976 the *General report* also contained the address given by the President of the Commission to the

European Parliament on the occasion of the presentation of the report on the past year, and an annexed memorandum setting out the Commission's programme for the coming year. Since 1977 this address and memorandum have been published separately in a booklet called *Programme of the Commission for* .... As a concise and comprehensive summary of Community activities and achievements, liberally provided in more recent issues with footnote references to the *Official journal* and other Community publications, the *General report* constitutes a valuable point of departure for more detailed study of specific areas of policy. Although not specifically mentioned in every instance, the *General report* must be considered one of the first sources of reference for study of those policy areas treated in subsequent chapters of this book.

Annual reports constitute a significant group of Community publications and are a rich source of information on most aspects of Community affairs. For the sake of convenience, annual reports may be divided into three main types. Firstly, there are those which, like the *General report*, describe the work of Community institutions. The *Review of the Council's work*, for instance, contains a record of meetings held and decisions taken by the Council of the European Communities during the year in question; the *Annual reports* published by the Economic and Social Committee and the European Investment Bank take stock of the work of these institutions in the past twelve months. More specialized committees, commissions and other Community bodies, such as the Mines Safety and Health Commission and the ACP–EEC Council of Ministers, also publish informative annual reports. Secondly, there are annual reports on the development of policy in particular Community sectors. Published in conjunction with the *General report* is the *Report on the development of the social situation in the Community*, the *Report on competition policy* and the *Report on the agricultural situation in the Community*. These publications, together with such similar sectoral policy reports as the *State of the environment* and the *Annual report on the development cooperation policies of the Community and its Member States*, are more fully described in appropriate policy chapters elsewhere in this book. Finally, there are mainly factual status reports which describe the present situation or state of integration in particular fields of policy. These too, an example of which is *The energy situation in the Community*, are treated in subsequent chapters of this book.

More current information on the whole spectrum of Community affairs than that contained in annual reports appears in the *Bulletin of the European Communities*, edited by the Secretariat-General of the Commission and published 11 times a year since 1968. Preceded by the *Bulletin de la Communauté européenne du charbon et de l'acier* and the *Bulletin de la Communauté économique européenne*, this monthly publication is divided into three main sections. Part 1 highlights topics of current concern; each issue contains brief articles on current affairs relevant to European integration, descriptions of recent Community legislation or summaries of significant Community publications and documents. Part 2 forms the main body of the *Bulletin*, consisting of a detailed summary of developments in each of the major policy fields during the month under review, of documents prepared and considered and of the work of Community institutions. Part 3 is concerned with Community documentation, consisting in the main of a monthly catalogue of Community publications. Of particular significance are the separately published Supplements to the *Bulletin of the European Communities*, which have increasingly been used to give wider publicity to significant Commission proposals, communications and memoranda. Although reference is made in subsequent chapters of this book to many such Supplements, a full list of those published between 1961 and 1971 appears in the *Catalogue des publications 1952–1971*, itself published as an unnumbered Supplement to the *Bulletin* in 1972.

The *Bulletin* and the progress reports referred to in earlier paragraphs provide valuable factual data, analysis and comment on Community affairs; they do not contain the texts of Community legislation or other Community documents. Serious research into European integration demands extensive use of the *Official journal of the European Communities*, the official gazette of the organization, which contains not only the texts of pieces of secondary legislation enacted in accordance with the process described in Chapter 1, but also draft legislation, official announcements and details of the work of the main Community institutions. First published on 30 December 1952 by the European Coal and Steel Community, the *Official journal* has since 1968 been divided into two separately published parts— *Information and notices* and *Legislation*. Both parts are numbered in sequences which begin anew at the beginning of each calendar year, distinguished one from the other by the use of the prefix 'C' in the case of *Information and notices*, taken from its French language title *Communications et informations*, and the prefix 'L' in the case of the *Legislation* series.

Information and notices is published at almost daily intervals (in 1978 313 issues were published); each issue is divided into up to three sections. The first, called 'Information', concerns the business of the main institutions. Published here are the minutes of proceedings of the European Parliament, including the texts of Resolutions adopted and parliamentary questions and answers, and details of cases presented to and decided by the Court of Justice of the European Communities. The second section, 'Preparatory Acts', contains the published texts of Commission proposals for legislation, including draft Regulations, Directives and Decisions. It also contains the Opinions of the Economic and Social Committee on such Commission proposals and other preparatory acts. The final section, 'Notices', consists of invitations to tender for works contracts and other official announcements. Since 1978, a separately published Supplement to the *Official journal*, often referred to as the 'S' series, has also contained invitations to tender for works contracts and notifications of open competitions.

Community law is promulgated by virtue of its publication in the *Legislation* series of the *Official journal*, each issue of which may contain as many as 20 or more separate pieces of secondary legislation. The 'L' series is published almost daily (there were 364 issues in 1978), and is divided into two parts. The first contains Regulations which, according to Article 191 of the EEC Treaty, 'shall be published in the Official Journal of the Community' and 'shall enter into force on the date specified in them or, in the absence thereof, on the twentieth day following their publication'. The second contains the texts of legislation whose publication is not obligatory, including Directives and Decisions. Each year the 'L' series contains the official texts of many thousands of separate pieces of Community legislation (in 1978, for instance, there were 3181 Regulations and 1041 Directives, Decisions and other legal acts), the identification of which is assisted by the separate publication of monthly and annual indexes providing numerical and broad subject access.

The task of consulting the mass of legislation enacted before the enlargement of the Communities in 1973, much of which remains central to the operation of

Community policies and institutions, has been greatly simplified by the publication of a Special Edition of the *Official journal* which contains, in chronological order, authentic English language texts of all secondary legislation published since 1952 and still in force on 31 December 1972. The ease with which legislative landmarks in the evolution of policy may be identified is improved by a number of other Community publications. *Europe today: state of European integration*, published by the European Parliament Secretariat's Directorate-General for Research and Documentation, consists of a concise summary of the legal position reached in various Community sectors, with reference to the most important pieces of legislation adopted. The *Documentation bulletin* prepared by the Commission's Central Archives and Documentation Service (SCAD) is also a useful bibliographical tool. Although the weekly issues of Series A constitute a useful current awareness service, it is the retrospective subject bibliographies published in Series B and C that are of particular value in the identification of legislation relevant to the development of policy in particular policy areas. The pages of the *General report* also contain helpful references to Community legislation and from time-to-time the Community publishes separate compendia of important legislative texts in a particular policy field, such as *Community energy policy: texts of the relevant legislation* (cat CH-22-76-132-EN-C), published by the Commission in 1976 and subsequently updated in 1979.

At the other end of the spectrum of Community publishing, there are free publications designed primarily for consumption by the casual reader rather than the committed researcher, which nevertheless constitute a useful introductory source of information on general Community development. Aimed primarily at the non-specialist, such publications form an integral part of the information policy pursued by the Commission of the European Communities through its Directorate-General for Information and its national information offices. Publications consist of newsletters such as *Euroforum*, designed to draw popular attention to topical events and to transmit news and information; leaflets and booklets which explain policy and describe the functions and work of Community institutions, and other publicity and promotional material. Such publications are usually well written and attract-ively produced and often, particularly in the case of items appearing in such series as *European documentation*, form helpful first introductions to unfamiliar topics.

More specialized reports and studies published by the European Communities are referred to in later chapters of this book, as are the many statistical serials issued by the Statistical Office of the European Communities, from which valuable factual data on general Community development can be derived. Bibliographical information on these and other Community publications is available from the *Catalogue des publications 1952–1971*, a cumulative catalogue replacing previous sales catalogues, published as an unnumbered Supplement to the *Bulletin of the European Communities* in 1972. This was followed by the multilingual *Catalogue of the publications of the European Community institutions 1972–1973*, issued in 1974. Since that time, a monthly catalogue called *Publications of the European Communities* has appeared in the *Bulletin of the European Communities* and as a separate offprint, subsequently cumulated into annual catalogues of the same title. The *List of additions to the Library*, an accessions bulletin from the Central Library of the Commission, also constitutes a valuable source of bibliographical information. Of particular value is the *Catalogue of European Community publications and documents received at the Commission Library 1978–1979*, published as a special issue in December 1979.

Bibliographical record

1 **Recommandations de la Commission en vue de l'accélération du rythme du Traité**
COM(60)16 final. 26 Feb 1960. 16p

In view of the encouraging performance of the EEC during its first two years and the promising economic situation, the Council invited the Commission to submit proposals for achieving the objectives of the Treaty of Rome faster than allowed for in the time-table established in the Treaty. In this document, the Commission considers the implications of this proposed action on the general equilibrium of the Community, on the economies of member states and on external relations. Having concluded that an acceleration is feasible and desirable, provided that certain conditions are observed, the Commission recommends the adoption of certain measures to this end. Accordingly, the Council decided on 12 May 1960 to speed up the implementation of the Treaty (*JO* 58, 12 Sept 1960, pp 1217–1220). As a consequence of this, and a similar acceleration in 1962 (*JO* 41, 28 May 1962, pp 1284–1286), the Commission was able to make recommendations for the complete abolition of duties and charges well ahead of schedule (*see* 4).

2 **La première étape du Marché commun**
Comm EEC, 1962. 128p (cat 8056)

The EEC Treaty made provision in Article 8 for the establishment of the common market during a transitional period in three stages each lasting three years; at the end of the first stage, the Council, on the basis of a report from the Commission, would decide whether sufficient progress had been made in the implementation of Treaty objectives to justify transition to the second stage. This report from the Commission, submitted in compliance with Article 8, looks back on the achievements of the Community during the first stage from January 1958 to January 1962. Divided into two main parts, the first section of the document is concerned with the internal development of the Community during that period. Separate parts deal in turn with the gradual creation of a common market, the evolution of common policies in such fields as regional and social affairs and the development of relations with the associated overseas states. The second section of the document is concerned with the external relations of the Community. It contains an account of the Community's relations with both non-member countries and developing countries, as well as a description of events culminating in applications for membership from the United Kingdom and Denmark, as well as negotiations for association agreements with other countries. The report was also published in an English language version called *The first stage of the Common Market: report on the execution of the Treaty (January 1958–January 1962)*. On 14 January 1962, the Council concluded that sufficient progress had been made to allow the Community to embark on its second stage (*JO* 10, 10 Feb 1962, p 164). (*See also* 3.)

3 **Mémorandum de la Commission sur le programme d'action de la communauté pendant la deuxième étape**
COM(62)300. 24 Oct 1962. 107p

A broad-ranging prospectus of tasks to be achieved by the Community during the second stage of the transitional period, produced by the Commission as a basis for discussion at the annual joint meeting between the Council, European Parliament and the Commission. This blueprint for the future development of the Community consists of eleven chapters in which the Commission outlines the steps that are necessary if Treaty objectives are to be achieved. These chapters refer to the internal market, competition policy, agricultural policy, transport policy, energy policy, social policy, economic policy, monetary policy, external relations, development aid and administration and finance. In each chapter, the Commission highlights the tasks to be accomplished and outlines means for their achievement. The report was published separately in 1962, with an English language version entitled *Memorandum of the Commission on the action programme of the Community for the second stage* (cat 8067). The report also appeared as *Community topics* No 10 under the title *The Common Market's action program.*

4 Initiative 1964
Community topics No 15

Recognizing the need for the EEC to maintain its vitality and momentum, the Commission considers the time ripe for new initiatives to speed up implementation of the common market. The first part of the memorandum deals with the customs union. As the timetable established in the Treaty for the progressive reduction of customs duties—a reduction of 30 per cent in each of the first two four-year stages and their complete abolition by 1970—has already been accelerated to the point where reductions have reached 60 per cent by 1 July 1963, two and a half years ahead of schedule, the Commission now proposes their complete abolition by 1 January 1967 and a third and final adjustment of the Common Customs Tariff on 1 January 1966. Further sections in the memorandum are concerned with the establishment of Community customs legislation on trade with non-member countries, and the abolition of frontier controls on trade between member countries. The gradual achievement of monetary union and social policy are also the subject of general proposals for action. As a result of the adoption of Council Decision 66/532/EEC of 26 July 1966 (JO 165, 21 Sept 1966, pp 2971–2972) and Council Regulation (EEC) No 950/68 of 28 June 1968 (JO L172, 22 July 1968, pp 1–102), the customs union was completed 18 months ahead of schedule on 1 July 1968. In March 1969, the Commission submitted to the Council a work programme in which it outlined its tasks for the next three years and identified the immediate priorities for 1969, published as a Supplement to the *Bulletin of the European Communities* 4-1969.

5 Financement de la politique agricole commune—ressources propres de la Communauté—renforcement des pouvoirs du Parlement européen
COM(65)320 final. 22 July 1965. 16p

See 364.

6 Communication de la Commission au Conseil concernant le remplacement des contributions financières des états membres par des

ressources propres et l'accroissement des pouvoirs budgétaires du Parlement européen
COM(69)700. 16 July 1969. 29p

EP Report: *Doc de séance* 102/69. 3 Oct 1969. H. Furler. 7p
EP Debate: *Annexe JO* No 117, 7 Oct 1969, pp 37–61
EP Resolution: *JO* C139, 28 Oct 1969, p 13

EP Report: *Doc de séance* 174/69. 8 Dec 1969. G. Spénale. 54p
EP Debate: *Annexe JO* No 120, 10 Dec 1969, pp 65–123
EP Resolution: *JO* C2, 8 Jan 1970, pp 13–25
ESC Opinion: *JO* C19, 13 Feb 1970, pp 23–28

A memorandum in which the Commission makes important proposals for replacing national financial contributions to the Communities by funds from the Communities' own resources, and in which it also supports a consequent increase in the budgetary powers of the European Parliament. An earlier proposal for the introduction of Community financing during the second phase of the transitional period had been instrumental in causing the Community crisis in 1965–66 (*see* 364). However, this document together with a package of proposals on financing the common agricultural policy (*see* 373), and a supplementary document containing specific proposals for amending Article 203 of the EEC Treaty on the budgetary powers of the European Parliament (COM(69)1020 final/2), were the subject of lengthy discussions in the Council which eventually led to the adoption of a number of important pieces of legislation. Of primary importance was Council Decision 70/243/ECSC, EEC, EURATOM of 21 April 1970, which provided for the phased replacement of financial contributions from member states by the Communities' own resources during an interim period from 1970 to 1974 leading to full Community financing from 1 January 1975 (*JO* L94, 28 Apr 1970, pp 19–22). On the following day, plenipotentiaries from the six member governments signed the *Treaty amending certain budgetary provisions of the Treaties establishing the European Communities and of the Treaty establishing a single Council and a single Commission of the European Communities* (*JO* L2, 2 Jan 1971, pp 1–11). All the major texts produced by the Commission, the European Parliament and the Council, including the document which forms the subject of this entry and the Council Regulation of 21 April 1970, in the progress towards Community financing and increased budgetary powers for the European Parliament, are reproduced with linking commentary in a European Parliament publication called *The European Communities' own resources and the budgetary powers of the European Parliament* (cat 5801) published in 1972. This is an abridged version of two earlier publications issued separately in Community languages, *Les ressources propres aux Communautés européennes et les pouvoirs budgétaires du Parlement européen: recueil de documents* (cat 4967) published in 1970 and *Les ressources propres aux Communautés européennes et les pouvoirs budgétaires du Parlement européen: les débats de ratification: analyse de documents* (cat 5399), published in 1971. (*See also* 7 & 8.)

7 Rapport du groupe ad hoc pour l'examen du problème de l'accroissement des compétences du Parlement européen
Bull EC Supp 4/72

An influential report was drawn up at the request of the Commission by an independent working party under the chairmanship of Georges Vedel, Honorary Dean of the Paris Faculty of Law and Economic Sciences, whose task was to examine the whole corpus of problems associated with strengthening the legislative and budgetary powers of the European Parliament. Prepared at a time when the Community had, as a result of Council Decision 70/243/ECSC, EEC, EURATOM of 21 March 1970 (*JO* L94, 28 Apr 1970, pp 19–22), made arrangements for financing the Community budget from its own resources, and had amended budgetary arrangements as a result of the Treaty of Luxembourg of 22 April 1970 (*JO* L2, 2 Jan 1971, pp 1–11), this report was intended to give the Commission guidance in its work in this area (*see* 6). The report opens with some discussion of the methodology adopted by the working party in the preparation and conduct of the investigation before proceeding in Chapter 2 to describe the state of the Community in 1972. Chapter 3 examines in closer detail the nature of the present institutions, their mode of operation and their suitability in the light of the tasks which confront the Community. On the basis of the analysis contained in Chapters 2 and 3, the working party then proceeds to examine the question of increasing the powers of the European Parliament and to make appropriate proposals. Election to the Parliament and its relationship with national parliaments are the subject of separate chapters. The working party also looks at the wider repercussions of a strengthened European Parliament on the Community's institutional framework and the adjustments that will have to be made. Finally, the report concludes with suggestions as to how the reforms proposed in the report can be implemented. On the basis of this and other preparatory work, the Commission was able to place firm proposals before the Council (*see* 8).

8 Strengthening of the budgetary powers of the European Parliament
COM(73)1000. 8 June 1973. 42p

EP Report: *Working doc* 131/73. 2 July 1973. G. Spénale. 15p
EP Debate: *Annex OJ* No 164, 4 July 1973, pp 123–157
EP Resolution: *OJ* C62, 31 July 1973, pp 29–31

EP Report: *Working doc* 175/73. 3 Oct 1973. G. Spénale. 84p
EP Debate: *Annex OJ* No 166, 4/5 Oct 1973, pp 8–49, 53–76
EP Resolution: *OJ* C87, 17 Oct 1973, pp 8–11

At the signing of the Budgetary Treaty on 22 April 1970, the Commission undertook to present fresh proposals for strengthening the budgetary powers of the European Parliament within two years of the Treaty's entry into force (*see* 6). In fulfilment of its obligation, the Commission presents in this document brief introductory notes and a draft Treaty designed to increase Parliament's budgetary powers and to replace the present Audit Board with a Court of Auditors with extensive powers to verify Community revenue and expenditure. After due consideration of the Commission's proposals, published as Supplement 9/73 to the *Bulletin of the European Communities*, representatives of the governments of the member states signed the Treaty on 22 July 1975 (*OJ* L359, 31 Dec 1977, pp 1–19). After ratification procedures were completed, the Treaty entered into force on 1 June 1977 and the Court of Auditors was set up in Luxembourg on 25 October

1977. Further information on the Court may be derived from its first annual report issued in 1978 (*OJ* C313, 30 Dec 1978, pp 1–234). In 1973 the European Parliament published a useful collection of papers on the topic in a volume called *The case for a European Audit Office* (cat 6159).

9 Report on European Union
COM(75)400. 25 June 1975. 68p

At the Paris summit conference in October 1972, the Heads of Government or State declared 'their intention of converting their entire relationship into a European Union before the end of this decade' and called upon Community institutions to prepare reports on the subject before the end of 1975 for submission to a further summit conference. This response from the Commission sets out its views on the essential features of a European Union, its institutional applications and the means for its achievement. As the phrase 'European Union' is open to a number of interpretations, the first part of the document concerns the scope and nature of European Union. In the second part, the Commission seeks to define the fields of competence and the scope of the powers of European Union. Separate sections deal with socio-economic matters, foreign policy, defence and the protection of human rights. Institutional considerations, and in particular how European Union would be translated into reality, are the subject of the third section. The document concludes with comments from the Commission on the means of proceeding with this objective. The document was published as Supplement 5/75 to the *Bulletin of the European Communities*. Reports on European Union prepared by the European Parliament, Court of Justice and Economic and Social Committee were published together in Supplement 9/75 to the *Bulletin of the European Communities*. (*See also* 11 & 13.)

10 Improvement of budgetary procedure and financial control
SEC(75)3599 final. 29 Oct 1975. 17p

In the first part of this document, the Commission enumerates the measures of a legislative and operational kind which it has taken to improve the budgetary procedures with regard to both forecasts and implementation. It also lists those measures proposed by the Commission but not yet adopted. The second part reviews the various mechanisms for exerting financial control, measures taken by the Commission to improve financial control and those Commission initiatives which have not been approved. (*See also* 15.)

11 European Union
Bull EC Supp 1/76

At the European Council meeting held in Paris in December 1974 Leo Tindemans, Prime Minister of Belgium, was invited to give the concept of European Union more precise definition and to make appropriate proposals, taking account of the views expressed by Community institutions (*see* 9), the opinions of member governments and other interested parties. The report, commonly referred to as the 'Tindemans' Report', has two objectives. Firstly, it seeks to define 'an overall approach providing a framework for relevant action in the member countries in coming years'; secondly, it highlights 'a number of practical measures which must be adopted simultaneously in the various directions entailed by the overall approach'. The report opens with a summary of Tindemans' findings on current attitudes towards the European concept, and the need to inject new vitality and momentum into the European ideal by the pursuit of defined policies within the overall framework of European Union. Subsequent chapters explore in more detail the exact nature of European Union in its various policy components. They are concerned with and make proposals on the external relations of the Community, economic and social policies and the protection of the rights of European citizens. The final chapter assesses the implications of the proposals made in the report for the Community's institutional machinery, and makes proposals designed to strengthen it and prepare it for its role in the progress towards European Union.

12 Report from the Commission on the establishment of a European Foundation
COM(77)600 final. 17 Nov 1977. 31p

The Tindemans Report recommends the establishment of a European Foundation whose object will be 'to promote, either directly or by assisting existing bodies, anything which could help towards greater understanding among our peoples by placing the emphasis on human contact: youth activities, university exchanges, scientific debates and symposia, meetings between the socio-professional categories, cultural and information activities' (*see* 11). At its meeting in March 1977, the European Council invited the Commission to compile a report on the terms of reference, nature and funding of such a Foundation, in response to which the Commission itself appointed a group of independent experts to assist its compilation. This report, prepared by the working group and approved by the Commission for submission to the European Council, outlines the main characteristics, objectives, working methods and structure of the proposed European Foundation. Part 1 outlines the tasks and objectives of the Foundation and the activities it might pursue with regard to youth work, scientific and research work, social and occupational groups, culture and information and external relations. The second part of the document is concerned with the structure and financing of such a Foundation. The document was published as Supplement 5/77 to the *Bulletin of the European Communities*. (*See also* 14.)

13 Commission report on European Union
1977   COM(77)623 final. 23 Nov 1977. 5p
1978   COM(78)653 final. 20 Nov 1978. 5p

After consideration of the Tindemans Report (*see* 11) at the European Council meeting at The Hague in November 1976, it was decided that the Ministers of Foreign Affairs and the Commission would be invited to prepare annual reports on the main results to date and the prospects for further progress towards European Union in the short term. In these subsequent annual reports, the Commission reviews developments made during the year under review and the areas in which immediate progress can be made. The 1977 report was published, together with the report by the Ministers of Foreign Affairs, in Supplement 8/77 to the *Bulletin of the European Communities*. The 1978 report, also in conjunction with the report from the Ministers of Foreign Affairs, was published in Supplement 1/79 to the *Bulletin of the European Communities*.

14 European Foundation
COM(78)51 final. 8 Feb 1978. 6p

EP Report: *Working doc* 575/77. 13 Mar 1978. R. Johnston. 8p
EP Debate: *Annex OJ* No 228, 14 Mar 1978, pp 36–46
EP Resolution: *OJ* C85, 10 Apr 1978, p 23

At its meeting in December 1977, the European Council decided in principle to create a European Foundation to promote exchanges and contacts between European citizens as visualized in the Tindemans Report (*see* 11) and the subsequent Commission document on the topic (*see* 12). In this communication, the Commission makes more precise its proposals on a number of aspects of the projected Foundation. In particular, it makes suggestions as to the scope of the work of the Foundation, its priority objectives, its structure and financing. The Commission subsequently submitted a draft Convention setting up a European Foundation (SEC(78) 1930 final).

15 Global appraisal of the budgetary problems of the Community
COM(78)64 final. 27 Feb 1978. 25p

EP Report: *Working doc* 3/78. 15 Mar 1978. M. Bangemann. 21p
EP Debate: *Annex OJ* No 228, 17 Mar 1978, pp 187–193
EP Resolution: *OJ* C85, 10 Apr 1978, pp 52–55

EP Report: *Working doc* 54/78. 11 Apr 1978. M. Bangemann. 30p
EP Debate: *Annex OJ* No 229, 14 Apr 1978, pp 275–280
EP Resolution: *OJ* C108, 8 May 1978, pp 63–65

At the European Council meeting in December 1975, it was agreed that each Spring a joint meeting of Ministers of Foreign Affairs would, together with the Commission, engage in a wide-ranging exchange of views on budget prospects and problems before the Commission commenced its task of drawing up a preliminary draft budget. This communication was prepared by the Commission for one such meeting, due to take place in the Spring of 1978. In the first part of the document, the Commission suggests some general guidelines for the years ahead, followed in the second part by suggestions for certain matters to be given priority from a medium-term budget point of view. A third section considers the main effect of the suggestions made in the previous two parts on the composition of the 1979 budget. More detailed consideration of the issues raised in the first two parts of the document is given in an annex on medium-term budget guidelines. The Commission later translated its thinking into practical proposals in the shape of a draft budget for 1979, published as Supplement 6/78 to the *Bulletin of the European Communities*.

16 Financing the Community budget—the way ahead
COM(78)531 final. 21 Nov 1978. 24p

Council Decision 70/243/ECSC, EEC, EURATOM of 21 April 1970 provides for the financing of Community activities from customs duties, agricultural levies and contributions from member states, later to be replaced by the proceeds of a Community rate of VAT of no more than 1 per cent (JO L94, 28 Apr 1970, pp 19–22). This memorandum from the Commission contains the Commission's views on what should happen when the Community budget outstrips these sources of revenue, a situation expected to occur in 1981. In its introduction to the document, the Commission explains why this will happen and examines the options available to the Community. It then examines in more detail the present system of financing the Community budget and explores the relationship between existing sources of finance and Community expenditure. The Commission then draws attention in turn to the institutional, technical and economic considerations that have to be taken into account before arguing the case for and against the principal possible sources of additional revenue for the Community budget. The Commission indicates that formal proposals will be forthcoming in due time. The communication was published as Supplement 8/78 to the *Bulletin of the European Communities*.

CHAPTER 3

Economic and financial affairs

Descriptive essay

The stated aim of the Treaty of Rome is to promote 'an ever closer union among the peoples of Europe' and, according to Article 2, by 'progressively approximating the economic policies of Member States, to promote throughout the Community a harmonious development of economic activities'. The Treaty goes on in Article 6 to state that 'Member States shall, in close cooperation with the institutions of the Community, coordinate their respective economic policies to the extent necessary to attain the objectives of this Treaty'. The general intention was to provide a framework within which the economies of member states could prosper and derive mutual benefit from their association and gradual integration. The objective was to be achieved by means of the establishment of a common market within which obstacles to economic activity across national boundaries would be eliminated, and by the evolution of common policies which would replace disparate national policies in a number of defined areas. Other chapters in this book look in some detail at the documentation generated by the Commission in the implementation of Treaty ideals; this particular chapter is concerned with the part played by the Commission in the management of the European economy and in the promotion of greater coordination between the economic policies of member countries.

Coordination of economic policies is more a question of guidance and advice than of regulation, of consultation than of law-making. Consequently, many of the documents prepared by the Commission are of a descriptive or analytical nature in which the Commission collates economic data and identifies economic trends as a basis for the discussion of means for coordinating policy. The role of the Commission is to monitor the performance of the European economy, to discern trends and to determine strategies for its overall development. Information received from member states on their short-term economic performance is collated, medium and long-term policy guidelines are prepared and studies on the state of the European economy at a particular point in time and its prospects for the future are undertaken. Three major fact-finding exercises have been undertaken on behalf of the Commission by panels of experts under the chairmanship of Pierre Uri for use as a backcloth against which to plan policy. The first was undertaken in 1958 at the time of the inception of the Community (see 17), the second in 1962 (see 19) and the third on the occasion of the tenth anniversary of the Community (see 24). A further stock-taking was undertaken by Pierre Maillet at the time of the enlargement of the Communities (see 27), shortly followed by an appraisal of economic performance and prospects carried out by the Commission (see 31).

Particularly influential in terms of the evolution of economic policy has been the series of medium-term economic policy programmes prepared by the Medium-Term Economic Policy Committee for submission by the Commission to the Council (*see* 61–73). The aim of these programmes is to provide medium-term guidelines for the development of economic policy in member countries over a five year period; they provide a broad strategy and perspective against which national policy decisions concerning the management of the economy can be taken.

Article 103 of the EEC Treaty declares that 'Member States shall regard their conjunctural policies as a matter of common concern. They shall consult each other and the Commission on the measures to be taken in the light of the prevailing circumstances'. The section of the chapter devoted to short-term policy illustrates the role of the Commission in this matter; it monitors the implementation and effects of national economic policies and issues guidelines for the conduct of economic policy both as a direct response to a particular set of circumstances and on a regular basis in the context of established consultative machinery. On the assumption that regular consultation will, in itself, gradually lead to closer coordination of policy, a number of pieces of Community legislation have been passed with a view to creating formal procedures and machinery to facilitate regular consultation. Notable in this respect is Council Decision 71/141/EEC of 22 March 1971 on the closer coordination of member states' short-term economic policies (*JO* L73, 27 Mar 1971, pp 12–13), Council Decision 74/120/EEC of 18 February 1974 on the attainment of a high degree of convergence of the economic policies of member states (*OJ* L63, 5 Mar 1974, pp 16–18), and Council Decision 74/122/EEC of 18 February 1974 setting up an Economic Policy Committee 'to promote coordination of Member States' short and medium-term economic policies' (*OJ* L63, 5 Mar 1974, pp 21–22).

A considerable amount of documentation on the short-term economic position of the Community has been produced as a consequence of the provisions of the Community acts referred to in the previous paragraph. Of particular significance is the *Annual report on the economic situation in the Community* which, on the basis of an assessment of the current economic situation, proposes guidelines for member states to follow in their short-term economic policy during the coming year (*see* 82). Other documents resulting directly from these pieces of legislation include the annual report to the Council, in which the Commission adjusts economic policy guidelines for the current year in the light of economic developments (*see* 91), an associated annual summary account of the economic policies pursued by member states in the previous year (*see* 92 & 96), and quantitative guidelines for the preparation of national budgets (*see* 94). The *Annual economic review*, prepared by the Commission as a separate background document to the annual economic report (*see* 101), is a particularly useful source of factual data on economic trends and the outlook for the coming year. Together with the *Annual report on the economic situation* it now forms the November issue of *European economy*, a thrice-yearly publication issued by the Commission. The other two issues, published in March and July, review the current economic situation in the Community, and contain reports and studies on problems of topical interest. Three separate supplements are also published. *Series A—Recent economic trends* consists of a monthly statistical commentary on the most recent trends in industrial production, consumer prices, unemployment, the balance of trade and exchange rates. *Series B—Economic prospects:*

business survey results reports monthly on the main results of opinion surveys of industrial managers in the Community, more fully recorded in the publication *Results of the business survey carried out among managements in the Community*. The third supplement, *Series C—Economic prospects: consumer survey results*, reports on the consumer survey carried out three times a year in the Community.

European economy is a relatively new publication, issued regularly since 1979. During the period covered by this guide, its function was fulfilled by its predecessor called *The economic situation in the Community*. Published quarterly, it devoted two issues to an analysis of the current economic situation in the Community, another to the Commission's proposal for an annual report on the economic situation in the Community (*see* 82), and a final issue to the Commission's annual communication on the adjustment of these guidelines for the coming year. Commission communications to the Council on the economic situation were often reproduced in this quarterly publication, which was supplemented by *Graphs and notes on the economic situation in the Community*, a monthly publication whose aim was to provide, by means of graphs and brief commentaries, a regular analysis of the development of short-term indicators.

Each issue of the *General report on the activities of the European Communities* contains a summary analysis of current economic trends and short-term prospects. Statistical data on short-term developments appear in *Eurostatistics: data for short-term economic analysis*, published in two three-language editions which appear alternately at the beginning and middle of each month. The aim of the publication is to present harmonized data on the main indicators useful for following short-term economic developments in the Community as a whole and in individual member countries. A series of country tables contains a selection of the economic indicators most often used in each country, together with data on the three candidate countries, the United States of America and Japan. Community tables provide comparable data on such indicators as national accounts, employment, industrial production, trade, prices and the balance of payments. Before 1979, the principal short-term indicators were published in the *Monthly general statistics bulletin*. Annual data on a wide range of topics which include population, national accounts, agriculture, energy, industry, trade and finance are published in *Basic statistics of the Community*, a handy pocket compendium of statistics.

ECONOMIC AND MONETARY UNION

It will be clear from an analysis of the entries in this chapter that regular disturbances in international monetary markets, particularly their disruptive effects upon the administration of such common policies as the common agricultural policy and their tendency to increase the divergence between national economies, have been a constant source of concern to the Commission. Surveys of the basic characteristics of the monetary instruments and policies of member states have been undertaken (*see* 18 & 25), general programmes for closer collaboration between member states have been put forward (*see* 20), and numerous short-term proposals have been drafted to deal with particular sets of circumstances (*see* 76 & 81 for instance).

In promoting the coordination of policy, the Commission has been assisted by the Monetary Committee established by the Treaty of Rome with a remit 'to keep under review the monetary and financial situation of the Member States and of the Community and the general payments system of the Member States and to report regularly thereon to the Council and to the Commission' (Article 105). A useful source of information on the work of the Monetary Committee is its annual report, published separately by the Committee and in the 'C' series of the *Official journal of the European Communities*. The 19th report for 1977, for instance, appears in the *Official journal of the European Communities* C156, 3 July 1978, pp 1–15. Amongst the several items published by the Monetary Committee, one of the most useful is the *Compendium of Community monetary texts* (cat CB-28-79-504-EN-C. ISBN 92-825-1148-0), reproducing the texts of important pieces of Community legislation on monetary affairs. The machinery of monetary cooperation also includes the Committee of Governors of Central Banks established in 1964, and the European Monetary Cooperation Fund established in 1973 to ensure that the Community exchange rate system operates satisfactorily and to manage short-term monetary support.

Much of the effort expended by the Commission in an attempt to minimize the disruptive efforts of monetary disturbances has been concerned with the promotion of a grand design for economic and monetary union (EMU). EMU is a concept which involves closer coordination of the economic policies of member states than hitherto experienced and fixed exchange rates between national currencies, leading progressively to a single European currency which would give some measure of protection against excessive exchange rate fluctuations on the international monetary markets. In the long-term, EMU implies a central monetary authority to which member states give up their power to conduct national monetary and budgetary policies. Further information on the concept of EMU and its policy implications may be gathered from the booklet on the subject prepared by Directorate-General X (Information) and issued as number 3/79 in the *European documentation* series.

The documents listed in the section of the chapter on EMU reflect the considerable activity concentrated on the concept from 1969 to 1972 when member states embraced the idea of EMU. Notable amongst these documents are the Barre Plan (*see 46*) and the Werner Report (*see 48 & 49*), on the basis of which the Commission submitted proposals which formed the basis for a phased programme for the introduction of EMU (*see 50*). However, despite the introduction of coordination procedures for national economic policies and the establishment of the European monetary snake, the economic and financial crisis following dramatic oil price rises prevented any significant progress towards EMU.

The concept was revived by Roy Jenkins, President of the Commission, in the first Jean Monnet Lecture at the European Institute in Florence on 27 October 1977, an intervention quickly followed by a Commission document, which aimed to give fresh impetus to the objective (*see 59*). After discussion on currency stabilization at its meeting in Brussels on 4 to 5 December 1978, the European Council adopted a Resolution on the introduction of a European Monetary System (EMS), the text of which, together with associated documents, is reproduced in *European economy* No 2, March 1979. The EMS is also the subject of attention in *European economy* No 3, July 1979. This issue contains a commentary on the background to and main elements of the EMS and a series of key documents, including the texts of European Council documents and relevant Community legislative acts.

Bibliographical record

17 Rapport sur la situation économique dans les pays de la Communauté
Comm EEC, 1958. 608p (cat 2079)

In response to the instruction contained in Article 245 of the EEC Treaty that 'upon taking up its duties, the Commission shall undertake the studies and arrange the contacts needed for making an overall survey of the economic situation of the Community', a working party of experts, under the chairmanship of Pierre Uri, was invited to prepare a general review of the structure of the economies of member states and of the trends that would determine their future development. This subsequent report of more than 600 pages constitutes a valuable factual record of the state of individual national economies on the eve of the establishment of the European Economic Community. The object was not to define economic policy or to indulge in economic forecasting but to provide the Commission with a sound factual base for use in evaluating the EEC's likely impact and in the identification of areas for future attention. The first part of the report consists of a synoptic review of the data accumulated during the course of the study, in which the working party picks out the salient features and inherent weaknesses of the European economy. The working party looks at the internal structure of the economies of member states in order to discover their potential for development and future competitive capacity, their trade relations with the outside world and financial policies. This digest is followed by separate chapters on each of the six member countries prepared by national experts and on the territories having special relationships with them, namely, Algeria, the Belgian Congo, Somalia, Dutch New Guinea and the overseas territories having special links with France. Prepared according to a common plan devised by the working party, each national survey analyses the structure of production, external economic relations and the financial and price system in the country under review. The whole text, published in English under the title *Report on the economic situation in the countries of the Community*, is liberally provided with supportive statistical tables. Following the enlargement of the European Communities in 1973, the Commission invited independent research institutes to prepare similar reports on the three new member states. The resultant study of the British economy, prepared by the National Institute of Economic and Social Research, was published by the Commission in 1975 in a volume called *The United Kingdom economy* (cat 8461), issued as number nine in the series *Studies—Economic and financial series*. A similar report called *The Irish economy* (cat 8462), prepared by Kieran A. Kennedy and Richard Burton of the Economic and Social Research Institute, Dublin, was also published in 1975 by the Commission as number ten in the same series.

18 **Les instruments de la politique monétaire dans les pays de la Communauté économique européenne**
Comm EEC, 1962. 279p (cat 8051)

A descriptive study of the instruments of monetary policy in member states for use by the Monetary Committee and the Commission in their discussions about the nature, use and effectiveness of such instruments. The study opens with an overview and comparative analysis of the basic characteristics of monetary policy and instruments in member states. This is followed by a systematic description of the instruments of monetary policy in each of the six member states. An English language version of the report was published under the title *The instruments of monetary policy in the countries of the European Community*. (*See also* 25.)

19 **Rapport sur les perspectives de développement économique dans la C.E.E. de 1960 à 1970**
Doc II/4344/62. n.d. 2 vols, 77p, 25p

In recognition of the fact that the approximation of economic policies referred to in Article 2 of the EEC Treaty must cover not only short-term measures but also the longer-term growth policies of member states, the Commission invited the same group of experts as had prepared the 1958 study (*see* 17) to look at the prospects for economic development in the Community during the period 1960 to 1970. This report, again prepared under the chairmanship of Pierre Uri, contains the working party's preliminary findings, submitted to the Commission in June 1962. Part 1 explains the methods used by the working group for making projections and the programme it adopted. Part 2 contains the provisional results of the projections conducted according to the principles explained in Part 1. These include estimates of the projected growth of the gross national product of member states in 1965 and 1970, together with a breakdown of these estimates into the main components of the national product. A separate volume contains a series of tables and graphs. The report was given full publication by the Commission in 1962; an English language version was entitled *Economic development prospects in the EEC from 1960 to 1970* (cat 8071).

20 **La coopération monétaire et financière au sein de la Communauté économique européenne**
II/COM(63)216 final. 19 June 1963. 20p

EP Report: *Doc de séance* 103/63. 4 Jan 1964. F.Vals. 12p
EP Debate: *Débs* No 69, 21 Jan 1964, pp 41–48
EP Resolution: *JO* 24, 8 Feb 1964, pp 409–410
ESC Opinion: *JO* 38, 5 Mar 1964, pp 652–655

A communication in which the Commission makes recommendations for closer collaboration between member states in monetary and financial affairs, prepared in compliance with Article 105 of the EEC Treaty, which requires the Commission to submit recommendations to the Council on how member states can 'provide for cooperation between their appropriate administrative departments and between their central banks'. The communication is composed of an introductory statement together with three specific recommendations supported by draft Decisions for their implementation. In the introductory statement, the Commission outlines the reasoning behind the three recommendations, with particular emphasis upon the growing interdependence between national monetary policies and economic integration in the European Economic Community and the need to extend monetary cooperation into both financial and budgetary policies and into international monetary relations. The first recommendation on collaboration between the central banks and the European Economic Community was adopted by the Council on 8 May 1964 in Council Decision 64/300/EEC (JO 77, 21 May 1964, pp 1206–1207); the second recommendation on cooperation in international monetary relations was adopted on the same date in Council Decision 64/301/EEC (JO 77, 21 May 1964, pp 1207–1208), and the third recommendation on cooperation between the competent government departments of member states in matters of budgetary policy was also adopted by the Council on 8 May 1964 in Council Decision 64/299/EEC (JO 77, 21 May 1964, pp 1205–1206). The communication was published in a Supplement to the *Bulletin of the European Economic Community* 7–1963.

21 Le développement d'un marché européen des capitaux
Comm EEC, 1967. 400p (cat 8181)

See 129.

22 Nécessité et modalités d'une action dans le domaine des capitaux
COM(69)200. 5 Mar 1969. 12p

See 131.

23 La politique du marché obligataire dans les pays de la CEE: instruments existants et leurs application de 1966 à 1969
Comm EC, 1970. 196p (cat 8320)

The report of a working party established by the Monetary Committee on 30 October 1967 to gather information on the ways in which equilibrium is established on the bond markets in each member state. Part 1 consists of an inventory of the procedures and instruments used by member states. Part 2 takes the form of a general account of the policies adopted by member states on their bond markets from 1966 to the middle of 1969. The report was also published in an English language version entitled *Policy on the bond markets in the countries of the EEC: current instruments and the use made of them from 1966 to 1969*.

24 Rapport sur la capacité concurrentielle de la Communauté européenne
Doc II/481/71. November 1971. 3 vols, 614p, 463p, 50p

A massive, three volume report from the study group set up by the Commission on the occasion of the tenth anniversary of the establishment of the European Economic Community to carry out an analysis of the competitive capacity of the European economy. Under the chairmanship of Pierre Uri, who had held a similar position on important working parties in 1958 (*See* 17) and in 1962 (*See* 19), it was the task of the working party to produce a report that would contribute to a better understanding of the problems to be faced and the policies that needed to be pursued as the Community moved out of its transitional phase. In the first volume, the working party takes stock of the resources available in the Community under such headings as manpower, capital and investment, natural resources and infrastructures, research and development. This first volume also looks at Community structures, regional development, markets, productivity and administration. Volume 2 deals with the costs of manpower, capital and public finance and with international relations. Volume 3 consists of a summary of chapters in the previous two volumes. It is also worth noting that the SOEC marked the tenth anniversary of the EEC by producing *Quelques chiffres: dix ans de Marché commun en tableaux 1958–1967* (cat 4486), a useful compilation of statistics designed to show how the economies of the Six expanded during this ten year period, also published in English as *The Common Market ten years on: tables 1958–1967*.

25 La politique monétaire dans les pays de la Communauté économique européenne
Comm EC, 1972. 451p (cat 8355)

A new study of the instruments of monetary policy in member states which brings up-to-date an earlier report compiled in 1962 (*see* 18). As in the previous study, the volume commences with a general review of the objectives of monetary policy and of the range and development of monetary policy instruments. This is followed by separate chapters on monetary policy in each of the six member countries. An English language version of the report was published as *Monetary policy in the countries of the European Economic Community: institutions and instruments*. In 1974 a supplementary volume of the same title was issued to cover the three new member countries, Denmark, Ireland and the United Kingdom (Doc II/213/74).

26 Organisations des relations monétaires et financières au sein de la Communauté
COM(72)50. 12 Jan 1972. 13p

See 51.

27 Fifteen years of Community policy
Comm EC, 1973. 69p (cat 8438)

A report prepared by Pierre Maillet, a Commission official, whose purpose was 'to analyse the effects of Community policy on the economies of member countries and on the Community as a whole in the period 1958–1970'. Prepared at the time of the enlargement of the Community, the report makes an assessment of how far Treaty objectives have been achieved, the effects of Community action and the capacity of the Community to cope with the problems it has had to face during this period. Rather than produce a straightforward historical review of the development of various policies, Mr Maillet decided to adopt a thematic approach to his subject. Consequently, the achievements of the past 15 years are considered under four main headings, the development of production structures; the development of incomes, standards of living and the use of the national product; the steadiness of the growth rate and the Community's contribution to the creation of a world economic order.

28 **Report from the Commission to the Council on the adjustment of short-term monetary support arrangements and the conditions for the progressive pooling of reserves**
COM(73)1099. 27 June 1973. 29p

See 86.

29 **European economic integration and monetary unification**
Doc II/520/1/73. Oct 1973. 311p

See 57.

30 **Report on the present or foreseeable impact of the energy supply situation on production, employment, prices, the balance of payments and the monetary reserves**
SEC(74)247 final. 30 Jan 1974. 10p

See 319.

31 **Inventory of the Community's economic and financial situation since enlargement and survey of future developments**
COM(74)1800 final. 25 Oct 1974. 31p

A report drawn up at the request of the Council in which the Commission makes an appraisal of the economic and financial position of the Community two years after its enlargement and endeavours to draw conclusions for the future. Divided into two parts, the report first considers the state of the European economy from 1972 to 1974, with comments on the Community's contribution during this period and forecasts of future economic prospects. The second part consists of a rather more detailed analysis of existing budgetary provisions and their foreseeable consequences up to and beyond 1979. The report was published as Supplement 7/74 to the *Bulletin of the European Communities*.

32 **Tripartite Conference: economic and social situation in the Community and outlook**
COM(75)540/2. 5 Nov 1975. 20p

See 532.

33 **The trend of public finance in the member states of the Community from 1966 to 1970**
Comm EC, 1976. 236p (cat 8713)

A study of the trend of public finance in the six original member countries from 1966 to 1970 published as number 11 in the series *Studies—Economic and financial series*. Part A consists of a comparative analysis of the trend of revenue and expenditure in government as a whole, followed in Part B by a comparison of the economic accounts of central government. The revenue and expenditure of local government is the subject of Part C, which is itself followed in Part D by a general review of the social security sector and a series of statistical tables on the economic accounts of each member state. This volume follows a similar report called

L'évolution des finances publiques dans les Etats-membres des Communautés européennes de 1957 à 1966 (cat 8291), published by the Commission in 1970 as number eight in the same series, a volume itself preceded in 1964 by number two in the series called *Les recettes et les dépenses des administrations publiques dans les pays membres de la CEE* (cat 8125).

34 Report of the study group 'problems of inflation'
Doc II/198/76. 3 Mar 1976. 41p

The final report from a group of experts under the chairmanship of R. Maldague, Head of the National Plan, Brussels, invited by the Commission to examine the problems of inflation in the Community. The working party emphasizes the deeply rooted nature of the problem and the need to undertake a programme of fundamental reforms and measures to achieve a more balanced economic, social and political structure. Chapter 1 establishes a general framework for this new structural approach. The three following chapters deal in turn with the problems raised by labour and employment policy, the means for achieving less inflationary consumption and new guidelines for the management of public finance. The final chapter is mainly concerned with the problems of organizing competition and containing meso-economic firms. It is worth noting that the SOEC published two useful volumes on inflation in 1976. The *Survey of retail prices 1975* contains the results of a survey designed to compare prices and consumer purchasing power parities of the national currencies in member states and *Consumer price indexes in the European Community*, written by Josef Stadlbauer, compares existing consumer price indexes in the Community.

35 Optica report 1976. Inflation and exchange rates: evidence and policy guidelines for the European Community
Doc II/855/76 final. 10 Feb 1977. 129p

The report of an independent group of experts under the chairmanship of Professor G. Basevi, invited by the Commission to verify and complete, mainly through statistical and econometric studies, the results contained in the report presented at the end of 1975 by the first Optica Group (Doc II/909/75). The report is divided into three chapters, reflecting the main themes of the study. Chapter 1 looks at the origins and consequences of exchange rate changes, Chapter 2 at enforcing purchasing power parity in the exchange markets, and Chapter 3 at the attractiveness of a European parallel currency.

36 Report of the study group on the role of public finance in European integration
Doc II/10/77. Apr 1977. 2 vols, 73p, 517p

A two volume report from the working group of independent experts, chaired by Sir Donald MacDougall, invited by the Commission at the end of 1974 to examine the future role of public finance at the Community level in the general context of European economic integration. Volume 1 contains the general report which includes an introduction and summary. Volume 2 contains a considerable quantity of more detailed data and evidence in the form of individual contributions from members of the study group and working papers submitted to the group. The report was subsequently published under the same title as number A13 (CB-N1-77-A13-EN-C) and B13 (CB-N1-77-B13-EN-C) in the series *Studies—Economic and financial series*.

37 Growth, stability and employment: stock-taking and prospects
COM(77)250 final. 23 May 1977. 16p

See 538.

38 The protection of savings in times of inflation and the question of indexation
COM(77)549 final. 10 Nov 1977. 99p

On 11 July 1975, the European Parliament adopted a Resolution in which it called upon the Commission 'to examine further the entire range of problems connected with index-linking and more particularly the protection of savings' (*OJ* C179, 6 Aug 1975, p 75). In this subsequent communication to the Parliament, the Commission makes a comprehensive survey of the question. The report opens with background information on the ways in which savings are badly affected in times of inflation, on the technical aspects of indexation and on the possible scope for the indexation of savings. The Commission then weighs up the pros and cons of indexing savings with reference to its impact on the economy and financial markets and with reference to the question of social justice. The most representative and recent cases of indexation in practice are cited before the Commission assesses the general attitude of both member states and the Community towards the indexation of financial assets. Although much remains to be done in this field, the Commission concludes with outline measures that might be taken to protect and encourage savings generally and to protect the savings of the less well-off in particular. A series of annexes include the text of the parliamentary committee report and Resolution which stimulated this communication, a series of legal texts relating to indexation and a bibliography. Other difficulties caused by inflation were examined by the Commission in a study called *The impact of rising prices on taxation and social security contributions in the European Community* (cat 8854), issued in 1976 as number 12 in the *Studies—Economic and financial series*.

39 Report of the study group on the new characteristics of socio-economic development: 'a blueprint for Europe'
Doc II/570/7/76. Dec 1977. 60p

The report of a working party of independent experts under the chairmanship of Giorgio Ruffolo, charged with the preparation of a broad assessment of economic problems and related matters in the Community, designed to highlight the most salient features of economic and social trends, the problems they pose and possible solutions. The report is divided into three parts. The first, entitled 'Europe at the crossroads', examines the principal characteristics of the steady growth phase which has marked the 25 year period since the Second World War, the structural changes which have taken place during this period, the factors behind the crisis which emerged in the late sixties and early seventies and the changes which this crisis have produced in economic and social development. The second part, entitled 'A blueprint for Europe', presents a scenario for the future in the form of a development model designed to meet the basic aspirations of an advanced society and compatible with foreseeable technological and ecological constraints. The final part, called 'A strategy for change', explains how to work towards this new development model, using such headings as the decentralization of government, the control of economic power, the development of social self-organization and the role of Community institutions.

40 Sectoral change in the European economies, from 1960 to the recession
Doc II/253/4/76. Jan 1978. 166p

The report of a group of independent experts under the chairmanship of R. Maldague, entrusted by the Commission with the task of studying the main characteristics of sectoral development in the economies of member states since the establishment of the EEC.

41 Working paper on the role of the tertiary (including public) sectors in the achievement of growth, stability and full employment
SEC(78)1526 final. 14 Apr 1978. 27p

See 545.

42 Report of the European planning study group
Doc II/210/4/78. May 1978. 81p

A report from a working party of independent experts under the chairmanship of Claude Gruson, charged by the Commission with an examination of the role longer-term Community planning should play in helping the Community to overcome its economic difficulties and the problems likely to arise in the future. After an introduction and definition of what is meant by planning, the working party moves on to summarize the experience of member states and the Community with regard to medium and long-term forecasting. The working party then proceeds to examine the provision, organization and use of indicative planning information before making certain recommendations concerning the possible future contribution planning can make to Community development. The report concludes with an annex which contains more detailed information on the planning experience of West Germany, Belgium, France, Italy, the Netherlands, the United Kingdom and the Community.

43 The economic implications of demographic change in the European Community: 1975–1995
Doc II/528/77. June 1978. 2 vols, 120p, 85p

A two volume report prepared by a group of independent experts under the chairmanship of Professor A. Kervyn de Lettenhove, on the economic implications of demographic change in the European Community. The prospect of a considerable increase in young people reaching working age during a period of recession, followed by a sharp fall in the number of young people coming on to the job market caused the Commission, in the context of its studies of medium-term economic assessments, to request this study. In the first volume, the working party looks first at population projections for each member state and forecasts of activity rates in member states during the period 1975 to 1995. The working group then makes some calculations as to the future size of the labour force and the effect of migration on the labour market in the European Community. The second volume consists of a technical annex in support of the findings recounted in the first volume. Comparable statistical data on population trends in the Community are available in the SOEC publication *Demographic statistics*.

44 Report on some structural aspects of growth
COM(78)255 final. 22 June 1978. 28p

A report prepared by the Commission for presentation to the European Council meeting at Bremen, following an agreement reached by Heads of Government or State at an earlier European Council meeting held in Copenhagen in April 1978, to draw up a common growth strategy to reverse the present recessionary trends in the European economy. In the first part of the document, the Commission comments upon the present situation and the outlook for the future. It then moves on to discuss the search for a growth strategy at the Community level before analysing the global and sectoral elements that are required of such a strategy.

45 Tripartite Conference of 9 November 1978
COM(78)512 final. 10 Oct 1978. 34p

See 546.

ECONOMIC AND MONETARY UNION

46 Mémorandum de la Commission au Conseil sur la coordination des politiques économiques et la coopération monétaire au sein de la Communauté
COM(69)150. 12 Feb 1969. 20p

EP Report: *Doc de séance* 229/68. 11 Mar 1969. C. Riedel. 9p
           Doc de séance 30/69. 5 May 1969. C. Riedel. 10p
EP Debate: *Annexe JO* No 114, 6 May 1969, pp 36–67
EP Resolution: *JO* C63, 28 May 1969, pp 9–10

A memorandum in which the Commission calls for the coordination of short and medium-term economic policies and the establishment of machinery for monetary cooperation, drawn up in clarification of points raised during Council discussion of an earlier Commission document on current economic and monetary problems (*see* 76). Often referred to as the 'Barre Plan', after Raymond Barre, the member of the Commission responsible for its preparation, the document falls into three main parts. In the first, the Commission recalls earlier initiatives designed to strengthen economic and monetary cohesion and emphasizes that the measures called for in this document are consistent with policies worked out over a number of years. In the second part, the Commission analyses the state and the short-comings of the present situation, with particular emphasis on the need for convergence of national medium-term economic policies. In the final part, the Commission calls for specific measures to coordinate medium and short-term economic policies and to establish Community machinery for monetary cooperation. The document concludes with a draft Council Decision on a consultation procedure on short-term economic policy, which was adopted by the Council on 17 July 1969 in Council Decision 69/227/EEC (JO L183, 25 July 1969, p 41). On the basis of proposals made in this memorandum, given formal publication as a Supplement to *Bulletin of the European Communities* 3-1969, the Council also adopted on 22 March 1971 Decision 71/142/EEC on closer cooperation between the central banks of member states (JO L73, 27 Mar 1971, p 14) and Decision 71/143/EEC setting up machinery for medium-term financial assistance (JO L73, 27 Mar 1971, pp 15–17). (*See also* 67.)

47 Communication de la Commission au Conseil au sujet de l'élaboration d'un plan par étapes vers une union économique et monétaire
COM(70)300. 4 Mar 1970. 19p

EP Report: *Doc de séance* 148/70. 5 Nov 1970. J.-E. Bousch. 15p
　　　　　 Doc de séance 187/70. 30 Nov 1970. J.-E. Bousch. 9p
EP Debate: *Annexe JO* No 131, 3 Dec 1970, pp 39–66
EP Resolution: *JO* C151, 29 Dec 1970, pp 23–25

In the final communiqué issued after the summit meeting held in The Hague on 1 and 2 December 1969, the Heads of State or Government 'reaffirmed their readiness to expedite the further action needed to strengthen the Community and promote its development into an economic union' (*Bull EC*, 1-1970, pp 11–16). This memorandum was prepared by the Commission in direct response to an instruction made by participants at that meeting that Community institutions should draw up in 1970, on the basis of the Commission's earlier memorandum (*see* 46), a plan for the establishment by stages of economic and monetary union. As an initial contribution, to be supplemented by further documentation as appropriate, this communication is restricted to a brief discussion of the guiding principles which the Commission believes should determine the nature of economic and monetary union, and the main features of each of the stages by which it should be introduced. In the first section, the Commission sets out its views on the objectives to be attained, the methods to be employed and other matters relating particularly to the need for consistency between policies, the stability of exchange rates, monetary unification and the international monetary system. In the second part of the document, the Commission outlines the measures which should be taken in each of three stages, the first stage consisting of preliminary measures during the period 1970 to 1971, the second stage of preparatory measures during the period 1972 to 1975, preceding the definitive establishment of economic and monetary union from 1976. The memorandum was published as a Supplement to the *Bulletin of the European Communities* 3-1970. After initial consideration of the paper the Council decided to establish a working party to examine the matter further (*See also* 48 & 49).

48 Rapport intérimaire au Conseil et à la Commission concernant la réalisation par étapes de l'union économique et monétaire de la Communauté

Doc 9.504/11/70. May 1970. 13p

EP Report: *Doc de séance* 148/70. 5 Nov 1970. J.-E. Bousch. 17p
EP Debate: *Annexe JO* No 131, 3 Dec 1970, pp 39–66
EP Resolution: *JO* C151, 29 Dec 1970, pp 23–25

On receipt of the Commission's communication on economic and monetary union (*see* 47), the Council decided on 6 March 1970 to establish a working party whose terms of reference were to 'draw up a report comprising an analysis of the various suggestions and enabling the fundamental choices to be made for the phased establishment of the economic and monetary union of the Community' (*JO* L59, 14 Mar 1970, p 44). This document consists of the preliminary report which the working party was instructed to present to the Council and to the Commission before the end of May 1970. Composed of the chairmen of the Monetary Committee, the Committee of Governors of Central Banks, the Medium-Term Economic Policy Committee, the Short-Term Economic Policy Committee and the Budget Policy Committee, together with a Commission representative, all meeting under the chairmanship of Pierre Werner, Prime Minister and Finance Minister of Luxembourg, the working party's aim in this document was to establish fundamental principles and to make some practical proposals to initiate the first stage of economic and monetary union. The report commences with a brief look at the current situation and then, by way of comparison, at the characteristics of the ultimate goal. The working party then proceeds to look in more detail at the measures to be enacted during the first three year stage of economic and monetary union. The document concludes with annexes which include the text of the final communiqué issued at the conclusion of The Hague summit conference, the terms of reference and composition of the working party and a brief memorandum on a European Exchange Stabilization Fund. The interim report, whose conclusions were adopted by the Council in June 1970, was published as a Supplement to the *Bulletin of the European Communities* 7-1970 and also reproduced in the *Journal officiel des Communautés européennes* C94, 23 July 1970, pp 1–11. A final report was submitted in October (*see* 49).

49 Rapport au Conseil et à la Commission concernant la réalisation par étapes de l'union économique et monétaire dans la Communauté
Doc 16.956/11/70. 8 Oct 1970. 74p

EP Report: *Doc de séance* 187/70. 30 Nov 1970. J.-E. Bousch. 9p
EP Debate: *Annexe JO* No 131, 3 Dec 1970, pp 39–66
EP Resolution: *JO* C151, 29 Dec 1970, pp 23–25

Popularly known as the 'Werner report', this final report from the working party set up by the Council in March 1970 under the chairmanship of Pierre Werner, Prime Minister and Finance Minister of Luxembourg, constitutes a major contribution to the discussions concerning the phased introduction of economic and monetary union. Incorporating material first presented in the interim report (*see* 48) together with a number of new chapters, the document describes the measures that member states will have to take to attain economic and monetary union and the consequences that will result from its achievement. In common with the interim report, the final report first compares the existing situation at the start of the process with what will replace it when final objectives have been achieved. The working party then proceeds to set out certain fundamental principles before describing specific proposals for initiating the process, with particular emphasis upon measures to be taken during the first phase to start on 1 January 1971. These proposals are considered under such headings as budget policy, fiscal policy, the policy for financial markets, domestic monetary and credit policy and external monetary policy. The working party also touches upon the institutional implications of its proposals. The document concludes with a number of annexes which include the text of the memorandum from the Committee of Governors of Central Banks of the Member States of the EEC to the working party. The report was published as a Supplement to the *Bulletin of the European Communities* 11-1970 and it also appeared in the *Journal officiel des Communautés européennes* C136, 11 Nov 1970, pp 1–38.

50 **Communication et propositions de la Commission au Conseil relatives à l'institution par étapes de l'union économique et monétaire**
COM(70)1250. 29 Oct 1970. 16p

EP Report: *Doc de séance* 187/70. 30 Nov 1970. J.-E. Bousch. 9p
EP Debate: *Annexe JO* No 131, 3 Dec 1970, pp 39–66
EP Resolution: *JO* C151, 29 Dec 1970, pp 23–25

A memorandum to the Council in which the Commission expresses its views on the Werner report (*see* 49) and makes a number of specific proposals for the phased introduction of economic and monetary union. The Commission confirms its general agreement with the conclusions reached by the working party and explains its reservations about certain aspects of the working party's findings. The memorandum is accompanied by a draft Council Resolution calling for the implementation of the first stage of economic and monetary union over a three year period starting on 1 January 1971, a draft Council Decision designed to strengthen the coordination of short-term economic policy between member states and a draft Council Decision on increased cooperation between the central banks of the Six. The memorandum was published in the *Journal officiel des Communautés européennes* C140, 26 Nov 1970, pp 20–26. On the basis of these proposals, the Council agreed to proceed to the first phase when it adopted a Resolution on 22 March 1971 in which representatives of member states expressed 'their political will to introduce, in the course of the next ten years, an economic and monetary union, in accordance with a phased plan commencing on 1 January 1971' (*JO* C28, 27 Mar 1971, pp 1–4). The Council also adopted on 22 March 1971 Decision 71/141/EEC on the coordination of short-term economic policies (*JO* L73, 27 Mar 1971, pp 12–13), and Decision 71/142/EEC on strengthening collaboration between central banks (*JO* L73, 27 Mar 1971, p 14).

51 **Organisations des relations monétaires et financières au sein de la Communauté**
COM(72)50. 12 Jan 1972. 13p

A memorandum from the Commission to the Council on the organization of monetary and financial relations within the Community, together with a draft

Council Resolution which includes recommendations for a reduction in the fluctuation margins of Community currencies. At its meeting on 31 January 1972, the Council expressed the wish that these proposals be placed in the context of economic and monetary union (*see* 52).

52 Vue d'ensemble sur les conditions de réalisation de la première étape de l'union économique et monétaire
SEC(72)622 final. 16 Feb 1972. 12p

A tabular presentation, compiled by the Commission in response to the Council's request that earlier proposals be placed in the context of economic and monetary union (*see* 51), of the achievements so far in the implementation of the first stage of economic and monetary union. The Commission examines in turn each of the specific provisions of the Council Resolution of 22 March 1971 (*JO* C28, 27 Mar 1971, pp 1–4), reporting on work in progress or already completed, problems encountered and still to be overcome and suggestions for further action. The report was published in the *Bulletin of the European Communities* 4-1972, pp 27–36.

53 Proposition de résolution du Conseil et des Représentants des Gouvernements des Etats membres relative à l'application de la Résolution du 22 mars 1971 concernant la réalisation par étapes de l'union économique et monétaire dans la Communauté
COM(72)250. 1 Mar 1972. 4p

EP Report: *Doc de séance* 1/72. 15 Mar 1972. W. Löhr. 9p
EP Debate: *Annexe JO* No 148, 16 Mar 1972, pp 101–103
EP Resolution: *JO* C36, 12 Apr 1972, pp 31–33

A proposal for a Council Resolution on the implementation of the Council Resolution of 22 March 1971 concerning the achievement by stages of economic and monetary union (*JO* C28, 27 Mar 1971, pp 1–4), in which the Commission sets out the principal measures which are needed to complete those already proposed by the Commission in the monetary and financial sectors. The Council approved the text at its meeting of 21 March 1972 (*JO* C38, 18 Apr 1972, pp 3–4). Divided into four parts, the Resolution first deals with increased coordination of member states' short-term economic policies. Part 2 is concerned with regional and structural measures, and Part 3 with measures to restrain the fluctuation of Community currencies on the foreign exchange markets. In the final part of the Resolution, the Council recognizes that priority must be given to Commission proposals on economic and monetary union, particularly those concerning tax harmonization and the evolution of a European capital market. In accordance with Part 3 of the Resolution and acting upon a proposal from the Commission (COM(73)68 final), the Council adopted on 3 April 1973 Regulation (EEC) No 907/73 establishing a European Monetary Cooperation Fund (*OJ* L89, 5 Apr 1973, pp 2–5). The task of the Fund was to ensure that the Community exchange rate system operated satisfactorily and to manage short-term monetary support.

54 Economic law of the member states of the European Communities in an economic and monetary union

Comm EC, 1973. 75p (cat 8408)

See 112.

55 Communication from the Commission to the Council on the progress achieved in the first stage of economic and monetary union, on the allocation of powers and responsibilities among the Community institutions and the member states essential to the proper functioning of economic and monetary union, and on the measures to be taken in the second stage of economic and monetary union
COM(73)570 final. 19 Apr 1973. 32p

EP Report: *Working doc* 107/73. 27 June 1973. Sir B. Rhys Williams. 6p
EP Debate: *Annex OJ* No 164, 4 July 1973, pp 157–170
EP Resolution: *OJ* C62, 31 July 1973, pp 31–32
ESC Opinion: *OJ* C115, 28 Sept 1974, pp 17–21

A document in which the Commission fulfils its promise, noted by the Council in its Resolution of 22 March 1971 (*JO* C28, 27 Mar 1971, pp 1–4), to table a report on the progress achieved in the first stage of economic and monetary union. It also takes the form of a response to the commitment entered into by Heads of State or Government at the Paris summit on 19 and 20 October 1972 to take the necessary measures during the course of 1973 to allow transition to the second stage of economic and monetary union on 1 January 1974, with a view to completing the process not later than 31 December 1980 (*Bull EC* 10-1972, pp 14–23). The document is divided into three main parts. In the first, the Commission reviews progress achieved in the first stage by comparing results attained with objectives pursued. The analysis also highlights the difficulties to be overcome and the lessons and conclusions to be drawn from the first stage. The second part consists of an outline action programme for the second stage to run from 1 January 1974 to 31 December 1976, which includes both guiding principles and practical proposals with regard to overall economic and structural policies. The final part examines the institutional implications of the measures with particular reference to the allocation of powers and responsibilities between Community institutions and member states. The document was published as Supplement 5/73 to the *Bulletin of the European Communities*.

56 Commission communication and proposals to the Council on the transition to the second stage of economic and monetary union
SEC(73)4200 final. 7 Nov 1973. 7p

EP Mot for Res: *Working doc* 260/73. 10 Dec 1973. 1p
EP Debate: *Annex OJ* No 169, 13 Dec 1973, pp 204–215
EP Resolution: *OJ* C2, 9 Jan 1974, pp 48–49
ESC Opinion: *OJ* C37, 1 Apr 1974, pp 5–7

A brief communication in which the Commission makes observations on the five specific proposals for the transition to the second stage of economic and monetary union submitted to the Council in a separate document (COM(73)1950) and later given full publication (*OJ* C114, 27 Dec 1973, pp 33–46). The Commission outlines the main areas in which progress is necessary, discusses the content of the specific proposals and urges the Council to take the necessary decisions to allow transition to the second stage. Although the Council was unable to adopt the draft Resolution on the implementation of the second stage (*OJ* C114, 27 Dec 1973, pp 33–35), other important decisions were taken on the basis of the Commission's proposals. On 18 February 1974, the Council adopted Decision 74/120/EEC on the attainment of a high degree of convergence of the economic policies of member states (*OJ* L63, 5 Mar 1974, pp 16–18), Directive 74/121/EEC on stability, growth and full employment in the Community (*OJ* L63, 5 Mar 1974, pp 19–20) and Decision 74/122/EEC setting up an Economic Policy Committee (*OJ* L63, 5 Mar 1974, pp 21–22).

57 European economic integration and monetary unification
Doc II/520/1/73. Oct 1973. 311p

A report from the Study Group on Economic and Monetary Union, established at the end of 1972 to examine the possibilities for, and means of, achieving economic and monetary union. The first part of the report, compiled by three Study Group rapporteurs, Professors Dosser, Magnifico and Peeters, summarizes the Group's main findings. It looks at the economics of monetary unification with regard to different exchange rate systems and the creation and role of a common European currency. Also considered are the economic and social policies for monetary unification and economic integration, with particular reference to stabilization policy, regional policy, employment policy, social policy, industrial policy and the Community budget. The second part of the report consists of substantial individual contributions from the ten members of the Study Group.

58 Report of the study group 'economic and monetary union 1980'
Doc II/675/3/74. 8 Mar 1975. 180p

The report of a group of experts under the chairmanship of Mr Marjolin, invited by the Commission to undertake an analysis of the problems raised by economic and monetary union, taking into account the major changes to be expected by 1980. The report is divided into four chapters. The first comprises a balance sheet of past developments, highlighting the reasons for slow progress and prospects for future development. The second chapter deals with the urgent problems which threaten the Community, particularly inflation, unemployment and balance of payments deficits. Chapter 3 consists of a short-term programme of measures to be implemented with particular emphasis upon financial and monetary problems. Finally, the working party examines the first steps towards economic and monetary union under such sub-headings as industrial policy, energy policy, capital markets policy and budgetary policy. Annexes bring together some individual contributions and provide details of the group's proposals relating to a Community unemployment benefit scheme.

59 Communication on the prospect of economic and monetary union
COM(77)620 final. 17 Nov 1977. 17p

A new initiative from the Commission in which it attempts to revive the concept of economic and monetary union as a means of achieving economic stability and growth in the Community. The document follows an influential speech given by Roy Jenkins, President of the Commission, at the first Jean Monnet Lecture held at the European Institute, Florence on 27 October 1977. In the first part of the document, the Commission argues the case for and the relevance of economic and monetary union, explains why the process has stagnated since 1972 and urges renewed efforts in this matter. In two further sections, the Commission reflects upon the means to be employed and outlines an action programme designed to lead, over a five year period, to a convergence of national economies, the achievement of a single market and the development of policies to meet structural and social problems in the Community.

60 Action programme for 1978
COM(78)52 final. 14 Feb 1978. 30p

In its communication on the prospects for economic and monetary union (*see* 59), favourably received by the European Council at its meeting in Brussels on 5 and 6 December 1977, the Commission proposed that detailed annual action plans should be drawn up within the framework of the overall five year programme. This document contains the Commission's proposals for 1978. The document is divided into four main chapters on convergence of national economies, the single market, structural policies and social policy. Each chapter begins with a general introduction, then lists the proposals already submitted before pinpointing other urgent matters to be dealt with by the Council during 1978. Although the document was not formally submitted to it for its opinion, the European Parliament nevertheless compiled a substantial report on the subject in November 1978 (*Working doc* 437/78).

MEDIUM-TERM ECONOMIC POLICY

61 Politique économique à moyen terme de la Communauté
11/COM(63)271 final. 25 July 1963. 23p

EP Report: *Doc de séance* 115/63. 14 Jan 1964. H. Dichgans. 17p
EP Debate: *Débs* No 69, 21 Jan 1964, pp 25–41
EP Resolution: *JO* 24, 8 Feb 1964, pp 408–409
ESC Opinion: *JO* 38, 5 Mar 1964, pp 643–651

A memorandum in which the Commission gives concrete expression to its view, stated earlier in its action programme for the second stage (*see* 3), that the Community needs a broad strategy extending over a number of years if it is to achieve the objectives defined in Article 2 of the EEC Treaty. Measures so far taken have been of a short-term character; policy must be given a medium-term perspective and plans must be laid for constructing a framework within which government and Community policy can be coordinated over several years. The memorandum explains why a medium-term view is needed, lists the main areas of economic policy in which advance planning is necessary and describes the nature of the Commission's proposals. The Commission recommends that economic forecasts projected over say, a five year period, be compiled by a group of independent experts and that these quantitative studies form the basis upon which to construct a programme of medium-term economic policy. A draft Council Decision attached to the memorandum recommends the establishment of a Medium-Term Economic Policy Committee, whose task would be to prepare such a programme. The Commission memorandum was published in a Supplement to the *Bulletin of the European Economic Community* 8-1963, pp 13–22. After discussion of this Commission initiative, the Council adopted on 15 April 1964 Decision 64/247/ EEC creating a Medium-Term Economic Policy Committee and decided to assemble a group of experts to prepare comprehensive medium-term economic projections to guide the Committee in its deliberations (*JO* 64, 22 Apr 1964, pp 1031–1033).

62 Avant-projet de premier programme de politique économique à moyen terme 1966–1970
Doc 787/11/1966 final. 25 Mar 1966. 93p

In accordance with Council Decision 64/247/EEC of 15 April 1964, a Medium-Term Economic Policy Committee was created in late 1964 (*JO* 64, 22 Apr 1964, pp 1031–1033). Composed of two members and two alternatives from each member state and from the Commission, the Council Decision gave the Committee specific responsibility for preparing 'in the light of all available information and in particular of the forecasts of a group of experts attached to the Commission, a preliminary draft of a medium-term economic policy programme outlining in broad terms the economic policies which the Member States and the institutions of the Community intend to follow during the period under consideration, and designed to ensure the coordination of such policies'. This document represents the Committee's preliminary draft programme for the period 1966 to 1970; it describes the main components of the programme after an initial reference to the overall concept of medium-term policy, its aims and the problems that need to be countered. The document indicates that although other sectors of economic policy will receive general attention, the programme will concentrate on three particular areas, employment policy, budgetary policy and regional policy.

63 Avant-projet de premier programme de politique économique à moyen terme 1966–1970
Doc 788/11/1966 final. 25 Mar 1966. 127p

This document contains the annexes to the draft programme submitted to the Commission on the same day (*see* 62). It contains a number of documents used as background material by the Medium-Term Economic Policy Committee in the preparation of its work. The first document, entitled *Problèmes de la politique de l'emploi et de la formation professionnelle*, considers the problems caused by the imbalance in the labour market. By collating and comparing data from each member state, the study is able to highlight difficulties and suggest options for their improvement. The first part looks at the means for increasing manpower resources, with particular reference to the position in member states regarding the age of commencement of work, retirement age, female employment, the length of the working week, immigration and emigration. The second part considers the means for achieving a better match between supply and demand in terms of both qualifications and geographical distribution. It reports on the position regarding vocational training and guidance in member states, professional and geographical mobility and the movement away from the land. The second document, entitled *Problèmes de la politique régionale*, describes the various types of region to be found in the EEC and the special problems associated with each area. It defines general principles for their solution and elaborates upon the objectives and instruments of regional policy in the Community and member countries. The text of the Council Decision establishing the Medium-Term Economic Policy Committee, a list of its members and the terms of reference of its various working groups constitute the third document. All three documents are included as annexes to the published version of the first programme, published in 1971 (*see* 64). A fourth background paper was submitted to the Council separately (*see* 65).

64 Projet de programme de politique économique à moyen terme (1966–1970)
COM(66)170. 29 Apr 1966. 21p

EP Report: *Doc de séance* 129/66. 28 Nov 1966. T. Elsner. 28p
EP Debate: *Débs* No 88, 30 Nov 1966, pp 110–157
EP Resolution: *JO* 232, 16 Dec 1966, pp 3907–3909
ESC Opinion: *JO* 92, 17 May 1967, pp 1789–1801

Council Decision 64/247/EEC of 15 April 1964 indicates that the Commission shall draw up a draft medium-term economic policy programme for submission to the Council on the basis of the work of the Medium-Term Economic Policy Committee and that 'this draft shall indicate the points in respect of which it differs from the preliminary draft of the Committee' (*JO* 64, 22 Apr 1964, pp. 1031–1033). In this communication to the Council, the Commission records its decision to endorse the Committee's draft programme (*see* 62) rather than prepare its own. The document contains observations from the Commission describing its reactions to the views of, and the conclusions reached by the Committee, and emphasizing the need for action in certain fields to be coordinated at Community level. On the basis of this document and the draft programme (*see* 62), the Council was able on 8 February 1967 to adopt a first medium-term economic policy programme for the period 1966 to 1970. Published in both the *Journal officiel des Communautés européennes* 79, 25 Apr 1967, pp. 1513–1567 and as a separate monograph called *Premier programme de politique économique à moyen terme 1966–1970* (cat 8344), the programme is divided into six separate chapters. The first three chapters are of a general nature, examining in turn the general objectives of medium-term economic policy, the general outlook for growth over the next few years and broad guidelines for economic policy over the same period. The remaining three chapters concentrate in more detail on matters relating to employment and vocational training, public finance and regional policy.

65 Perspectives de développement économique dans la CEE jusqu'en 1970
COM(66)170 annexes. Apr 1966. 2 vols, 122p, 184p

In addition to its observations on the draft programme proposed by the Medium-Term Economic Policy Committee (*see* 64), the Commission decided to send the

Council this report drafted by the working group of independent experts, whose task it was to prepare the medium-term economic projections upon which the Medium-Term Economic Policy Committee would base its programme. The report deals with economic development prospects in the Community as far as 1970, with particular emphasis upon the prospects for employment, the domestic product and its use in each member country.

66 Projet de second programme de politique économique à moyen terme
COM(68)148 final. 20 Mar 1968. 2 vols, 184p, 207p

EP Report: *Doc de séance* 155/68. 20 Nov 1968. T. Elsner. 34p
EP Debate: *Annexe JO* No 108, 27/28 Nov 1968, pp 82–86, 103–115, & 122–131
EP Resolution: *JO* C135, 14 Dec 1968, pp 15–17

A memorandum in which the Commission forwards to the Council the draft second medium-term economic policy programme prepared by the Medium-Term Economic Policy Committee and endorsed by the Commission, together with introductory comments and observations on each of its main chapters. Intended as a supplement to the first programme (*see* 64), this second programme concentrates upon problems treated only generally in the first programme. An introductory chapter is followed by consideration of measures to encourage industry to adapt to structural change, with particular reference to shipbuilding and electronics. Further chapters are concerned with agricultural policy and the need for an active research and development policy to ensure that Community industry remains competitive. The expansion of savings, the financing of investments and incomes policy are also covered. A number of special studies are annexed to the draft programme. These consist of analyses of the problems experienced by the shipbuilding and electronics industries, a report from a working party on guidelines for promoting research and development, the text of a Resolution adopted by the Council on 31 October 1967 on the problems of scientific and technical research, and a list of the members of the Medium-Term Economic Policy Committee and its working groups. The programme was approved by the Council on 12 December 1968 and published, without its annexes in the *Journal officiel des Communautés européennes* L129, 30 May 1969, pp 1–96, and with its annexes in a separate volume called *Second programme de politique économique à moyen terme* (cat 8345).

67 Mémorandum de la Commission au Conseil sur les orientations globales à moyen terme (1971–1975) de la politique économique dans la Communauté
COM(69)1250. 15 Dec 1969. 25p

A memorandum in which the Commission gives substance to the proposals for medium-term policy outlined in February 1969 (*see* 46) and establishes a framework of guidelines for the preparation of a third medium-term economic policy programme. As its introductory passages indicate, the memorandum draws 'pertinent lessons from the economic development of the Community in the last ten years, indicates the main problems now confronting it and in terms of indicative orders of magnitude, suggests possible guidelines of overall economic policy for the coming years'. The memorandum was published as a Supplement to the *Bulletin of the European Communities* 2-1970. In January 1970, the Council decided to instruct the Commission, acting in close collaboration with the Medium-Term Economic Policy Committee, to draw up by the Autumn of 1970 a draft third programme containing quantified economic indicators for the period 1971 to 1975. (*See* 68.)

68 Projet de troisième programme de politique économique à moyen terme
COM(70)1200. 21 Oct 1970. 73p

EP Report: *Doc de séance* 189/70. 2 Dec 1970. E. Lange. 11p
EP Debate: *Annexe JO* No 131, 3 Dec 1970, pp 66–87
EP Resolution: *JO* C151, 29 Dec 1970, pp 26–28
ESC Opinion: *JO* C36, 19 Apr 1971, pp 17–21

In line with the procedure established in Council Decision 64/247/EEC of 15 April 1964 (*JO* 64, 22 April 1964, pp 1031–1033), the Medium-Term Economic Policy Committee prepared and submitted to the Commission a preliminary draft programme covering the years 1971 to 1975. The Commission subsequently endorsed it without amendment and in this document submitted it, together with an introduction explaining the reasons behind the proposals and a draft Council Decision, to the Council. The programme is described in three chapters. By way of introduction, the first chapter establishes the need for a coherent medium-term strategy to act as a framework for economic development in the Community. The second chapter provides quantified medium-term target figures for the main indicators of economic development, namely, the balance of trade and payments, prices, gross national product and employment. The third chapter on guidelines for economic policy outlines the general and structural measures that are necessary if national economies are to develop along compatible lines. The Council formally adopted this third medium-term programme on 9 February 1971 (*JO* L49, 1 Mar 1971, pp 1–39).

69 Perspectives pour 1975: évolution globale et problèmes de politique économique dans la Communauté
Doc 20791/11/1970. Mar 1971. 2 vols, 191p, 108p

A two volume report on the work carried out by the Study Group on Medium-Term Economic Forecasts since 1966 on quantitative analysis and overall economic projections within the Community framework. The first volume examines trends apparent in the economic policy of member states and evaluates the Community's macro-economic prospects up to 1975. The second volume is concerned with medium-term projections for individual member countries.

70 Fourth medium-term economic policy programme: draft
COM(76)530 final. 8 Oct 1976. 91p

EP Report: *Working doc* 579/76. 7 Mar 1977. H. Schwörer. 30p
EP Debate: *Annex OJ* No 214, 10 Mar 1977, pp 95–120
EP Resolution: *OJ* C83, 4 Apr 1977, pp 27–30
ESC Opinion: *OJ* C56, 7 Mar 1977, pp 56–65

A draft medium-term economic policy programme drawn up by the Commission on the basis of a preliminary draft prepared by the Economic Policy Committee, set up by Council Decision 74/122/EEC of 18 February 1974 to take the place, amongst others, of the Medium-Term Economic Policy Committee (*OJ* L63, 5 Mar 1974, pp 21–22). In the foreword to the programme, the Commission indicates that it 'must be seen as the framework for Community action in the economic field between 1976 and 1980. It lays down the economic development to be aimed at in the medium-term and the economic policy consequences which arise from this'. In this document, the Commission diagnoses the causes of the Community's present poor state of economic health, lays down a series of both quantitative and qualitative objectives and recommends guidelines for their achievement in such areas as public finance, employment policy, incomes policy, consumer policy, investment policy and competition policy. The programme consists of three parts. The first is concerned with sketching the background, with particular reference to the current economic crisis and the inadequacies of Community policy. The second part examines medium-term problems, describes guidelines for the development of medium-term economic policy and outlines a strategy for applying these guidelines, whose implementation is the subject of the third part of the document. The Council adopted the fourth medium-term programme on 14 March 1977 by Decision 77/294/EEC (*OJ* L101, 25 Apr 1977, pp 1–40).

71 **Situation of, and prospects for, the world economy: the Community's dependence and influence**
Doc 11/46/1/76. Dec 1976. 86p

A report prepared by an independent group of experts under the chairmanship of A. Kervyn de Lettenhove, invited by the Commission to examine trends in world medium-term economic prospects and their likely impact upon Community medium-term economic development. The first chapter consists of a broad survey of the current world economic situation, with reference to inflation, the collapse of the Bretton Woods monetary system, the threat to free trade, the increasing politicization of international economic relations and the role of the Community in the world economy. The second chapter is devoted to a consideration of the Community's medium-term economic prospects. The working party looks at the uncertainty surrounding medium-term economic development in the Community and at the implications of a high and a low medium-term growth rate. The role of exchange rates and the problems of balance of payments disequilibria are the subject of the third chapter. This is followed by consideration of various aspects of international economic relations, including trade relations between nations, the migration of labour, economic relations between industrialized and developing countries and East–West economic relations. In the final chapter, the working party looks at the implications of the international economic situation and the role of the Community with reference to still unresolved problems and the measures needed to promote sustained economic growth and a more stable international monetary system.

72 **Report on the present economic situation and the medium-term outlook**
COM(77)431 final. 14 Sept 1977. 18p

At the same time as it adopted the fourth medium-term economic policy programme (*see* 70), the Council invited the Commission, with the assistance of the Economic Policy Committee, to undertake a series of investigations into such topics as employment, investment and external payments. In this report, the Commission uses data from these studies to present an overall picture of current economic conditions and to formulate a strategy designed to revive and sustain the European economy. The document is divided into three main sections. The first two briefly analysing the present situation and its inherent problems, are followed by a more substantial series of guidelines designed to produce conditions under which there would be lasting growth without attendant problems of inflation.

73 **Outlook 1980: one year after drawing up the fourth programme of medium-term economic policy for the Community**
Doc 11/236/3/77. 26 Sept 1977. 86p

A report from the Study Group on Medium-Term Economic Assessments, set up by the Commission to assist in the preparation of medium-term programmes by making and updating medium-term projections and by examining associated statistical and model-building problems. The Study Group assesses the Community's medium-term economic outlook one year after the preparation of the fourth medium-term economic policy programme (*see* 70) and highlights the difficulties, particularly with regard to employment, likely to be experienced in the medium-term. Chapter 1 explains the approach adopted by the Study Group, Chapter 2 is devoted to the economic problems presented by the projections and Chapter 3 is concerned with threats to the achievement of the guidelines laid down in the fourth programme and the scope for a return to full employment. The report concludes with a number of graphs and statistical tables.

SHORT-TERM ECONOMIC POLICY

74 **Mémorandum de la Commission relatif à la mise au point des instruments de politique conjoncturelle en vue de la lutte contre une recession éventuelle ou un affaiblessement caractérisé de l'expansion économique**
1/COM(62)276 final. 28 Nov 1962. 24p

A memorandum in which the Commission recommends that member governments make contingency plans to combat effectively and swiftly any sharp fall off in economic growth or the appearance of recessionary trends. Based largely on surveys undertaken by the Economic Policy Committee in collaboration with the Monetary Committee, these recommendations include specific proposals for the adjustment of instruments of monetary and budgetary policy, price and incomes policy and investment to give them the necessary flexibility and effectiveness.

75 **Politique susceptible d'être poursuivie au sein de la Communauté pour surmonter les difficultés provenant de la situation économique en France**
COM(68)600. 15 July 1968. 14p

A memorandum in which the Commission seeks to adjust short-term economic policy to assist the French government in the restoration of equilibrium in the face of the consequences of the May/June 1968 disturbances, and to minimize the impact of these disturbances on the Community as a whole. Acting within the framework of the procedure provided by Article 108 of the EEC Treaty, the Commission makes recommendations for preventing the development of an inflationary situation in France and for granting France the mutual assistance provided for in that Article. On 20 July 1968, the Council adopted Directive 68/310/EEC to this end (*JO* L189, 1 Aug 1968, pp 13–14).

76 **Mémorandum de la Commission au Conseil au sujet de la politique susceptible d'être poursuivie au sein de la Communauté pour faire face aux problèmes économiques et monétaires actuels**
SEC(68)3958. 5 Dec 1968. 28p

In response to disturbances and speculation in the international money markets and to diverging trends in prices and balances of payments, the Commission submitted this memorandum to the Council on the policy which should be followed in the Community to deal with current economic and monetary problems. The document highlights the need to prevent a revival of speculation, to attain rapid economic growth during 1969 and to promote the balanced development of prices and production costs in the Community. The Commission also announced that it would, before 15 February 1969, submit proposals for the establishment of machinery for monetary cooperation in the Community (*see* 46).

77 **Mémorandum de la Commission au Conseil relatif au maintien des conditions d'une croissance equilibrée dans la Communauté**
COM(69)650. 9 July 1969. 24p

Despite the measures proposed by the Commission at the end of 1968 (*see* 76) and in February 1969 (*see* 46), continuing economic problems, fresh monetary disturbances and increasing inflationary pressures caused the Commission to prepare this new memorandum on the ways in which Community countries can maintain balanced economic growth. The Commission reviews the position of the Community as a whole and of individual member states, draws attention to the problems inherent in the current situation and urges that both the Community and member states mobilize their resources and take vigorous action to bring inflationary tendencies under control. The communication concludes with a number of statistical annexes. The memorandum was published in the *Journal officiel des Communautés européennes* C8, 20 Jan 1970, pp 12–21 and in English as an annex to the quarterly publication *The economic situation in the Community* 3/4-1969.

78 **Mémorandum de la Commission au Conseil sur la politique conjoncturelles de la Communauté pour 1970**
COM(69)1350. 22 Dec 1969. 16p

A memorandum on short-term economic policy for 1970 in which the Commission draws attention to the continued existence of inflationary trends and the need for urgent action to slow down the expansion of domestic demand. Divided into three brief sections, the document first recalls the main features of economic development during the second half of 1969, then comments on the economic outlook and the problems facing both the Community and member countries during 1970. On the basis of this assessment, the Commission advances in the third section a number of guidelines for short-term economic policy, which were approved by the Council at its meeting on 26 January 1970. The memorandum was published in English as an annex to the quarterly publication *The economic situation in the Community* 1-1970. A similar memorandum prepared later in 1970 was published in English as an annex to *The economic situation in the Community* 3/4-1970.

79 Mémorandum de la Commission au Conseil sur la situation conjoncturelle de la Communauté
COM(70)1400 final. 2 Dec 1970. 24p

EP Report: *Doc de séance* 14/71. 19 Apr 1971. A. Oele. 17p
EP Debate: *Annexe JO* No 137, 21 Apr 1971, pp 67–97
EP Resolution: *JO* C45, 10 May 1971, pp 22–24

Similar in aim and arrangement to previous memoranda on short-term policy (*see* 78), this document identifies trends in the present economic situation, assesses short-term prospects for both the Community as a whole and for individual member states and urges member states to adopt uniform guidelines for the determination of their economic policy over the coming months. The communication was published in English in *The economic situation in the Community* 1-1971.

80 Mémorandum de la Commission au Conseil sur les orientations de la politique économique à court terme, les éléments essentiels des budgets économiques et les orientations quantitatives des budgets publics pour ...
1971/72   COM(71)626. 2 June 1971. 16p
1972/73   SEC(72)2113 final. 14 June 1972. 23p
1973/74   COM(73)1030 final. 20 June 1973. 72p

A memorandum presented annually to the Council in accordance with Decision 71/141/EEC of 22 March 1971, Article 3 of which requires the Commission to propose to the Council guide figures for the draft public budgets in advance of their final adoption (*JO* L73, 27 Mar 1971, pp 12–13). In the light of available data, the Commission makes recommendations concerning public finance policy, monetary and credit policies to be followed in the coming year. (*See also* 94.)

81 Communication de la Commission au Conseil sur les problèmes posés par la situation monétaire actuelle
COM(71)1050 final. 9 Sept 1971. 5p

A brief communication to the Council in which the Commission sets out its proposals for restoring stability to international monetary affairs. Accepted by the Council as a basis for a common Community position in the Group of Ten and the International Monetary Fund, the document supports the principle of fixed parities, concerted action on international capital movements and joint action by the central banks in the exchange markets.

82 Rapport annuel sur la situation économique de la Communauté
COM(71)1100. 14 Sept 1971. 73p
COM(72)1100 final. 8 Sept 1972. 24p
COM(73)1560 final. 18 Sept 1973. 35p
SEC(74)3355 final. 18 Sept 1974. 36p
COM(75)520 final. 15 Oct 1975. 37p
COM(76)557 final. 20 Oct 1976. 45p
COM(77)494 final. 18 Oct 1977. 46p
COM(78)529 final. 19 Oct 1978. 17p

An annual report on the economic situation in the Community and in member countries presented to the Council by the Commission for its approval in accordance with Council Decision 71/141/EEC of 22 March 1971 on the closer coordination of member states' short-term economic policies (*JO* L73, 27 Mar 1971, pp 12–13). On the basis of an assessment of the present economic situation, each report proposes guidelines for member states to follow in their short-term economic policy during the coming year. Provision is made for the report, once adopted by the Council, to be brought to the attention of national parliaments so that it might be taken into account during their budget debates. Although officially available in English only since 1973, the report has since its inception appeared in English as the third quarterly issue of *The economic situation in the Community*, or since 1979, as the November issue in its successor *European economy*. Once adopted by the Council, the report is also published in the *Official journal of the European Communities*. (*See also* 91.)

83 Conséquences pour la Communauté de la situation actuelle dans les domaines monètaires et commerciaux
SEC(71)3274 final. 15 Sept 1971. 33p

An assessment of the effects of the present crisis in international economic relations and particularly of moves to reflate the American economy, on the Community's economic activity, its policies and institutions. Part 1 summarizes the action taken by the United States to reflate the American economy. Part 2 analyses the repercussions of these steps on Community economic activity and the working of Community machinery. Part 3 examines the consequences of American measures on development aid. Annexes include a more detailed description of the American measures, a report on the conclusions of the GATT Working Party on the U.S. Trade Measures Surcharge and a number of statistical tables. The report was published in Supplement 6/71 to the *Bulletin of the European Communities*.

84 Rapport spécial de la Commission au Conseil sur les conséquences de la situation actuelle sur la politique agricole commune
SEC(71)3407 final. 27 Sept 1971. 10p

See 378.

85 Communication de la Commission au Conseil concernant l'adaption des orientations de la politique économique pour 1972
COM(72)300. 8 Mar 1972. 21p

In accordance with the procedure laid down in Council Decision 71/141/EEC of 22 March 1971 (JO L73, 27 Mar 1971, pp 12–13), this report contains the Commission's proposals for adjusting the guidelines for short-term economic policy for 1972. In addition to consideration of monetary and budgetary policy, the Commission looks at the problems of inflation, upon which the Council adopted a Resolution on 5 December 1972 (JO C133, 23 Dec 1972, pp 12–15). (*See also* 91.)

86 Report from the Commission to the Council on the adjustment of short-term monetary support arrangements and the conditions for the progressive pooling of reserves
COM(73)1099. 27 June 1973. 29p

EP Report: *Working doc* 189/73. 15 Oct 1973. K. Arndt. 6p
EP Debate: *Annex OJ* No 167, 19 Oct 1973, pp 205–218
EP Resolution: *OJ* C95, 10 Nov 1973, pp 27–28

A report presented to the Council in accordance with the request made by Heads of State or Government at the Paris summit on 19 and 20 October 1972 that Community institutions should prepare a report on the development of short-term monetary support by 30 September 1973, and on the terms for the progressive pooling of reserves by 31 December 1973. In view of the effects of monetary disturbances and the need to accelerate progress, the Council subsequently invited the Commission to prepare a report on both topics by 30 June 1973. The report outlines the Commission's views on the Community monetary system and makes proposals for the achievement of a lasting and stable monetary system, focused on an enhanced role for the European Monetary Cooperation Fund, established by Council Regulation (EEC) No 907/73 of 3 April 1973 (OJ L89, 5 Apr 1973, pp 2–5). The report was published as Supplement 12/73 to the *Bulletin of the European Communities*.

87 Situation of the Community: urgent measures
COM(74)100 final. 23 Jan 1974. 4p

A brief report from the Commission concerning the emergency measures to be taken in the light of severe economic disruptions caused by the dramatic increase in oil prices.

88 Declaration on the state of the Community
COM(74)150 final. 31 Jan 1974. 9p

A rallying call from the Commission in which it urges Heads of Government to 'honour by their deeds their decision to unite Europe' and to meet the challenges currently facing the Community by concerting their efforts and policies through the institutions of the European Communities. The Commission points to the failure to establish a European Regional Development Fund, to move to the second stage of economic and monetary union and to define a common energy policy, before emphasizing the need for a common response to current difficulties.

89 Urgent economic and monetary measures
COM(74)1000. 5 June 1974. 3p

A brief memorandum prepared by the Commission for a forthcoming meeting of the Council of Finance Ministers in which it presses for the adoption of a limited number of urgent practical measures to arrest the deterioration in the economic situation, as evidenced by the increasing pace of inflation and balance of payments deficits. The document contains the main elements of a similar document presented to the Council at the beginning of the same year (*see* 87).

90 The economic situation in the Community
COM(74)1925. 14 Nov 1974. 9p

A working document prepared for the Council meeting on 18 November 1974, in which the Commission points to the actions that are needed to meet the structural problems experienced by the economies of member states in the present economic climate.

91 Communication of the Commission to the Council concerning the adjustment of the economic policy guidelines for ... and proposal for a Council Decision
1976   COM(76)82 final. 3 Mar 1976. 26p
1977   COM(77)58 final. 4 Mar 1977. 35p
1978   COM(78)102 final. 13 Mar 1978. 23p

An annual report submitted to the Council in compliance with Council Decision 74/120/EEC of 18 February 1974 on the attainment of a high degree of convergence of the economic policies of member states (*OJ* L63, 5 Mar 1974, pp 16–18). Article 2 of that Decision provides that on the first of the three occasions during the year when the Council shall hold meetings to examine the economic situation in the Community it shall, on the basis of a proposal from the Commission, adjust economic policy guidelines for the current year as required by economic developments. Each report reviews economic progress in the Community in relation to the objectives set in the annual economic report (*see* 82) and makes proposals for their adjustment as necessary. The text of the communication is published in the first quarterly issue of *The economic situation in the Community*, and that of the subsequent Council Decision concerning the adjustment of economic policy guidelines in the 'L' series of the *Official journal of the European Communities*.

92 Summary account of the economic policies pursued in 1974
COM(75)92 final/2. 17 Mar 1975. 12p

An annual summary report on the economic policies pursued in the previous year by member states, submitted to the Council in conjunction with a proposal for adjustments to economic policy guidelines (*see* 91). This complied with Article 2 of Council Decision 74/120/EEC of 18 February 1974 on the attainment of a high degree of convergence of the economic polices of member states (*OJ* L63, 5 Mar 1974, pp 16–18). The report consists of four chapters on budgetary policy, monetary policy, exchange-rate policy and incomes policy. The report was published in *The economic situation in the Community* 1-1975. (*See* 96 for subsequent annual reports.)

93 Report on the application of the Council Decision of 18 February 1974 on the attainment of a high degree of convergence of the economic policies of the member states of the European Economic Community and the conformity of the policies pursued with the objectives set
COM(75)93 final/2. 17 Mar 1975. 6p

Article 12 of Council Decision 74/120/EEC of 18 February 1974 requires the Commission to present to the Council for its meeting in the first quarter of the year, a report on the application of the Decision and on the degree to which the economic policies pursued by member states are consistent with the objectives laid down (*OJ* L63, 5 Mar 1974, pp 16–18). This report contains the Commission's review of the application of each of the Decision's articles and draws attention to those areas where there have been marked differences between policies and objectives. The report was published in *The economic situation in the Community* 1-1975. (*See* 96 for later annual reports.)

94 Communication by the Commission to the Council on economic policy to be followed in ... and on the preparation of public budgets for ...
1975/1976   COM(75)341 final. 2 July 1975. 23p
1976/1977   COM(76)325 final. 23 June 1976. 29p
1977/1978   COM(77)315 final. 7 July 1977. 36p

In accordance with Article 3 of Council Decision 74/120/EEC of 18 February 1974 on the attainment of a high degree of convergence of the economic policies of member states, the Council is, in its second annual examination of the economic situation, to fix guidelines for the draft public budgets for the following year (*OJ* L63, 5 Mar 1974, pp 16–18). This communication is submitted by the Commission as a contribution to that debate. Divided into two main parts, the report first makes a descriptive assessment of the current economic situation in the Community and its outlook. In the light of this analysis, the Commission makes proposals in the second part for economic policy guidelines for the coming year. The document concludes with statistical data and with a proposal for a Council Decision on the preparation of public budgets in the coming year, which when adopted by the Council, is published in the 'L' series of the *Official journal of the European Communities*. (*See also* 80.)

95 Tripartite Conference: economic and social situation in the Community and outlook
COM(75)540/2. 5 Nov. 1975. 20p

See 532.

96 Summary account and degree of convergence of the economic policies pursued in the member countries in the Community in ...
1975   COM(76)81 final. 3 Mar 1976. 23p
1976   COM(77)63 final. 4 Mar 1977. 19p
1977   COM(78)103 final. 13 Mar 1978. 54p

A two part annual report in which the Commission, in compliance with Article 2 of Council Decision 74/120/EEC of 18 February 1974 (*OJ* L63, 5 Mar 1974, pp 16–18), first submits a report on the economic policies pursued in member states in the previous year. It then, in accordance with Article 12 of the same Decision, describes the implementation of the Decision in the year under review and assesses the compatability of the policies actually pursued with the objectives established. The report has been regularly published in the first quarterly issue of *The economic situation in the Community* until the replacement of that journal by *European economy* in 1979. (*See* 92 & 93 for earlier reports.)

97 The economic situation in the Community
COM(77)7 final. 27 Jan 1977. 118p

An assessment of the Community's short-term position, in the first part of which the Commission analyses the overall situation in the Community and compares it with the world situation. The second part of the document consists of a more detailed assessment of the position in each member country. The document concludes with an annex on diverging price and cost trends in the Community and another annex consisting of a report to the Council and the Commission on the meeting of the Economic Policy Committee on 6 October 1976. The document was published in *The economic situation in the Community* 4-1976.

98 Economic situation in the Community
COM(77)310 final. 24 June 1977. 6p

A brief communication prepared for the European Council meeting in London on 29 and 30 June 1977 in which the Commission outlines the main characteristics of current economic trends and assesses prospects for the remainder of the year. The document concludes with statistical tables on industrial production, employment, consumer prices and the balance of trade in member states and the Community.

99 Improving co-ordination of the national economic policies
COM(77)443 final. 5 Oct 1977. 7p

A communication in which the Commission suggests a number of ways in which the machinery and procedures established by Council Decision 74/120/EEC of 18 February 1974 on the coordination of short-term economic policy (*OJ* L63, 5 Mar 1974, pp 16–18) may be made more effective. The document indicates the areas in which adjustments, most of which require changes in the legal framework, are necessary.

100 The economic situation in the Community
COM(77)640 final. 25 Nov 1977. 7p

A brief document prepared for the European Council meeting in Brussels on 5 and 6 December 1977 in which the Commission summarizes its views on the present state of the economic situation in the Community, and assesses the outlook for the immediate future. The document concludes with a number of statistical tables of short-term economic indicators.

101 Annual economic review 1978–1979
SEC(78)4033 final. 19 Oct 1978. 166p

A detailed factual study of the main features of recent economic developments in the Community, submitted to the Council in conjunction with, and as background material to, the annual report on the economic situation in the Community (*see* 82). The scope of the report is indicated by the fact that separate chapters are devoted to the growth of demand and output, employment and unemployment, prices and incomes, convergence and divergence in the economy, budgetary trends and policies, monetary trends and policies, the balance of payments and structural changes before and since the 1973 oil crisis. The text contains over 30 statistical tables and is followed by a statistical annex containing a time series of annual data for the period 1958 to 1977 or 1978 on such main economic indicators as domestic product, consumer prices, employment and public expenditure.

CHAPTER 4

The common market

Descriptive essay

In popular usage the term 'common market' has come to be used as a synonym for the European Economic Community or, more expansively, the European Communities. However, in the language of economics the phrase has a more precise meaning. More ambitious than either a free trade area within which trade barriers are eliminated, or a customs union which additionally involves the creation of a common external tariff as protection against imports from third countries, a common market takes the concept one stage further by adding to the characteristics of a customs union free movement of factors of production, that is, labour, capital and services.

The establishment of a common market within which the European economy can flourish is a fundamental objective of the EEC, indeed, the objective most readily associated with the organization. Article 2 of the EEC Treaty talks of 'establishing a common market' in part fulfilment of Community objectives and Article 3 of 'the elimination, as between Member States, of customs duties and of quantitative restrictions on the import and export of goods, and of all other measures having equivalent effect' during a 12 year transitional period provided for in Article 8. It is clearly recognized, however, that the removal of customs duties and quantitative restrictions on intra-Community trade and the establishment of a Common Customs Tariff is not in itself sufficient to create a homogeneous economic unit displaying the same characteristics and offering the same opportunities as a domestic market. Consequently, provision is also made in the Treaty for the removal of other economic barriers and the creation of conditions within which European industry can take full advantage of a wider internal market on an equal basis.

This chapter is concerned with various ways in which the Treaty seeks to remove tariff and non-tariff barriers to free trade across national frontiers within the Community, and to establish the conditions under which the European economy can take full advantage of opportunities afforded by an enormously increased domestic market. However, it should be noted at the outset that policy in many of these areas is laid down in the Treaty itself. The role of Community institutions is largely to implement, by means of secondary legislation, already established rules. In other words, the essential task of Community institutions is to make law rather than to define policy, in marked contrast to other areas of the Treaty where only the briefest reference is made to the make-up of a number of common policies. Almost all of the considerable amount of documentation generated by the Commission concerning the creation of a single market takes the form of specific legislative proposals submitted within the general policy framework established in the Treaty of Rome and is consequently excluded from this bibliographical guide. It goes without saying, however, that the lack of genuine policy documents is not a reflection of a lack of achievement in this sector. As mentioned, many of the Community's practical achievements have been in the areas of policy concerned with the introduction of the common market.

FREE MOVEMENT OF GOODS, PERSONS, SERVICES AND CAPITAL

The four freedoms referred to in Part II of the Treaty of Rome, the free movement of goods, persons, services and capital constitute the principal foundations upon which the EEC is based. Of these, the free movement of goods provided for in Articles 9–37, is by far the most fundamental. The remaining three freedoms are largely concerned with creating the conditions under which there can be a free flow of goods across national boundaries within the common market. Article 9 of the EEC Treaty states that 'the Community shall be based upon a customs union which shall cover all trade in goods and which shall involve the prohibition between Member States of customs duties on imports and exports and of all charges having equivalent effect, and the adoption of a common customs tariff in their relations with third countries'. In further Articles, the Treaty sets out quite a detailed scheme for the elimination of customs duties between Member States (Articles 12–17) and for the elimination of quantitative restrictions between member states (Articles 30–37) according to a precise time-table. In point of fact, the elimination of customs duties between member states was achieved ahead of schedule in July 1968.

Since policy is established in the Treaty, and Community institutions are simply required to give effect to it by creating Community law, none of the considerable bulk of customs legislation designed to remove tariff barriers to trade and quantitative restrictions is represented in this bibliographical guide. Neither does it adequately reflect the considerable amount of work invested by Community institutions in an effort to harmonize national customs laws and procedures. However, some of the documents listed in this chapter do confirm the Commission's concern to eliminate controls on intra-Community trade, (*see* 132 & 135) and to simplify customs formalities and procedures (*see* 134 & 137). The chapter also contains reference to a useful document in which the Commission takes stock of the customs union at the end of the five year transitional period laid down in the Treaty of Accession for new member countries (*see* 138). During December of the same year, the Commission organized a conference in Brussels on the achievements and prospects for the customs union. A record of the proceedings of the conference was published by the Commission in 1978 under the title *The customs union: today and tomorrow* (cat CB-24-78-047-EN-C. ISBN 92-825-0297-X).

There are two main facets to a customs union. In addition to the abolition of internal barriers to trade, a customs union also involves the introduction of a Common Customs Tariff (CCT) for external trade. Articles 18 to 29 of the Treaty of Rome make detailed arrangements for the progressive implementation of the CCT during the transitional period, a task which was accomplished ahead of schedule on 1 July 1968. The CCT is drawn up annually by the Council for the following year and published in the 'L' series of the *Official journal of the European Communities* towards the end of the year. An immense amount of work is undertaken and a mountain of often technical documentation generated by Community institutions in the constant refinement and updating of a tariff which at present contains about 3700 headings. Technical progress calls for regular revision of CCT nomenclature and classification and the description of tariff items, whilst changing economic and commercial conditions necessitate close supervision and regular updating of rates of duty, exemptions and suspensions from duty on hundreds of individual products. The *Official journal of the European Communities*, not this bibliographical guide, is the source of this information. However, it should be noted that the Commission publishes loose-leaf *Explanatory notes to the Customs tariff in the European Communities* (cat CB-24-77-205-EN-C) intended as a guide to the classification of goods in the CCT, and another loose-leaf publication called *Tariff classifications* (cat 8684) which is a compendium of Community legislative instruments relating to the classification of goods in the nomenclature of the CCT.

Customs duties and quantitative restrictions are not the only impediments to free trade within the Community. In addition to specific provision for aligning policy in such areas as customs (Article 27), movement of workers (Article 49), establishment (Article 54), provision of professional services (Article 57), taxation (Article 99) and export aids (Article 112), the Treaty of Rome makes provision in Article 100 for the approximation of those legislative and administrative provisions which 'directly affect the establishment or functioning of the common market', and in Articles 101 and 102 for eliminating distortions of 'the conditions of competition in the common market'. Although a general programme for eliminating technical barriers to trade was adopted in 1969 (*see* 130), the task of aligning differing national standards on such matters as health and safety, packaging and labelling, consumer protection, quality control and environmental protection for hundreds of different products or groups of products is necessarily a long-term and difficult undertaking. In reflection of the nature of the operation, the documentation of the subject is considerable, often complex and highly specific. Although this documentation is not represented here, the progress made by Community institutions in removing technical barriers to trade may be traced from the tables listing Directives adopted by the Council and proposals submitted by the Commission, published each year in the *General report on the activities of the European Communities*. A bibliography of Community legislation relating to the elimination of technical barriers to trade in industrial products has been published as *Documentation bulletin B/1* and another on foodstuffs as *Documentation bulletin B/6*. In 1979 the Commission published a *Recapitulatory list of directives and proposals for directives relating to the elimination of technical barriers to trade for industrial products* (cat CB-29-79-110-EN-C. ISBN 92-825-1401-3), which lists, with references to the *Official journal*, 122 Directives adopted by the Council, 21 Directives adopted by the Commission and 40 proposals for Directives submitted by the Commission but not yet adopted by the Council, as well as many modifications and amendments to these legislative acts. It should also be noted that a list of measures taken by Community institutions on the approximation of legislation in such economic sectors as agriculture, industry, and transport is published periodically as a Supplement to the *Bulletin of the European Communities*.

If the European Economic Community is to become a single economic entity, then it is equally necessary that workers have the freedom to move between Community countries and the right to take up employment in any Community country without fear of discrimination on the basis of nationality or loss of privileges to which they would be otherwise entitled in their own country. Articles 48 to 51 of the EEC Treaty are designed to ensure that workers and their families may move about freely within the Community and may take up offers of jobs anywhere within the Community. Treaty provisions define the basic rights to be accorded, enumerate the methods to be used and establish a time-table for their achievement. Since it is the task of Community institutions simply to implement clearly established principles, the documentation of this subject is almost entirely legislative and consequently falls outside the scope of this bibliographical guide. The texts of the instruments which give legal effect to these provisions have, in addition to their original appearance in the *Official journal of the European Communities*, been brought together into useful, occasionally updated compendia, the latest of which *Freedom of movement for workers within the Community* (cat 8961) contains, amongst others, the texts of Regulation (EEC) No 1612/68 of 15 October 1968 which effectively introduced full freedom of movement some 18 months ahead of schedule (JO L257, 19 Oct 1968, pp 2–12). This Regulation, together with associated implementing measures and two important Regulations introducing earlier phases of implementation in 1961 (JO 57, 26 Aug 1961, pp 1073–1084) and in 1964 (JO 62, 17 Apr 1964, pp 965–980) are listed in the *Bibliography on free movement of persons and services* published in *Documentation bulletin* B/17. Further information on the progressive implementation of the principle of mobility of labour and its effects on the labour market appears in the annual reports *La libre circulation de la main-d'oeuvre et les marchés du travail dans la CEE*, published by the Commission during the period 1966 to 1970.

Articles 48 to 51 (referred to above) relate to the free movement of wage-earners. The right of the self-employed and professional classes to carry on their business or profession in Community countries other than their own, without fear of discrimination on the basis of nationality, is provided for in Articles 52 to 66 under the right of establishment and the freedom to provide services. Here the task of eliminating barriers to free movement is made much more difficult because of differing and often jealously guarded academic and professional standards and qualifications. Consequently, in addition to the removal of restrictions based on nationality, the Treaty of Rome provides for the Council to issue Directives 'for the mutual recognition of diplomas, certificates and other evidence of qualification'. It also provides for the Commission to draw up general programmes for the abolition of existing restrictions on freedom of establishment and freedom to supply services (*see* 124) and to submit proposals to the Council for their progressive implementation.

Since the Treaty provides the policy framework within which Community institutions are to operate, policy proposals from the Commission have not been required. Rather, it has been the task of the Commission to draft and submit numerous proposals for Directives on the right of establishment of self-employed persons and a considerable number on the mutual recognition of diplomas, certificates and other professional qualifications for professional occupations which include lawyers, engineers, architects, doctors, dentists, pharmacists, veterinary surgeons, opticians, midwives, general nurses, accountants and journalists. Clearly, this documentation is often highly specific, legislative in nature and therefore outside the compass of this book. However, individual proposals for legislation and acts adopted by the Council on the removal of restrictions are listed in the *General report on the activities of the European Communities* and periodically in Supplements to the *Bulletin of the European Communities*, the latest of which, Supplement 9/72, covers the period 1 January 1958 to 31 December 1971. The most up-to-date information on Community proposals and acts appears in a document called *Schedule of Community acts concerning right of establishment and freedom to provide services* (Doc 111/1418/77). Further comprehensive lists of proposals and legislation appear in the *Bibliography on free movement of persons and services* published as *Documentation bulletin B/17*, giving the position as at March 1979.

Companies are particularly affected by the rules regarding the rights of establishment. As part of its policy of encouraging joint ventures between companies in different member states, helping them to become more competitive and to take advantage of expanded markets, the Commission has submitted a number of proposals for harmonizing national company law. Four important Directives on the harmonization of national legislation have been accepted. The first concerns safeguards for the parties and third parties in public limited companies (*JO* L65, 14 Mar 1968, pp 8–12); the second relates to the capital of public limited companies (*OJ* L26, 31 Jan 1977, pp 1–13); the third concerns mergers between public limited companies (*OJ* L295, 20 Oct 1978, pp 36–43) and the fourth is to do with the harmonization of the annual accounts of limited companies (*OJ* L222, 14 Aug 1978, pp 11–31). Neither these nor the Commission's proposals for a fifth, sixth, seventh and eighth Directive on company law fall within the purview of this guide. However, it should be noted that a number of the most important proposals for legislation in this field have been published as Supplements to the *Bulletin of the European Communities*. These include the Commission's proposal for a fifth Directive on the structure of sociétés anonymes (Supplement 16/72); the proposal for a seventh Directive on group accounts (Supplement 9/76) and the proposal for an eighth Directive on the qualifications of the auditors of company accounts (Supplement 4/78). Also published in this form are the Commission's proposals for a Regulation on the European Co-operation Grouping (Supplement 1/74) and the draft Convention on the international merger of sociétés anonymes (Supplement 13/73).

COMPETITION POLICY

Companies are also subject to Community rules designed to eliminate practices which distort the free play of competition between firms and thus prejudice the advantages of operating within a much expanded internal market. Although the Treaty of Rome does not positively define the concept of competition, it does identify a number of undesirable practices which interfere with it. Article 85 prohibits as incompatible with the common market 'all agreements between undertakings, decision by associations of undertakings and concerted practices which may affect trade between Member States and which have as their object or effect the prevention, restriction or distortion of competition within the common market'. It goes on expressly to prohibit agreements based on such restrictive practices as price-fixing, market-sharing, exclusive dealing and unequal pricing, although dispensations are allowed in certain circumstances.

Article 86 is concerned with the abuse of economic power by firms that enjoy a dominant market position. Such abuse may, in particular, consist of:

(a) directly or indirectly imposing unfair purchase or selling prices or other unfair trading conditions;

(b) limiting production, markets or technical development to the prejudice of consumers;

(c) applying dissimilar conditions to equivalent transactions with other trading parties, thereby placing them at a competitive disadvantage;

(d) making the conclusion of contracts subject to acceptance by the other parties of supplementary obligations which, by their nature or according to commercial usage, have no connection with the subject of such contracts.

Article 87 instructs the Council to adopt legislation to give effect to the principles established in Articles 85 and 86, as a result of which it subsequently adopted Regulation 17 of 6 February 1962, a detailed set of rules, later amended several times, governing the way in which the Commission should implement Treaty provisions (*JO* 13, 21 Feb 1962, pp 204–211). Article 88 is concerned with interim arrangements until the implementing legislation referred to in Article 87 is adopted, and Article 89 specifically grants to the Commission responsibility for the practical application of the principles laid down in Articles 85 and 86.

A substantial body of documentation has been generated by the Commission in the execution of its considerable powers of supervision over competition policy in the common market. The Commission vigorously enforces observance of the rules of competition by taking direct action against firms which engage in restrictive practices or exploit their market dominance, backed up, if necessary, by the imposition of hefty fines and by rulings from the Court of Justice. Over the past 20 years, direct Commission intervention of this kind has resulted in the accumulation of a sizable corpus of competition law consisting of individual rulings on specific cases brought before the Commission. Such legislation, much of which is referred to in the bibliography on competition policy published as *Documentation bulletin* B/12, is not represented in this bibliographical guide. Such is the explicit nature of the rules governing competition, as defined in the Treaty of Rome, and the executive role reserved for the Commission, that policy documents of the kind which constitute the subject of this book are inappropriate and unnecessary in this field; the role of the Commission in this case is not to formulate and initiate policy but to enforce policy governed by rules already established in the founding Treaties.

However, cases brought before the Commission, together with more general developments relating to the evolution and prosecution of policy, are reported upon in a regular chapter on competition policy in the *General report on the activities of the European Communities*. Significant cases and developments are also described in the monthly *Bulletin of the European Communities*. Such matters are more fully dealt with in the annual *Report on competition policy*, published since 1972 as a separate annex to the *General report* as a result of the European Parliament's request for such an annual review. Although each volume contains a separate section on the application of the rules of competition as regards firms in the Community, the first annual report is particularly useful in view of the fact that it takes a retrospective look at the development of competition policy as a whole from its inception up to the end of 1971. This first report was accompanied by *Competition law in the European Economic Community and in the European Coal and Steel Community* (cat 8395), a compilation of legislative texts relating to the application of competition law up to 31 December 1971.

The *Report on competition policy* also contains a section on the development of concentration in the European Communities. The Treaty of Rome does not prohibit monopolies as such. Monopolies may arise from a simple lack of competitors in a particular sector, or from rationalization motivated by desire to increase competitiveness and efficiency. However it is clearly recognized that monopolies can be exploited to the detriment of the consumer and in contravention of the founding principles of the common market. Consequently, the Commission, which set out its general position on concentration in 1965 (*see* 103), has sought to check potential abuses of market dominance by using the powers at its disposal. In July 1973, for instance, the Commission made controversial proposals, as yet not approved, for controlling mergers between undertakings (*OJ* C92, 31 Oct 1973, pp 1–7). Other proposals and rulings from the Commission are described in the *Report on competition policy*, an annex to which lists, with *Official journal* references, all of the legislative decisions taken by the Commission during the year under review.

In order to base its policy on a thorough knowledge of the structure of individual economic sectors, the Commission has undertaken considerable empirical research on concentration. More than 40 reports on concentration in specific industries ranging from classical records to the food processing industry have been published in the *Evolution of concentration and competition series*. In 1976 the Commission published *Methodology of concentration analysis applied to the study of industries and markets*, by Remo Linda, Head of the Commission's Market Structure Division, which describes the background to, and methodology of, these studies and illustrates the salient features and principal objectives of the research. The titles of individual publications are listed in an annex to the *Report on competition*.

The Treaty of Rome also recognizes the disruptive potential of certain state aids in a common market based on the principles of free and fair competition. Article 92 declares as incompatible with the common market 'any aid granted by a Member State or through State resources in any form whatsoever which distorts or threatens to distort competition by favouring certain undertakings or the production of certain goods'. However, the Treaty does recognize that certain defined types of aid are acceptable and may, with the Commission's agreement, be granted by member states. Although this chapter includes reference to a general statement of Commission policy on sectoral aid schemes (*see* 122), it should be noted that documents relating to specific aids are dealt with in the chapters relating to these sectors. Regional aids, for instance, are treated in Chapter 10 and aids to the coal industry in Chapter 5. A picture of the position regarding state aids and of the watchdog role pursued by the Commission may be constructed from the pages of the *Report on competition policy*, each annual issue of which contains a section on state intervention.

TAXATION

Fiscal frontiers, caused by differences in taxes between member states, can be as real a barrier to free trade as customs duties or restrictive practices. Recognizing the need to prevent taxes from hindering the establishment and functioning of the common market, the Treaty of Rome makes provision in Article 99 for the Commission to 'consider how the legislation of the various Member States concerning turnover taxes, excise duties and other forms of indirect taxation, including countervailing measures applicable to trade between Member States, can be harmonized in the interest of the common market' and invited the Commission to make appropriate proposals to the Council. Consequently, early documents and publications from the Commission reflect this initial concern with tax rules liable to distort competition. Reports were received from a number of committees and working groups of experts invited by the Commission to study and make recommendations on the means of giving best effect to Treaty provisions. In the light of these deliberations, particularly the reports from the Fiscal and Financial Committee (*see* 139) and the three working groups set up to examine alternative approaches to tax harmonization (*see* 140), the Commission ultimately tabled formal proposals for replacing the various forms of turnover tax currently in force in member states by a common system of value added tax.

The progressive implementation of a common value added tax system, achieved so far by means of six Council Directives (*see* 140), has been accompanied by the preparation of numerous studies and reports, mostly compiled by independent academic experts, on various aspects of value added tax and its effects on different sectors within the Community. A number of these studies have been published in the *Studies—Competition: approximation of legislation* series. They include *Conséquences budgétaires, économiques et sociales de l'harmonisation des taux de la TVA dans la CEE avec une analyse quantitative pour les Pays-Bas* (cat 8316) published as number 16 in 1970; *Rapport sur l'application de la TVA aux opérations immobilières au sein de la Communauté* (cat 8433), published as number 21 in 1971; *Les opérations financières et bancaires et la taxe sur la valeur ajoutée* (cat 8434), published as number 22 in 1973; *Etude sur l'application de la taxe sur la valeur ajoutée aux petites entreprises dans les six anciens Etats membres de la Communauté* (cat 8435), published as number 23 in 1973 and *Etude des problèmes particuliers posés par l'application de la taxe sur la valeur ajoutée au secteur agricole des pays de la Communauté européenne* (cat 8436), published as number 24 in 1973.

It was recognized from the outset that excise duties could have the same disruptive effect as turnover taxes on the free movement of goods within the common market. Particular attention was given to the harmonization of excise duties during the early 1970s when the movement towards economic and monetary union stimulated a batch of draft Directives on the subject. However, a document submitted to the Council in 1977 reveals that apart from tobacco duty, progress has so far been disappointing (*see* 148).

Authority for Community action in the field of direct taxation derives from Article 100, which gives the Council the power, acting on proposals from the Commission, to issue Directives 'for the approximation of such provisions laid down by law, regulation or administrative action in Member States as directly affect the establishment or functioning of the common market'. In 1967 the Commission prepared a programme of work in the field of direct taxation (*see* 141), which was quickly followed by a more substantial memorandum on the subject of the approximation of direct tax systems in member states (*see* 142). Although the Commission submitted a number of proposals on company taxation and a memorandum on international tax evasion (*see* 145), progress has been slow and will probably accelerate only in the context of economic and monetary union.

The considerable effort invested by the Commission in the drafting of numerous specific proposals for legislation relating to direct and indirect taxes is not adequately reflected in a bibliographical guide of this kind. However, detailed bibliographical information on measures adopted and proposed in this field is available from a document entitled *State of harmonisation of fiscal legislations* (Doc xv 577/78) and from the bibliography on fiscal matters issued in the *Documentation bulletin* B/5. The characteristics of those taxes subject to Commission attention, including their basis for assessment and methods of collection, are given in the *Inventory of taxes*, prepared by the Directorate-General for Financial Institutions and Taxation (DG XV) every two years or so. *Tax statistics* contains statistical data on taxes levied by member states.

Bibliographical record

102 Politique économique et problèmes de la concurrence dans la CEE et dans les pays membres de la CEE
Doc 3650-2/IV/65. n.d. 132p

As part of its preparatory work on competition policy, the Commission invited a number of academic experts to prepare studies on the role of competition policy in the general economic policies of member states. This report, prepared by Professor J. Zijlstra, formerly Dutch Minister of Economic and Financial Affairs, is a synthesis of these country reports together with observations on the future development of competition policy and its relationship with economic policy in the Community. Part 1 is based on the country reports; it examines similarities and differences in current ideas on competition policy and economic policy in member countries. Part 2 considers the likely impact that the Community's further development will have on economic policy in member countries and Part 3 studies economic and competition policies in the light of Community economic objectives. The report was given formal publication in a volume of the same title published by the Commission in 1966 as number two in the series *Etudes—Série concurrence* (cat 8176).

103 Le problème de la concentration dans le marché commun
SEC(65)3500. 1 Dec 1965. 46p

A memorandum in which the Commission explains its position on industrial combination and describes the difficulties which can arise from the concentration of firms in such areas as company law, tax law and competition. Taking as its starting point sections 25 and 26 of the Action Programme for the Second Stage (*see* 3), and amplifying the principles of policy identified by Commissioner Hans von der

Groeben in a speech to the European Parliament (*Débs* No 79, 14/18 June 1965, pp 102–111), the Commission recognizes the need for much larger units of production but is equally aware of the dangers of monopoly dominance of markets. Part 1 deals with the economic problems of concentration. It looks at the benefits to be derived from large-scale mass production in the context of the enlarged domestic market and at the obstacles that face firms that wish to cooperate or to merge. Equally, it considers the dangers inherent in situations in which firms have dominant positions in a particular market. In the second part of the document, the Commission looks more closely at the positive and negative effects of company and fiscal law on concentration. The Commission also explains its views on the applicability of Articles 85 and 86 to the question of concentration and makes suggestions to alleviate the position of small and medium-size firms. The document was published by the Commission in 1966 in a volume of the same title as number three in the series *Etudes—Série concurrence* (cat 8182). The attitude of the High Authority of the ECSC to concentration was explained in a memorandum entitled *La politique de la Haute Autorité en matière d'ententes et de concentrations*, published in the *Bulletin de la Communauté européenne du charbon et de l'acier*, No 47, 1964.

104 **Table ronde sur l'entreprise dans la Communauté économique européenne, Milan, 22–23 septembre 1966**
Doc 11783/X/66. n.d. 24p

A keynote speech delivered by Guido Colonna di Paliano, member of the Commission, at the opening session of the Round Table on the Firm in the European Economic Community, held in Milan in September 1966, in which he urges increased efforts to eliminate such obstacles to free movement of industrial products as monopolies, state aids, technical barriers and disparate customs legislation. Extracts from the speech appear in the *Bulletin of the European Communities* 11-1966, pp 10–15.

105 **Mémorandum de la Commission de la Communauté économique européenne sur la création d'une société commerciale européenne**
SEC(66)1250. 22 Apr 1966. 54p

A memorandum in which the Commission considers various solutions to the mainly legal difficulties that presently make it difficult for companies to combine together and to take full advantage of new domestic markets beyond national frontiers. Introductory remarks describe the ways in which the existence of different legal systems can hinder business activity across national boundaries, and how companies created according to uniform legal provisions applicable in all member states can largely remove these obstacles. The adequacy of the legal provisions made in the Treaty of Rome to allow companies to operate in any Community country and to facilitate international mergers are the subject of discussion in the second part of the document. In the third part, the Commission considers how the creation of a new type of European company, with a uniform legal base, might eliminate the problems discussed earlier in the document. The Commission considers two alternative solutions. Firstly, it considers the creation of a European company incorporated under a uniform law to be introduced in all member states. Secondly, it examines the creation of a European company under European law by virtue of a convention complementary to the Treaty of Rome. In its conclusions, the Commission gives support to the notion of a European company but delays a choice between the two alternatives until further studies have been completed. The memorandum was published as a Supplement to the *Bulletin of the European Economic Community* 9/10-1966. The Commission subsequently submitted a proposal for a Regulation embodying a statute for European companies (*see* 109). (*See also* 106 & 107.)

106 Projet d'un statut des sociétés anonymes européennes
Doc 16.205/IV/66. Dec 1966. 206p

In December 1965 the Commission invited a group of independent experts, under the chairmanship of Professor Pieter Sanders, to look at the questions of principle raised by the concept of a European company and to draft a set of rules to govern such a new legal entity. This subsequent piece of work consists of a detailed introduction in which the group discusses the difficult matters of principle raised by the creation of European joint stock companies and a draft statute for such a company. The report was published by the Commission in 1967 in a volume of the same title, issued as number six in the series *Etudes—Série concurrence* (cat 8213).

107 Contribution à l'étude des modes de représentation des intérêts des travailleurs dans le cadre des sociétés anonymes européennes
Comm EC, 1970. 64p (cat 8278)

A report prepared by Professor G. Lyon-Caen with other independent experts on the ways in which workers' interests can be adequately represented in a European company. Prepared at the invitation of the Commission, as a contribution to its work on the preparation of a draft statute for a European company, the report contains a critical examination of the section devoted to this matter in Sanders' model statute (*see* 106) and makes detailed observations and suggestions on the matter.

108 Grandes lignes d'une politique de concurrence en matière de structures de l'industrie sidérurgique
SEC(70)30 final. 13 Jan 1970. 10p

See 197.

109 Société anonyme européenne
COM(70)600 final. 24 June 1970. 609p

EP Report: *Doc de séance* 178/72. 30 Nov 1972. M. Pintus. 171p
           Working doc 67/74. 26 June 1974. P. Brugger. 160p
EP Debate: *Annex OJ* No 179, 10 July 1974, pp 126–210
EP Resolution: *OJ* C93, 7 Aug 1974, pp 22–24
ESC Opinion: *JO* C131, 13 Dec 1972, pp 32–48

Following preparatory studies conducted by and for the Commission (*see* 105–107), this document contains the Commission's formal proposal for a Regulation embodying the statute of a European company, whose uniform nature, valid throughout the Community, would allow business to take full advantage of opportunities offered by the enlarged domestic market. Although an amended proposal was tabled in 1975 (COM(75)150 final), the text of which was published as Supplement 4/75 to the *Bulletin of the European Communities*, the proposal is still before the Council.

110 **Première communication de la Commission au Conseil sur l'état d'ouverture des marchés publics et des marchés des entreprises chargées d'un service d'intérêt économique général en ce qui concerne les fournitures**
SEC(72)2601 final. 24 July 1972. 48p

A first memorandum from the Commission on the current situation with regard to the liberalization of public contracts and of contracts with firms responsible for providing services of economic interest in respect of supplies. The Commission recalls the obligations embodied in the Treaty of Rome, assesses past progress in opening up public contracts and proposes a number of measures to alleviate difficulties that still apply. The Commission pays particular attention to capital goods and items of advanced technology, where much remains to be done. The assessments made in this document were updated in 1975 (*see* 118).

111 **Communication de la Commission au Conseil sur la création d'un bureau de rapprochement des entreprises dans la Communauté**
SEC(72)2596 final. 20 Sept 1972. 12p

A communication in which the Commission makes proposals for the creation of an office to assist firms, particularly small and medium-size firms, seeking to cooperate with counterparts in other Community countries. It is proposed that the office's activities should include the dissemination of information, the establishment of contact between interested undertakings and the notification of obstacles in the way of cross frontier cooperation. The Council approved the budget for establishing the office on 16 April 1973 and it began its operations on 2 May 1973. (*See also* 114 & 120.)

112 **Economic law of the member states of the European Communities in an economic and monetary union**
Comm EC, 1973. 75p (cat 8408)

An interim report, with provisional conclusions and recommendations, on the place of the economic law of member states in an economic and monetary union, prepared on behalf of the Commission by Professor P. Verloren Van Themaat, Utrecht State University. The report is based on more detailed country reports produced according to a common schema by other academic experts. Chapter 1 contains introductory material relating to the aim of the study and the methodology used to achieve its stated objectives. Chapter 2 uses the data supplied by the national reports to summarize and compare the national systems of economic law and to formulate a number of general conclusions for the coordination of the economic law of member states. In Chapter 3, the author highlights the principal similarities and differences between the economic law of member states and discusses their importance for Community policy. Chapter 4 summarizes the principal conclusions to be drawn from the report. The report was published as number 20 in the series *Studies—Competition: approximation of legislation series*. Also published as number 20 in this series are the country reports for Germany (cat 8425), France (cat 8426), Italy (cat 8427), the Netherlands (cat 8428), the United Kingdom (cat 8429), Denmark (cat 8633) and Ireland (CG-SP-77-007-EN-C).

113 Report on takeover and other bids
Doc XI/56/74. n.d. 122p

A report by Professor R. R. Pennington, Special Adviser to the EEC, on the phenomenon of takeover bids as a technique for gaining control of companies without the need to negotiate a merger. The report first explains the nature of takeover bids, before examining in some detail existing law and practice in member states. The report highlights the common features in national systems and makes proposals for their harmonization. The report concludes with a draft proposal for a Council Directive on the subject.

114 Annual report of the Business Cooperation Centre [title varies]
1973	SEC(73)4979 final. 11 Jan 1974. 9p
Nov 1973 – Oct 1974	SEC(75)435 final. 7 Feb 1975. 14p
Nov 1974 – Oct 1975	*See* 120
Nov 1975 – Oct 1976	COM(77)277 final. 28 July 1977. 10p
1977	COM(78)328 final. 19 July 1978. 9p

An annual review of the activities of the Business Cooperation Centre and of its achievements during the period under review. The report contains factual data and comments upon the volume and nature of the Centre's activities. It also provides some indication of the Centre's future plans. (*See also* 111 & 120.)

115 Competition policy as an element of European agricultural policy
Doc X/469/74. June 1974. 21p

See 384.

116 Memorandum from the European Commission to the Council of Ministers on the changed conditions of competition in certain sectors of agriculture resulting from the new situation on the energy market
SEC(74)2200 final. 12 June 1974. 103p

See 385.

117 Public purchasing in the Common Market
SEC(74)4272. 6 Nov 1974. 113p

The report on a study of procedures and practices relating to the award of public and semi-public contracts in Community countries prepared by G. Charpentier and Sir R. Clarke at the invitation of the Commission. Appointed in November 1973 to make a review of 'the reasons underlying the low and stagnant level of intra-Community public procurement' and to make suggestions for improvement, the authors divide their report into two parts. In the first, the openness of government, regional and local authority purchasing practice are investigated; in the second, public utilities in their purchasing policies and practices are examined. (*See also* 118.)

118 First communication from the Commission to the Council on progress in liberalizing public contracts and contracts awarded by undertakings responsible for the operation of services of general economic interest in respect of supplies
COM(75)285 final. 16 June 1975. 37p

A document in which the Commission brings up-to-date its earlier memorandum on progress in liberalizing public contracts and contracts awarded to undertakings responsible for the operation of services of a general economic interest in respect of supplies (*see* 110). Since the general conclusion of the previous report was that 'although the gradual abolition of customs duties and quantitative restrictions had led to vigorous trade in the Community in all products bought by private firms or private individuals, the same was not true of capital goods and articles of advanced technology generally bought by public administrations and undertakings responsible for operating economic services of general interest', this document concentrates upon progress made since 1972 with regard to capital goods and articles of advanced technology. The document takes the form of notes additional to the information contained in the original document on electro-medical and x-ray instruments, data-processing, civil aviation, equipment for power stations, railway equipment and telecommunications equipment. (*See also* 117.)

119 Employee participation and company structure in the European Community
COM(75)570 final. 12 Nov 1975. 118p

See 576.

120 Report to the Council of Ministers on the activities of the Business Cooperation Centre
COM(75)694 final. 23 Dec 1975. 13p

A review and assessment of the first three years work of the Centre submitted to the Council as a basis upon which to discuss confirmation or modification of the Centre's terms of reference. As a result of the exercise, the Centre's status was confirmed and strengthened by the addition of certain coordinating functions concerning sub-contracting. (*See also* 111 & 114.)

121 Memorandum on the creation of an EEC trade mark
SEC(76)2462 final. 6 July 1976. 41p

As the introduction states, the object of this memorandum is to present the views of the Commission on the creation of a Community system of trade mark law since 'the creation of an EEC trade mark enjoying protection on a uniform basis throughout the territory of the common market is a necessary step towards attaining the objectives of the Community'. After an introductory section in which the Commission reviews the work carried out so far, with particular reference to the pre-liminary draft of a Convention for a European Trade Mark prepared in 1964 by the

Trade Mark Working Group, the memorandum explains the reasons for creating a Community system of trade mark law and its main objectives. The fundamental concepts and principles upon which the proposed law is based are explained in the third section, which is followed by a final section in which the Commission considers in more detail the principles of substantive trade mark law and procedure. The document was published as Supplement 8/76 to the *Bulletin of the European Communities*. In presenting the memorandum at this time, the Commission hoped to take advantage of the promising climate generated by the signing of the Convention for the European Patent for the Common Market (*OJ* L17, 26 Jan 1976, pp 1–43). During the period of discussion preceding this agreement, the Council had published in 1973 a *Draft Convention for the European Patent for the Common Market*, upon which the Commission had delivered opinions in 1974 (*OJ* L109, 23 Apr 1974, pp 34–36) and in 1975 (*OJ* L261, 9 Oct 1975, pp 26–30). This Community Patent Convention itself followed the signing in 1973 of the Convention on the Grant of European Patents by 21 European countries, including the Nine, as a result of which the European Patent Office opened in Munich on 1 January 1978.

122 Commission policy on sectoral aid schemes
COM(78)221 final. 25 May 1978. 9p

A statement of Commission policy on sectoral aid schemes prepared as a basis for an exchange of views with the Council. Having underlined the fact that the Treaty of Rome grants to the Commission responsibility for ensuring the compatibility of state aids with the common market, the Commission proceeds to outline Treaty policy on competition, its development and relevance to current economic problems. The document explains Commission policy and methods with particular reference to the problems created by industries in crisis or enjoying a period of rapid growth.

FREE MOVEMENT OF GOODS, PERSONS, SERVICES AND CAPITAL

123 Synthèse des rapports établis en 1960 sur la situation actuelle du service social des travailleurs migrants dans les six pays membres de la C.E.E.
Doc V/5664/1/60. n.d. 68p

See 547.

124 Note de commentaires sur le programme général de libération de l'établissement
Doc III/C/573/60. 22 Mar 1960. 76p

A commentary on the proposal for a general programme for the abolition of existing restrictions on the freedom of establishment, submitted by the Commission to the Council in accordance with Article 54 of the EEC Treaty, which states that 'the programme shall set out the general conditions under which freedom of establishment is to be attained in the case of each type of activity and in particular the stages by which it is to be attained'. Divided into four main chapters, the memorandum opens with a discussion of the programme's fields of application. The second chapter spells out in more detail the nature of the obstacles to be eliminated. The structure of the programme and the priorities identified are the subject of the third chapter. Finally the Commission highlights problems which merit the Council's attention. The programme was subsequently adopted by the Council and published in the *Journal officiel des Communautés européennes* 2, 15 Jan 1962, pp 36–46. A similar programme for the removal of restrictions on the freedom to supply services, submitted by the Commission in accordance with Article 63 of the EEC Treaty, was also adopted by the Council and published in the *Journal officiel des Communautés européennes* 2, 15 Jan 1962, pp 32–35. (*See also* 133.)

125 Le projet d'un premier programme commun pour favoriser l'échange de jeunes travailleurs
COM(63)14 final. 3 Apr 1963. 49p

EP Report: *Doc de séance* 95/63. 27 Nov 1963. L.-E. Troclet. 16p
　　　　　Doc de séance 100/63. 27 Nov 1963. L.-E. Troclet. 6p
EP Debate: *Débs* No 67, 28 Nov 1963, pp 162–171
EP Resolution: *JO* 182, 12 Dec 1963, pp 2908–2909

An action programme submitted by the Commission to the Council in compliance with Article 50 of the EEC Treaty, which declares that 'Member States shall, within the framework of a joint programme, encourage the exchange of young workers'. As a consequence of this initiative, the Council adopted on 8 May 1964 a programme aimed at fostering exchanges within the EEC of young workers with basic qualifications who want to complete training in another member country while gainfully employed (*JO* 78, 22 May 1964, pp 1226–1228).

126 Suites données à 'la recommandation de la Commission aux états membres concernant l'activité des services sociaux à l'égard des travailleurs se déplacant dans la Communauté'
Doc 6936/1/V/64. n.d. 138p

See 552.

127 La sécurité sociale des pays membres de la Communauté et les travailleurs migrants des pays tiers
HA doc 4657/66. n.d. 90p

See 554.

128 Les aspects économiques de la liberté d'établissement et de prestation de services dans la Communauté économique européenne
Comm EC, 1967. 219p (cat 8221)

The published proceedings of an international conference on the economic implications of freedom of establishment and of freedom to supply services, held at Pont-à-Mousson, France, on 9 and 10 June 1967. The publication contains the texts of the general reports and individual papers presented at the conference and a summary of the main discussion. A series of annexes includes a tabular list of

Commission proposals to the Council in this field together with appropriate references.

129 Le développement d'un marché européen des capitaux
Comm EEC, 1967. 400p (cat 8181)

The report of a group of independent experts charged by the Commission with making a study of the problems confronting the capital markets of the Community. Popularly referred to as the 'Segré Report' after Professor Claudio Segré, chairman of the working party, this report looks at conditions, methods and probable implications of setting up a European capital market and obstacles that would be encountered. The report is divided into five main parts. Part 1 defines the bases and conditions for developing a European capital market, highlights the structural problems common to the markets of member states and examines the existing links between capital markets. Part 2 sets out to show how the establishment of a European capital market can be facilitated by certain adjustments in the way in which the economic policies of member states are applied. Part 3 contains recommendations for widening the scope of medium and long-term credit for industry and for local authorities' capital expenditure. The integration of securities markets and the obstacles which may impede the development of a European capital market form the subject of the final two chapters. The report, also published in English under the title *The development of a European capital market*, concludes with a considerable statistical annex.

130 Programme général pour l'élimination des entraves techniques aux échanges résultant de disparités entre législations nationales
COM(68)138 final. 5 Mar 1968. 39p

EP Report: *Doc de séance* 114/68. 25 Sept 1968. A. Armengaud. 44p
EP Debate: *Annexe JO* No 106, 3 Oct 1968, pp 175–183
EP Resolution: *JO* C108, 19 Oct 1968, pp 39–40
ESC Opinion: *JO* C132, 6 Dec 1968, pp 1–5

In recognition of the fact that a single internal market requires the elimination, not only of customs and quota restrictions on free trade, but also the elimination of non-tariff barriers, the Commission submitted to the Council this systematic action programme for the removal of technical obstacles to trade resulting from differences in domestic legislation between one country and another. The central feature of the document is an outline programme to be adopted in three phases between 1 July 1968 and 1 July 1969. The proposal contains specific measures for the first phase concerning motor vehicles, agricultural tractors and machinery, glassware, electrical machinery and equipment, measuring instruments, dangerous substances and oil pipelines (*JO* C48, 16 May 1968, pp 24–31). The Council adopted the programme by way of a Resolution on 28 May 1969 (*JO* C76, 17 June 1969, pp 1–10). Just how much progress has so far been achieved may be deduced from an extremely useful publication called *Recapitulatory list of directives and proposals for directives relating to the elimination of technical barriers to trade for industrial products* (cat CB-29-79-110-EC-C. ISBN 92-825-1401-3).

31 **Nécessité et modalités d'une action dans le domaine des capitaux**
COM(69)200. 5 Mar 1969. 12p

A brief memorandum to the Council in which the Commission presses for the adoption of various measures to facilitate the freedom of movement of capital in the member states of the EEC. The Commission first recalls Treaty provisions before considering the problems to be overcome in this area. Finally, the Commission explains the nature and extent of the action it envisages to improve the mobility of capital. A document on the taxation aspects of capital liberalization was submitted to the Council at the same time (*see* 143).

32 **Suppression des contrôles sur les échanges intracommunautaires**
SEC(70)283 final. 16 Apr 1970. 44p

EP Report: *Doc de séance* 80/71. 28 June 1971. A. Califace. 7p
EP Debate: *Annexe JO* No 140, 6 July 1971, pp 58–63
EP Resolution: *JO* C78, 9 Aug 1971, p 48

EP Report: *Doc de séance* 109/72. 31 Aug 1972. C. A. Bos. 30p
EP Debate: *Annexe JO* No 154, 9 Oct 1972, pp 20–26
EP Resolution: *JO* C112, 27 Oct 1972, pp 10–12

A report on the controls to which member states still subject intra-Community trade and the conditions under which controls could be eliminated. The Commission considers in turn such obstacles to free trade as customs, fiscal and technical controls. A second report was prepared in 1973 (*see* 135).

33 **Etat d'application des directives du Conseil en vue de la réalisation de la liberté d'établissement et de la libre prestation des services dans les Etats membres**
SEC(70)277 final/2. 30 Apr 1970. 31p

EP Report: *Doc de séance* 234/70. 9 Feb 1971. S. Dittrich. 32p
EP Debate: *Annexe JO* No 133, 12 Feb 1971, pp 234–239
EP Resolution: *JO* C19, 1 Mar 1971, pp 35–36

A progress report on the application in member states of the 32 Directives so far adopted by the Council in furtherance of the general programme for the elimination of restrictions on the freedom of establishment, and a similar general programme for the elimination of restrictions on the freedom to supply services adopted by the Council in December 1961 (*see* 124). In separate sections for each member country, the Commission lists the Directives adopted and the legislative and other action taken by member governments to comply with their provisions. This document follows a report on the implementation of the general programmes as at 30 April 1967 submitted to the Council on 3 July 1967 (SEC(67)2387 final).

34 **Communication of the Commission to the Council concerning the simplification of customs formalities and procedures**
SEC(73)2334 final. 20 June 1973. 11p

Continuing customs formalities and administrative procedures at national frontiers within the EEC remain an obstacle to free trade, and are incompatible with the concept of an internal market within which movement is as unfettered as in a domestic context. The aim of this document is 'to ascertain the main causes of existing difficulties and to find out to what extent any improvement may be made in the current situation in the near future'. The Commission looks first at the causes of the present complexity of customs procedures and formalities. A second part, reviewing the action already taken to simplify customs procedures, is followed by a final part in which the Commission assesses the possibilities for improving the situation in the near future. A further communication on simplification procedures was tabled in December 1973 (SEC(73)4870), following which the Council adopted on 27 June 1974 a Resolution concerning measures to be taken with a view to simplifying the tasks of customs administrations (*OJ* C79, 8 July 1974, pp 1–2). (*See also* 137.)

135 Second report of the Commission to the Council concerning the elimination of controls on intra-Community trade—situation as at 1 June 1973
SEC(73)1661 final. 13 July 1973. 46p

In 1970 the Commission drew up a report on the controls to which intra-Community trade was still subject despite the customs union, and the conditions that would lead to their elimination (*see* 132). This new version reflects the situation as at 1 June 1973. It throws into relief the progress made since 1970 and outlines the measures that remain to be taken in the medium and long-term if the movement of goods is to be as free as in a domestic market. Separate chapters deal with customs controls, fiscal controls, exemptions from customs and fiscal duties, the controls inherent in trade policy, controls applied for financial reasons and controls in the agricultural and transport sectors.

136 Action programme in favour of migrant workers and their families
COM(74)2250. 18 Dec 1974. 27p

See 498.

137 Simplification programme
COM(75)67 final. 25 Feb 1975. 28p

EP Report: *Working doc* 135/75. 16 June 1975. K. Mitterdorfer. 21p
EP Debate: *Annex OJ* No 193, 7 July 1975, pp 14–24
EP Resolution: *OJ* C179, 6 Aug 1975, pp 7–9

A 'comprehensive work programme for the simplification of customs procedures, customs legislation and institutional methods for dealing with customs matters'. This simplification programme, supplementing two earlier communications on the topic (*see* 134) and complementing a legislative programme submitted to the Council in April 1971 (SEC(71)682 final), seeks to reduce the barriers to free trade by simplifying customs formalities. A brief introductory section is followed by a series of more lengthy annexes, the first of which outlines the content of the simplification programme. A second annex contains suggestions for improvements in the relevant procedural arrangements. A time-table for action and a summary of the work undertaken in the execution of the 1971 general programme for the approximation of customs laws also appear as annexes. A progress report on the implementation of the simplification programme was included as an appendix to a report produced in 1977 (*see* 138).

138 Communication of the Commission to the Council and to the European Parliament on the state of the customs union of the European Economic Community
COM(77)210 final. 13 June 1977. 43p

EP Report: *Working doc* 557/77. 3 Mar 1978. K. Nyborg. 63p
EP Debate: *Annex OJ* No 229, 11 April 1978, pp 82–91
EP Resolution: *OJ* C108, 8 May 1978, pp 29–31

As July 1977 marks the end of the transitional period laid down in the Treaty of Accession for new member countries, the Commission decided that this would be an appropriate moment to take stock of the state of the customs union. In the first section of the report, the Commission recalls the essential part played by the customs union in the process of European integration. This is followed by a description of the instruments of the customs union, that is, the Common Customs Tariff and customs legislation and of the problems facing the customs union today. On the basis of this assessment, the Commission then proceeds to outline what action should be taken to improve the functioning of the customs union in both the short and the long-term. A series of appendices include progress reports on the general programme for the approximation of customs legislation adopted by the Commission in 1971 (SEC(71)682 final) and on the simplification programme adopted by the Commission in 1975 (*see* 137).

TAXATION

139 Rapport du Comité fiscal et financier
Comm EEC, 1962. 150p (cat 8070)

A report from the Fiscal and Financial Committee established by the Commission on 5 April 1960 under the chairmanship of Professor F. Neumark, with a mandate to 'a) study if and to what extent the differences currently existing in the finances of Member States partly or even entirely hinder the establishment of the Common Market bringing into being and guaranteeing conditions analagous to those of an internal market, b) study to what extent it is possible to eliminate those differences which more considerably hinder the development and functioning of the Common Market'. The report opens with background information about the Committee's composition and terms of reference and with statistical data on the current economic and financial situation in member states. The Committee then gives its attention to basic considerations concerned with the disparities arising from the tax systems in member countries. The Committee makes proposals for quantitative and qualitative harmonization of certain taxes and outlines a proposed time-table. A series of annexes include statistical data and papers on tax systems for holding companies, investment companies and investment funds by Dr J. Kauffman, on the influence of member states' economic growth on problems of tax harmonization, by Professor A. Barrère and on the harmonization of taxes on companies and on dividends by Professor B. Schendstok.

140 **Rapport général des sous-groupes A, B et C crées pour examiner différentes possibilités en vue d'une harmonisation des taxes sur le chiffre d'affaires**
Doc 3310/IV/62. Jan 1962. 165p (cat 8049)

This document contains reports from three sub-groups appointed on 23 February 1960 at a meeting of Commission staff and government experts on fiscal matters to take a more detailed look at three methods of achieving closer tax harmonization within the European Communities. Sub-Group A, invited to examine the possibility of removing physical inspection of goods at the frontier in relation to turnover tax, considers substituting a system of periodical declarations by importers and exporters which member states could verify by an *a posteriori* check on their accounts. The reports from Sub-Group B, invited to study the possibilities of introducing a single general tax levied at the stage prior to retail trade combined with a tax on retailers and Sub-Group C, instructed to look at the possibility of introducing a common tax applied at the production stage or an added value tax, are preceded by general remarks common to both reports and followed by a comparison of the most important features of the different systems studied by the two groups. The document concludes with an assessment of the consequences of changing from one taxation system to another. In the light of the experts' rejection of single-stage retail, wholesale and production taxes in favour of a system of taxation on value added, of the opinion of the Fiscal and Financial Committee (*see* 139) and in accordance with the provisions of Articles 99 and 100 of the EEC Treaty, the Commission subsequently placed before the Council draft Directives for the introduction of a common value added tax. On 11 April 1967 the Council adopted Directive 67/227/EEC on the harmonization of legislation concerning turnover taxes, which provided for the introduction of a common system of VAT by 1 January 1970 (*JO* 71, 14 Apr 1967, pp 1301–1302). This was accompanied by Council Directive 67/228/EEC outlining procedures for its application (*JO* 71, 14 Apr 1967, pp 1303–1312). Important pieces of legislation on VAT adopted later by the Council include Decision 70/243/ECSC/EEC/EURATOM of 21 April 1970, which provided for up to 1 per cent of VAT revenue to be allocated to the Community budget (*JO* L94, 28 Apr 1970, pp 19–22) and Council Directive 77/388/EEC of 17 May 1977, which introduced a uniform basis of assessment and provided for the Community budget to be totally financed from its own resources as from 1 January 1978 (*OJ* L145, 13 June 1977, pp 1–40). As national procedures were not completed in time, the date of application was later changed to 1 January 1979.

141 **Programme d'harmonisation fiscale**
SEC(67)385 final. 7 Feb 1967. 6p

A work programme for the harmonization of both direct and indirect taxes in which the Commission outlines the measures which need to be taken both before and after 1 July 1968, when the customs union is due to be completed and the common agricultural policy fully established. Together with a more discursive memorandum presented to the Council in June 1967 (*see* 142), the work programme was given full publication as a Supplement to the *Bulletin of the European Economic Community* 8-1967.

142 Programme d'harmonisation des impôts directs
SEC(67)1480 final. 23 June 1967. 34p

This programme for the harmonization of direct taxes follows on from an earlier calendar of measures submitted to the Council in February 1967 (*see* 141). As the introduction suggests 'the aim of the programme is to describe in detail the conditions under which certain current tax problems arise and to propose solutions to these problems'. The Commission begins by explaining why there is need for a certain approximation of the system of direct taxation in member countries and by enumerating the long-term objectives of the programme. A second section draws attention to a number of urgent problems associated with the liberalization of capital movements, the tax problems raised by industrial combination and depreciation and makes appropriate suggestions. Both the schedule of work prepared in February and the programme were subsequently published as a Supplement to the *Bulletin of the European Economic Community* 8-1967.

143 Mesures d'aménagement en matière d'impôts directs en vue de faciliter le développement et l'interpénétration des marchés de capitaux dans la Communauté économique européenne
COM(69)201. 5 Mar 1969. 14p

A document in which the Commission gives consideration to measures for adjusting direct taxes with a view to facilitating the development and interpenetration of the capital markets of the European Communities. The memorandum, prepared in response to a request from the Council, proposes a number of measures designed to prevent taxation from determining capital movements, mainly concerning the withholding tax imposed by most member states on incomes both from variable yield securities and from bonds and debentures. The memorandum was presented to the Council along with an associated memorandum on action in the capital markets (*see* 131).

144 Rapport de la Commission au Conseil sur l'exécution des travaux décidés par le Conseil le 27 janvier 1970 en relation avec la proposition de première directive du Conseil concernant l'aménagement des systèmes nationaux de taxes sur les vehicules utilitaires
SEC(71)2911 final. 28 July 1971. 325p

See 422.

145 Report on the tax arrangements applying to holding companies
COM(73)1008 final. 18 June 1973. 10p

A report on the tax status of holding companies within the Community, prepared as a result of Council concern about their potential use for the purpose of tax evasion. Part 1 looks at the possibilities of using such companies as financing and letter-box companies; Part 2 considers the problems these companies raise in the Community.

The document concludes with proposals for measures to limit their potential as sources of tax evasion. In the following year, the Commission sent to the Council a brief memorandum and draft Council Resolution on the problems of international tax evasion and avoidance (COM(74)1971) on the basis of which the Council adopted a Resolution on 10 February 1975 (*OJ* C35, 14 Feb 1975, pp 1–2).

146 Tax policy and investment in the European Community
Comm EC, 1975. 504p (cat 8457)

A two part study undertaken on behalf of the Commission by the Institute of Fiscal Studies and Institute of Economic Research at the Erasmus University, Rotterdam. As the foreword indicates, 'the first part describes and analyses the various tax instruments aimed at influencing private investment in the nine countries of the European Community. The second part is an attempt to discover how indicators of the relative efficiency of instruments of tax policy can be given a basis in economic theory'. The report was published as number one in the *Studies—Taxation series*.

147 Action programme for taxation
COM(75)391 final. 23 July 1975. 17p

Despite the prominent place given to fiscal harmonization in the Council Resolution of 22 March 1971 on economic and monetary union (*JO* C28, 27 Mar 1971, pp 1–4) and reaffirmed in the Council Resolution of 21 March 1972 (*JO* C38, 18 Apr 1972, pp 3–4), disappointing progress has been attained to date. In this action programme, the Commission seeks to give new impetus to taxation policy by urging the Council to adopt a series of measures according to a defined time-table. The action programme is divided into two parts; in the first part the Commission draws attention to those measures that are necessary in the tax field if economic and monetary union is to be successfully introduced. The Commission looks first at value added tax and in particular at the need for rapid Council action on the Commission's proposal for a sixth Council Directive on the subject, the text of which was published as Supplement 11/73 to the *Bulletin of the European Communities*. The Commission also considers the progress attained, the proposals already before the Council and the measures still to be taken with regard to excise duties, direct taxes, international tax evasion and avoidance and tax exemption for individuals. In each case, useful bibliographical references are given to Commission proposals and enacted legislation. The second part of the action programme is more concerned with the long-term preparation for closer European integration. The Commission explains why such alignment of fiscal policy is necessary to the achievement of a genuine common market and outlines its general proposals under headings for value added tax, excise duties and direct taxes. The document concludes with a time-table by which measures referred to in Part 1 should be implemented. Just how successful the Community has been in achieving fiscal harmonization may be gleaned from a document entitled *State of harmonisation of fiscal legislations*, the latest version of which, prepared in January 1978 (Doc XV/77/78), lists Commission proposals submitted to and adopted by the Council on this matter.

148 Problems posed by excise harmonization
COM(77)338 final. 27 July 1977. 6p

A memorandum in which the Commission explains why there is need for harmonization in the field of excise duties and makes suggestions as to how and in what order of priority the Council, having expressed a willingness to re-commence work in this area, should deal with those Commission proposals already submitted. The memorandum opens with an account of the specific proposals tabled in pursuance of the Council Resolution of 22 March 1971 on economic and monetary union (JO C28, 27 Mar 1971, pp 1–4) and with the long-term aim of abolishing fiscal frontiers. These measures included a framework Directive to govern the harmonization of consumer taxes other than VAT and proposals for Council Directives on the harmonization of excise duties on alcohol, beer, wine and mixed beverages submitted to the Council in February 1972 (COM(72)225), the texts of which appeared in the *Journal officiel des Communautés européennes* C43, 29 Apr 1972, pp 23–42 and as Supplement 3/72 to the *Bulletin of the European Communities*. The Commission describes the response to these proposals, explains why the disappointing results so far must be rectified and makes recommendations to the Council as to how it should proceed in this matter. It is also worth noting that a study called *Cigarette tax harmonisation* (cat 8857), carried out by Metra Consulting Group Ltd. in the context of Council Directive 72/464/EEC of 19 December 1972 on the harmonization of taxes on manufactured tobacco (JO L303, 31 Dec 1972, pp 1–3), was published by the Commission in 1975 as number two in the *Studies—Taxation* series.

CHAPTER 5

Industry

Descriptive essay

The Treaty of Rome does not make explicit provision for the establishment of a common policy for industry. It was expected that application of the Treaty's general rules concerning the creation of a single market on the basis of free and fair competition, referred to in the previous chapter, would lead spontaneously to the gradual alignment of the industrial policies pursued by individual member states. However, during the 1960s, it became increasingly clear that market forces alone would be insufficient to bring about the anticipated transformation of Community industry. Consequently during the 1970s, the Commission placed new emphasis upon the evolution of an overall industrial strategy, as illustrated particularly in the Colonna Report (*see* 151), a major blueprint on industrial policy and an important memorandum (*see* 153) and action programme submitted in 1973 (*see* 154). As the documents listed in the first part of this chapter represent, in the main, an attempt to provide an overall framework for the individual components of industrial policy treated in the previous chapter, any study of industrial policy must take in documents from both chapters.

The gradual shift of emphasis from the prosecution of industrial policy on a sectoral basis to the formulation of a coherent and comprehensive industrial policy may be followed through the pages of the annual *General report on the activities of the European Communities*. The change of emphasis is well illustrated in this publication by virtue of the fact that in recent years the previously separate chapter on industrial policy has been replaced by one called 'Internal Market and Industrial Affairs'. The *Bulletin of the European Communities* also provides useful information on the development of industrial policy and the performance of European industry. On the same theme but rather more specialized is *Results of the business surveys carried out among managements in the Community*, a monthly source of information on the well-being of Community industry and its prospects for the future. Based on a questionnaire survey of some 20 000 managers, this publication contains tables and graphs recording their expectations for orders, production, prices and employment in the coming months. A summary of the main results of the survey appears in a separate monthly supplement to *European economy* under the title *Series B—Economic prospects: business survey results*. During the years 1962 to 1975, the results of the survey were published in less detail three times a year in *Report of the results of the business surveys carried out among heads of enterprises in the Community*.

During the period covered by this bibliographical guide, the main source of statistical data on industrial performance has been the *Quarterly bulletin of industrial production*, before 1976 simply called *Industrial statistics*. Published quarterly by the Statistical Office of the European Communities with a separate yearbook, the bulletin contained until 1978 monthly and annual indices of industrial production for all industrial sectors, except building and civil engineering, and quarterly and annual figures on the production of certain raw materials and manufactured goods. However, a rationalization of industrial statistics led in 1978 to the much speedier publication of the production indices and other indicators of industrial activity in a new monthly bulletin called *Industrial short term trends*, leaving the *Quarterly bulletin* to concentrate on data concerning the production of basic materials and manufactured goods.

Statistical data of a more specialized nature appear in the publication called *Annual investments in fixed assets in the industrial enterprises of the member countries of the European Communities*, which presents information drawn from the annual enquiry carried out by national statistical offices into capital investment in industry in accordance with Council Directive 64/475/EEC of 30 July 1964 (JO 131, 13 Aug 1964, pp 2193–2212). Volumes covering the years 1972 to 1974 and 1973 to 1975 were published separately by the Statistical Office in 1976 and 1977 respectively. Results for 1971 to 1973 appeared in *Statistical studies and surveys* 2-1975 and for 1970 to 1972 and 1964 to 1970 in issues 2-1974 and 2-1972 of the same serial respectively. The results of special investigations into specific aspects of industrial activity appear from time-to-time in the more general statistical publications. An example is the massive volume of statistical data on different branches of industry generated by the 1963 census of Community industry published in *Etudes et enquêtes statistiques* 2-1969.

Many of the documents prepared by the Commission reflect that institution's concern with the problems of particular branches of industry. The development problems experienced by individual industrial sectors have always engaged the attention of the Commission and have led to the preparation of a large number of sectoral reports and studies. Over the years, the Commission has paid particular attention to the problems experienced by advanced technology industries in which limited financial resources, particularly to support the high cost of research and development, make it difficult for European firms to compete with the giant conglomerates of America and Japan. Equal concern has been shown for the well-being of traditional but declining industrial sectors in which major structural change is necessary if they are to remain competitive. Consequently, separate sections of this chapter are devoted to individual industrial sectors. The aerospace and data processing industries have been selected to represent advanced technology industries and the textile and shipbuilding industries are taken as important examples of long-established European industries suffering from major retraction. Special attention is paid to the coal and steel industries in view of the integral role they have played in the movement towards European integration. The nuclear power industry is dealt with separately in Chapter 7 on energy policy; information on the work of the Commission in branches of industry not covered in this guide may be obtained from the *General report on the activities of the European Communities*.

COAL AND STEEL

Although the main purpose of this bibliographical guide is to review the documentation generated by the Commission of the European Communities under powers vested in it by the EEC Treaty, no chapter on industrial policy would be complete without some reference to the work of the institution within the legal and institutional framework provided by the European Coal and Steel Community. The purpose of this first experiment in European economic integration was to establish a common market in coal and steel, an objective whose implementation was to be principally the responsibility of the High Authority, an institution given much wider rule-making powers than either of the other two executives with which it later merged in 1967 to form the Commission of the European Communities. It was the duty of the High Authority to implement, then administer, the rules and regulations established in the Treaty of Paris and to manage the common market for coal and steel on a day-to-day basis. The High Authority had powers to deal directly with coal and steel undertakings and to superintend certain aspects of their activities; it also had an independent source of income from the ECSC levy on coal and steel production to spend on such matters as the retraining and redeployment of surplus manpower, the modernization of plant and the redevelopment of areas in decline.

Clearly, in fulfilment of these and other duties, the High Authority generated a great deal of documentation whose characteristics reflect the role allocated to that institution. Unlike the EEC Treaty, which does no more in most instances than create a framework upon which Community institutions are left to build common policies, the ECSC Treaty is essentially a Treaty of rules and regulations to govern the operation of a common market in just two, albeit important, industrial sectors. The role of the High Authority is largely administrative and supervisory; it is to make and execute law rather than to formulate and initiate policy. Consequently, much of the documentation generated by the High Authority, and later by the Commission, concerns the short-term administration and regulation of the coal and steel industries and the constant adjustment of policy to match changing economic and market circumstances. Such documentation, most of which features in the *Official journal of the European Communities*, is excluded from this chapter, in which entries are restricted to a relatively small number of policy and related documents concerning the management of the Community's heavy industries on a macro rather than a micro level, and a medium and long-term rather than short-term basis.

Many of the documents listed in this chapter represent expressions of concern about adverse economic conditions in the Community coal and steel industries. After an initial period of growth during the years 1953 to 1957, the Community coal industry suffered a long period of decline characterized by falling output and rising unemployment, a trend only arrested after the 1973 oil crisis. Documents listed in this chapter (*see* 165, 168 & 172) show that the High Authority, and later the Commission, was as mindful of the social as much as the economic consequences of a slump whose repercussions are well described in a useful commentary on the common market for coal called *Twenty-five years of the common market for coal 1953–1978* (cat CD-22-77-847-EN-C. ISBN 92-825-0007-1),

82

published by the Commission in 1977. In the iron and steel industry, the High Authority and Commission has had to cope with problems connected with excess supply over demand and has kept a watching brief over the availability of raw materials (*see* 187 & 195) and on competition from third countries (*see* 186). The worst steel crisis since the Second World War caused a flurry of activity during the mid 1970s in an attempt to minimize the economic and social disruption caused by a massive fall in demand (*see* 203–206).

Other documents represented in this chapter illustrate some of the ways in which the Community has responded to the problems experienced by the coal and steel industries. Schemes were devised for allowing state aids to the coal industry (*see* 163, 174, 178 & 181) and a subsidy scheme was introduced to guarantee adequate supplies of Community coke and coking coal for the iron and steel industries (*see* 162, 173 & 175). In accordance with Article 55 of the ECSC Treaty, the High Authority made available funds for 'research relating to the production and increased use of coal and steel and to occupational safety in the coal and steel industries' and also used its financial resources to make loans, loan guarantees and grants, for the rejuvenation of the coal and steel industries.

Long-term forecasts of the trend of supply and demand and of market conditions are necessary for sound economic management in any industrial sector. Article 46 of the ECSC Treaty stipulates that the High Authority shall 'periodically lay down general objectives for modernization, long-term planning of manufacture and expansion of productive capacity' so as to provide industrial undertakings with a framework within which to construct appropriate plans for future industrial activity. Consequently, documents prepared by the High Authority in accordance with Treaty objectives are characterized by a series of periodic reports for both the steel industry (*see* 185, 189, 194, 198, 202 & 207) and the coal industry (*see* 166, 171 & 177), all similar in aim and arrangement but each revised to take account of current statistical data and best estimates of future requirements. The general purpose of such documents is to provide guidelines for forward planning of long-term production and investment levels in the coal and steel industries.

Equally necessary for the efficient management of industry are regular short-term forecasts of supply and demand and market conditions. Until the end of 1971, the High Authority, then the Commission of the European Communities, published quarterly forecasts in the *Official journal of the European Communities* under the title *Programme provisionnel 'charbon'*. These forecasts, based on quarterly meetings between the High Authority and representatives from member states, relate to the current situation in the coal market and prospects for the immediate future with respect to production, sales, imports, exports, supply and demand. The High Authority, now the Commission of the European Communities, also compiles an annual balance sheet comparing the situation in the coal industry for the coming year with that of the past year, with regard to production, sales, imports, exports and trade. Although compiled since 1958, the balance sheet has received full publication in the *Official journal of the European Communities* only since 1970, replacing, from 1971, the quarterly forecasts which then ceased to be published. The 1977/78 balance sheet, for instance, published under the title *The Community coal market in 1977 and forecasts for 1978*, was published in the *Official journal of the European Communities* C118, 22 May 1978, pp 1–45.

As far as steel is concerned short-term forecasts, usually referred to as 'forward programmes', have varied in frequency of publication according to the well-being of the industry. During 1956 to 1971 forward programmes were published quarterly in the *Official journal of the European Communities*. Then from 1972, as the situation improved and in order to allow trends to emerge more clearly, annual forward programmes were published in the *Official journal of the European Communities*, usually with half-yearly reappraisals. However, during the steel crisis of 1975, there was a reversion to quarterly forecasts.

An additional source of statistical data is the range of publications issued by the Statistical Office of the European Communities. The *Quarterly iron and steel bulletin*, formerly called *Iron and steel*, is the principal source of regular series on production, consumption, orders and deliveries, internal and external trade. An associated yearbook provides summarized annual data on the same range of topics. Similar provision is made for coal in the *Quarterly bulletin of energy statistics*, formerly *Energy statistics* and in an annual publication called *Coal statistics* which contains summarized balance sheets for various types of coal. Short-term movements in the two industries are recorded in *Coal: monthly bulletin* and in *Iron and steel monthly bulletin*, both of which provide rapid publication of the most important short-term economic indicators. Information on past and future investment in the Community coal and steel industries is published in *Investment in the Community coalmining and iron and steel industries*, each issue of which contains the results of an annual survey of actual and proposed investment in the coal and steel industries. A summary report for 1956 to 1965 was published in 1966 (cat 3875), and another for 1966 to 1973 in 1974 (cat 8422).

Finally, it should be recorded that in addition to the publications referred to in this introduction, the High Authority, later the Commission, has published a considerable number of more specialized technical and research reports concerning the coal and steel industries in the Community. Many have appeared in such monograph series as *Recueils de recherches 'charbon'*, *Etudes techniques 'charbon'* and *Recherches techniques 'acier et mines de fer'*, individual volumes within which are listed, together with many Euronorms devised to promote technical harmonization, in the *Catalogue des publications 1952–1971* and its subsequent annual updates. Research and technical reports and papers are also listed and summarized in *Euro abstracts. Section II Coal and steel*.

Bibliographical record

149 Enquête sur la situation des petites et moyennes entreprises industrielles dans les pays de la CEE
SEC(65)3600. 1 Dec 1965. 218p

A report on the problems experienced by small and medium-size firms in Community countries, prepared by Professor Woitrin of the Catholic University of Louvain, from data collected by research institutes in each member country. Discussion of the report's findings and of information from member states relating to measures taken in their countries in favour of small and medium-size firms subsequently formed the basis for proposals incorporated by the Commission in the second medium-term economic policy programme (*see* 66). The synthesis prepared by Professor Woitrin was published in 1966 by the Commission in a volume of the same title (cat 8183), issued as number four in the series *Etudes—Série concurrence*.

50 Mémorandum sur la politique industrielle de la Communauté
SEC(67)1201 final. 4 July 1967. 23p

A memorandum in which the Commission takes stock of the achievements in industrial policy, reviews the various policy instruments provided by the EEC Treaty and places those specific measures already in train in the context of an overall framework. Part 1 concerns the objectives of industrial policy and includes an outline action programme. Part 2 concentrates in more detail upon means of action both general and sectoral.

51 La politique industrielle de la Communauté
COM(70)100 final. 18 Mar 1970. 5 vols, 35p, 70p, 119p, 92p, 39p

EP Report: *Doc de séance* 226/70. 3 Feb 1971. G. Springorum. 33p
EP Debate: *Annexe JO* No 133, 9/10 Feb 1971, pp 63–94 & 96–102
EP Resolution: *JO* C19, 1 Mar 1971, pp 21–23
ESC Opinion: *JO* C59, 11 June 1971, pp 9–19

A major blueprint, popularly known as the 'Colonna Report' after Mr Guido Colonna di Paliano, member of the Commission responsible for its preparation, in which the Commission presents for the first time an overall assessment of the problems of industrial development in the Community and makes proposals for an integrated industrial strategy, so taking advantage of the opportunity afforded by the merger of the three executives. Intended as a basis for discussion with Community institutions and member states, the document comprises a general memorandum and a supporting document divided into four separate parts. The general memorandum is concerned with the broad principles of industrial policy and with basic guidelines for the determination of policy. It highlights and describes in turn five fundamental objectives whose attainment would give the EEC a more efficient and competitive base, namely, the creation of a single market, improvements in the institutional framework within which firms operate, the restructuring of Community industry, adaptability to change and closer ties in international economic relations. The first part of the supporting document describes in some detail the current position of Community industry and draws unfavourable comparisons between the strength and efficiency of Community industry and that of its main industrial competitors, particularly the United States of America. The remaining three parts look more closely at areas where remedial action is necessary, namely, the environment within which firms operate, the ability of Community industry to adapt to change and the promotion of advanced technology industries. The general memorandum was published as a Supplement to the *Bulletin of the European Communities* 4-1970 and together with the supporting documents in a publication of the same title, an English language version of which was issued under the title *Industrial policy of the Community* (cat 8314). The Commission later submitted to the Council a number of specific proposals designed to give effect to the principles outlined in the memorandum. These included a proposal for the creation of joint undertakings within the scope of the EEC Treaty (COM(71)812 final) and a proposal on the implementation of Community industrial development contracts (COM(72)710 final).

152 Note de synthèse sur les actions de la Communauté économique européenne intéressant les petites et moyennes entreprises
SEC(72)650. 18 Feb 1972. 88p

Requested by COREPER to assist with its deliberations, this document consists of a synoptic analysis in tabular form of measures taken by each member state in favour of small and medium-size firms together with an explanatory memorandum. The Economic and Social Committee also investigated the difficulties experienced by small firms during this period and in 1974 produced a substantial report on the situation (ESC 714/74), published separately by the Committee in 1975 under the title *The situation of small and medium-sized undertakings in the European Community: study.*

153 Memorandum from the Commission on the technological and industrial policy programme
SEC(73)1090 final. 3 May 1973. 39p

EP Report: *Working doc 277/73.* 12 Dec 1973. P. B. Cousté. 19p
EP Debate: *Annex OJ* No 171, 11 Feb 1974, pp 23–34
EP Resolution: *OJ* C23, 8 Mar 1974, pp 10–11
ESC Opinion: *OJ* C115, 28 Sept 1974, pp 8–16

Responding to the impetus generated by the Paris summit in October 1972, the final declaration of which invited Community institutions to submit an action programme before 1 January 1974, this memorandum outlines in general terms the measures the Commission intends to take to create the unfettered framework within which Community industry can flourish. Five main sections sketch the Commission's intentions in those areas singled out for particular attention at the Paris summit, namely, abolition of technical barriers to trade in foodstuffs and industrial products, the gradual extension of rights to tender for public contracts, the promotion of advanced technology industries and of industries in sectors experiencing particular problems and the harmonization of industrial policy with other Community objectives. A series of annexes include a time-tabled programme of decisions to be taken in these priority areas over the next five years. The memorandum was published as Supplement 7/73 to the *Bulletin of the European Communities.* The Commission later submitted more concrete proposals to the Council on the basis of the contents of this memorandum (*see* 154).

154 Programme of action in the field of technological and industrial policy
SEC(73)3824 final. 30 Oct 1973. 19p

A document submitted to the Council by the Commission in response to a Council request for formal proposals on the technological and industrial policy programme outlined in general terms earlier in the year (*see* 153). Presented in the form of a draft Council Resolution, the proposed action programme closely follows the contents of the earlier memorandum but modifies the time-table in the light of developments over the past six months. The draft Resolution contains sections on the removal of technical barriers to trade, of restrictions on bidding for public contracts, of fiscal barriers which impede cooperation between enterprises and the promotion of advanced technology industries and those in need of modernization. A series of annexes list the proposals to be adopted by the Council within specified time limits. After examination of this document, the Council was able to adopt a Resolution on industrial policy on 17 December 1973 (*OJ* C117, 31 Dec 1973, pp 1–14) and a statement concerning the removal of legal barriers to the linking of undertakings (*OJ* C117, 31 Dec 1973, p 15).

55 Multinational undertakings and Community regulations
COM(73)1930. 7 Nov 1973. 49p

EP Report: *Working doc* 292/74. 24 Oct 1974. F. Leenhardt. 28p
EP Debate: *Annex OJ* No 184, 12 Dec 1974, pp 204–230
EP Resolution: *OJ* C5, 8 Jan 1975, pp 37–39
ESC Opinion: *OJ* C116, 30 Sept 1974, pp 14–18

A response from the Commission to the growing influence of multinational companies on the economic, social and political life of Community countries and to the disquiet caused by the inability of national legal, fiscal, economic and monetary rules to control their large-scale, widely spread activities. The document presents a general policy framework and an index of measures designed to alleviate a number of particular problems. Proposals for specific measures are collected into seven chapters concerning protection of the general public, protection of workers' interests, the maintenance of competition, takeover methods, equality of conditions of reception, protection of developing countries and the improvement of information. A series of annexes include a draft Resolution on measures to be taken and an analysis of the problems raised by the development of multinational companies, highlighting the repercussions of foreign investment on the host country and on countries of origin (*OJ* C114, 27 Dec 1973, p 28). The memorandum was published as Supplement 15/73 to the *Bulletin of the European Communities*. In 1976 the Commission published *A survey of multinational enterprises* (cat 8818), a synopsis of the findings of a study of the nature and activities of multinational corporations based on information supplied by the companies themselves.

56 Report by the Commission on the behaviour of the oil companies in the Community during the period from October 1973 to March 1974
COM(75)675. 10 Dec 1975. 157p

See 326.

57 Report from the Commission to the Council on the implementation of the industrial policy programme (resolution of 17 December 1973)
COM(76)199 final. 10 May 1976. 17p

A report from the Commission on the practical measures taken to implement the industrial policy programme envisaged in the Council Resolution of 17 December 1973 (*see* 154). Short sections review progress in each of the nine action areas identified in the Council Resolution. Reasons are advanced to explain why many of the time limits have not been met and suggestions made as to how progress can be accelerated.

158 **Complement to the address by Mr Davignon, Member of the Commission, to Parliament, given on 16 February 1978, on the occasion of Parliament's examination of the proposal for a resolution on questions relating to small and medium-sized firms in the Community**
COM(78)137 final. 4 Apr 1978. 13p

Small and medium-sized undertakings have a vital part to play in the economic life of the Community. In this communication, the Commission offers its observations on the Resolution adopted by the European Parliament (*OJ* C63, 13 Mar 1978, pp 38–41) on the basis of an earlier parliamentary committee report on small and medium-sized undertakings in the Community (*Working doc* 518/77). The memorandum begins by outlining the objectives and principles which the Commission intends to follow in this field and then offers comments on the main points raised in the Resolution of the European Parliament. Since no Community country has a legal definition of what constitutes a small or medium-sized firm, the Commission's Directorate-General for Industrial and Technological Affairs prepared in 1976 a document collating the most widely used definitions in member states (Doc 413/III/76).

COAL

159 **Rapport spécial de la Haute Autorité à l'Assemblée parlementaire européenne concernant la question charbonnière (31 janvier au 15 mai 1959)**
HA ECSC, 1959. 80p (cat 2226)

A special report to the European Parliamentary Assembly in which the High Authority recalls the initiatives it has taken during the first half of 1959 in an attempt to check the continuing slump in the coal industry. In particular, the report refers to the High Authority's plan to invoke Article 58 of the ECSC Treaty, which, in the event of a decline in demand and in a period of 'manifest crisis', empowers the High Authority to reduce production by the introduction of a system of production quotas, and Article 74 of the ECSC Treaty, which allows for measures to safeguard the Community and its objectives. The High Authority also reports on the inability of the Council of Ministers to approve these emergency measures. A series of annexes contain statistical data, together with the texts of the principal documents prepared by the High Authority during this period of intense activity.

160 **Politique de recherche technique de la Haute Autorité**
HA doc 3061/3/61. 15 July 1961. 15p

See 231.

161 **Approvisionnement en charbon du secteur foyers domestiques 1953–1962**
HA doc 5227/1/64. 8 Jan 1965. 37p

The domestic heating sector constitutes an important market for coal. This report reviews the position coal has occupied in this sector over the ten year period 1953 to 1962. (*See also* 170.)

162 L'approvisionnement en charbon à coke dans la Communauté avec référence spécial à l'industrie sidérurgique
HA doc 6744/2/64. 17 Feb 1965. 48p

A first study of Community supplies of coking coal, prepared by the High Authority in response to the reference made to the topic by governments of member states in the Protocol of Agreement on energy problems, signed on 21 April 1964, Article 12 of which states that 'the Council must give particular attention to the problem of long-term supplies of coking coal to the Community' (*JO* 69, 30 Apr 1964, pp 1099–1100). The High Authority makes particular reference to the iron and steel industry, in view of that industry's large-scale consumption of coal and coke in its manufacturing processes. Part 1 consists of an assessment of the current position as regards coking coal supplies to Community consumers in general and to the iron and steel industry in particular. In Part 2 the High Authority looks at other factors that will influence the coking coal market in the near future, particularly the demands likely to be made by the iron and steel industry. The likely effects of imports of coking coal from America on the cost of iron and steel production in the Community are considered in Part 3. The report, modified, extended and re-submitted to the Council in 1966 (HA doc 1625/1/66), confirmed the need for a subsidy system to guarantee adequate supplies of Community coke and coking coal for the iron and steel industry and to protect the product against cheaper foreign imports. On 16 February 1967 the governments of member states adopted a Protocol of Agreement on coking coal and coke for use in the Community iron and steel industry (*JO* 36, 28 Feb 1967, p 561), which was quickly followed by High Authority Decision 1/67/ECSC of 21 February 1967 introducing a subsidy system to enable 'coal firms to reduce the price of coking coal and to make blast furnace coke to be sold to Community steel enterprises, in order to promote the sale of these items' (*JO* 36, 28 Feb 1967, pp 562–567). Intended to be of two years' duration in the first instance, the scheme was later extended by a year in Commission Decision 2177/68/ECSC of 27 December 1968 (*JO* L315, 31 Dec 1968, p 1). At the same time, the Council asked the Commission to prepare a thorough analysis of the position regarding coke and coking coal for the steel industry before 31 March 1969 (*see* 173).

163 Mémorandum de la Commission au Conseil sur les mesures financières des états membres en faveur de l'industrie houillère pour l'année ...

1965	HA doc 5248/1/65. 10 Sept 1965. 97p
1966	HA doc 2000/1/66. 21 Apr 1966. 85p
1967	HA doc 700/67. 21 June 1967. 117p
1968	SEC(68)2607 final. 29 July 1968. 142p
1969	SEC(69)2915 final. 25 July 1969. 150p
	SEC(69)3716 final. 14 Oct 1969. 20p
1970	SEC(70)2711 final. 22 July 1970. 51p
1971	SEC(71)3580 final. 13 Oct 1971. 73p

1972	SEC(72)2360 final. 6 July 1972. 81p
	SEC(73)2272 final. 19 June 1973. 36p
1972/73	SEC(74)1377 final. 18 Apr 1974. 139p
1973/74	SEC(75)1104 final. 24 Mar 1975. 79p
1975	COM(75)360 final. 15 July 1975. 30p
1976	COM(77)127 final. 12 Apr 1977. 40p
1977	COM(77)570 final. 15 Nov 1977. 37p
1978	COM(78)367 final. 28 July 1978. 34p

A series of annual reports, published in English since 1973 under the title *Memorandum on the financial aid awarded by the Member States to the coal industry*, in which the Commission reports on the compatibility of the financial assistance granted by member states to their coal industries with the provisions of the aid schemes established by the European Communities and with the proper functioning of the common market. Each report refers to the economic and financial problems facing coal undertakings, the competitive situation in the coal market and the compatibility of individual measures with the aid scheme in operation at that time. Three such regimes for the payment of state subsidies to coal undertakings have been introduced. The first scheme was introduced by High Authority Decision 3/65/ECSC of 17 February 1965 (*JO* 31, 25 Feb 1965, pp 480–484) and, extended by Commission Decision 27/67/ECSC of 25 October 1967 (*JO* 261, 28 Oct 1967, pp 1–2), remained in force until 31 December 1970. The second series of guidelines was introduced by Commission Decision 3/71/ECSC of 22 December 1970 and lasted until 31 December 1975 (*JO* L3, 5 Jan 1971, pp 7–14). The third and current piece of legislation was adopted on 25 February 1976 when Commission Decision 528/76/ECSC introduced an aid system to last for ten years from 1 January 1976 (*OJ* L63, 11 Mar 1976, pp 1–10). (*See also* 174.)

164 L'action de la Haute Autorité dans le domaine de la recherche technique
HA doc 7005/1/65. Nov 1965. 55p

See 233.

165 Aspects sociaux du problème charbonnier
HA doc 2366/66. n.d. 10p

A brief document in which the High Authority investigates the social problems caused by recession in the coal industry. The first part examines the problems posed by a reduction in employment; the second part looks at means of assuring a sufficient, young, stable and qualified work-force in the coal-mining industry. (*See also* 168 & 172.)

166 Mémorandum pour le Comité Consultatif sur l'objectif de production charbonnière 1970 et sur la politique charbonnière
HA doc 1805/66. 9 Mar 1966. 49p

Article 46 of the ECSC Treaty declares that the High Authority shall 'periodically lay down general objectives for modernisation, long-term planning of manufacture and expansion of productive capacity'. Although preliminary objectives were established by the High Authority in 1955 (*JO CECA* 16, 19 July 1955, pp 822–832) and new targets for 1975 were established in 1957 (*JO CECA* 16, 20 May 1957, pp 195–220), the current fluidity of the energy sector makes new general objectives for coal particularly difficult at this time. However, in the light of information derived from the 1966 energy balance sheet and from the High Authority's review of the long-term energy outlook for the Community (*see* 274), both confirming the continued structural decline of coal, the High Authority decided to submit to the Consultative Committee this document in which it draws attention to the main trends in the coal market and makes appropriate proposals. The memorandum begins with a description of the current position of the coal industry in the Community and of its medium-term development prospects. In the light of the imbalance in the coal sector, the High Authority then proceeds to propose revisions to former production targets and to outline a suitable strategy for production and marketing up to 1970. A substantial annex provides a considerable body of statistical and other data upon which the memorandum's analyses are based. The annex begins with an assessment of the present situation and recent trends in the Community energy market as they affect coal. Consideration is then given to Community coal output in the light of the likely supply of and demand for energy in 1970 and to production prospects for 1980. The Consultative Committee subsequently issued a Resolution on the matter (*JO* 123, 8 July 1966, pp 2282–2284).

167 Analyse de la situation charbonnière de la Communauté
HA doc 1793/66. 11 Mar 1966. 76p

A mainly statistical assessment of developments in the coal economy since 1958 with certain projections for 1970. The document begins with a general statistical review of trends since 1957 under such headings as production, manpower, imports and exports and prices. Subsequent sections consider the financial position of coal undertakings in a number of Community countries and review the financial assistance accorded to these undertakings by both the High Authority and member governments.

168 La situation de la main-d'oeuvre dans les charbonnages de la Communauté
HA doc 2160/66. 24 Mar 1966. 14p

The downward trend in coal production, accompanied by increased mechanization, the closure of some undertakings and the rationalization and concentration of others, has led to a steady decline in manpower in the industry. In this document the High Authority describes the main features of the declining workforce in the coal industry during the period 1957 to 1965. Attention is given to such aspects as recruitment and qualifications, migrant labour and the age structure of the industry. (*See also* 165 & 172.)

169 Possibilités d'action en faveur du charbon communautaire
HA doc 2164/66. 31 Mar 1966. 9p

Measures to assist the Community coal industry have so far centred on the 1964 Protocol of Agreement on energy problems (*JO* 69, 30 Apr 1964, pp 1099–1100) and the system of financial assistance adopted in the following year (*see* 163). In this memorandum the High Authority takes the opportunity to look more closely at the possibilities for assistance under the terms of Article 57 of the ECSC Treaty, which refers, in the sphere of production, to the 'indirect means of action' at the High Authority's disposal, in particular, 'cooperation with Governments to regularise or influence general consumption, particularly that of the public services' and 'intervention in regard to prices and commercial policy as provided for in this Treaty'. Separate sections of the document are devoted to consideration of the possibilities for cooperation with governments, intervention on prices, commercial policy and intra-Community trade.

170 **Evolution du marché des foyers domestiques de la Communauté et de son approvisionnement en combustibles solides**
HA doc 2760/66. 21 Apr 1966. 26p

A country-by-country analysis of the state of the domestic market for solid fuels in all member states except Italy, drawn up by the High Authority at a time when the market shows signs of regression and on the basis of information supplied by questionnaires circulated to appropriate authorities. During the same month, the High Authority submitted to the Council detailed statistical information based on the questionnaire returns (HA doc 2824/66). (*See also* 161.)

171 **L'évolution de l'économie charbonnière de la Communauté de 1966 à 1970**
HA doc 4489/66. 7 July 1966. 18p

A summary of quantitative forecasts concerning the development of the coal industry in the Community in the period up to 1970. (*See also* 166.)

172 **Aspects sociaux de la politique charbonnière (dans le cadre d'une politique énergetique communautaire)**
COM(69)148. 26 Feb 1969. 8p

Recession in the coal industry and the associated need for modernization have considerable social implications. In this document, the Commission takes a look at the social problems facing the industry and offers certain guidelines for Community policy in this field. (*See also* 165 & 168.)

173 **Rapport de la Commission au Conseil concernant la question des charbons à coke et cokes destinés à la sidérurgie de la Communauté**
SEC(69)1154 final. 25 Mar 1969. 90p

The subsidy scheme introduced in 1967 to maintain Community production of coke and coking coal at a level sufficient to supply the needs of the Community iron and steel industry, and to facilitate the marketing of these products, was due to lapse at the end of the year (*see* 162). This comprehensive appraisal of the position regarding coke and coking coal in the Community is intended to provide the Council with a factual basis upon which to base its deliberations on what arrangements, if any, to make for the future. Chapter 1 is devoted to an analysis of the present situation and the likely impact of new processes in the manufacture of pig iron and steel on demand for coke and coking coal over the next ten years. In Chapter 2, the

Commission evaluates the overall level of demand for coke and coking coal from the world steel industry and the means of meeting these requirements up to 1980. Chapter 3 considers the contribution the Community's coal-mining industry can make to satisfying the needs of the Community iron and steel industry. Finally, in Chapter 4, the Commission considers the impact of the existing subsidy system on the provision of supplies for the Community industry. The report was published in a volume of the same title in 1969, an English version of which was entitled *Report on the question of coking coal and coke for the iron and steel industry of the Community* (cat 4799). After due consideration of the report, the Council decided on 19 December 1969 in Decision 70/1/ECSC to extend the existing aid scheme until 31 December 1972 (JO L2, 6 Jan 1970, pp 10–15). (*See also* 175.)

174 **Etude sur la question de l'approvisionnement en charbon et de la production houillère dans la Communauté**
SEC(70)2399 final. June 1970. 125p

A detailed factual study of coal production and supply in the Community prepared to assist discussion of what measures should be taken when the Community's first system of financial aid to the coal industry, introduced by High Authority Decision 3/65/ECSC of 17 February 1965 (JO 31, 25 Feb 1965, pp 480–484) and extended by Commission Decision 27/67/ECSC of 25 October 1967 (JO 261, 28 Oct 1967, pp 1–2), expires on 31 December 1970 (*see* 163). Chapter 1 places coal in the context of the Community's overall energy balance sheet and looks at the position as regards the supply of coking coal, domestic coal and steam coal. It also gives consideration to the question of security of supply. In Chapter 2 the Commission turns its attention to conditions of supply for both Community and imported coal, and in the final chapter it deals with fluctuations in demand and the possibility of adjusting supply. The Council later agreed with the Commission's conclusions that aids to the coal industry were still needed. The Commission accordingly adopted Decision 3/71/ECSC of 22 December 1970 introducing a new legal basis for granting aid to the coal industry until 31 December 1975 (JO L3, 5 Jan 1971, pp 7–14). (*See also* 178.)

175 **Deuxième étude sur l'approvisionnement de l'industrie sidérurgique de la Communauté en charbons à cokes et cokes**
SEC(72)2427 final. 12 July 1972. 159p

A second report on the supply of coke and coking coal to the steel industry following an earlier report in 1969 (*see* 173), prepared by the Commission in advance of the expiry of the existing aid system on 31 December 1972. Chapter 1 consists of an appraisal of the present position and of the possibilities for developing new techniques for making caste iron, steel and coke. In Chapter 2 the Commission looks at the problems of satisfying the iron and steel industry's needs for adequate supplies. It examines the trends in world production of iron and steel and the demand for coke and for coking coal. Further chapters consider price implications and the supply of coal from third countries. Discussion of the report led to the adoption on 25 July 1973 of Commission Decision 73/287/ECSC introducing a new system of aids to run until 1978 (OJ L259, 15 Sept 1973, pp 36–42), extended to the end of 1981 by Commission Decision 1613/77/ECSC of 15 July 1977 (OJ L180, 20 July 1977, pp 8–9).

176 **Medium-term research aid programme (1975 to 1980) under Article 55 ECSC Treaty**
SEC(74)1423 final. 18 Apr 1974. 16p

Article 55 of the ECSC Treaty stipulates that 'the High Authority shall promote technical and economic research relating to the production and increased use of coal and steel and to occupational safety in the coal and steel industries'. In order to coordinate research activities and to channel resources into areas of research where tangible results may be expected, the Commission sets out in this document the criteria by which it will judge applications for financial assistance and specifies sectors in which it will be concentrated in the period 1975 to 1980. This document, later published in the *Official journal of the European Communities* C60, 25 May 1974, pp 16–26, followed two earlier research aid programmes established for the periods 1967 to 1970 (SEC(68)2514 final) and 1970 to 1974 (*JO* C99, 31 July 1970, pp 1–16), revised in 1972 (*JO* C74, 10 July 1972, pp 1–16). Earlier still, in 1963, the High Authority had made known the principal areas of research that it proposed to support (*Bull CECA* No 41, 1963). In the same year, the High Authority also established the administrative procedures for the submission and examination of applications for grants, in which it set out the terms and conditions under which such aid was to be granted and the position regarding the disclosure and dissemination of research results (*JO* 70, 9 May 1963, pp 1433–1440). The document was reproduced at the time of the establishment of guidelines for a second medium-term technical research programme (*JO* C99, 31 July 1970, pp 9–16) and an amended version issued when the third such programme was devised in 1974 (*OJ* C139, 12 Nov 1974, pp 1–8).

177 **Medium-term guidelines for coal 1975–1985**
COM(74)1860 final. 21 Nov 1974. 51p

EP Report: *Working doc* 147/75. 27 June 1975. F. Burgbacher. 22p
EP Debate: *Annex OJ* No 193, 8 July 1975, pp 44–69
ER Resolution: *OJ* C179, 6 Aug 1975, pp 15–16
CC ECSC Opinion: *OJ* C10, 15 Jan 1975, pp 1–2

A memorandum in which the Commission seeks to re-assess the role coal can play in supplying the Community's future energy needs up to 1985, in the light of the dramatic economic consequences of the 1973 oil crisis. The document attempts to quantify the contribution coal can make to the general objective of reducing dependence on imported crude oil and thereby to define the main guidelines of a Community coal policy for the period 1975 to 1985. Chapter 1 looks in detail at the place of coal in the new energy supply structure. It estimates demand for hard coal from power stations, coking plants and other sources up to 1985 and the likely level of supplies from both Community production and imports from non-member countries. Chapter 2 is concerned with defining the elements of a coal policy for the Community. It looks at the problems of market equilibrium, the need to create a stable and regular market for coal and measures to secure adequate coal supplies for the future. Chapter 3 consists of a summary of the main lines of coal policy for the period from 1975 to 1985. Two annexes to the memorandum consist of a draft Council Resolution on the matter and a brief communication on measures to monitor coal imports. The memorandum, minus its annexes, was published in the *Official journal of the European Communities* C22, 30 Jan 1975, pp 1–18.

178 Aids to the Community's coal industry (experience and prospects)
COM(75)370 final. 10 Sept 1975. 54p

EP Report: *Working doc* 133/76. 10 June 1976. G. Springorum. 16p
EP Debate: *Annex OJ* No 204, 17 June 1976, pp 192–205
EP Resolution: *OJ* C159, 12 July 1976, pp 33–35

A general review of how Community aids to the coal industry have worked since 1965, together with suggestions for measures to take effect when the existing aid scheme expires on 31 December 1975 (*see* 174). In Chapter 1 the Commission takes stock of the application of Commission Decision 3/71/ECSC of 22 December 1970 on aids to the Community coal industry, with particular reference to the practical difficulties concerning its application (*JO* L3, 5 Jan 1971, pp 7–14). In the following chapter, the Commission discusses the nature of the provision that needs to be made for assisting the coal industry in the context of the new energy supply situation. Chapter 3 consists of a number of conclusions and guidelines. The document is completed by an annex tracing the development of aid schemes between 1965 and 1974 and a series of statistical tables on the subject. A new aid regime to cover the ten years from 1 January 1976 was subsequently adopted on 25 February 1976 by Commission Decision 528/76/ECSC (*OJ* L63, 11 Mar 1976, pp 1–10).

179 The position of the Community's coal industry
COM(76)667 final. 9 Dec 1976. 2p

A brief document in which the Commission draws attention to the progressive deterioration in the position of the coal industry in relation to the objectives set in 1974 (*see* 177).

180 The Community coal market situation
COM(77)41 final. 25 Feb 1977. 18p

An appraisal of the present situation in the coal market, following an earlier warning that the steep rise in coal stocks and imports threatened to endanger attainment of the targets set for 1985 (*see* 179). The Commission reviews the Community situation and attempts to evaluate the interrelationship between Community coal production and imports of coking coal from third countries. The Commission identifies the problems concerning imports from third countries and makes suggestions for achieving a balance between the interests of coal producers and coal consumers. On 7 November 1977 the Council adopted Council Decision 77/707/ECSC, whose intention was to improve the system of collecting information on imports of coal originating in non-member countries and intended for electricity generation (*OJ* L292, 16 Nov 1977, p 11).

181 Introduction of a Community aid system for intra-Community trade in power station coal
COM(78)70 final. 22 Feb 1978. 6p

EP Report: *Working doc* 199/78. 3 July 1978. L. Ibrugger. 21p
EP Debate: *Annex OJ* No 232, 5 July 1978, pp 172–181
EP Resolution: *OJ* C182, 31 July 1978, pp 38–40

A brief communication in which the Commission seeks to explain why there is a need for a Community aid system in support of intra-Community trade in power station coal. The document begins with a general justification of aid measures in the present difficult economic climate, before outlining a plan for an aid scheme to apply for three years from 1 January 1979. This document was followed in September 1978 by a formal proposal for a Council Regulation establishing such a scheme (COM(78)364 final). However, neither this proposal nor an earlier proposal for a Council Regulation on financial measures to promote the use of coal for electricity generation (COM(76)648 final) has yet been adopted by the Council.

182 ECSC redevelopment policies
SEC(78)4351 final. 13 Dec 1978. 45p

See 209.

STEEL

183 Note succincte sur la politique sidérurgique
HA doc 1683/58. 14 Feb 1958. 24p

An early discussion document in which the High Authority identifies the general areas in which it wishes to achieve progress. Separate chapters are devoted to four main themes around which iron and steel policy should be evolved. These chapters are concerned with supply and the conditions for expansion, including policies for scrap, coke and iron ore; the structure of the industry, especially the degree of concentration and specialization; prices, investment and markets and the social aspects of steel policy, including recruitment, vocational training, wage structure and job security.

184 Politique de recherche technique de la Haute Autorité
HA doc 3061/3/61. 15 July 1961. 15p

See 231.

185 Mémorandum sur la définition des objectifs généraux acier de la Communauté
JO 24, 5 Apr 1962, pp 729–773

A document in which the High Authority attempts to construct a series of guidelines to assist long-term planning in the steel industry, prepared in accordance with Article 46 of the ECSC Treaty, which requires the High Authority to 'periodically lay down general objectives for modernization, long-term planning of manufacture and expansion of productive capacity'. The document follows two earlier, more tentative sets of general objectives established in 1955 (*JO CECA* 16, 19 July 1955, pp 821–832) and in 1957 (*JO CECA* 16, 20 May 1957, pp 195–220) and benefits from the work of various committees and working parties set up to examine these earlier projections and to refine methodological techniques. Relating essentially to 1965, although including data for 1970 mainly as background, the memorandum contains three substantial chapters. They deal with the future demand for steel in terms of both internal demand and exports to third countries; production capacity targets for the various stages of iron and steel production and manpower problems, including recruitment and qualifications. The memorandum was published in March 1962 as an unnumbered Supplement to the *Bulletin de la Communauté européenne du charbon et de l'acier* and also as the first volume in a monograph series called *Collection objectifs généraux 'acier'* (cat 3017). This latter publication also contains a paper entitled *Les méthodes utilisées et leur appréciation; les résultats obtenus*, in which the High Authority describes methods used to define general objectives and presents some results not reproduced elsewhere in the memorandum. This monograph also contains the four principal reports compiled by working parties of experts set up to look at the probable trend in internal steel requirements, export prospects for 1965, developments in iron and steel-making techniques and manpower problems. It concludes with a compilation of basic statistical data, a list of the members of the various working groups and an analytical index. (*See also* 189.)

186 Importations d'aciers laminés en provenance des pays tiers
HA doc 2982/2/63. 17 May 1963. 36p

In response to a request from the Council of Ministers, the High Authority considers the reasons why imports of laminated steel products have grown and assesses their impact upon the general development of the steel market. In a series of chapters, the High Authority looks at such aspects of the question as the causes of this trend, its effects on Community prices, the situation in the export market, the evolution of raw steel production and the maintenance of equilibrium between supply and demand.

187 Mémorandum sur la situation des mines de fer de la Communauté
HA doc 5800/63. 9 Sept 1963. 53p

A descriptive document which aims to assist discussion of the present difficulties being experienced by the Community iron ore industry. Part 1 looks at trends in the production and consumption of iron ore in the Community from both the economic and social angles. This is followed by an analysis of the causes and effects of a trend which has seen a decline in demand for Community ore in the face of growing competition from high-grade third country ores. In Part 3 the High Authority looks at the question of security of supply. A final section contains a number of proposals for remedial action.

188 La situation de la Communauté dans l'économie sidérurgique mondiale
HA doc 6943/63. 29 Oct 1963. 42p

A comparative study in which the High Authority seeks to facilitate better evaluation of the Community iron and steel industry's prospects by placing the industry in a world context. The document highlights imbalances between supply and demand and distortion in the conditions of competition. Statistical information is used to compare the situation in the Community with that pertaining in the United Kingdom, United States and Japan. In the first part of the document, the High Authority looks at the disequilibrium between supply and demand, with reference to structural aspects of the problem, world trade, the imbalance in the Community and the extent of penetration of steel from third countries. In the second part of the document, the High Authority examines distortion in the conditions of competition.

189 **Rapport sur l'état d'exécution des derniers objectifs généraux acier pour l'année 1965**
HA doc 7846/1/63. Apr 1964. 28p

A status report prepared half-way through the period covered by the current set of general objectives (*see* 185), in which the High Authority takes stock of progress achieved and makes a critical assessment of results as compared with forecasts. Following the same order as the original document, the report contains sections on future steel needs, production capacity targets and manpower problems. It traces the development of the iron and steel industry through the first three years of the period and seeks explanations for the gaps between predictions and realizations. The report was also published in a volume of the same title issued as number two in the series *Collection objectifs généraux 'acier'* (cat 3553). (*See also* 194.)

190 **L'évolution et les caractéristiques de l'emploi dans la sidérurgie de la Communauté**
HA doc 3196/64. 26 May 1964. 22p

A document in which the High Authority traces the main features of employment trends in the Community iron and steel industries. Chapter 1 is concerned with employment trends in each member country. In Chapter 2 the High Authority highlights various aspects of the employment situation in the industry, including the structure of personnel, manpower needs and recruitment.

191 **La situation sur les marchés sidérurgiques dans les pays tiers**
HA doc 2450/65. n.d. 239p

A general and substantial analysis of the world steel market in which the High Authority first looks at the general trends of supply and demand and then follows this with commentaries and statistical tables on the market situation in each of 25 third countries. This document was subsequently given full publication by the High Authority in 1965 in a volume of the same title (cat 11780). A supplementary document was produced in 1967 in which the High Authority turns its attention to investment plans and the growth of production potential in steel producing countries (HA doc 1500/67).

192 **L'approvisionnement en charbon à coke dans la Communauté avec référence spéciale à l'industrie sidérurgique**
HA doc 6744/2/64. 17 Feb 1965. 48p

See 162.

193 L'action de la Haute Autorité dans le domaine de la recherche technique
HA doc 7005/1/65. Nov 1965. 55p

See 233.

194 Mémorandum sur le définition des objectifs généraux 'acier', de la Communauté 1970
JO 244, 30 Dec 1966, pp 4097–4160

A new set of general objectives for the steel industry drawn up by the High Authority with the help of four expert committees of employers, consumers, government representatives and trade union representatives. The document takes account of the considerable changes in the trend of demand and the shape of the world market since the last set of objectives was published in 1962 (*see* 185). Arranged in four main parts, the memorandum first looks at the future need for steel in the Community in 1970 and the corresponding need for raw materials. The High Authority then considers how far the Community steel industry can satisfy these needs, with reference to the productive capacity of the industry in the context of the new techniques being introduced into steel-making. In the third part of the document, the High Authority turns its attention to the reorganization and modernization that is necessary in the industry if it is to be competitive. The manpower problems inevitably associated with major structural change are the subject of the final part. The memorandum was published in the *Bulletin de la Communauté européenne du charbon et de l'acier* No 65, 1967 and separately in 1967 as number three in the series *Collection objectifs généraux 'acier'* (cat 4126). This latter publication also contains a number of technical annexes which provide detailed data as background to the main report. Also prepared in conjunction with the general objectives for 1970 was *Les exportations de biens d'équipement de la Communauté; essai de prévisions jusqu'en 1970*, in which the High Authority seeks to evaluate the quantities of steel used in the manufacture of capital goods, except motor vehicles and ships, exported to non-member countries in the past and likely up to 1970. The report was published in 1967 as number 3A in the series *Collection objectifs généraux 'acier'* (cat 12885) and summarized in *Informations statistiques* 1-1967, pp 69–79. (*See also* 198.)

195 Etude sur l'approvisionnement en minerai de fer de l'industrie sidérurgique de la Communauté
HA doc 2985/2/67. 20 Oct 1967. 2 vols, 92p, 41p

A study of the current situation regarding iron ore supplies for the Community steel industry and the outlook for the next ten years. Part 1 consists of a descriptive analysis of the current situation, in which the High Authority considers such elements of the situation as competition between imported and indigenous ore, the implications of new processes in steel production and supplies of iron ore from third countries. In Part 2 the High Authority makes forecasts for the next ten years. It estimates Community needs, the world market for iron ore, the probable evolution of competition between imported and indigenous ore. A second volume contains a considerable amount of statistical data.

196 **Rapport de la Commission au Conseil concernant la question des charbons à coke et cokes destinés à la sidérurgie de la Communauté**
SEC(69)1154 final. 25 Mar 1969. 90p

See 173.

197 **Grandes lignes d'une politique de concurrence en matière de structures de l'industrie sidérurgique**
SEC(70)30 final. 13 Jan 1970. 10p

In view of the expansion in steel production and consequent organizational changes in the steel industry, the Commission decided to issue this document on competition policy with regard to the structure of the steel industry. In the document the Commission explains the criteria it will adopt in application of Article 66 of the ECSC Treaty. The document was also published in the *Journal officiel des Communautés européennes* C12, 30 Jan 1970, pp 5–8.

198 **Mémorandum sur les objectifs généraux de la sidérurgie de la Communauté pour l'années 1975–1980**
SEC(71)1090/4. 31 Mar 1971. 187p

The first set of medium-term guidelines for the steel industry to be prepared since the merger of the three executives created a single Commission of the European Communities. As in previous forecasts (*see* 194), the accent is upon general guidelines formulated on the basis of economic and structural prospects rather than on concrete proposals on steel policy. The document is divided into five main parts which deal in turn with quantitative and qualitative estimates of steel requirements, factors of production, the balancing of supply and demand, manpower and ways and means of pursuing a medium-term iron and steel policy. The memorandum was published in the *Journal officiel des Communautés européennes* C96, 29 Sept 1971, pp 1–82 and separately as number four in the series *Collection objectifs généraux 'acier'* (cat 8361). (*See also* 202.)

199 **Deuxième étude sur l'approvisionnement de l'industrie sidérurgique de la Communauté en charbons à cokes et cokes**
SEC(72)2427 final. 12 July 1972. 159p

See 175.

200 **Commission communication to the representatives of the governments of the member states meeting in the Council**
COM(75)299 final. 19 June 1975. 8p

A short report presented to the Council by the Commission on the situation in the scrap metal market, with reference to short-term trends and measures to remove restrictions on the export of scrap to non-member countries.

201 **Repercussions on employment of the steel programme**
SEC(75)3156 final. 26 Sept 1975. 15p

A memorandum in which the Commission refers in general terms to the action it has taken in recent months to improve employment prospects in member countries and in particular, to the measures to alleviate the repercussions on employment of the economic recession in the steel industry. Statistical tables summarize the first returns resulting from the application of Council Decision 1870/75/ECSC of 17 July 1975, which obliged steel companies to furnish information on recent developments in employment (*OJ* L190, 23 July 1975, pp 26–27). An annex to the document explains the provisions made in Article 56 of the ECSC Treaty to deal with employment problems.

202 General objectives steel 1980–1985
SEC(75)4062/3. 10 Dec 1975. 292p

The first set of general objectives to include the new member states, this document follows the pattern set in previous documents (*see* 198) by providing governments, undertakings and other interested parties with an assessment of the steel industry's long-term prospects to assist them with their production and investment planning. Following an introductory chapter in which the Commission looks at the objectives and instruments of long-term steel policy, the Commission then turns its attention to long-term trends in steel demand by way of an analysis of historical developments and forecasts of steel consumption in 1980 and 1985. In the following chapter, the Commission takes stock of the world steel market and the Community's export trade, with estimates of the likely future balance between demand and production. In view of the increasing competition from the newer producing countries, the Commission also devotes attention to improvements in steel grades, steel products and techniques. Equally, in reflection of the current situation, there is greater emphasis than formerly on forecasts for labour requirements in 1980. Additional chapters are devoted to an examination of financing problems, the supply and consumption of raw materials and energy. The memorandum was published in the *Official journal of the European Communities* C232, 4 Oct 1976, pp 1–141. In 1977 the Commission gave notice of its intention to revise certain chapters in the light of the profoundly changed circumstances caused by the steel crisis and to extend projections to 1990 (*OJ* C103, 27 Apr 1977, p 4). (*See also* 207.)

203 Consultation with the Council on the possibility of introducing a measure under Article 61(b) of the ECSC Treaty, including minimum prices within the common market for steel products
COM(75)700. 10 Dec 1975. 38p

The Article in question gives the Commission the power to resort to a system of minimum pricing if a situation of 'manifest crisis' exists or is imminent. In this paper the Commission takes a close look at the situation in the industry, with particular regard to such aspects as the state of the market, employment and the financial position of undertakings, and reviews measures the Commission has taken in 1975 to alleviate the situation. On the basis of this assessment, the Commission recommends implementation of the powers available under Article 61(b) of the Treaty. Supportive statistical data on production, new orders, prices and other indicators appear in a series of annexes.

204 Problems in the steel industry
SEC(76)2813 final. 21 July 1976. 10p

Prepared in the wake of the most serious steel crisis since the War, this document from the Commission draws lessons for the future from the experience of the 1975 steel crisis and reviews the impact of the measures taken in response to it. The Commission begins with a brief description of the crisis, its effects on the steel industry and action taken by the Commission during the crisis. In view of the likely recurrence of serious difficulties in the steel industry, the remainder of the memorandum is devoted to proposals designed to give the Commission powers to take quick and effective remedial action whenever necessary. These proposals may be divided into permanent measures relating to investment and the statistical monitoring of the steel market and crisis measures which would have much speedier impact than those already allowed under the provisions of the ECSC Treaty. The document concludes with brief reference to relations with third countries and to the social and regional problems consequent upon crises of this nature.

205 Common steel policy
SEC(76)4143 final/2. 1 Dec 1976. 15p

A reiteration of the broad policy guidelines outlined earlier in the year (*see* 204), expanded to take account of questions left unanswered at that time and of the comments generated by that earlier document. The Commission outlines the nature of both the permanent measures that need to be taken with regard to investment and the statistical monitoring of the steel market and the crisis measures concerning production and prices to be activated only in times of severe difficulty. The Commission also looks briefly at relations with third countries in the steel market and at social and regional problems. The document concludes with a series of technical annexes. The memorandum was published in the *Official journal of the European Communities* C303, 23 Dec 1976, pp 3–5. As a consequence of the steel crisis, the Commission decided on 20 December 1976 to implement the first anti-crisis measures (*OJ* C304, 24 Dec 1976, p 5), which were later extended in both 1977 and 1978.

206 Restructuring of the steel industry: methods and organization
COM(77)688 final. 9 Dec 1977. 3p

The crisis in the steel industry highlighted the need to adapt production capacity to the long-term trend in demand and to improve competitiveness by reducing production costs. In this brief document, the Commission announces its intention to formulate a restructuring programme at the Community level as a blueprint for the recovery of the Community steel industry.

207 General objectives for steel 1980, 1985 and 1990
SEC(78)3205 final. 20 July 1978. 35p

In 1977 the Commission gave notice of its intention to revise certain chapters of the current general objectives for steel in the light of changed circumstances and to extend them to 1990 (*see* 202). This document fulfils that promise by up-dating those chapters concerning 'the growth in Community steel consumption, the

Community's external trade in steel, the equilibrium between supply and demand and the supply of raw materials', where original hypotheses have been largely invalidated by events in recent years. The intention is 'to establish new estimates of the maximum production potential required for the various categories of finished products, for crude steel and for each steelmaking process and to provide a general outline for the reorganization of steel undertakings'. The Commission makes it clear that other chapters in the current set of general guidelines concerning competitiveness, labour requirements and finance will be revised at a later stage.

08 Social aspects of the iron and steel policy
COM(78)570 final. 31 Oct 1978. 25p

EP Report: *Working doc* 603/78. 12 Feb 1979. J. Laurain. 25p
EP Debate: *Annex OJ* No 239, 15 Feb 1979, pp 169–171 & 180–196
EP Resolution: *OJ* C67, 12 Mar 1979, pp 38–40

Restructuring will have serious consequences for employment in the steel industry. In anticipation of such problems and in an effort to coordinate policy, the Commission reviews in this document existing Community aid measures and examines means of adapting them to new social objectives. The document begins with an analysis of the present employment situation in the steel industry and of the outlook up to 1980. The Commission then takes stock of the aid measures currently at its disposal, including aid under Articles 54, 55 and 56 of the ECSC Treaty. In the third chapter the Commission considers budgetary implications.

09 ECSC redevelopment policies
SEC(78)4351 final. 13 Dec 1978. 45p

A review of the problems encountered in those regions where ECSC industries are in decline, and of the measures taken by the Commission to alleviate their worst consequences. The document begins with a description of the problems, using employment figures for the coal and steel industries as a yardstick. The Commission then considers present Commission policy, with reference to the allocation of reconversion loans, finance from the European Regional Development Fund and research designed to solve the problems caused by this phenomenon.

AEROSPACE

10 Les industries aéronautiques et spatiales de la Communauté comparées à celles de la Grande-Bretagne et des Etats-Unis
Comm EC, 1971. 5 vols, 1000p (cat 8284)

An exhaustive and well-documented survey of the Community aerospace industry as it compares with those of the United Kingdom and the United States, carried out on behalf of the Commission by a group of experts and published as number four in the series *Etudes—Série industrie*. Based mainly on interviews with representatives of government, industry and the airlines, the survey team was able to build up a detailed country-by-country picture of the structure of the industry, its development over a ten year period and of government policies in this field. The national surveys covered such aspects as turnover and investment, labour force, degree of concentration of firms and financial structures. Significant individual firms in member countries were used as case studies. The general report consists of five separate volumes. In volume 1 the group of experts compare the organization of research and development in the Community from 1960 to 1967 with the situation in the United Kingdom and the United States. Volume 2 provides a composite picture of the structure of the industry, with reference to such aspects as the process of production, the structure of firms and tlhe points of comparison with the British and American situation. The space activities and programmes of the United States and the United Kingdom are compared with those of European space agencies and of individual member countries in volume 3. Volume 4 is devoted to an investigation of the main components of the market for civil and military aircraft, and volume 5 considers the role of the industry in the economy as a whole. Ten further volumes annexed to the report, but not published with it, are mostly composed of detailed national surveys. The general report was also published in English under the title *The aeronautical and space industries of the Community compared with those of the United Kingdom and the United States.*

211 Communication de la Commission au Conseil concernant les actions de politique industrielle et technologique de la Communauté à entreprendre dans le secteur aéronautique
COM(72)850. 12 July 1972. 117p

A three part document containing a communication, a number of implementing texts and a series of annexes. In the first chapter of the communication, the Commission examines the difficulties currently facing the industry and its prospects for the future. This is followed in the next chapter by proposals from the Commission designed to emphasize that the long-term well-being of the industry depends upon greater coordination of the presently fragmented European aircraft construction industry, and the establishment of guidelines for a concerted industrial strategy. In Chapter 3 the Commission makes recommendations for urgent remedial action to deal with the present difficulties. The implementing texts consist of a draft Recommendation on the coordination of development policies and the structural reorganization of companies, a communication on the framework of aids given to transnational civil aircraft projects, a draft Directive on the adoption of common provisions for insurance credits, exchange guarantees and guarantees against cost increases in export operations to non-member countries of Community civil aircraft projects on a transnational basis, and a communication on present tariffs for aero products. A series of annexes provide more detailed descriptive data on various aspects of the industrial scene, including the main characteristics of the market for commercial transport aircraft and air transport, the structure of European production and its comparison with that of the United States and the United Kingdom, cooperative aeronautical projects and aids made available to the industry by individual member governments.

212 Action programme for the European aeronautical sector
COM(75)475 final. 1 Oct 1975. 72p

EP Report: *Working doc 303/76.* 5 July 1976. O. Guldberg. 48p

EP Debate: *Annex OJ* No 205, 6 July 1976, pp 12–34
EP Resolution: *OJ* C178, 2 Aug 1976, pp 8–11
ESC Opinion: *OJ* C131, 12 June 1976, pp 1–7

A communication in which the Commission makes proposals for industrial policy in the civil and military aerospace sectors on the basis of a detailed analysis of the situation in, and outlook for, the industry. Prepared as a result of a request for such a study made by the Council in its Resolution of 4 March 1975 (*OJ* C59, 13 Mar 1975, pp 1–2), the document consists of a general communication supported by a series of more detailed annexes and implementing texts. In the communication the Commission first examines the industry's current development problems with much of the detail presented in the form of a supporting annex on the subject. The document emphasizes that future prospects depend upon the establishment of a common Community policy. To that end the Commission proposes a joint action programme, different aspects of which, including research and development, the structure of companies, employment and productivity are described in more detail in a series of annexes. The document concludes with a draft Council Decision on the creation of a common policy in the civil aircraft and aviation sectors (*OJ* C265, 19 Nov 1975, pp 2–4), subsequently amended in 1977 (*OJ* C40, 17 Feb 1977, pp 11–12), and a draft Council Resolution relating to the purchase and development of aircraft weapon systems. The whole document was published as Supplement 11/75 to the *Bulletin of the European Communities*. However, the only tangible result from this Commission initiative so far has been the Council statement of 14 March 1977 on industrial policy in the aeronautical sector, in which it determined certain criteria for the establishment of a joint programme (*OJ* C69, 19 Mar 1977, p 6).

13 **Action programme for aeronautical research**
COM(77)362 final. 26 July 1977. 47p

EP Report: *Working doc* 454/77. 5 Jan 1978. G. Carpentier. 19p
EP Debate: *Annex OJ* No 225, 17 Jan 1978, pp 33–44
EP Resolution: *OJ* C36, 13 Feb 1978, p 13
ESC Opinion: *OJ* C59, 8 Mar 1978, pp 16–18

An action programme whose purpose is to set up a number of initial, short-term projects and to make some contribution to the definition of a long-term strategy. By way of introduction the Commission first looks back to earlier initiatives in 1975 (*see* 212) and at the expressed views of other institutions. The Commission then describes the proposed short-term projects concerning helicopters and airframes before devoting some attention to procedures for the development of future programmes and a long-term strategy. The document concludes with proposals for financing and managing the programme. More detailed information on the planned projects appears as an annex to two draft Council Decisions adopting the programme and a time-table of action (*OJ* C210, 2 Sept 1977, pp 8–9).

14 **Commission communication to the Council with a view to concerted action on aircraft programmes provided for in the resolution of 4 March 1975 and the statement of 14 March 1977**
COM(78)211 final. 23 June 1978. 13p

A document in which the Commission appraises the Council of the current position as regards civil aircraft programmes in member countries and defines the role which the Community might play in supporting the development of the European aircraft industry, bearing in mind the position adopted by the Council in its Resolution of 4 March 1975 (*OJ* C59, 13 Mar 1975, pp 1–2) and in its statement of 14 March 1977 (*OJ* C69, 19 Mar 1977, p 6). After initial remarks about the relatively healthy state of the industry and a review of past Community initiatives, the Commission looks at present cooperative ventures and, stressing the need for continuing concerted action, at the scope for Community contributions in the future. Current European aerospace programmes are described in an annex to the document.

DATA PROCESSING

215 Systèmes à grande puissance de traitement automatique de l'information: besoins et applications dans la Communauté européenne et au Royaume-Uni vers les années soixante-dix
Comm EC, 1971. 60p (cat 8332)

A condensed version of an original five volume report prepared by the Soris Institute of Turin into the demand for, and applications of, extra large electronic data processing systems in the Community and in the United Kingdom during the 1970s. This summary report, published as number six in the series *Etudes—Série industrie*, explains the methods of data collection and analysis and the forecasting methods used by the Institute, before outlining the general conclusions reached in three main areas of research, namely, the supply of hardware and software, the development of computer installations and the prospects for new applications in each of six specific industries. The report was also published in English under the title *Demand for and applications of extra large electronic data processing systems in the European Community and the United Kingdom in the seventies.* In 1973 the Commission published as number seven in the series mentioned above *Investigation on the development of software: report of the synthesis* (cat 8439), a report by external consultants on software technology.

216 Community policy on data processing
SEC(73)4300 final. 21 Nov 1973. 33p

EP Report: *Working doc* 153/74. 2 July 1974. P.-B. Cousté. 32p
EP Debate: *Annex OJ* No 179, 8 July 1974, pp 54–58 (withdrawn)
ESC Opinion: *OJ* C255, 7 Nov 1975, pp 4–7

The Commission's first broad statement on the need for a common policy for the data processing industry. In the two main sections of the communication, the Commission focuses attention on the need to build a strong and flourishing European-based industry in both hardware and software and upon the promotion of effective application of data processing to the needs of the European user. In a third part the Commission highlights certain additional measures that would generate a favourable environment for the industry. The document concludes with economic data on the industry and a draft Council Resolution on the matter. On 15 July 1974 the Council adopted a Resolution on data processing in which it encouraged the Commission to formulate an overall medium-term programme to promote the industry and computer applications (*OJ* C86, 20 July 1974, p 1).

17 Initial proposals for priority projects in data-processing
COM(75)35 final. 5 Mar 1975. 63p

EP Report: *Working doc* 199/75. 31 Aug 1975. P.-B. Cousté. 36p
EP Debate: *Annex OJ* No 194, 23 Sept 1975, pp 41–56
EP Resolution: *OJ* C239, 20 Oct 1975, pp 16–17
ESC Opinion: *OJ* C263, 17 Nov 1975, pp 44–46

A first but limited action programme prepared in accordance with the Council Resolution of 15 July 1974 (*see* 216), in which the Commission outlines the nature of its six proposals with particular reference to their financial implications. Three of the five proposed projects were later adopted by the Council on 22 July 1976 by Decision 76/632/EEC (*OJ* L223, 16 Aug 1976, pp 11–15), and a sixth proposal for the creation of an advisory committee on data processing projects was also adopted on the same day by Council Decision 76/633/EEC (*OJ* L223, 16 Aug 1976, p 16). (*See also* 220.)

18 Community policy for data-processing
COM(75)467 final. 10 Sept 1975. 105p

EP Report: *Working doc* 462/75. 12 Jan 1976. P.-B. Cousté. 23p
EP Debate: *Annex OJ* No 198, 12 Jan 1976, pp 8–25
EP Resolution: *OJ* C28, 9 Feb 1976, pp 6–7
ESC Opinion: *OJ* C131, 12 June 1976, pp 8–11

A reflection of a more systematic overall approach to the development of the industry in which the Commission combines an initial and necessarily partial exposition of broad strategy over the medium-term with a second series of specific proposals for immediate implementation (*see* 217 for the first series). In the first part of the communication, the Commission proposes a number of measures designed to maintain an open and competitive market, with particular emphasis on such key areas as support for the development of cooperative projects, standardization, software portability and the coordination of public procurement policies. A second part deals with measures to support the industry, notably, the provision of a financial mechanism for financing sales. Appended to the document are four specific proposals for priority actions upon which the Council later adopted a number of Decisions (*OJ* L255, 6 Oct 1977, pp 22–34).

19 A four-year programme for the development of informatics in the Community
COM(76)524 final. 27 Oct 1976. 4 vols, 46p, 120p, 141p, 16p

EP Report: *Working doc* 235/77. 31 Aug 1977. P.-B. Cousté. 39p
EP Debate: *Annex OJ* No 220, 14/15 Sept 1977, pp 150–163 & 216–219
EP Resolution: *OJ* C241, 10 Oct 1977, pp 41–44

A substantial multi-volume blueprint in which the Commission outlines a four-year programme to apply in the data processing, telecommunications and electronic components industries between 1978 and 1981. Volume 1 describes the objectives and summarizes the content of the programme. It provides for various measures to establish a genuine common market and to support the Community data processing industry. Volume 2 consists of a series of supporting technical annexes, and volume 3 of a factual analysis of the industry used by the Commission in the preparation of its specific proposals. Volume 4 consists of a communication on the current state of the electronic components industry, with particular emphasis upon its weaknesses and the kind of Community action that is necessary if the industry is to meet successfully the challenge from America and Japan.

220 Community data processing policy. First priority activities: three joint projects on computer applications. First annual report
COM(78)761 final. 15 Jan 1979. 13p

A progress report on the application of Council Decision 76/632/EEC of 22 July 1976 concerning three specific projects in the field of data processing concerning public health, improvements in the retrieval of legal documentation and future developments in computer-aided design techniques for the benefit of advanced electronics and construction (*OJ* L223, 16 Aug 1976, pp 11–15). The report describes the nature and management of the projects and the work achieved since their inception. It also makes some reference to the Community's second set of priority projects. (*See also* 217 & 218.)

TEXTILES

221 Structure, évolution et perspectives de l'industrie textile dans la C.E.E.
Doc III/2786/1/59. Jan 1960. 115p

A detailed examination of the textile industry in the European Economic Community and its place in the European economy, in which the Commission outlines its development in terms of production, trade and prospects for the future. The study concludes with a substantial number of statistical appendices.

222 Note de la Commission aux gouvernements des états membres sur la situation et les problèmes de l'industrie textile communautaire
COM(66)27 final. 9 Feb 1966. 27p

A memorandum in which the Commission describes the current state of the textile industry in the Community, the objectives of a concerted structure policy and the instruments available for its achievement. A number of statistical annexes include data on production, imports and exports.

223 L'industrie textile de la CEE: analyse et perspectives (1975)
Comm EC, 1969. 218p (cat 5885)

A fact-finding study prepared for the Commission by the Paris Centre for the Study of Modern Economic Techniques under the direction of Professor J. De Bandt, which analyses the evolution of productivity in the industry, looks at the structure, competitiveness and capital resources of the industry and estimates the prospects for consumption, production and employment in the future.

24 Politique sectorielle pour le textile
SEC(71)2615 final. 22 July 1971. 10p

A general assessment of the position of the industry in the European economy together with guidelines for the promotion of productivity and competitiveness. Aspects given particular attention include commercial policy, the coordination of research, use of the reformed Social Fund and the creation of an Economic Observation Centre for accurate forecasting of capital investment, production and supply. The guidelines were partially implemented in the following year when, as a result of Council Decision 72/429/EEC of 19 December 1972, persons employed in the textile industry were allowed to derive benefit from the European Social Fund (*JO* L291, 28 Dec 1972, pp 160–161). On 21 March 1974 the Council adopted Decision 74/214/EEC by which it accepted the Arrangement regarding International Trade in Textiles negotiated within the context of GATT, and whose objective was the expansion of the textile trade (*OJ* L118, 30 Apr 1974, pp 1–10). This 'Multifibre Agreement' has resulted in the conclusion of a large number of bilateral agreements with non-member countries. Also in 1974, and again in an effort to give practical expression to the sentiments expressed in the 1971 communication, the Commission presented to the Council a proposal for a programme of technological research in the textile sector (COM(74)1440 final), which subsequently led to Council Decision 75/266/EEC of 14 April 1975 establishing a programme of research in the textile sector (*OJ* L111, 30 Apr 1975, pp 34–36).

25 General guidelines for a textile and clothing industry policy
COM(78)362 final. 20 July 1978. 33p

As stated in the introduction 'this paper sets out the Commission's proposals for general guidelines for adapting the textile and clothing industries to the conditions of international competition', in reply to a declaration from the European Council meeting held in December 1977 that 'with the aim of adapting the European production machine to the new conditions on the Community and world markets, solutions to the structural problems which are common to all Member States must increasingly be sought at Community level, particularly for the iron and steel, textile and shipbuilding industries'. The document proper opens with an outline of the main features of the sector and of the difficulties currently being experienced. It then briefly defines a number of general objectives designed to allow the industry to compete internationally and to provide substantial employment opportunities before describing in more detail a number of specific guidelines for their achievement, including the adaption of commercial structures, increased coordination of national policies, technological development and the promotion of exports. The document concludes with a number of annexes, the first of which consists of a commentary and statistics on the main characteristics of the clothing and textile industry. Other annexes consist of papers on the textile imports regime, with reference to the many agreements negotiated with non-member countries and on state aids to the textile industry.

SHIPBUILDING

226 Rapport sur l'évolution à moyen et à long terme du marché de la construction navale
Comm EC, 1972. 177p (cat 8302)

A report prepared for the EEC Shipbuilding Liaison Committee by a working group under the chairmanship of Mr de Mas Latrie, in accordance with suggestions made by the Medium-Term Economic Policy Committee. The first part of the report, based on an overall and a sectoral approach so as to minimize deficiencies in the available statistical data, estimates medium-term (1975) and long-term (1980) trends in demand for additional tonnage to expand and replace the world merchant fleet. Forecasts for newbuilding requirements are based on an analysis of the foreseeable volume of sea-borne trade in 1975 and 1980 and of the capacity of the world merchant fleet needed to carry this level of trade. The second part of the study concerns the future trend of supply in the industry in the medium-term only, looking at the development of production capacity, the foreseeable trend in newbuilding and its comparison with expected demand. The document concludes with a short memorandum from the working group revising forecasts in the light of data made available since the report was first issued in 1969. The report was published in English in a volume entitled *Report on the long and medium term development of the shipbuilding market.*

227 Proposals from the Commission to the Council on the shipbuilding industry
COM(73)1788 final. 24 Oct 1973. 42p

EP Report: *Working doc* 68/74. 8 May 1974. L. Krall. 14p
EP Debate: *Annex OJ* No 177, 13 June 1974, pp 175–198
EP Resolution: *OJ* C76, 3 July 1974, p 41
ESC Opinion: *OJ* C97, 16 Aug 1974, pp 40–47

A series of proposals prepared by the Commission in accordance with Council Directive 72/273/EEC of 20 July 1972 on aids to the shipbuilding industry, Article 7 of which requires the Commission to undertake a study of trends in supply and demand and of the overall effect of aids on competition and trade in the shipbuilding market (*JO* L169, 27 July 1972, pp 28–30). The document consists of two separate memoranda and a specific proposal on aids. The first memorandum concerns guidelines for industrial policy with reference to investment support, conversion and social policy, research and development and improved marketing methods. The second paper on procedures for action in the industry recommends the creation of a permanent information system so as to provide the Commission with data essential for the study of supply and demand and of procedures for granting and coordinating investment aid to the industry. Two annexes contain a brief summary of various analyses of supply and demand and an examination of the factors giving rise to an imbalance between the two. The document concludes with a draft Council Directive on aids to the shipbuilding sector (*OJ* C114, 27 Dec 1973, pp 23–27), intended as a replacement for Council Directive 72/273/EEC of 20 July 1972 (*JO* L169, 27 July 1972, pp 28–30) which was due to expire on 31 December 1973 and which itself replaced Council Directive 69/262/EEC of 28 July 1969 (*JO* L206, 15 Aug 1969, pp 25–26) on 1 January 1972. In the event, the Council found it impossible to adopt the draft Directive in time. Instead it extended the period of validity of Directive 72/273/EEC for a period of six months on each of three occasions until, on the basis of a new proposal from the Commission (COM(75)195 final) the Council was at last able to adopt Directive 75/432/EEC of 10 July 1975 (*OJ* L192, 24 July 1975, pp 27–29) valid until 31 December 1977. In October of that year the Commission submitted a new proposal for aid to the shipbuilding industry (COM(77)517 final).

228 Communication from the Commission to the Council on shipbuilding
COM(76)224 final. 26 May 1976. 34p

A document in which the Commission makes suggestions concerning the ways in which the productive capacity of the industry can be reduced to compensate for the serious decline in demand. The Commission describes and discusses the problems facing the industry, particularly that of over-production, and prescribes remedial action to achieve an orderly and coordinated reduction of Community production and to effect the modernization and restructuring of remaining facilities. Concrete proposals are promised for a later date.

229 Communication from the Commission to the Council on the Community's relations with non-member countries in shipping matters
COM(76)341 final. 30 June 1976. 19p

See 442.

230 Reorganization of the Community shipbuilding industry
COM(77)542 final. 6 Dec 1977. 36p

EP Report: *Working doc* 182/78. 3 July 1978. J. Prescott. 105p
EP Debate: *Annex OJ* No 232, 5 July 1978, pp 122–146
EP Resolution: *OJ* C182, 31 July 1978, pp 29–32
ESC Opinion: *OJ* C269, 13 Nov 1978, pp 53–55

A memorandum in which the Commission explores means for alleviating the severe problems experienced by Community shipyards as a result of the world-wide structural imbalance between productive capacity and demand. The first chapter summarizes the causes of the present crisis, examines its consequences for the Community and the measures currently in hand to provide work for the shipbuilding industry at national, international and Community levels. The second chapter outlines the objectives of Community policy in this area, with particular reference to the need to make Community shipyards more competitive on the world market by adapting production structures, redeploying labour and stimulating demand. In the third chapter the Commission describes the action it intends to take to realize these objectives. Appended to the document are brief papers on the characteristics of the crisis in the shipbuilding industry and an inventory of finance requirements for reorganizing the industry. The document also contains a proposal for a Council Decision setting up a Shipbuilding Committee (*OJ* C10, 12 Jan 1978, pp 5–6). The memorandum was published as Supplement 7/77 to the *Bulletin of the*

European Communities. On the basis of these proposals from the Commission, the Council was able on 19 September 1978 to adopt a Resolution concerning the reorganization of the industry (*OJ* C229, 27 Sept 1978, pp 1-2).

CHAPTER 6

Science and research

Descriptive essay

The Treaties establishing the three European Communities specifically apportion responsibility for research in the coal, steel and nuclear sectors but say nothing about the need for a coordinated scientific and technological policy to solve Europe's general research and development problems at the Community level. Consequently, the resolve to establish European scientific cooperation found its first expression in those sectors in which responsibility for research policy was clearly defined. Many of the documents listed in this chapter reflect the sectoral approach characteristic of the early years of Community development, during which time, Community institutions looked for progress in the fields of coal and steel research, where activities were designed to improve the competitive capacity of those industries, and nuclear research, where the aim was to foster the speedy growth of a strong nuclear industry.

Initial Community research activities were undertaken under the authority of the ECSC Treaty, Article 55 of which declares that the 'High Authority shall promote technical and economic research relating to the production and increased use of coal and steel and to occupational safety in the coal and steel industries'. Early documents from the High Authority acknowledge the value of research as an essential component of the Community's efforts to create a strong industrial base and explain how the High Authority proposes to execute its Treaty obligations in this regard (*see* 231 & 233). Reference is also made to the High Authority's responsibility to promote cooperation between research bodies and to make technical improvements more widely known by issuing opinions on research programmes and major investment projects, publishing reports and organizing symposia.

Since its establishment in 1952, the European Coal and Steel Community has made a significant impact upon industrial research in the coal and steel industries. Research funds have been made available to finance both pure and applied research, usually in the context of medium-term research programmes which form the general framework for research activities, provide the criteria and establish the priorities by which numerous individual submissions for ECSC assistance are judged (*see* 176). Documents concerning individual research projects are not represented in this bibliographical guide. However, information on the many industrial research projects funded by the European Coal and Steel Community and the scientific and technical publications arising from such work may be obtained from *Euro abstracts*, Section II of which has, since 1975, been devoted to coal and steel research. This valuable bibliographical source contains brief descriptive details of research programmes recently granted financial support, annual progress reports on current research contracts in the coal, steel and related social sectors (industrial hygiene, safety and medicine) and abstracts of those scientific and technical publications and patents arising from the successful completion of research contracts. The scientific and technical publications listed in *Euro abstracts* are released in a separate report series covering such additional topics as nuclear science, energy and the environment, in which each item is identified by the prefix EUR together with a unique report number. EUR reports are not listed in this book, but it should be noted that the annual index to *Euro abstracts* Section II contains a cumulative list of EUR reports announced in the bulletin during the previous two years. Research activities are also reported in monographs published in such series as *Recherches techniques 'acier et mines de fer', Recueils de recherches 'charbon'* and *Etudes techniques 'charbon'*.

In order to create the most favourable conditions for the rapid growth of a strong civil nuclear industry in the Community, provision is made for the promotion of research in Articles 4–11 of the EAEC Treaty. Article 4 declares that the Commission 'shall be responsible for promoting and facilitating nuclear research in the Member States and for complementing it by carrying out a Community research and training programme'. Subsequent Articles refer to some of the ways in which the Commission is to discharge this responsibility. In order to discourage unnecessary duplication of effort and to direct research into productive areas, the Commission is empowered to invite member states or enterprises to submit details of their research programmes, to express an opinion on them and with the consent of interested parties, to publish them. Provision is also made for direct Community involvement in research activities through the work of its own research centres at Ispra (Italy), Geel (Belgium), Petten (Netherlands) and Karlsruhe (West Germany) and for indirect action through the provision of financial assistance for teams of researchers in member countries.

Much of the research work undertaken under the aegis of Euratom has been conducted within the overall framework of multi-annual research programmes. Article 215 of the EAEC Treaty makes provision for a research and training programme, details of which are given in Annex V to the Treaty. Although a second multi-annual programme was adopted for 1963 to 1967, conflicting national interests led the Council to adopt only interim, annual programmes during the period 1968 to 1972, which inevitably created uncertainty and disillusionment and severely limited the effectiveness of Euratom's activities (*see* 236). In 1968 the Commission made a critical appraisal of Euratom's achievements over the past ten years (*see* 238), and in the following year submitted proposals designed to give fresh impetus to the organization (*see* 240). It was not until 1973 however, that the Council was able to agree to a new multi-annual research programme to cover the years 1973 to 1977 (*see* 244), which was itself revised in 1975 (*see* 250). After preparatory work in 1975, the Commission submitted in the following year formal proposals for a new multi-annual programme for the period 1977 to 1980, on the basis of which the Council was able in 1977 to adopt a new programme (*see* 254).

Documents relating to individual research projects and to multi-annual research programmes in such specific fields as controlled thermonuclear fusion and plasma physics, are not included in this chapter. Details of individual programmes and projects are published in the *Official journal of the European Communities*, and the main results of Euratom research work are published in the EUR report series mentioned in an earlier paragraph. *Euro abstracts*, Section I of which has since 1975 been devoted to Euratom and EEC research, is a useful source of information on individual projects and any consequent publications. Although aimed primarily at the informed general public *Eurospectra : scientific and technical review of the Commission of the European Communities* includes technical notes on current research projects and brief details of newly published EUR reports.

The problems of Euratom and the Joint Research Centre have increasingly been considered in the wider context of the evolution of a common science and research policy which, because of the lack of a clear Treaty mandate and lukewarm political commitment, has made only fitful progress over the past 20 years. Although important reports were prepared by the Working Party on Scientific and Technical Research (PREST) during the 1960s (*see* 239 & 243), it was the political commitment to a common scientific and technological policy expressed by member states at The Hague summit, and more particularly at the Paris summit in 1972, that provided the vital impetus. After a number of attempts to stimulate progress, notably in 1970 (*see* 242) and in 1972 (*see* 244), the Commission was able to take advantage of the positive climate generated by the enlargement of the Communities to submit a major package of proposals in the summer of 1973 (*see* 247). As a result of this initiative, the Council was able in January 1974 to adopt a number of Resolutions of far-reaching importance, one of which provided for scientific and technological research in sectoral policy areas not specifically referred to in the founding Treaties. In 1977 the Commission tabled fresh guidelines for the development of a common scientific and technological policy up to the end of the 1970s (*see* 259).

Although reference is made in other chapters to major research and development programmes in such sectors as energy and the environment, documents relating to individual projects and specific research programmes are not included in this bibliographical guide. However, an extremely useful document prepared by the Scientific and Technical Research Committee (CREST) in 1978 contains texts relating to the common policy as a whole and those research and development programmes which have been adopted by the Council since 1974. Entitled *Acts published in the Official journal of the European Communities concerning Community scientific and technical research Jan 1974 to March 1978* (CREST/19/78), the document incorporates all the communications, Decisions and Resolutions of Community institutions relating to scientific research and development that have been published in the *Official journal of the European Communities* since 1 January 1974. More general comment and analysis on the components of the common policy is published in the *General report on the activities of the European Communities* and in the *Bulletin of the European Communities*.

Bibliographical record

231 Politique de recherche technique de la Haute Autorité
HA doc 3061/3/61. 15 July 1961. 15p

First issued in 1961 then revised in 1963, this document constitutes the first written outline of the High Authority's policy on technical research, prepared in response to requests for such a statement from the European Parliament in its Resolution of 1 July 1960 (*JO* 49, 27 July 1960, pp 1073–1074), the Consultative Committee and the Council of Ministers. The High Authority recognizes the indispensable contribution research can make to the improvement of industrial production and of standards of living and describes the way in which the High Authority is able to support, encourage and initiate research activities. The document then proceeds to examine the aims and principles of research policy both generally and as they relate specifically to the coalmining, iron and steel industries. This is followed by discussion of the ways in which the High Authority has been able to promote the coordination of research activities, particularly through the creation of expert committees, and to disseminate research results. The memorandum was published in the *Bulletin de la Communauté européenne du charbon et de l'acier* No 41 1963.

232 Progrès technique et Marché commun: perspectives économiques et sociales de l'application des nouvelles techniques, Bruxelles, Palais des Congrès, 5–19 décembre 1960
Comm EEC, Comm ECSC, Comm EAEC, 1962. 2 vols, 354p, 736p (cat 8018)

See 484.

233 L'action de la Haute Autorité dans le domaine de la recherche technique
HA doc 7005/1/65. Nov 1965. 55p

A retrospective review, conducted by the High Authority on the eve of the merger of the three executives, of the role it has played over a ten year period in the promotion and coordination of research activities in the coalmining, iron and steel industries. Main chapters are devoted to the principles and procedures adopted by the High Authority in pursuit of the objectives of Article 55 of the ECSC Treaty, to the general trend of research in the industries concerned and to an outline of research completed, in hand and planned. Existing research programmes are described in a series of detailed annexes. The report appeared in the *Bulletin de la Communauté européenne du charbon et de l'acier* No 62 1966.

234 Réflexions sur des expériences acquises par Euratom en matière de politique communautaire de recherche scientifique et technique
EUR/C/3935/66. 5 Oct 1966. 49p

A report prepared on behalf of the Commission of the EAEC by P. de Groote, which recalls the responsibilities and functions assigned to Euratom in this area, and the contribution Euratom has made to overall science and research policy. Observations regarding the resources needed for research activities and the means for their organization are drawn from the Community's past experience in organizing a Community research policy.

235 Mémorandum sur les problèmes que pose le progrès scientifique et technique dans la Communauté européenne
EUR/C/1711/2/67. 20 Mar 1967. 27p

EP Report: *Doc de séance* 146/67. 22 Nov 1967. G. Bersani. 11p

EP Report: *Débs* No 96, 27 Nov 1967, pp 20–46
EP Resolution: *JO* 307, 18 Dec 1967, pp 6–7

EP Report: *Doc de séance* 112/68. 25 Sept 1968. G. Bersani. 18p
EP Debate: *Annexe JO* No 106, 1 Oct 1968, pp 61–94
EP Resolution: *JO* C108, 19 Oct 1968, pp 22–23

A communication from the three executives in which they welcome the Council's declared intention to devote a special session to the problems of scientific and technical research and offer their own contribution to the discussions. Intended more as a synthesis of significant strands from various interested sources, including the European Parliament (*Docs de séance* 97/66 & 107/66), the Inter-Executive Working Party on Scientific and Technical Research set up in October 1965 and member governments, than as a definitive statement of policy, the memorandum first considers the problems facing member states, with emphasis on the importance of scientific and technical progress for continued economic growth. The three executives analyse the reasons for the widening technological gap between Europe and the more technologically advanced countries and reflect upon the measures that should be adopted to promote research and industrial innovation. The promised special Council meeting took place in October 1967, at the conclusion of which the Council adopted an important Resolution in which member countries affirmed their common will to reinforce and promote scientific research and industrial innovation, the text of which was published in the *Bulletin of the European Economic Community* 12-1967, pp 5–6. It also appears as an annex in the Second Medium-Term Economic Policy Programme (*see* 66).

36 Activités futures d'Euratom en matière de recherches
COM(68)160. 6 Mar 1968. 2 vols, 37p, 105p

Article 215 of the EAEC Treaty provided for an initial five year research and training programme, details of which are elaborated in Annex V to the Treaty. On 23 July 1962 the Council adopted a second five year programme which expired on 31 December 1967 (*JO* 70, 6 Aug 1962, pp 2008–2015) and which was replaced by an interim programme of one year's duration as a result of Council Decision 67/42/EURATOM of 8 December 1967 (*JO* 311, 21 Dec 1967, p 23). This detailed discussion document is designed to assist in the preparation of a new multi-annual research programme. It suggests a number of principles which should govern Euratom's future activities; it deals with the options open to the Community regarding the methods to be employed to introduce greater coordination between research and development programmes and it suggests the areas of research to be pursued. In volume 1 the Commission makes general proposals for action in such areas as reactor development, fundamental research, public service research and assesses the potential of the Joint Research Centre (JRC). In volume 2, the Commission explains in much more detail its proposals in each of the areas highlighted in volume 1. Despite this preparatory work and a specific submission for a new multi-annual programme (COM(68)801), uncertainty and disagreement about Euratom's future research activities caused the Council to adopt only interim, annual research programmes during the period 1968 to 1972. (*See also* 240.)

237 **Poursuite des travaux en matière de coopération technologique**
SEC(68)1524 final. 15 May 1968. 21p

A memorandum in which the Commission offers its views on the fundamental problems associated with technological cooperation in Europe. The Commission applauds existing cooperative efforts and seeks ways of promoting further collaboration both within the Community and in other European countries.

238 **Rapport d'ensemble sur la politique nucléaire de la Communauté**
COM(68)800. 9 Oct 1968. 92p

Prompted by uncertainty and disagreement over Euratom's future, the Commission uses this opportunity to take stock of the Community's performance during the past decade. The report seeks to explain why Euratom has made such disappointing progress towards creating favourable conditions for the growth of a strong nuclear industry in the Community and draws lessons for the future. Part 1 consists of a critical analysis of past nuclear development in its energy, industrial, technological and research aspects. Part 2 contains details of a proposed programme designed to remedy the situation, whose projects include the industrial promotion of reactors, cooperative efforts in reactor research and development work and a common policy for the supply of nuclear fuels. The communication was published as a Supplement to the *Bulletin of the European Communities* 9/10-1968.

239 **La coopération scientifique et technique entre pays européens: possibilités dans sept secteurs**
Doc 7301/11/69. 9 Apr 1969. 185p

A report prepared by the Working Party on Scientific and Technical Research Policy (PREST) in accordance with the wishes of the Council of Ministers, as expressed in its Resolutions following meetings on 31 October and 10 December 1968, the texts of which are appended to this document. These Resolutions invite PREST to examine the possibilities for cooperation in six defined fields and to examine the prospects for its extension to other areas. The bulk of the document consists of a series of proposals, divided into those which are ready for a Council Decision and those which require further study, in each of the agreed sectors. These are information science and telecommunications, new means of transport, oceanography, metallurgy, nuisances and meteorology. The Working Party draws attention to the problems pertaining in each sector, describes the nature and objectives of the proposed projects, the grounds and methods for cooperation and assesses to what extent they provide a solution to the problems.

240 **Activités futures d'Euratom**
COM(69)350. 23 Apr 1969. 160p

EP Report: *Doc de séance* 64/69. 24 June 1969. A. Oele. 19p
EP Debate: *Annexe JO* No 116, 1 July 1969, pp 41–71
EP Resolution: *JO* C97, 28 July 1969, pp 30–31

Following an abortive attempt to introduce a new multi-annual research programme in 1968 (*see* 236) and the subsequent approval of a one year programme for 1969 (JO L64, 14 Mar 1969, pp 6–13), the Commission attempts in this initiative to inject new vigour into the Community's scientific research policy by announcing proposals for a new multi-annual research and training programme whose separate elements include reactor research, basic nuclear research and projects of public interest in the nuclear field. For the first time the programme also includes proposals for non-nuclear research activities, particularly relating to information science, the abatement of nuisances and the creation of a Central Bureau of Standards. The document also establishes principles and criteria for achieving an industrial policy in the nuclear field. A series of 22 annexes provide technical data in support of the proposals made in the document, which was subsequently published as a Supplement to the *Bulletin of the European Communities* 6-1969. However, despite this Commission initiative, the Council could not agree on a new multi-annual programme. Instead, a series of annual programmes was approved. In 1972 the Commission tabled another set of proposals for a multi-annual programme (*see* 244).

241 Note de la Commission au Conseil sur les suites à donner au §9 du communiqué de la Haye relatif au développement technologique de la Communauté
SEC(70)2083 final. 17 June 1970. 23p

The final communiqué of The Hague summit conference states that 'Heads of State or Government reaffirmed their desire to pursue more vigorously the activity of the Community in regard to the coordination and promotion of industrial research and development in the principal sectors of importance, in particular by Community programmes, and to provide financial resources for this purpose'. Taking advantage of this positive climate of opinion, the Commission outlines in this document a number of proposals concerning the most urgent problems in the main sectors of cooperation and urges adoption of a procedure for consultation between member states on major R & D projects.

242 Note de la Commission au Conseil concernant une action communautaire d'ensemble en matière de recherche et de développement scientifique et technologique
SEC(70)4250. 11 Nov 1970. 22p

EP Report: *Doc de séance* 17/71. 19 Apr 1971. A. Oele. 25p
EP Debate: *Annexe JO* No 137, 21 Apr 1971, pp 104–116
EP Resolution: *JO* C45, 10 May 1971, pp 24–26

A critical appraisal of the current state of development of scientific and technological research and development policy in which the Commission draws particular attention to the lack of coordination between bodies responsible for preparing R & D programmes and the dire need for a reorganization of the Joint Research Centre (JRC). Using this assessment as a basis, the Commission makes a number of specific recommendations, including one for the creation of a European Research and Development Committee (CERD) to coordinate R & D programmes on a Community level, and another for the establishment of a European Research and Development Agency to implement the executive action to be worked out by

CERD. The document also makes observations on the spheres of activity in which the Community should be engaged and on the financing and administration of projects. The document was published as Supplement 1/71 to the *Bulletin of the European Communities*. CERD was established on 14 June 1972, and as a result of Commission Decision 71/57/EURATOM of 13 January 1971, the JRC was reshaped to give it greater management autonomy, closer links with industry and to allow it to develop its activities to cover technology in general (*JO* L16, 20 Jan 1971, pp 14–16).

243 Pour une politique de recherche et d'innovation dans la Communauté: rapport du Groupe de travail 'politique de la recherche scientifique et technique'
In Second programme de politique économique à moyen terme. Comm EC, 1971. 122p (cat 8345)

An abridged version of the report submitted in July 1967 by the Working Party on Scientific and Technical Research (PREST), established on 5 March 1965 by the Medium-Term Economic Policy Committee with a mandate to study the problems involved in the elaboration of a coordinated or common policy for scientific and technological research and to make proposals. Published as an annex to the second medium-term economic policy programme (*see* 66), the report is popularly referred to as the 'Maréchal Report' after Mr Maréchal, chairman of the Working Party. The first part of the report is concerned with the factors governing the general promotion of research and innovation and the creation of a favourable economic climate. In the second part the Working Party looks at measures to favour research and the elements of a policy of cooperation. The report concludes with recommendations for future action.

244 Objectifs et moyens pour une politique commune de la recherche scientifique et du développement technologique
SEC(72)700. 14 June 1972. 96p

A comprehensive document in which the Commission seeks to take advantage of a new political climate generated by enlargement to urge the Council to cast off the restrictive interpretation of Community R & D policy and to take a much broader view of Community involvement in this sector. By way of an analysis of the current situation, with particular reference to the place of Europe as a world technological force, the demands increasingly made upon science and technology by society, the impact of large-scale research programmes and the limits of national resources, the Commission aims to demonstrate the need for the Community to build a common R & D policy to rationalize the use of, and increase the efficiency of, national and Community resources. The Commission supports this conclusion with lessons for the future from past experience gained in cooperative ventures in scientific and fundamental research. The Commission considers, in the light of this analysis, the general features of a common R & D policy and their practical implementation in terms of the harmonization of national policies, common and Community projects and the adoption of a common attitude towards the outside world. The Commission then proceeds to describe the instruments that would be needed to implement such a policy and devotes special attention to the bodies that would need to be created to plan, implement and control R & D policy and the instruments that would be needed to stimulate R & D activities. The document concludes with a draft Council Resolution on the matter and three annexes on the future role of the JRC and on research activities concerning the environment and materials. The document was published as Supplement 6/72 to the *Bulletin of the European Communities*. The Commission later gave practical expression to its views in a series of proposals for a new multi-annual research programme for 1973 to 1977 (COM(72)1500 – COM(72)1510 and COM(73)659 final). The Council approved the programme on 6 February 1973 and adopted it formally by means of a number of Decisions taken on 14 May 1973 on direct action to be taken by the JRC (*OJ* L153, 9 June 1973, pp 1–18), and on 18 June 1973 by a further series of Decisions on direct and indirect action (*OJ* L189, 11 June 1973, pp 30–44). In 1974, in accordance with the provisions of the programme, the Commission made proposals for a revision of the programme to take account of changed circumstances and priorities (*See* 250).

45 Research, science and education: scientific and technical information
CAB/X/17/73. n.d. 27p

A working document presented to the Commission by Ralf Dahrendorf, member of the Commission, as a contribution to the debate on scientific and technological policy. On the basis of a review of the state of Community scientific research and development, Dahrendorf offers guidelines for medium-term objectives. The document was subsequently used as a basis for the preparation of a formal Commission initiative on the matter (*see* 247).

46 Working programme in the field of research, science and education
SEC(73)2000/2. 23 May 1973. 33p

See 589.

47 Scientific and technological policy programme (Parts 1 & 2)
COM(73)1250 final. 25 July 1973. 99p

EP Report: *Working doc* 219/73. 13 Nov 1973. G. Flämig. 19p
EP Debate: *Annex OJ* No 168, 15 Nov 1973, pp 216–228
EP Resolution: *OJ* C108, 10 Dec 1973, pp 58–60

A memorandum submitted to the Council in response to the initiative taken by Heads of State or Government at the Paris summit conference in October 1972, when, in their final declaration they stated that 'objectives should be defined and the development of a common scientific and technological policy ensured ...' and requested that an action programme and time-table be drawn up before 1 January 1974. Based largely on preparatory work undertaken by Ralf Dahrendorf (*see* 245) and an earlier statement of objectives (*see* 244), this initiative consists of a major package of proposals and projects. In Part 1 the Commission focuses attention upon six areas of activity, namely, the coordination of national policies, the promotion of basic research, measures in support of Community policies, scientific and technical information, tasks in connection with public services and the outlook for long-term research. In each section an explanatory memorandum fills in the background, sometimes supported by draft Council Decisions and Resolutions as appropriate. Part 1 concludes with an overall survey and detailed time-table of measures to be taken. In Part 2 the Commission outlines a number of proposals for projects in support of Community policies in such areas as social affairs, energy, development aid and the environment. The memorandum was published as Supplement 14/73 to the *Bulletin of the European Communities*. The outcome of Council deliberations on this document was the adoption on 14 January 1974 of four major Council Resolutions, which together represent a significant step forward in the field of scientific and technological policy. The first Resolution on the coordination of national policies and the definition of scientific and technological projects of interest to the Community provides for the creation of a Scientific and Technical Research Committee (CREST) to coordinate national research policies and to assist the Commission in the preparation of proposals for projects (*OJ* C7, 29 Jan 1974, pp 2–4). A second Resolution concerns Community participation in the European Science Foundation (*OJ* C7, 29 Jan 1974, p 5), and a third concerns an initial action programme for science and technology (*OJ* C7, 29 Jan 1974, p 6). The fourth Council Resolution on the development of a Community programme for technological forecasting (*OJ* C7, 29 Jan 1974, pp 7–9) led to the formation of a 'Europe + 30' team whose report was submitted to the Commission in 1975 (*see* 252).

248 Medium-term research aid programme (1975 to 1980) under Article 55 ECSC Treaty
SEC(74)1423 final. 18 Apr 1974. 16p

See 176.

249 Energy for Europe: research and development
SEC(74)2592 final. 17 July 1974. 3 vols, 22p, 57p, 65p

See 286.

250 Revision of the multi-annual research programme of the JRC and new proposals for the Petten Establishment
COM(74)2200 final. 18 Dec 1974. 151p

EP Report: *Working doc* 522/74. 10 Mar 1975. G. Flämig. 22p
EP Debate: *Annex OJ* No 189, 7 Apr 1975, pp 6–19
EP Resolution: *OJ* C95, 28 Apr 1975, p 7

Since the Council was unable to agree to revise the multi-annual research programme adopted in 1973 (*see* 244) on the basis of a proposal submitted to the Council on 3 April 1974 (COM(74)500 final), this document contains fresh proposals on the JRC's multi-annual programme modified in the light of opinions expressed by the Council, particularly as regards the Petten Establishment. The new programme contains proposals for a reassessment of the allocations for each objective identified in the original programme, for additional activities for the Petten Establishment and for measures to facilitate the preparation of future programmes. An annex to the document contains draft proposals for Council Decisions on the matter. A separate volume of technical annexes provides much more detailed information on the Commission's proposals. The Council approved the revision by a series of Decisions taken on 25 August 1975 (*OJ* L231, 29 Jan 1975, pp 1–28).

51 Programme of research and development actions in the field of energy
COM(74)2150 final. 8 Jan 1975. 85p

See 289.

52 The Europe Plus Thirty report
Doc XII/694/75. n.d. 418p

In its Resolution of 14 January 1974, the Council approved a one year programme of research on technological forecasting, assessment and methodology, in which it declared that 'in order to ensure the development of a Community policy in the scientific and technological field the European Communities must try to determine how existing scientific and technological capacity can best be used for the purpose of keeping the objectives and instruments of a common policy under constant review' (*OJ* C7, 29 Jan 1974, pp 7–9). As a consequence, a team of experts headed by Lord Kennet was asked to investigate the feasibility of a Community study entitled 'Europe + 30' whose aim would be to anticipate those developments over the next 30 years likely to affect the progress of Europe, and to report on the desirability of creating a technology assessment office to evaluate the implications of scientific and technological developments on the society and economy of the Community. Part 1 emphasizes the need for, and usefulness of, a long-term forecasting capacity within the Community and reviews existing methodological techniques. In Part 2 the group illustrates the type of results that could be obtained in 16 specific fields of forecasting. Part 3 is concerned with technological assessment and the question of the long-term socio-economic consequences of technological advance. Finally, in Part 4 the group make proposals for an instrument for carrying out long-term forecasting and technology assessment at the Community level. (*See also* 258.)

53 Proposal for a multi-annual environmental research and development programme of the European Economic Community (indirect action) (1976–1980)
COM(75)353 final. 15 July 1975. 30p

See 477.

54 Overall concept for the next multi-annual research programme of the Joint Research Centre
COM(75)529 final. 22 Oct 1975. 22p

EP Report: *Working doc* 49/76. 20 Apr 1976. G. Flämig. 17p
EP Debate: *Annex OJ* No 203, 11 May 1976, pp 65–78
EP Resolution: *OJ* C125, 8 June 1976, pp 16–18

Prepared at the request of the Council, the Commission attempts in this document to define in general terms the role the JRC will play in the next multi-annual research programme. This initial outline, to be followed in 1976 by a detailed and quantified programme, is consistent with the overall design for research and development policy enunciated in another document prepared at the same time (*see* 255). The Commission opens with a critical appraisal of the current role of the JRC and of the weaknesses inherent in its structure. This is followed by some discussion of the shape to be given to a new programme, the broad guidelines to be followed in its construction, its duration and size. As a consequence of formal proposals tabled by the Commission in May 1976 (COM(76)171 final) based upon the opinions expressed in this and its associated document (*see* 255), the Council was able on 18 July 1977 to approve Council Decision 77/488/EEC introducing a new multi-annual research programme for the JRC to extend from 1977 to 1980 (*OJ* L200, 8 Aug 1977, pp 4–9).

255 Objectives, priorities and resources for a common research and development policy
COM(75)535 final. 29 Oct 1975. 30p

EP Report: *Working doc* 71/76. 10 May 1976. P. Krieg. 20p
EP Debate: *Annex OJ* No 203, 11 May 1976, pp 65–78
EP Resolution: *OJ* C125, 8 June 1976, pp 18–19

Prepared at the request of the Council as a basis for discussion on the guidelines to be adopted and objectives to be set for science and technology policy in the medium-term (1975–1980). The Commission identifies medium-term objectives and priorities, establishes criteria for the choice of projects and calculates the level of expenditure needed to complete the proposed projects. The Commission makes it clear that it intends to concentrate its attention on energy resources, the environment, economic and industrial development and social questions. The document briefly examines the role of the JRC, although this is dealt with in much more detail in an associated document (*see* 254), before concluding with annexes which list the programmes adopted by the Commission and Council since January 1974 and a time-table of financial estimates for 1976 to 1980. The document was given full publication as Supplement 4/76 to the *Bulletin of the European Communities*.

256 Proposal for a Council Decision reviewing the energy research and development programme adopted by the Council's Decision of 22 August 1975 (75/510/EEC)
COM(76)395 final. 23 July 1976. 22p

See 297.

257 Science and European public opinion
Doc XII/922/77. n.d. 98p

A report on the main results of an opinion survey conducted by the Community into the relationship between scientific research and public opinion.

258 Communication from the Commission to the Council concerning the follow-up to the 'Feasibility Study' Europe + 30
COM(77)218 final. 22 June 1977. 10p

A brief document from the Commission in which it describes the background to, and the main findings of, the Europe + 30 report produced by an independent project team under the guidance of Lord Kennet in 1975 (*see* 252). The Commission also describes how it intends to follow up the report with an initial five year pilot phase, which was placed before the Council on 30 June 1977 (*OJ* C187, 5 Aug 1977, pp 7–9).

259 Common policy in the field of science and technology
COM(77)283 final. 30 June 1977. 82p

EP Report: *Working doc* 361/77. 14 Nov 1977. E. Holst. 38p
EP Debate: *Annex OJ* No 223, 17 Nov 1977, pp 181–198
EP Resolution: *OJ* C299, 12 Dec 1977, pp 41–43
ESC Opinion: *OJ* C59, 8 Mar 1978, pp 19–24

Guidelines for the development of the common policy for science and technology during the period 1977 to 1980, in which the Commission 'outlines the objectives, general conditions, constraints and the criteria for the selection of projects'. The document 'describes the priority scientific and technical programmes which exist or are to be developed' and 'specifies the levels and methods of coordination within the framework of the common scientific and technological policy'. The Commission first explains why a common research policy is so necessary for the well-being of the Community over the next four years before sketching the main features of the programme, the criteria upon which it is based and the parameters within which it must operate. Special attention is given to the role and programme of the JRC. After describing the main elements of the programme, the Commission then proceeds to consider industrial research, the coordination of national research and technological policies, the mechanics of conducting a common policy and international cooperation. The document also refers to the management and dissemination of research results and to long-term priorities for research and development policy. A number of annexes contain graphs and diagrams, a draft Council Resolution on the guidelines for a common policy (*OJ* C187, 5 Aug 1977, pp 3–4), two draft Council Decisions (*OJ* C187, 5 Aug 1977, pp 5–9) and a brief analysis of public funding for research and development. The document was published as Supplement 3/77 to the *Bulletin of the European Communities*.

260 Action programme for aeronautical research
COM(77)362 final. 26 July 1977. 47p

See 213.

261 Work within the COST framework: European cooperation in the field of scientific and technical research
COM(78)156 final. 12 Apr 1978. 14p

A document in which the Commission takes stock of cooperation with some ten non-member European countries conducted within the committee of senior national officials established in 1971 and known as COST (Coopération Scientifique et Technique). The document begins with background information on the development of this form of intergovernmental cooperation, then describes the four main categories of research project at present carried out within the COST framework. The Commission describes a number of problems concerning COST projects, particularly as regards the definition and implementation of programmes involving cooperative research with non-member countries, financing, ratification and secretarial services. A number of annexes include the opinion of the Scientific and Technical Research Committee (CREST) on the development of scientific and technical cooperation within COST and a list of COST projects.

CHAPTER 7

Energy

Descriptive essay

Although progress towards the practical implementation of a common energy policy has been extremely modest, the mere number of entries in this chapter reveals that this derives more from a lack of political will than from a paucity of policy initiatives from the Commission of the European Communities and its three predecessor executives. The Commission has made a number of notable attempts to elaborate an overall policy but has met with little more than declarations of intent and general agreements on principles and objectives. During the early years of Community development, progress towards a concerted policy was hampered by the fact that the founding Treaties allocated responsibility for coal to the High Authority of the European Coal and Steel Community, for nuclear energy to the Commission of the European Atomic Energy Community and for all other sources of energy to the Commission of the European Economic Community. These institutional difficulties were alleviated by the creation of the Inter-Executive Working Party on Energy which, together with its various working groups, gave energy policy much of its early impetus and which was responsible for the first major blueprint on energy policy (ser 271).

The replacement of the High Authority of the European Coal and Steel Community, the Commission of the European Economic Community and the Commission of the European Atomic Energy Community in 1967 by a single Commission of the European Communities offered the first real opportunity to consider a fully integrated approach to Community energy policy. The new executive lost no time in preparing a detailed programme for a common policy embracing all energy sectors (see 275) on the basis of which numerous practical proposals were later tabled (see 277). The guidelines were updated and further amplified in 1972 (see 278 & 279).

A new phase of energy policy was ushered in by the oil crisis in 1973, in response to which the Commission undertook a major review of policy objectives and priorities (see 285). The message was that the vulnerability of the Community to sharp reductions in oil supplies and dramatic increases in prices must be reduced by promoting policy objectives that emphasize economy in the use of energy and reduce the Community's dependence on imported energy. Although its quantitative targets have been subsequently revised (see 288), the validity of the document's general objectives has remained intact and has guided the Commission in its subsequent activities. After consideration of this and associated documents (see 287 & 288), the

Council adopted a number of important Resolutions which together form the legal basis for subsequent Community action (*OJ* C153, 9 July 1975, pp 6–8).

The Community response to the oil crisis was to adopt plans to reduce dependence on imported energy from its existing level of 61 per cent in 1973 to 50 per cent and, if possible, 40 per cent by 1985, progress in the implementation of which is recorded in a series of annual reports (*see* 294, 303 & 309). The various elements of the strategy devised to achieve this general objective are represented by entries in this chapter of the book. One aspect of the policy was to reduce total demand for energy and to encourage its more efficient use. An action programme for the rational use of energy was devised (*see* 287 & 295) and finance made available for projects to promote energy savings (*see* 310). Another objective was to promote the use of indigenous sources of energy and thereby reduce dependence on imported supplies. The Commission's views on the contribution to be made to the Community's energy supply position by various energy sectors is represented in documents on nuclear energy (*see* 341 & 343), electricity (*see* 342), hydrocarbons (*see* 321) and coal (*see* 177). Provision was also made for research and development to ensure better use of existing forms of energy and the use of new sources of energy (*see* 286, 289 & 297).

It will also be noted from the documents listed in this chapter that the new energy strategy has an important international aspect. The extreme supply difficulties experienced by many industrialized countries in 1973 not surprisingly led to talk of mutual cooperation between energy-importing countries, a practical expression of which was the conference on energy held in Washington in February 1974 (*see* 316). This initiative led in turn to the formulation of an International Energy Programme and the creation of an International Energy Agency to implement it (*see* 322). At the same time the Community sought to establish a regular dialogue with the oil-producing countries so as better to protect its future supplies. A forum for such consultation was provided when, in December 1975, the Conference on International Economic Cooperation (CIEC) met in Paris (*see* 322 & 323). Composed of both industrialized and developing countries, one of its four commissions was concerned with energy.

Much effort has also been expended, particularly since the oil crisis, in an attempt to improve the quality of information available to the Commission on the short-term energy situation in the Community. Laws have been passed, for instance, to require member states to provide the Commission with quarterly data on energy balance sheets (*see* 276) and on crude oil and natural gas imports (*see* 324); short-term targets have been set for the achievement of energy policy objectives (*see* 290 & 293); numerous reports have been prepared for the Council on the current energy situation (*see* 300, 305, 306 & 308, for instance). Short-term trends are also described in *The energy situation in the Community* (*see* 270), an annual report on the market situation in each main energy sector. More general information on all aspects of energy policy appears in the *General report on the activities of the European Communities* and in the *Bulletin of the European Communities*.

In addition to short-term indicators for the day-to-day management of the energy economy, the Commission needs to have some appreciation of long-term trends in supply and demand for use in the formulation of general policy. Consequently, the Commission has on a number of occasions sought to make use of the best available data to forecast levels of demand and production in the long-term.

The first such study took place in 1956 (*see* 262), followed in 1962 by a report containing projections for 1965, 1970 and 1975 (*see* 272). This report was updated to take account of recent developments in 1966 (*see* 274) and itself revised in 1972 (*see* 280). Liberally provided with tables, graphs and other data, these quantitative studies are a valuable source of factual information. Additional statistical information is published by the Statistical Office of the European Communities. The main source of data for the period covered by this book is the *Quarterly bulletin of energy statistics* and its predecessor, *Energy statistics*, which contain figures on the overall energy balance sheet together with separate quarterly balance sheets and monthly statistical series for each main source of energy. In 1977 the *Quarterly bulletin* was replaced by a series of monthly bulletins, including *Hydrocarbons: monthly bulletin* and *Electrical energy: monthly bulletin*, each of which contains the main short-term indicators for the appropriate energy sector. The *Yearbook* formerly published in conjunction with the *Quarterly bulletin* and *Energy statistics* has similarly been replaced by separate annuals called *Gas statistics* and *Electrical energy statistics*. The contribution of coal to the energy economy is dealt with in Chapter 5.

Bibliographical record

262 Etude sur la structure et les tendances de l'économie énergetique dans les pays de la Communauté
HA doc 5880/4/56. n.d. 104p

The first important statistical study of the energy market and of future energy requirements, this report emerged from the work of the Joint Committee established in 1953 between member governments and the High Authority as a permanent forum for the examination and coordination of general economic policy. Part 1 outlines the present state of the energy economy on the basis of the limited amount of data available for the period 1950 to 1955. Part 2 makes use of this information to forecast levels of demand and production for 1965 and 1975. The report was published by the High Authority in a volume of the same name in 1957 (cat 1944), and its contents were summarized in an English language publication issued by the High Authority in the following year, called *A problem for Europe: the supply of energy* (cat 2004).

263 Rapport de la Commission 'modes de fixation et structure des prix de l'énergie'
HA doc 3215/59. 15 Feb 1959. 43p

A comparative study of methods used to determine energy prices in each energy sector and the conditions of sale attaching to different categories of consumer, compiled by one of the two sub-committees of the Joint Committee set up to investigate certain conditions of competition between the different energy sectors.

264 Rapport de la Commission 'réglementations fiscales et douanières applicables aux différents produits énergetiques'
HA doc 3216/59. Apr 1959. 39p

A report compiled by a sub-committee of the Joint Committee on the effects of tax and tariff regulations applied by Community countries on the competitiveness of the various energy sources.

265 Premier rapport sur une politique coordonnée dans le domaine de l'énergie
HA doc 3024/59. 22 Apr 1959. 105p

A detailed appraisal by the Joint Committee of the Community energy market and of prevailing attitudes and policies. The report examines energy policy in Community countries and the structure of the energy market, with emphasis upon such aspects as prices, production and the security of supply.

266 Tendances de l'évolution de l'économie énergetique dans la Communauté
HA doc 5682/59. 11 Sept 1959. 40p

A report on medium and long-term trends in the energy economy, prepared by the High Authority for the Inter-Executive Working Party on Energy, a body which emerged from the cooperation envisaged in the Protocol concluded between the Council of Ministers and the High Authority on 8 October 1957 (*JO CECA* 35, 7 Dec 1957, pp 574–578). This declaration of intent gives to the High Authority, in consultation with the Joint Committee and with the full participation of the executives of the European Economic Community and the European Atomic Energy Community as soon as they are created, responsibility for initiating studies and subsequently for presenting proposals for a coordinated energy policy. Although largely procedural in content, the Protocol assumed symbolic significance as the first step towards a common energy policy.

267 Premier rapport sur la portée et les effets des mesures prises dans le domaine de la politique énergétique
HA doc 8055/59. 30 Nov 1959. 30p

A review of energy policy measures taken by Community countries undertaken by three ad hoc working groups set up by the Inter-Executive Working Party on Energy to study short-term energy balance sheets, competitive conditions in the energy field and the general problems of a coordinated policy.

268 Aide-mémoire au sujet de la mise en oeuvre d'une coordination des politiques énergetiques
HA doc 6892/1/59. 3 Dec 1959. 2p

A brief document concerning organizational arrangements for cooperation between the High Authority and the Commissions of the European Economic Community and the European Atomic Energy Community on energy matters.

269 Coordination des politiques énergetiques: note intérimaire
HA doc 1557/1/60. 4 Mar 1960. 22p

Prepared for the Inter-Executive Working Party on Energy by its ad hoc working groups, and submitted to the Council of Ministers as a basis for discussion, this report advocates the principle of coordination and outlines initial proposals on how national energy policies might be aligned. During the course of the year, the memorandum was supplemented by five annexes, details of which are given in the *Ninth general report on the activities of the European Coal and Steel Community*, pp 91–93, and a number of practical proposals as a first step towards the implementation of a coordinated energy policy (HA doc 7920/1/60). The measures include initial proposals to harmonize commercial policy and the rules of competition, and a proposal for increased consultation on energy policy matters.

70 Perspectives de la consommation d'énergie de la Communauté en 1960
HA doc 1634/1/60. 21 Mar 1960. 64p

The first short-term energy balance sheet, compiled by an ad hoc working group of the Inter-Executive Working Party on Energy. In 1961 it was decided to undertake such quantitative examinations on an annual basis, with the result that in 1961 the European Coal and Steel Community published *Rapport sur la situation énergetique de la Communauté et perspectives d'approvisionnement d'énergie dans la Communauté en 1961* (cat 7664), and another of the same title in the following year for 1962 (cat 2893). In 1963 this annual survey of the energy market changed its title to *La conjoncture énergetique dans la Communauté*. Published in English since 1973 under the title *The energy situation in the Community*, each volume assesses the market situation in each main energy sector during the year under review and comments upon the outlook for the coming year.

71 Mémorandum sur la politique énergetique
Bull CECA. Second numéro hors série. 1962. 34p

EP Report: *Doc de séance* 70/63. 4 Oct 1963. V. Leemans. 18p
             Doc de séance 78/63. 11 Oct 1963. V. Leemans. 5p
EP debate: *Débs* No 66, 17 Oct 1963, pp 87–127
EP Resolution: *JO* 157, 30 Oct 1963, pp 2634–2635
ESC Opinion: *JO* 189, 29 Dec 1963, pp 3059–3073
CC ECSC Opinion: *JO* 8, 22 Jan 1964, pp 110–111

EP Report: *Doc de séance* 116/63. 14 Jan 1964. V. Leemans & S. A. Posthumus. 4p
EP Debate: *Débs* No 69, 22 Jan 1964, pp 105–116
EP Resolution: *JO* 24, 8 Feb 1964, pp 415–416

The first major policy initiative on the definition of an overall Community policy for energy, drafted by the Inter-Executive Working Party on Energy under the chairmanship of Pierre Lapie. The memorandum seeks to define the general aims and objectives of a common policy and the means for its implementation. An introduction describing the background from which the document has emerged is followed by an assessment of the position in, and outlook for, the main energy sectors, with particular reference to security of supply. A third section draws long-term policy conclusions from this analysis and makes proposals for the establishment of a common market to be created in three stages, a preparatory period to end on 1 January 1964, a transitional period to run from 1 January 1964 to

1 January 1970, and a final period to begin on 1 January 1970. The memorandum was also published separately in 1962 (cat 5051) and reproduced in full in the *Eleventh general report on the activities of the European Coal and Steel Community*, pp 180–209. Detailed examination and lengthy discussion of the memorandum resulted in the signing of the *Protocole d'accord relatif aux problèmes énergetiques intervenu entre les gouvernements des états membres des Communautés européennes, à l'occasion de la 94ᵉ session du Conseil spécial de ministres de la Communauté européenne du charbon et de l'acier tenue le 21 avril 1964 à Luxembourg* (JO 69, 30 Apr 1964, pp 1099–1100), a significant if limited agreement in which member states expressed their political will to work towards a common energy policy.

272 Etude sur les perspectives énergetiques à long terme de la Communauté européenne
Bull CECA. Troisième numéro hors série. 1962. 197p

The most comprehensive analytical and quantitative forecast of future long-term trends in Community energy demand so far compiled. Liberally provided with tables, graphs and statistical annexes, the document reviews the total energy requirements of the Community, traces the changing patterns of supply and demand and considers the outlook in each major energy sector, generally using 1970 as a reference point but whenever possible giving corresponding figures for 1965 and 1975. As such, its long-term projections form an essential background to the policies outlined in the 1962 memorandum (*see* 271). The report was published separately in a volume of the same title in 1964 (cat 3365), an English version of which was called *Study on the long-term energy outlook for the European Community*. (*See also* 274.)

273 Information sur les mesures de politique énergetique prises dans les principaux pays industriels
HA doc 3943/1/63. 2 Oct 1963. 106p

A collation of data on energy policy measures taken by the United States of America, Russia, Canada, the United Kingdom and Japan and on the supply and demand situation in each of these industrialized countries. The document was prepared as a measure of comparison with the Community situation as described in 1962 (*see* 272).

274 Nouvelles réflexions sur les perspectives énergetiques à long terme de la Communauté: évolution récente, perspectives pour 1970, tendances jusqu'en 1980
HA doc 7803/4/65. Apr 1966. 89p

A detailed study of long-term trends in the energy market in order to bring up-to-date the contents of the 1962 report on the subject (*see* 272). Projections are extended to 1980 and placed in a world-wide framework; figures are revised to take account of recent developments, additional information and more sophisticated forecasting techniques. The study was also published in the *Bulletin de la Communauté européenne du charbon et de l'acier* No 61 1966. A review of world energy trends, used as a background study for this analysis, was published by the Commission of the

European Economic Community in 1968 in a volume called *Tendances énergetiques mondiales* (cat 4253).

Première orientation pour une politique énergetique communautaire
COM(68)1040. 18 Dec 1968. 2 vols, 26p, 216p

EP Report: *Doc de séance* 191/69. 10 Feb 1970. V. Leemans. 83p
EP Debate: *Annexe JO* No 113, 13 Mar 1969, pp 99–103
         Annexe JO No 123, 11 Mar 1970, pp 80–103
EP Resolution: *JO* C40, 3 Apr 1970, pp 25–26

A seminal document on Community energy policy in which the Commission, thanks to the merger of the three Community executives, is able for the first time to formulate a general concept of energy policy based on an overall rather than a sectoral assessment of the Community energy market. Introductory remarks, recognizing the value of the work already accomplished by the three separate executives, precede paragraphs in which the Commission explains why an energy policy is so necessary, outlines its aims and the ways in which they can be realized. The main body of the report consists of three sections. In the first the Commission makes proposals for the creation of a framework of action designed to give coherence to the lengthy process of policy implementation, just as the general objectives do for coal and steel and the target programmes for nuclear energy. The second section contains technical proposals for the establishment of a common market in the energy sector, including measures to remove obstacles to trade, freedom of establishment and the harmonization of rules governing competition. The third section contains measures for an energy supply policy and recommendations on commercial policy and investment. A series of graphs and two substantial working documents are annexed to the memorandum. The first, *La situation actuelle du marché de l'énergie dans la Communauté*, constitutes a detailed factual account of contemporary developments in the overall energy market, and of supply and demand conditions in each individual sector. The second working document, *Problèmes fondamentaux d'une politique énergetique communautaire*, looks at the problems to be resolved if the objectives of a common energy policy are to be realized, and at the available means of action. The document, minus its annexed working documents, was published as a Supplement to the *Bulletin of the European Communities* 12-1968. The complete document was also issued as a separate monograph in 1969 (cat 8259).

Bilans énergetiques: situation ... estimations ... prévisions ...
1969–1970–1971   Doc XVII/20626/70 final. Jan 1971. 116p
1970–1971–1972   Doc XVII/407/71. Jan 1972. 70p
1971–1972–1973   Doc XVII/329/72. Jan 1973. 70p
1972–1973–1974   SEC(74)280 final. 14 Jan 1974. 41p

Short-term statistical data on the supply situation in the Community and its member countries. Each annual balance sheet consists of a country-by-country analysis of supply and demand, broken down by consumer sector and form of energy, for the past year with estimates for the current year and forecasts for the coming year. As a result of difficulties experienced during the oil crisis of 1973, the

Council adopted on 30 January 1974 Regulation (EEC) No 293/74 which required member states to supply the Commission with sufficient information for the preparation of quarterly energy balance sheets (*OJ* L32, 5 Feb 1974, pp 1–2).

277 Mémorandum sur la mise en oeuvre de la première orientation pour une politique énergetique communautaire
COM(71)810 final. 22 July 1971. 40p

A brief review of measures framed in accordance with the guidelines established in the 1968 memorandum (*see* 275). Three annexes to the document contain further specific proposals on minimum stocks of crude oil (*JO* C106, 23 Oct 1971, pp 1–2), which was adopted by the Council on 19 December 1972 in Directive 72/425/EEC (*JO* L291, 28 Dec 1972, p 154); on joint ventures in the hydrocarbons sector (*JO* C106, 23 Oct 1971, pp 2–5), adopted by the Council on 9 November 1973 in Regulation (EEC) No 3056/73 (*OJ* L312, 13 Nov 1973, pp 1–3) and borrowing to finance nuclear power stations (*JO* C106, 23 Oct 1971, p 5).

278 Progrès nécessaires de la politique énergetique communautaire
COM(72)1200 final. 4 Oct 1972. 35p

EP Report: *Working doc* 36/73. 7 May 1973. P. Giraud. 45p
EP Debate: *Annex OJ* No 162, 8 May 1973, pp 45–51 & 66–90
EP Resolution: *OJ* C37, 4 June 1973, pp 19–21
ESC Opinion: *OJ* C101, 23 Nov 1973, pp 15–21

An attempt on the part of the Commission to stimulate progress on the implementation of a common energy policy. The document adjusts and amplifies the analyses made in 1968 (*see* 275) to take account of trends in the energy market since 1968 and of a new study of energy outlook up to 1985 (*see* 280). In Part 1 the Commission outlines measures considered to be necessary in certain areas of current concern, namely, environmental protection, the rational use of energy, scientific and technical research, relations between importing and exporting countries and between importing countries themselves. Part 2 contains specific proposals for the oil, natural gas, coal, electricity and nuclear energy sectors. The document was published as Supplement 11/72 to the *Bulletin of the European Communities* and also separately, along with an associated document (*see* 279), in a volume entitled *Problems, resources and necessary progress in Community energy policy 1975–1985* (cat 8416).

279 Les problèmes et les moyens de la politique de l'énergie pour la période 1975–1985
COM(72)1201. 4 Oct 1972. 33p

EP Report: *Working doc* 36/73. 7 May 1973. P. Giraud. 45p
EP Debate: *Annex OJ* No 162, 8 May 1973, pp 45–51 & 66–90
EP Resolution: *OJ* C37, 4 June 1973, pp 19–21
ESC Opinion: *OJ* C101, 23 Nov 1973, pp 15–21

A document in which the Commission attempts to anticipate the energy problems likely to occur in the period up to 1985, and to highlight the available options, using as a base the study of prospects for energy demand (*see* 280) and reports on supply outlook for the principal sources of energy (*see* 313 & 314). In this respect, the document contains the basic reasoning underlying the measures proposed in an associated document (*see* 278). Main chapters are concerned with the prospects for demand up to 1985, the likely availability of energy sources, the problems of energy policy and the available means of action. The document was published along with its associated document (*see* 278) in a volume entitled *Problems, resources and necessary progress in Community energy policy 1975–1985* (cat 8416).

Perspectives de la demande d'énergie primaire dans la Communauté (1975–1980–1985)
SEC(72)3283 final. 4 Oct 1972. 127p

The aim of this study of future trends, similar to that of earlier studies in 1956 (*see* 262), 1962 (*see* 272) and 1966 (*see* 274), is to provide a sound factual base upon which to evaluate the various policy options. An introductory chapter, explaining the purpose, methodology and general concepts involved, is followed by one which charts the way in which energy trends have evolved over the past decade. Chapter 3 contains forecasts of prospects for energy demand up to 1985 on the basis of sectoral and global projections. More detailed results of forecasts for such major sectors of consumption as the iron and steel industry, chemical industry, transport and the domestic sector are given in a series of substantial annexes which also include tables and statistical data. Additional estimates for the new member states were made in 1973 (SEC(73)128). The report was published separately in 1974, the English language version of which was entitled *Prospects of primary energy demand in the Community (1975–1980–1985)* (cat 8415).

Guidelines and priority activities under the Community energy policy
SEC(73)1481 final. 19 Apr 1973. 10p

A document which briefly outlines the Commission's general strategy for securing adequate long-term energy supplies. Recognizing that energy policy must be placed in a global context, the Commission proposes broad guidelines for the regulation of relations between oil-importing and oil-exporting countries. The Commission also makes general recommendations on the organization of the Community oil market and priority actions required in the fields of nuclear energy, coal, natural gas and environmental protection. The Commission later tabled concrete proposals for hydrocarbons (*see* 315) and for nuclear energy (*see* 341) on the basis of this memorandum.

Communication from the Commission to the Council on initial implementation of the 'Guidelines and priorities for a Community energy policy'
COM(73)1320. 25 July 1973. 39p

See 315.

Communication from the Commission to the Council on the

implementation of the 'Guidelines and priority measures for a Community energy policy'
COM(74)10 final. 1 Feb 1974. 14p

See 341.

284 **Memorandum from the European Commission to the Council of Ministers on the changed conditions of competition in certain sectors of agriculture resulting from the new situation on the energy market**
SEC(74)2200 final. 12 June 1974. 103p

See 385,

285 **Towards a new energy policy strategy for the European Community**
COM(74)550 final/2. 26 June 1974. 63p

EP Report: *Working doc* 184/74. 10 July 1974. J. F. Pintat. 17p
EP Debate: *Annex OJ* No 179, 11 July 1974, pp 243–274
EP Resolution: *OJ* C93, 7 Aug 1974, pp 79–80
ESC Opinion: *OJ* C125, 16 Oct 1974, pp 58–60
         OJ C15, 22 Jan 1976, pp 21–37
CC ECSC Opinion: *OJ* C133, 29 Oct 1974, pp 2–3

A sharp reduction in oil supplies, and the dramatic increase in prices brought about by the oil crisis in late 1973, highlighted the vulnerability of the Community supply position and further emphasized the need for concerted action in the field of energy. In the light of these developments, and following the lead given by Heads of Government or State at the summit conference held in Copenhagen in December 1973, the Commission undertook a major review of energy policy objectives and priorities. This extremely influential study of the implications of the oil crisis for energy policy outlines an overall strategy for the future; it forms the blueprint upon which subsequent initiatives are based and upon which the Council later adopted a Resolution (*OJ* C153, 9 July 1975, pp 1–2). In Chapter 1 the Commission postulates a number of long-term objectives for an energy supply structure, and the conditions to be met for their achievement by the end of the century. The major part of the chapter is, however, devoted to the solution of more pressing short-term and medium-term supply problems. The Commission re-examines the validity of hypotheses upon which previous objectives were based (*see* 280), establishes a series of new quantified targets for 1985 and examines their financial implications. In Chapters 2 to 5 the Commission outlines the broad lines of policy for electricity and nuclear energy, coal, oil and natural gas. In the following chapter the Commission looks briefly at ways of implementing the strategy. A series of annexes contain specific proposals to restrict power stations in their use of natural gas, adopted by Council Directive 75/404/EEC of 13 February 1975 (*OJ* L178, 9 July 1975, pp 24–25), and petroleum products, adopted by Council Directive 75/405/EEC of 14 April 1975 (*OJ* L178, 9 July 1975, pp 26–27), a proposal for a harmonized system of imports and exports for hydrocarbons and a brief memorandum on the rational use of energy (*see also* 287). The memorandum was published as Supplement 4/74 to the *Bulletin of the European Communities*.

Energy for Europe: research and development
SEC(74)2592 final. 17 July 1974. 3 vols, 22p, 57p, 65p

EP Report: *Working doc 447/74*. 31 Jan 1975. M. Vandewiele. 16p
EP Debate: *Annex OJ* No 186, 20 Feb 1975, pp 206–223
EP Resolution: *OJ* C60, 13 Mar 1975, p 36
ESC Opinion: *OJ* C62, 15 Mar 1975, pp 3–8

A call from the Commission for a research and development programme whose contribution to the new energy strategy will be the better use of existing forms of energy and the use of new sources of energy. In the memorandum the Commission establishes guidelines for research priorities and makes proposals for a programme of action centred upon a number of priority areas upon which specific proposals are promised before the end of the year (*see* 289). The views expressed by the Commission are based on preparatory work already undertaken on scientific and technological policy (*see* 247), and more particularly on the findings of two special committees whose reports are annexed to the Commission's proposals in two separate volumes. The first report, presented to the Commission by Dr P. della Porta on behalf of the European Committee for Research and Development (CERD), is entitled *An initial energy R & D programme for the European Community: an interim report to the E.C. Commission*. The second special report is the *Report of the Energy Program Group Mark 11 (modified)*, prepared for the Commission by the Group under the chairmanship of Professor R. Lindner. The Commission memorandum, minus these specialized annexes, was published as Supplement 5/74 to the *Bulletin of the European Communities*.

A Community action programme and a draft Council resolution on the rational utilization of energy
COM(74)1950 final. 27 Nov 1974. 65p

Following up its brief memorandum on the subject prepared earlier in the year (*see* 285), the Commission explains in more detail in this document how it proposes to find better and more efficient ways of using energy. In the first section of the memorandum, the Commission outlines an action programme whose general aim is to reduce the level of energy input for the same level of output. The Commission highlights basic objectives, the criteria for the choice of projects to form part of the action programme and the means for their implementation. In the second part of the document, the Commission describes in some detail the priority measures that need to be carried out in the domestic and small-scale consumption sector and in the transport, industrial and energy industry sectors. A number of summary tables and charts is followed by a draft Council Resolution on the matter. After due consideration of the proposed action programme, the Council was able on 17 December 1974 to adopt an important Council Resolution on the rational use of energy, the objective of which was to reduce the long-term rate of growth in energy consumption in the Community without prejudicing economic progress (*OJ* C153, 9 July 1975, p 5). The Commission later prepared a report on the progress achieved in the implementation of this action programme (*see* 295).

Community energy policy objectives for 1985

COM(74)1960 final. 27 Nov 1974. 20p

EP Report: *Working doc* 524/74. 10 Mar 1975. J. F. Pintat. 16p
EP Debate: *Annex OJ* No 188, 13 Mar 1975, pp 115–129
EP Resolution: *OJ* C76, 7 Apr 1975, pp 30–31

Prepared in readiness for the meeting which the Council promised to hold before the end of 1974 in order to state its position on the targets set for 1985 in an earlier document (*see* 285), this document from the Commission revises those targets to take account of more recent forecasts from member states. The Commission comments on the nature and scope of the stated objectives and suggests a general course of action for each energy sector. Measures to achieve these objectives are more fully examined in separate documents on coal (*see* 177), hydrocarbons (*see* 321), electricity (*see* 342) and nuclear energy (*see* 343). After consideration of the document, the Council adopted on 17 December 1974 an important Resolution in which it resolved to reduce Community dependence on imported energy from its level of 63 per cent in 1973 to 50 per cent, and if possible 40 per cent, by 1985 (*OJ* C153, 9 July 1975, pp 2–4). On 13 February 1975 the Council adopted another Resolution on measures to be implemented to achieve the Community energy objectives adopted in the December 1974 Resolution (*OJ* C153, 9 July 1975, pp 6–8). The Commission later prepared progress reports on the achievement of these energy objectives (*see* 294, 303 & 309).

289 Programme of research and development actions in the field of energy
COM(74)2150 final. 8 Jan 1975. 85p

EP Report: *Working doc* 526/74. 10 Mar 1975. Lord Bessborough. 18p
EP Debate: *Annex OJ* No 188, 13 Mar 1975, pp 110–129
EP Resolution: *OJ* C76, 7 Apr 1975, pp 27–28
ESC Opinion: *OJ* C263, 17 Nov 1975, pp 30–34

A document in which the Commission presents to the Council the practical proposals for research and development work relating to the use of energy promised in an earlier memorandum (see (*see* 286). The document is arranged according to the strategic areas listed in that memorandum. In Part 1 the Commission constructs an outline programme of action for each strategic area, in which priorities are established and a time-table defined. In Part 2 the Commission presents a more detailed and sometimes technical breakdown of the R & D projects to be undertaken. The communication concludes with a proposal for a Council Decision adopting a research programme (*OJ* C54, 6 Mar 1975, pp 26–29). After consideration of this document, the Council adopted Decision 75/510/EEC of 22 August 1975 concerning a research programme in five specific areas, namely, energy conservation, the production and use of hydrogen, solar energy, geothermal energy and systems analysis (*OJ* L231, 2 Sept 1975, pp 1–5). The Commission reviewed progress in the implementation of the research programme in 1976 and later made proposals for its continuation beyond 30 June 1979, when the four year programme was due to expire (*see* 297).

290 Energy savings: short term targets
COM(75)22 final. 31 Jan 1975. 23p

A document in which the Commission explains how immediate savings of energy can be made over the following two years. The annexes contain a proposal for a Council Directive which was subsequently superseded by a draft Resolution on fixing short-term objectives for the reduction of oil consumption (COM(75)118 final), which the Council adopted on 26 June 1975 (*OJ* C153, 9 July 1975, p 9).

Financing of the energy policy by the Community
COM(75)245 final. 11 June 1975. 25p

A document in which the Commission estimates the amount of investment required to finance measures to conserve and make more efficient use of energy and to develop alternative and more reliable sources of supply. The Commission reviews the present situation as regards investment and makes suggestions for the better financing of energy policy in the future.

Main foci of a policy for the development of energy resources in the Community and within the larger framework of international cooperation
COM(75)310. 11 June 1975. 9p

EP Report: *Working doc* 530/76. 2 Feb 1977. P. Giraud. 36p
EP Debate: *Annex OJ* No 212, 8 Feb 1977, pp 45–56 & 64–76
EP Resolution: *OJ* C57, 7 Mar 1977, pp 25–27

A document in which the Commission seeks to establish guidelines for promoting investment in energy sources available in the Community as another means of achieving the targets for 1985, and for cooperation on an international basis in this area.

Energy savings: short term objectives 1976–1977
COM(75)474 final. 17 Sept 1975. 12p

A document in which the Commission reviews the results of efforts to save energy in 1975 and sets targets for 1976 and 1977. An appended draft Council Resolution on the matter was adopted by the Council on 9 December 1975 (*OJ* C289, 17 Dec 1975, pp 1–2).

Report on the achievement of the Community energy policy objectives for 1985
COM(76)9. 16 Jan 1976. 52p

EP Report: *Working doc* 530/76. 2 Feb 1977. P. Giraud. 35p
EP Debate: *Annex OJ* No 212, 8 Feb 1977, pp 45–56 & 64–76
EP Resolution: *OJ* C57, 7 Mar 1977, pp 25–27

A report on the achievements so far of the energy policy objectives set for 1985 in the Council Resolution of 17 December 1974 (*see* 288). The report consists of a factual comparison of the most recent energy forecasts received from member states with Community objectives set in the Council Resolution. It opens with a short memorandum describing the position regarding the demand for energy and the state of Community energy supplies. The document concludes with a series of statistical tables outlining each member country's supply and demand forecasts up to 1985, and an appendix which offers a more detailed statistical comparison of national forecasts and Community objectives. (*See also* 303.)

295 First periodical report on the Community action programme for the rational use of energy and draft recommendation of the Council
COM(76)10. 16 Jan 1976. 2 vols, 31p, 81p

EP Report: *Working doc* 314/76. 30 Sept 1976. R. T. Ellis. 29p
EP Debate: *Annex OJ* No 207, 15 Oct 1976, pp 234–237
EP Resolution: *OJ* C259, 4 Nov 1976, pp 45–46

A report prepared by the Commission in response to an invitation from the Council to report on the situation in member states as regards realization of the objectives embodied in the Council Resolution of 17 December 1974 on the rational use of energy (*see* 287). Derived largely from the work of the Steering and Coordination Group set up in conjunction with the action programme, the Commission uses the results of this review to propose a fresh programme of action, including five recommendations for specific measures which were adopted by the Council on 4 May 1976 (*OJ* L140, 28 May 1976, pp 11–19). The document also contains a comparative table showing the specific measures adopted by member states as part of the programme for the rational use of energy, and a separate documentary annex containing the interim reports from the eight expert groups whose work forms the basis for the specific recommendations. The report was published separately in a volume of the same title in 1976 (cat CH-22-76-116-EN-C). (*See also* 299.)

296 Implementation of the energy policy guidelines drawn up by the European Council at its meeting in Rome 1 and 2 December 1975
COM(76)20. 16 Jan 1976. 21p

EP Report: *Working doc* 530/76. 2 Feb 1977. P. Giraud. 35p
EP Debate: *Annex OJ* No 212, 8 Feb 1977, pp 45–56 & 64–76
EP Resolution: *OJ* C57, 7 Mar 1977, pp 25–27
ESC Opinion: *OJ* C197, 23 Aug 1976, pp 29–32

A response to the attempt by the European Council meeting in Rome in December 1975 to give new impetus to energy policy, in which the Commission draws attention to those measures already proposed in the three areas highlighted by the European Council, namely, Community solidarity in the event of oil supply difficulties, energy conservation and the development of Community energy resources. The Commission also outlines a package of fresh proposals in these fields.

297 Proposal for a Council Decision reviewing the energy research and development programme adopted by the Council's Decision of 22 August 1975 (75/510/EEC)
COM(76)395 final. 23 July 1976. 22p

EP Report: *Working doc* 403/76. 15 Nov 1976. J.-F. Pintat. 9p
EP Debate: *Annex OJ* No 209, 16 Nov 1976, pp 71–76
EP Resolution: *OJ* C293, 13 Dec 1976, pp 17–18

A document in which the Commission evaluates progress so far in the implementation of the research and development programme adopted in 1975 (*see* 289). The Commission describes the position regarding each of the five programme objectives and suggests a number of minor amendments to be embodied in a new Council Decision on the subject, which was adopted by the Council on 21 December 1976 in Decision 77/54/EEC (*OJ* L10, 13 Jan 1977, pp 28–31). In 1978 the Commission tabled proposals for a second four year research and development programme to take effect when the present programme expired on 30 June 1979 (COM(78)388 final).

8 Community energy policy
COM(76)508 final. 30 Sept 1976. 13p

A communication in which the Commission draws the Council's attention to the extremely modest progress made towards the main objectives of Community energy policy, particularly self-sufficiency and security of supply. In Part 1 the Commission explains the reasons for the failure of the Community to reach targets for reduced dependence on imported energy and reviews its proposals for protecting and encouraging Community energy resources and for effecting energy savings. In Part 2 the Commission outlines a number of salient points concerning the security of imported supplies. The document concludes with a series of conclusions, statistical tables and graphs.

9 An intensification of the Community's programme for energy saving
COM(77)39 final. 24 Feb 1977. 7p

A communication in which the Commission expresses its concern at the size of the shortfall now likely in the production of energy from indigenous sources and urges that a major effort be made to intensify the Community's energy saving programme. The document reviews progress so far and highlights those areas in which rapid progress is essential. A work programme is outlined, and a number of areas identified in which the Commission intends to submit proposals for concrete action before the summer recess. One such subsequent proposal was concerned with energy savings from the modernization of existing buildings (COM(77)186). A further series of practical proposals on the rational use of energy was tabled in May 1977 (COM(77)185 final). Both the Commission communication and these specific proposals, together with interim reports from the eight expert groups set up in conjunction with the original action programme (*see* 287), were published in 1977 in a volume called *Second report on the Community programme for the rational use of energy* (cat CB-24-77-326-EN-C). A first report was published in 1976 (*see* 295). As a result of the communication and proposals from the Commission, the Council adopted on 25 October 1977 Recommendations 77/712/EEC and 77/713/EEC on measures to save heating in new buildings and industrial undertakings (*OJ* L295, 18 Nov 1977, pp 1–4) and Recommendation 77/714/EEC on the creation of advisory bodies to promote energy economy (*OJ* L295, 18 Nov 1977, pp 5–6). On 13 February 1978 the Council adopted Directive 78/170/EEC on the performance of heat generators and hot water systems in non-industrial buildings (*OJ* L52, 23 Feb 1978, pp 32–33).

300 The energy situation of the Community
COM(77)38 final. 24 Feb 1977. 3p

A brief communication in which the Commission expresses its concern over the deterioration that has taken place in the energy situation since the last Council meeting on energy discussed an earlier Commission document (*see* 298). The Council is asked to note the serious implications of present energy trends and to consider the detailed proposals already submitted by the Commission.

301 Protection and promotion of energy-related investments—guaranteed minimum price for energy produced in the Community
COM(77)188 final. 27 May 1977. 6p

A working document in which the Commission considers the implications of the need for large sums of money to be invested in the development of energy resources over the next ten years. The Commission recognizes that if industry is to finance investment on the scale that is necessary, then ways must be found for this investment to be assured an economic return through prices which will cover the long-term development costs of the new energy resources. The Commission looks at the various schemes for establishing a price-guarantee mechanism in the Community, sets out the various procedures which could be used and points out their respective advantages and disadvantages. (*See also* 302 & 310.)

302 First reflections on the development and the protection of energy investment in the Community
COM(77)184 final. 1 June 1977. 10p

A brief paper in which the Commission reflects on ways in which the instruments by which the Community gives support to investment in the energy sector can be strengthened. The Commission looks at forecasts of the amount of investment likely to be needed and the factors that make it difficult to realize such high levels of investment. Three ways in which the Community can assist are identified, namely, additional lending and loan guarantees and the encouragement of long-term contracts. Annexes to the document contain an analysis of current and possible future uses of loan finance from Community sources in the energy sector and some samples of long-term contracts.

303 Second report on the achievement of Community energy policy objectives for 1985
COM(77)395 final. 28 July 1977. 61p

EP Report: *Working doc* 433/77. 9 Dec 1977. J. H. Osborn. 30p
EP Debate: *Annex OJ* No 224, 12 Dec 1977, pp 13–32
EP Resolution: *OJ* C6, 9 Jan 1978, pp 12–13
ESC Opinion: *OJ* C101, 26 Apr 1978, pp 23–28

A second progress report drawn up in accordance with the request made by the Council in its Resolution of 17 December 1974 that it be regularly informed of progress towards the achievement of energy policy targets (*OJ* C153, 9 July 1975, pp 2–4). Based on energy programmes drawn up by member states in the first quarter of 1977, the report compares the situation forecast by member states for 1985 with the objectives set in 1974 (*see* 288) and the situation described in the first progress report in 1976 (*see* 294). The aim of the report is to highlight any deficiencies in national programmes and to identify areas where joint action would be beneficial to the achievement of Community objectives. A number of primarily statistical annexes contain a factual analysis of member states' energy forecasts for 1985, a series of graphs and tables on energy balances in 1973, 1976, 1980 and 1985 and a study of energy investments in the Community from 1976 to 1985. (*See also* 309.)

Energy prices in the Community
COM(77)481 final. 6 Oct 1977. 3p

A brief review of the problems raised by energy prices with regard to both supply and demand, in which the Commission describes work in progress and outlines a number of guidelines for future action.

The energy situation in the Community and in the world
COM(77)483 final. 6 Oct 1977. 6p

A status report on the energy market in the Community and the world. In the first part the Commission takes stock of the present energy situation and the outlook for 1977. In Part 2 the Commission describes the main features of the world energy scene.

The Community and world energy situation
COM(78)101 final. 9 Mar 1978. 15p

A brief analysis of the energy situation in the Community in 1977 and of the outlook for 1978, with reference to energy demand and the position in the oil, natural gas, electricity and nuclear energy sectors. The Commission draws a number of policy conclusions from this assessment and identifies a number of practical measures deserving of immediate attention. The document concludes with a number of statistical appendices.

Cooperation with developing countries in the field of energy
COM(78)355 final. 31 July 1978. 18p

A Community action programme designed to help developing countries to realize their energy potential, submitted by the Commission in recognition of the need for international cooperation in the energy field, particularly between industrialized and developing countries. Divided into three main sections, the document first considers the reciprocal advantages of such cooperation against the background of the existing economic and energy situation and in the context of world economic growth. In the second part, the Commission identifies and examines some of the areas in which cooperation can provide a useful contribution to the satisfaction of the energy requirements of developing countries. Part 3 outlines a framework for Community action, describes the instruments required for its implementation and specifies the areas in which the Community can take action. The Commission announces its intention to submit more detailed proposals on specific aspects of the subject after discussion with other Community institutions. The document concludes with a brief analysis of the possible contribution of the Joint Research Centre.

308 The energy situation in the Community: prospects and policy
COM(78)464 final. 21 Sept 1978. 7p

A brief communication in which the Commission draws the Council's attention to the main trends in the present energy situation and highlights the areas in which Community action is needed. The Commission calls on the Council to endorse the policy outlined and to take action on its proposals.

309 Energy objectives for 1990 and programmes of the Member States
COM(78)613 final. 16 Nov 1978. 39p

A third annual examination of progress towards achievement of the energy policy objectives laid down by the Council in December 1974 (*see* 288), following previous reports in 1976 (*see* 294) and 1977 (*see* 303). The Commission reports on the implementation of the 1985 objectives and sets new aims to be pursued between now and 1990. The Commission comments upon the forward figures and programmes submitted by member states in mid 1978 and outlines the problems and options concerning the 1990 targets, on which it promises to make proposals at a later date with a view to fixing specific targets.

310 Demonstration projects in the field of energy-saving and exploitation of new energy sources
COM(78)672 final. 4 Dec 1978. 41p

Proposals for financing demonstration projects to promote energy saving had been submitted by the Commission in May 1977 (COM(77)187 final). In accordance with the consequent Council Regulation (EEC) No 1303/78 of 12 June 1978 on the granting of financial support (*OJ* L158, 16 June 1978, pp 6–9), the Commission published a call for interested parties to submit applications for support by 30 September 1978 (*OJ* C158, 4 July 1978, pp 2–4). This document records the response to that call and explains the ways in which the Commission made its selections from the applications received. It also gives details of the 16 successful projects covering energy savings, and the 30 successful projects involving alternative sources of energy.

OIL AND GAS

311 Problèmes et perspectives du gaz naturel dans la Communauté
Comm EEC, 1965. 74p (cat 8133)

A report on the prospective contribution of natural gas to the Community energy economy, stimulated in part by a European Parliament report on the subject (*Doc de séance* 126/62). The memorandum places the gas sector in the general energy context, provides an inventory of natural gas resources available both inside and outside the Community, and examines the economic conditions which regulate the use of natural gas. A series of conclusions examine the prospects for future development of natural gas and its wider energy implications.

Première note de la Commission au Conseil sur la politique de la Communauté en matière de pétrole et de gaz naturel
SEC(66)469. 14 Feb 1966. 41p

EP Report: *Doc de séance* 106/66. 12 Oct 1966. V. Leemans. 16p
EP Debate: *Débs* No 87, 20 Oct 1966, pp 162–180
EP Resolution: *JO* 201, 5 Nov 1966, pp 3467–3468

A communication from the Commission to the Council concerning those energy sources that fall within the scope of the Treaty of Rome. In the first section the Commission analyses the structure of the market for oil and natural gas. This is followed by proposals for a series of measures to give effect to the objectives established in the *Protocole d'accord relatif aux problèmes énergetiques intervenu entre les gouvernements des états membres des Communautés européennes, à l'occasion de la 94ᵉ session du Conseil spécial de ministres de la Communauté européenne du charbon et de l'acier tenue le 21 avril 1964 à Luxembourg (JO 69, 30 Apr 1964, pp 1099–1100).* The document was published as a Supplement to the *Bulletin of the European Economic Community* 7-1966.

Prévisions et orientations à moyen terme pour le secteur pétrolier dans la Communauté
SEC(72)3173 final. 25 Sept 1972. 102p

A compendium of data on the oil sector and its medium-term prospects which together with a similar document for natural gas (*see* 314), and a more general evaluation of the prospects for energy demand (*see* 280), provide a useful basis for the formulation of policy. Three main chapters deal in turn with the problems of supply, market organization and industrial structure. A series of annexes are concerned with prospects for consumption, the availability of oil resources, maritime transport, refining, distribution and the financial structure of the industry. The document was published separately in 1974 in a volume entitled *The Community oil sector medium-term forecast and guidelines* (cat 8414).

Prévisions et orientations à moyen terme pour le secteur du gaz dans la Communauté
SEC(72)3182 final. 28 Sept 1972. 101p

EP Report: *Working doc* 213/73. 12 Nov 1973. J. E. Bousch. 12p
EP Debate: *Annex OJ* No 168, 13 Nov 1973, pp 69–103
EP Resolution: *OJ* C108, 10 Dec 1973, pp 21–22

A detailed analysis of the gas sector and its prospects for the next 10 or 15 years, in which the Commission describes the general supply structure and the trend of supply and demand. Aspects of the industry given particular attention include supply, consumption, production, transport, distribution and storage, capital investment, aid, prices and the structure of gas undertakings. The report concludes with a discussion of problems highlighted by the analysis. The report was published by the Commission in 1974 in a volume entitled *Medium-term prospects and guidelines in the Community gas sector* (cat 8413). A comparative study of gas prices compiled from data received from over 20 census points was published in *Etudes et enquêtes statistiques* 3-1971. A comparative statistical study of the real prices, as opposed to the list or post prices, paid by consumers of oil, coal and gas in the Community between 1955 and 1970 was published as an unnumbered supplement to *Energy statistics* 1-1974.

315 Communication from the Commission to the Council in initial implementation of the 'Guidelines and priorities for a Community energy policy'
COM(73)1320. 25 July 1973. 39p

EP Report: *Working doc* 220/73. 12 Nov 1973. T. Normanton. 33p
EP Debate: *Annex OJ* No 168, 13 Nov 1973, pp 69–103
EP Resolution: *OJ* C108, 10 Dec 1973, pp 18–20
ESC Opinion: *OJ* C37, 1 Apr 1974, pp 8–16

A document from the Commission in which it submits to the Council the first set of concrete proposals on a common supply policy as promised in an earlier communication (*see* 281). In an explanatory memorandum, the Commission elaborates upon the relationship to be established between the Community and both the oil importing and oil exporting countries, and explains the reasoning behind the six specific proposals on hydrocarbons annexed to the document (*OJ* C92, 31 Oct 1973, pp 10–22). After consideration of the document, the Council adopted Regulation (EEC) No 388/75 of 13 February 1975 whose aim was to provide the Commission with improved information on the export of crude oil and gas to third countries (*OJ* L45, 19 Feb 1975, pp 1–5), and Regulation (EEC) No 3254/74 of 17 December 1974 on imports of the same from non-member countries (*OJ* L349, 28 Dec 1974, pp 1–2).

316 Cooperation with the United States in the energy field
SEC(74)68 final. 9 Jan 1974. 2p

A brief document compiled by the Commission in order to help the Council define its position in readiness for the conference of oil-consuming countries held, on American initiative, in Washington in February 1974. The memorandum was reproduced in the *Bulletin of the European Communities* 1-1974, pp 15–16. Also published in the *Bulletin of the European Communities* 2-1974, pp 13–22 were statements made on behalf of the Community at the conference and the final communiqué. As a result of the conference, a draft Agreement on an International Energy Programme was produced in September 1974 with the support of all Community countries except France, Canada, Japan, Norway and the United States of America. In November 1974 the International Energy Agency (IEA) was established as an autonomous body within the OECD framework to implement the Programme.

317 Communication from the Commission to the Council on measures to be adopted in consequence of the present energy crisis in the Community
COM(74)40 final. 16 Jan 1974. 6p

EP Report: *Working doc* 357/73. 12 Feb 1974. H. Lautenschlager. 20p
EP Debate: *Annex OJ* No 171, 14 Feb 1974, pp 246–253
EP Resolution: *OJ* C23, 8 Mar 1974, pp 47–48

Prepared in response to a request made by the Heads of State or Government at the Copenhagen summit meeting for urgent measures to deal with the developing oil crisis, this memorandum consists of proposals for six short-term measures, four of which had already been submitted (COM(74)20 final) and all of which were later withdrawn. The statement on energy annexed to the final communiqué of the Copenhagen summit was reproduced in the *Bulletin of the European Communities* 12-1973, pp 11–12.

8 Relations between the Community and the energy-producing countries
COM(74)90. 23 Jan 1974. 8p

Prompted by the concern shown at the Copenhagen summit for the establishment of a stable relationship with energy-producing countries, this memorandum from the Commission explores the implications of such cooperation at both the Community and the national level, the mutual benefits and responsibilities such cooperation would bring and the ways in which it might be achieved.

9 Report on the present or foreseeable impact of the energy supply situation on production, employment, prices, the balance of payments and the monetary reserves
SEC(74)247 final. 30 Jan 1974. 10p

An initial report on the implications of the energy crisis for the European economy, derived from the information made available by member states in anticipation of the application of Council Regulation (EEC) No 293/74 of 30 January 1974 on comprehensive energy balance sheets for the Community (*OJ* L32, 5 Feb 1974, pp 1–2).

0 Report from the Commission to the Council on the implementation of Directive 72/425 imposing an obligation on member states to increase the minimum level of their stocks of crude oil and/or petroleum products to 90 days consumption not later than 1 January 1975
SEC(74)4324 final. 14 Nov 1974. 12p

A summary of information received by the Commission from member states in compliance with Article 2 of Council Directive 72/425/EEC of 19 December 1972 (*JO* L291, 28 Dec 1972, p 154).

1 A Community policy in the hydrocarbons sector and draft Resolution of the Council
COM(74)1961 final. 27 Nov 1974. 16p

EP Report: *Working doc* 122/75. 17 June 1975. S. Leonardi. 32p
EP Debate: *Annex OJ* No 194, 23 Sept 1975, pp 56–77
EP Resolution: *OJ* C239, 20 Oct 1975, pp 18–19

A memorandum from the Commission on the problems of a Community supply policy for hydrocarbons, following earlier documents on two other main facets of hydrocarbons policy, namely, relations with energy importing and exporting countries (*see* 315 & 318). The memorandum contains broad recommendations on various aspects of supply policy, including the efficient use and development of reliable resources, commercial policy, investment and pricing policy. The document concludes with a draft Council Resolution on the subject.

322 Commission communication to the Council on the activities of the International Energy Agency, the preparation of the consumer/producer dialogue
COM(75)5 final. 10 Jan 1975. 2p

One of a number of brief communications submitted by the Commission to the Council in January and February 1975 in preparation for the forthcoming dialogue between energy consumer and producer countries, a preparatory meeting of which was planned for 1975. Other documents are concerned with practical details for the conference (COM(75)7 final), the principles of a common stance to be adopted by members of the Community (COM(75)72 final), and the systems consumer countries could set up to give practical expression to their solidarity on the development of alternative sources of energy (COM(75)74 final). (*See also* 323.)

323 Energy questions to be determined at the Community level
COM(75)6 final. 15 Jan 1975. 6p

A brief document in which the Commission draws to the attention of the Council the areas in which a common stance is necessary in advance of the preparatory conference of oil importing and exporting countries. The Commission pays particular attention to the question of the development of indigenous energy resources and energy savings in the short-term. After two preparatory meetings in April and September 1975, known as Kleber I and II, the full Conference on International Economic Cooperation (CIEC) met in December 1975. Although one of its four commissions was concerned with energy, disappointing results had been achieved by the time of the final ministerial meeting in early summer 1977. (*See also* 674.)

324 Commission report to the Council on imports of crude oil into the Community
COM(75)440 final. 10 Sept 1975. 11p

A statistical report on past and future hydrocarbon imports into the Community, compiled from returns made by member states in accordance with Council Regulation (EEC) No 1055/72 of 18 May 1972 on notifying the Commission of imports of crude oil and natural gas (JO L120, 25 May 1972, pp 3–6). The report summarizes information relating to the past year on the basis of which trends are forecast for the coming year. A report on estimated import levels for the first half of 1976 was submitted in July 1976 (COM(76)406 final).

325 Report on the state of implementation of Council Directive 68/414/EEC amended by Council Directive 72/425/EEC imposing an obligation on

member states of the EEC to maintain minimum stocks of crude oil and/or petroleum products
COM(75)606 final. 28 Nov 1975. 6p

A report on the progress made by member states in compliance with Council Directive 68/414/EEC of 20 December 1968 (JO L308, 23 Dec 1972, pp 14–16), modified by Council Directive 72/425/EEC of 19 December 1972 (JO L291, 28 Dec 1972, p 154), which require member states to maintain minimum stocks of petroleum products at a level equivalent to at least 90 days consumption in the previous year.

Report by the Commission on the behaviour of the oil companies in the Community during the period from October 1973 to March 1974
COM(75)675. 10 Dec 1975. 157p

An investigation into the role played by the major oil companies during the oil supply crisis, with particular regard to the repercussions of their dominant position on the application of the Community's rules of competition. In Part 1 the Commission explains the nature of the enquiry and in Part 2 provides background information on the structure of the oil industry and on the events leading up to the crisis. This is followed in Part 3 by an investigation of the relationship between oil companies and public authorities, national governments and national enterprises. The effects of the crisis upon the availability of supplies and on prices is the subject of Part 4. Finally, the Commission considers the consequences of the crisis for the smaller, independent distributors.

Report from the Commission to the Parliament and the Council on the application of Regulation (EEC) No 3056/73 on the support of Community projects in the hydrocarbons sector
COM(76)709 final. 23 Dec 1976. 33p

A report on the application to date of Council Regulation (EEC) No 3056/73 of 9 November 1973 on the support of Community projects in the hydrocarbons sector OJ L312, 13 Nov 1973, pp 1–3). The document reviews the various development projects granted support in conjunction with the Regulation's aim to encourage technological development activities directly connected with exploration, the storage and transport of hydrocarbons.

Report by the Commission to the Parliament and to the Council upon the application of Council Directive of 4th May 1976 regarding a Community procedure for information and consultation on the prices of crude oil and petroleum products in the Community
COM(78)416 final. 8 Sept 1978. 11p

A report submitted by the Commission in accordance with Council Directive 76/491/EEC of 4 May 1976 (OJ L140, 28 May 1976, pp 4–10). The Directive provides for the submission for each of the three years following 1 January 1977, a report on the results of the Directive's implementation.

ELECTRICITY AND NUCLEAR ENERGY

329 Un objectif pour Euratom
Comm Euratom, 1957. 118p

A report compiled by Louis Armand, Franz Etzel and Francesco Giordani who, on 16 November 1956, were commissioned by the governments of the Six to prepare a study 'on the amount of nuclear energy which can be produced in the near future in the six Euratom countries and the means to be employed for this purpose'. The report, drafted after consultations with governments and industrial interests in member countries, the United States, the United Kingdom and Canada, makes an ambitious estimate of the nuclear power capacity that can be accommodated in the next ten years and makes recommendations for its achievement, with particular reference to cooperation with the United States, the United Kingdom and Canada, the type of reactor to be used, its fuel requirements and the overall cost of nuclear energy. A series of annexes include papers on the overall energy economy in the Community, the prospects and scope for nuclear power over the next ten years and the growth of electricity output in the Community.

330 Rapport sur la situation des industries nucléaires dans la Communauté
Doc EUR/C/593/2/58. 30 June 1958. 189p

A general survey of the position of the nuclear industry in the Community, prepared in accordance with Article 213 of the EAEC Treaty, which invited the Commission to submit such an overview to the Assembly within six months. The report describes the national and international organizations established to deal with the new problems arising from the use of nuclear power. It reviews the uranium and thorium ore resources within the Community and the means employed for their extraction in member states. The Commission then goes on to examine the nuclear fuel cycle from the time the fuel is used, to its reprocessing after irradiation and the disposal of unusable wastes. After some technical analysis of the various reactors and their use, the report concludes with consideration of the industrial uses of nuclear energy, of the foreseeable trends in power requirements and of the relative costs of conventional and nuclear electricity. The report was published separately under the same title in 1958, an English language version of which was called *Report on the position of nuclear industries in the Community* (cat 8412).

331 Les perspectives de l'énergie nucléaire
Doc EUR/C/4191/3/60. 20 July 1961. 42p

An interim study, prepared by Dr H Michaelis, on the economic outlook for nuclear energy over the next 20 years. The report, to be revised as improved data becomes available, forecasts electricity requirements up to 1980 and examines the contribution nuclear power can make to satisfying this demand.

332 Le prix de vente de l'énergie électrique dans les pays de la Communauté économique européenne: rapport
Doc II/6536/62 final. 13 Sept 1962. 2 vols, 127p, 86p

A comparative study of electricity prices in each of the Community countries compiled at the Commission's request by four independent experts, G. Destanne de Bernis, L. Duquesne de la Vinelle, A. Mertara and T. Wessels. The report collates data on price formation gathered in each member country, offers explanations for the differences observed in price levels and makes some general observations on these price variations. A series of annexes briefly describe the situation in each member country. The report was published separately by the Commission in 1962 as number one in the series *Etudes—Série économique et financière* (cat 8075).

3 Situation et perspectives de l'énergie nucléaire dans la Communauté européenne de l'énergie atomique
Comm Euratom, 1964. 126p (EUR 1887)

Prepared by Dr H. Michaelis on behalf of the Commission, this fact-finding study extends earlier investigations into the present position of nuclear energy in the Community and its development potential over the years ahead. The report looks at the cost structure of the electricity industries in member countries, at the costs attracted by proven-type power reactors and at the outlook for their economic operation as compared with coal and oil-fired power stations. Other chapters deal with the probable trend of nuclear energy capacity and production in the Community, nuclear fuel supply problems and the development of advanced-type converters and fast-breeder reactors.

4 Premier programme indicatif pour la Communauté européenne de l'énergie atomique
Doc EUR/C/1000/3/65. Mar 1966. 39p

EP Report: *Doc de séance* 77/66. 27 June 1966. N. Hougardy. 7p
EP Debate: *Débs* No 86, 30 June 1966, pp 169–175
EP Resolution: *JO* 130, 19 July 1966, pp 2446–2447
ESC Opinion: *JO* 47, 18 Mar 1966, pp 637–672

Prepared in accordance with Article 40 of the EAEC Treaty, which states that 'in order to stimulate action by persons and undertakings and to facilitate coordinated development of their investment in the nuclear field, the Commission shall periodically publish illustrative programmes indicating in particular nuclear energy production targets and all the types of investment required for their attainment'. The programme, published in the *Journal officiel des Communautés européennes* 77, 28 Apr 1966, pp 1145–1172, establishes quantitative targets for nuclear energy production during the period 1970 to 1979 and outlines the level and type of investment required to attain such targets. The Commission analyses the various development models that are possible, and considers the repercussions of the programme on such related activities as uranium extraction and heavy water production. It also makes some tentative forecasts for nuclear energy in the 1980s. The document was published separately by the Commission of the EAEC in 1966 (EUR 2773) in a volume which also contains a substantial documentary annex, based on earlier work conducted by Dr H. Michaelis (*see* 333), which contains a vast amount of technical and economic data to support the general conclusions reached in the target programme. Estimates are made of the foreseeable trend of supply and demand for electricity and nuclear energy up to the end of the century, and consideration is given to the industrial potential of the nuclear industry. The technical and economic prospects of various reactor types are examined, as are nuclear fuel supply requirements during the various stages of development. (*See also* 338.)

335 **Rapport d'ensemble sur la politique nucléaire de la Communauté**
COM(68)800. 9 Oct 1968. 92p

See 238.

336 **Situation de l'approvisionnement en combustibles nucléaires**
Doc XVII/8690/69. n.d. 56p

A report from a special working party set up by the Council in December 1967 within Euratom's Consultative Committee on Nuclear Research to investigate the long-term supply of enriched uranium in the Community. The report first looks at the nuclear fuel supply position, with regard to Community requirements and the position concerning supplies of natural uranium, enriched uranium, plutonium and thorium. In the second part of the document, the working party looks at the supply situation in the western world, with particular emphasis on the United States. The study, which was later used by the Commission in the preparation of proposals for the Council (*see* 337), was published separately by the Commission in 1970 in a volume issued as number three in the series *Etudes—Série énergie* (cat 8290).

337 **Approvisionnement à long terme en uranium enrichi**
COM(69)387 final. 22 May 1969. 34p

Based on the findings of the special working group of the Consultative Committee on Nuclear Research (*see* 336), this document from the Commission contains a statement of the principles upon which a common policy should be based and proposals designed to secure the creation of an enrichment capacity in the Community. It also seeks to improve the conditions of supply from the United States. The Commission envisages a three phase exercise leading to the commissioning of the plant by 31 December 1978. The Council subsequently referred the document to the special working group of the Consultative Committee on Nuclear Research for further investigation. (*See also* 339.)

338 **Deuxième programme modificatif pour la Communauté européenne de l'énergie atomique**
Comm EC, 1972. 323p (EUR 5011)

A second target programme for the production of electricity by nuclear fusion, intended by the Commission to take account of the general energy situation and developments in nuclear technology since the first such programme was prepared in 1966 (*see* 334). In Part 1 the Commission places nuclear energy in the general Community energy context with reference to the contribution nuclear energy can make to the achievement of Community energy policy objectives. The Commission then proceeds to look more closely at the scope for using nuclear energy and at the growth in electricity production. The objectives of the target programme are outlined and the resources available for achieving these objectives, that is the reactor families, are reviewed. The Commission also assesses the extent of the potential market, the investment required and the conditions necessary for the achievement of the programme. In Part 2 the Commission examines long-term prospects for the period 1985 to 2000. The document concludes with a number of technical annexes.

9 Création d'une capacité communautaire d'enrichissement de l'uranium
COM(72)693 final. 23 June 1972. 8p

EP Report: *Working doc* 296/72. 26 Feb 1973. L. Noe'. 11p
EP Debate: *Annex OJ* No 160, 14 Mar 1973, pp 133–141
EP Resolution: *OJ* C19, 12 Apr 1973, pp 42–43

A document in which the Commission revises the plan for the creation of a European enrichment capacity outlined in an earlier document (*see* 337). This modified version takes account of recent developments and the opinion of the special working group of the Consultative Committee on Nuclear Research that supplies of enriched uranium could not be guaranteed after 1980. The Commission urges the Council to take measures before the end of 1974 to promote the creation of a Community uranium enrichment capacity sufficient to meet a significant proportion of its requirements from the beginning of the next decade. In response to this Commission initiative, the Council instructed the special working group of the Consultative Committee on Nuclear Research to prepare a report to enable the Council to adopt a position on the Commission's proposals. (*See also* 340.)

0 Creation of a Community uranium enrichment capacity
COM(73)408 final. 20 Mar 1973. 10p

EP Report: *Working doc* 38/74. 16 Apr 1974. L. Noe'. 20p
EP Debate: *Annex OJ* No 175, 23 Apr 1974, pp 57–67
EP Resolution: *OJ* C55, 13 May 1974, pp 25–27

A revision of the proposals submitted by the Commission in 1972 for the creation of a Community uranium enrichment capacity (*see* 339) to take account of a report on the earlier proposals by the special study group of the Consultative Committee on Nuclear Research, and of changes in the commercial and contractual policy to be pursued by the United States Atomic Energy Commission with regard to the provision of uranium enrichment facilities. The document consists of a brief memorandum and a draft Council Resolution, on the basis of which the Council adopted on 22 May 1973 a Resolution confirming the need for a Community uranium enrichment capacity. To this end, the Council established a Standing Committee on Uranium Enrichment (COPENUR) to undertake studies of the enriched uranium market, to collect data, review measures for promoting the required Community capacity and to facilitate coordination between the parties concerned. On the basis of a report from this Committee, the Commission submitted new proposals to the Council on 29 November 1973 (SEC(73)4065) upon which the Council adopted a Resolution on 4 June 1974, in which it again underlined the need for the Community to acquire an enrichment capacity to cover an increasing proportion of Community requirements by the beginning of the 1980s (*OJ* C69, 14 June 1974, pp 1–2).

341 Communication from the Commission to the Council on the implementation of the 'Guidelines and priority measures for a Community energy policy'
COM(74)10 final. 1 Feb 1974. 14p

EP Report: *Working doc* 42/74. 22 Apr. 1974. G. Springorum. 6p
EP Debate: *Annex OJ* No 175, 23 Apr 1974, p 67 (no debate)
EP Resolution: *OJ* C55, 13 May 1974, p 27
ESC Opinion: *OJ* C116, 30 Sept 1974, pp 26–30

A communication in which the Commission develops the role to be played by nuclear energy in the general strategy outlined by the Commission in 1973 (*see* 281). The Commission's general intention is to speed up the development of nuclear energy as a means of reducing Community dependence on external sources of supply. A programme of action to promote the use of nuclear energy and a time-table of action are proposed, with particular reference to public health and conservation of the environment, the industrial, scientific and technological base and the problems of fuel supply. The document concludes with a draft Council Resolution promoting the use of nuclear power (*OJ* C44, 19 Apr 1974, pp 12–13).

342 Guidelines for the electricity sector in the Community: the role of electricity in a new energy policy strategy
COM(74)1970 final. 27 Nov 1974. 56p

EP Report: *Working doc* 200/75. 31 Aug 1975. J. F. Pintat. 23p
EP Debate: *Annex OJ* No 194, 23 Sept 1975, pp 77–89
EP Resolution: *OJ* C239, 20 Oct 1975, pp 20–21

A document in which the Commission considers the medium-term aims for electricity in the context of the new energy policy strategy, as elaborated in an earlier document, (*see* 288) and the means for their achievement. The Commission defines broad objectives for the electricity sector under such headings as economic prospects, electricity demand, electricity production, the structure of the industry and its investment and financing. On the basis of this analysis of the objectives of the sector and of its problems, the Commission then proceeds to lay down a number of guidelines for the implementation of an energy policy in the electricity sector. The document concludes with a statistical annex on electricity demand and production in the Community from 1950 to 1990.

343 Towards a Community nuclear fuel supply policy
COM(74)1963 final. 27 Nov 1974. 36p

EP Report: *Working doc* 25/75. 7 Apr 1975. P. Giraud. 18p
EP Debate: *Annex OJ* No 189, 10 Apr 1975, pp 159–164
EP Resolution: *OJ* C95, 28 Apr 1975, p 34.

A report in which the Commission reviews the practical consequences for fuel supply policy of the enhanced role reserved for nuclear energy in the new energy policy strategy, as outlined in an earlier document (*see* 288). In Part 1 the Commission outlines the main characteristics and principal problems of the nuclear fuel supply situation, with particular reference to natural and enriched uranium and plutonium. Part 2 is concerned with the essential features of a supply policy and an action programme devised in the light of the situation described in the first part of the document. The document concludes with a draft Council Resolution on the development of nuclear energy in the Community.

Communication from the Commission to the Council on technological problems of nuclear safety: draft resolution
COM(75)60 final. 25 Feb 1975. 41p

EP Report: *Working doc* 49/75. 5 May 1975. W. Müller. 17p
EP Debate: *Annex OJ* No 191, 15 May 1975, pp 131–140
EP Resolution: *OJ* C128, 9 June 1975, pp 24–25

In view of the enhanced role to be played by nuclear energy in the new energy context, as illustrated in the action programme submitted in early 1974 (*see* 341), there is an urgent need to investigate the special safety problems associated with the development of atomic energy. In this document the Commission recognizes the need for vigilance in this matter and outlines some of the problems to be overcome, with special reference to the dangers inherent in the fact that safety techniques are being developed disparately from country to country. The Commission urges the necessity for measures at the Community level to harmonize safety techniques, to standardize equipment and to encourage the coordination of applied research programmes. A draft Council Resolution on the subject (*OJ* C99, 2 May 1975, pp 4–5) is followed by a substantial annex which consists of a detailed report on the technological problems relating to nuclear safety. On 22 July 1975 the Council adopted a Resolution on the matter (*OJ* C185, 14 Aug 1975, pp 1–2).

Situation and prospects of the industries producing heavy electrical engineering and nuclear equipment for electricity generating in the Community
SEC(75)2770 final. 23 July 1975. 64p

The first thorough study of this sector carried out by the Commission in which it takes stock of the position and prospects of the heavy electromechanical equipment industry concerned with the production of energy in the Community. The Commission estimates electricity consumption and the number of power stations to be installed during the period 1975 to 1985, before making observations about the structure of the industry and its place in the Community energy context. The Commission also evaluates the Community market, the economic situation in the sector and its employment and social aspects. In 1975 the Commission also published a *Study of the European market for industrial nuclear power stations for the mixed production of steam and electricity* (cat 8608), issued as number eight in the *Studies— Industry* series.

Draft Council Resolution concerning consultation at Community level on the siting of power stations. Proposal for a Council Regulation. The introduction of a Community consultation procedure in respect of power stations likely to affect the territory of another Member State
COM(76)576 final. 10 Dec 1976. 35p

EP Report: *Working doc* 145/77. 14 June 1977. Mrs H. Walz. 21p
EP Debate: *Annex OJ* No 219, 7 July 1977, pp 260–271
EP Resolution: *OJ* C183, 1 Aug 1977, pp 56–57
ESC Opinion: *OJ* C114, 11 May 1977, pp 22–24

A document in which the Commission looks at the problems surrounding the choice of sites for power stations, conventional as well as nuclear, with particular reference to the need for member countries to incorporate power station planning into their land use planning and environmental protection policy programmes and to coordinate their action on a Community basis. The document explains the background to the two specific measures placed before the Council, a draft Resolution on the creation of a consultative body for Community cooperation on the siting of power stations, and a draft Regulation on a Community consultation procedure in respect of power stations likely to affect the territory of another member state (*OJ* C31, 8 Feb 1977, pp 3–5). The European Parliament had earlier prepared a substantial report and documentary annex on the criteria for a Community policy on the siting of nuclear power stations in terms of their acceptability to the general population (*Working doc* 392/75). On 20 November 1978 the Council adopted a Resolution on the matter (*OJ* C286, 30 Nov 1978, p 1).

347 The Community and the international nuclear environment
COM(77)163 final. 13 May 1977. 11p

A brief position statement in which the Commission surveys and gives its opinion on the problems facing the Community in the context of the current international debate on nuclear energy problems. The Commission makes particular reference to the American attitude, as recently outlined by the President, and to the likely repercussions of American policy on Community policy. The Commission also announces its intention to forward further communications on specific aspects of nuclear policy in the near future (*see* 350, 351 & 352).

348 Technological problems of nuclear safety: progress report
COM(77)168 final. 24 May 1977. 21p

A report on progress made at the Community and national level in the field of nuclear safety, submitted to the Council in accordance with the provisions of the Council Resolution of 22 July 1975 on technological problems of nuclear safety (*OJ* C185, 14 Aug 1975, pp 1–2). The Commission first considers measures designed to harmonize safety techniques and equipment for reactors which have reached a high degree of industrial development. It then looks at activities concerning the coordination of applied research programmes and at the safety of sodium-cooled fast reactors in the light of the work of the Safety Working Group within the Fast Reactor Coordinating Committee and the Working Group on Codes and Standards. Also given consideration in the document are measures relating to plutonium recycling and radioactive waste disposal and action on the transport of radioactive materials.

349 The nuclear problems
COM(77)199 final. 27 May 1977. 4p

A working document prepared by the services of the Commission as a basis for a general debate by the Council on current nuclear problems. The document looks at the present state of the nuclear programme, at the development of fast breeder and high temperature reactors, at the nuclear fuel cycle and at research and development. The Commission indicates its intention to come forward with specific proposals for action in due course.

0 **Points for a Community strategy on the reprocessing of irradiated nuclear fuels**
COM(77)331 final. 2 July 1977. 17p

In line with the promise made earlier in the year to submit to the Council additional documents on various aspects of nuclear policy (*see* 347), this communication from the Commission contains proposals for Community guidelines on the reprocessing of used nuclear fuels. Having first explained what constitutes reprocessing, the Commission then emphasizes the need for its consideration as an essential component of an overall Community policy as regards nuclear energy. Particular attention must be paid to protection of the population and the environment against any possible dangers, and to safeguards against the use of nuclear fuels for purposes other than those for which they are intended. The Commission then proceeds to outline the difficulties as regards reprocessing before discussing the considerations that need to be taken into account when evolving a Community strategy. The document concludes with a draft Council Decision setting up an ad hoc committee on the reprocessing of irradiated nuclear fuels (*OJ* C199, 20 Aug 1977, pp 2–3).

1 **The fast breeder option in the Community context—justification, achievements, problems and action perspectives**
COM(77)361 final. 28 July 1977. 28p

EP Report: *Working doc* 519/77. 8 Feb 1978. L. Noe'. 27p
EP Debate: *Annex OJ* No 226, 16 Feb 1978, pp 225–235
EP Resolution: *OJ* C63, 13 Mar 1978, pp 45–47

One of a series of papers on nuclear policy promised by the Commission in an earlier document on the subject (*see* 347). In the first part of this discussion paper on the possible role of nuclear energy in the Community energy context, the Commission underlines the need for nuclear fission to maintain and improve its contribution in view of the increasingly unstable and costly situation as regards supply of hydrocarbons. Having discussed the question of dependence on hydrocarbon and uranium imports, the Commission looks at the nuclear option and the contribution that fast breeder reactors can make beyond the year 2000. This is followed by a description of the present state of fast breeder reactor development in the Community, with reference to member states' programmes and to Community policy. Having discussed the potential and actual state of development of fast breeder reactors, the Commission then considers the problems in the way of their introduction and use and the action that is needed to solve them. In an annex to the document, the Commission describes the work of the Fast Reactor Coordinating Committee.

352 **Communication from the Commission to the Council on a Community plan of action in the field of radioactive wastes**
COM(77)397 final. 24 Aug 1977. 21p

The third of a series of papers on various aspects of nuclear policy promised by the Commission earlier in the year (*see* 347). If the use of nuclear energy is to be extended in the new energy context then a Community attitude needs to be established as regards the management and disposal of radio-active wastes. After establishing the need for such a plan of action and reviewing the work already in hand, the Commission proceeds to outline a six point plan of action to extend Community policy to deal with the problems of nuclear waste. An annex to the document contains a draft Council Resolution which itself includes a proposal for the establishment of a high-level committee of experts to assist the Commission on matters concerning implementation of the plan (*OJ* C249, 18 Oct 1977, p 11).

353 **Conclusions drawn by the Commission from the public debates on nuclear energy**
COM(78)129 final. 31 Mar 1978. 10p

In November 1977 and in January 1978, Mr Guido Brunner, member of the Commission, chaired open discussions on nuclear energy. In this communication the Commission draws conclusions from these debates and takes the opportunity to place before the Council new proposals intended to meet some of the opinions expressed during those public sessions. The Commission draws the Council's attention to a number of proposals which have already been submitted and indicates a number of areas in which it intends to make new proposals. A record of the discussion at the meetings was published in 1978 in a volume called *Open discussions on nuclear energy organised by the Commission of the European Communities* (cat CD-ND-78-006-6A-C).

CHAPTER 8

Agriculture and fisheries

Descriptive essay

Agriculture is the sector in which the greatest degree of integration has been achieved. In recognition of the wide divergence between national agricultural policies and the insuperable difficulties that mere harmonization would cause, the Treaty of Rome provides for the replacement of national agricultural policies during a transitional period extending up to 31 December 1969 by a common policy for agriculture to apply throughout the Community. Article 39 declares the objectives to be to increase agricultural productivity; to ensure a fair standard of living for the agricultural community; to stabilize markets; to assure the availability of supplies and to ensure reasonable consumer prices. The remaining Articles pertaining to agriculture refer generally to some of the methods to be used to achieve these aims.

An enormous amount of documentation has been generated by Community institutions in the construction and day-to-day administration of a policy whose provisions now cover more that 90 per cent of the Community's agricultural production and which consumes more than 70 per cent of the total Community budget. In view of the explicit provision in the Treaty of Rome for a common agricultural policy with declared objectives and general means for their achievement, the majority of policy proposals are intended merely to implement or to further refine already established policy guidelines. The number of major blueprints in which the Commission outlines its general strategy for the long-term development of policy as a whole are relatively few but, nevertheless, constitute important landmarks in the evolution of policy. Such initiatives occurred notably in 1960, when the Commission first defined its concept of a common agricultural policy and tabled its thoughts on how to realize Treaty objectives (see 355); in 1968, when the Commission made plans for the rejuvenation of Community agriculture by means of a radical farm modernization programme (see 369–371); in 1973 (see 383) and again in 1975 (see 386), when growing dissatisfaction with certain aspects of the common agricultural policy prompted the Commission to recommend modifications and improvements.

However, more characteristic of agricultural documentation are the sectoral documents which deal with specific aspects of policy and subsequent legislative documentation concerning the implementation and day-to-day administration of policy in various agricultural sectors. This is particularly true of market and price policy, the determination and regulation of which has caused the construction of a vast edifice of Community legislation. Article 40 of the Treaty of Rome envisages the gradual assimilation of agricultural products into Community contról during the transitional period by means of the introduction of common marketing and price arrangements for each sector of agricultural activity. Guaranteed minimum price levels are established for key agricultural products at an annual review; they are maintained on the domestic market by intervention if threatened by over-supply and by the imposition of variable import levies on cheaper imports from third countries. The common organization of markets was achieved progressively product by product, until by the end of 1968 common price and marketing arrangements applied to almost all the major agricultural products.

During the transitional period, the Commission directed its main attention to the gradual extension of the number of agricultural products subject to common market organization. In view of the large number of individual commodities, and the overriding concern of this bibliographical guide with general policy formulation, this documentation is not directly represented in this chapter. There is, however, reference to the Commission's first package of proposals on the subject (*see* 355) and a review of the first year of operation of a series of measures relating to a number of defined product areas (*see* 358). In recognition of the significance of cereals as the first common regime to be introduced, and its subsequent use as a model for other products, the chapter also includes a memorandum on pricing policy in the commentary to which reference is made to the basic legislation regulating the cereals market (*see* 360).

The Commission's increasing preoccupation with the problems attendant upon the expanding common organization of markets is also reflected in the chapter. In 1971, for instance, the Commission presented to the Council a special report on the disruptive effect of the monetary crisis, a consequence of which was the introduction of monetary compensatory amounts (MCAs) and green currencies as a means of reducing the effects of currency fluctuations (*see* 378). The problems of surplus production also exercized the Commission, as witnessed by its memorandum to the Council on the subject in 1969 (*see* 374), and the references to the problems of market equilibrium made in later policy initiatives in 1973 (*see* 383) and 1975 (*see* 386).

Although the market for each commodity tends to be governed by no more than one or two basic Council Regulations, the actual management of these common markets on a day-to-day basis involves the adoption of an endless stream of implementing legislation, designed both to administer the complex series of price support mechanisms (whose aim is to stimulate production, stabilize prices and ensure an acceptable level of farm incomes) and to adjust them in response to fluctuations in costs, monetary values and other market forces. Hundreds of administrative Regulations are made each year by the Commission using decision-making powers delegated to it by the Council, the exercise of which is controlled by a series of Management Committees in which member states are represented. In 1976, for instance, of 3237 Regulations promulgated, no less than 2164 were adopted by the Commission of the European Communities. They concerned such routine administrative matters as the fixing and altering of import levies, the determination of market prices and the establishment and adjustment of monetary compensatory amounts. Roughly comparable with Statutory Instruments in the United Kingdom national context, this documentation is highly specific and often technical; its long-term significance in terms of policy formation is minimal, and as such, it is not represented in this bibliographical guide.

Statistical data on the application of these price mechanisms may be obtained from the range of statistical serials published by the European Communities. *Agricultural markets: prices* provides regular information on the guide or target price at which products are expected to sell on the open market, the intervention price at which national intervention boards are obliged to purchase the product and the threshold, sluice-gate or reference price below which imports attract an appropriate import levy. (Price terminology varies according to the product under review.) Divided into two separately published sections since 1970, *Agricultural markets: prices: vegetable products* records fixed prices agreed by the Community for a defined period, market prices which vary according to market forces and import levies for cereals, rice, oils and fats, wine, sugar and isoglucose. *Agricultural markets: prices: livestock products* does the same for pigmeat, eggs, poultry, beef and veal, milk and milk products. Statistics for each product are preceded by an explanatory note which provides a handy summary of the main legislation upon which that particular common market is based. Additional price data may be obtained from *Agricultural statistics*, which has since 1976 been replaced by a series of separate publications, one of which is entitled *Agricultural price statistics*, and from the *Yearbook of agricultural statistics*.

Other documents listed in this chapter reflect the Commission's long-held view that even if market and price policy is properly considered to be the cornerstone of the common agricultural policy, then it must go hand-in-hand with farm modernization if the fundamental problems of Community agriculture are to be solved. The Commission recognized the need for an agricultural structure policy as early as 1960 (*see* 355), although measures were restricted in the first instance to the coordination of national structure policies, mainly through the Standing Committee on Agricultural Structure, established by Council Decision of 4 December, 1962 (*JO* 136, 17 Dec 1962, pp 2892–2895), and financial support from the Guidance Section of the European Agricultural Guidance and Guarantee Fund (EAGGF or more commonly FEOGA according to its French initials) (*see* 362). The chapter reveals that it was in 1968 that the Commission took a major initiative on structural policy when it tabled a seminal policy blueprint, popularly known as the 'Mansholt Plan' after Sicco Mansholt, then the Commissioner responsible for agricultural policy in which it unfolded a radical plan to change the face of Community agriculture over a ten year period (*see* 369). In addition to the main report on structural reform, the dossier also includes a descriptive analysis of existing structural policies in member states (*see* 371). Other documents in the chapter emphasize the Commission's view that the inherent weaknesses of Community agriculture will not be alleviated without an overall policy framework to embrace both prices policy and structural policy (*see* 374 & 376). The fact that the Mansholt Plan was given a rather cautious welcome by member states is illustrated by the fact that it was not until 1972 that the Council adopted a number of limited measures designed to implement some of the Plan's provisions (*see* 375), reports on the application of which are also included in the chapter (*see* 388 & 392).

In addition to the valuable information embodied in the policy documents referred to in the preceding paragraphs, descriptive data on the shape and pattern of Community farming appear in other Community publications. The large-scale survey of farming structures conducted by the Commission from 1966 to 1968 in compliance with Council Regulation 70/66/EEC of 14 June 1966 (*JO* 112, 24 June

1966, pp 2065–2080) resulted in a massive 13 volume publication called *Enquête su la structure des exploitations agricoles 1966/67*, containing data on such matters as th type and size of agricultural holdings, the use of land, farming methods and th labour employed. More regular comparative data on farm incomes, economi conditions and other aspects of farm management appear in the reports on th survey results obtained by the Farm Accountancy Data Network (*see* 379). Furthe statistical data on structural policy appear in *Agricultural statistics* and more recentl in *Agricultural structure 1950–1976*, which contains facts and figures on the size o agricultural holdings, agricultural manpower and farm machinery, generall calculated on an annual basis.

Other facets of agricultural policy are also represented in this chapter. Th Commission's concern, for instance, with giving a social dimension to agricultura policy is illustrated (*see* 356 & 357), as are the efforts to provide an adequate financia base for administration of the policy (*see* 362, 364, 368 & 373). The progressiv implementation of these and other aspects of policy may be followed through th pages of the *Agricultural situation in the Community*, an annual review and genera commentary on the position in the agricultural sector, published in conjunctio with the *General report on the activities of the European Communities* (*see* 372). Als useful in this respect, though less comprehensive by far, is the *Newsletter on th common agricultural policy*, each issue of which deals with one particular topic Specialized monographs on diverse aspects of agricultural policy and associate agricultural problems appear regularly in the series *Studies—Agricultural series*, i *Etudes—Série informations internes sur l'agriculture* and its successor series *Information sur l'agriculture*.

Preservation of the world's dwindling fish stocks became a major internationa issue during the early 1970s. The documents listed in the section of this chapte devoted to fishing are mainly concerned with two aspects of the matter. Firstly there are those documents concerned with discussions about the regulation of fishin conducted on an international plane in the United Nations Conference on the Lav of the Sea (*see* 403 & 405), despite which countries took unilateral action to exten their fishing limits to 200 miles, a trend followed by the Community on 1 Januar 1977 in the interests of its fishermen (*see* 402). Secondly, there are document concerned with the internal management and control of fishing within th Community 200 mile limit, with regard to the conservation of fish stocks and th negotiation of reciprocal agreements with third countries (*see* 404). However, it wi be clear from other documents listed in this section that conflicting national interest and traditions have so far precluded the establishment of a common fisheries polic (*see* 406 & 409).

Bibliographical record

AGRICULTURE

354 Recueil des documents de la conférence agricole des Etats membres de l Communauté économique européenne à Stresa du 3 au 12 juillet 1958
Comm EEC, 1959, 250p (cat 2116)

A collection of the main documents emanating from the conference called by the Commission to Stresa from 3 to 11 July 1958 in accordance with Article 43 of the EEC Treaty, which stipulates that 'in order to evolve the broad lines of a common agricultural policy, the Commission shall, immediately this Treaty enters into force, convene a conference of the Member States with a view to making a comparison of their agricultural policies, in particular by producing a statement of their resources and needs'. The conference was attended by national delegations from each member country, headed by the Minister of Agriculture and composed of government officials and experts, together with observers from international agricultural organizations already active in the Six. Inaugural speeches delivered by the Italian Minister of Agriculture as host and by the President and Vice-President of the Commission of the European Economic Community are followed by reports from each of the six Ministers of Agriculture in which they paint a broad picture of the state of agriculture in their own countries, with particular regard to the problems a common agricultural policy will need to solve. These national reports are followed by reports from each of the three working parties into which the conference was divided. The first looks at the state of agriculture and agricultural policy in member states; the second considers the possible repercussions of the application of the Treaty of Rome on agriculture in the Six, and the third looks at the aims and long-term evolution of the common agricultural policy, with particular reference to relations with non-member countries. The general conclusions of the conference are embodied in the final Resolution (*JO* 11, 1 Aug 1958, pp 281–283). The publication concludes with the closing speeches and a list of delegates.

55 Proposition concernant l'élaboration et la mise en oeuvre de la politique agricole commune en vertu de l'article 43 du traité instituant la CEE
COM(60)105. 30 June 1960. 350p

EP Report: *Doc de séance* 70/60. 5 Oct 1960. R. Boscary-Monsservin. 8p
EP Debate: *Débs* No 32, 13/14 Oct 1960, pp 56–108 & 129–156
EP Resolution: *JO* 71, 16 Nov 1960, pp 1378–1384

Presented to the Council in compliance with Article 43 of the EEC Treaty, which declares that 'within two years of the entry into force of this Treaty, the Commission shall submit proposals for working out and implementing the common agricultural policy', this document contains the Commission's first considered views on the introduction of a common agricultural policy. Derived from an analysis of the state of agriculture and agricultural policy in member states based on discussions with member governments, Community institutions and the conclusions of the Conference of Stresa (*see* 354), this wide-ranging document identifies a number of basic elements of policy to be pursued. The Commission proposes measures to improve the structure of agriculture, including the creation of a farm fund to provide financial assistance, together with a range of measures relating to market policy, commercial policy and social policy in the agricultural sector. A series of proposals are tabled for the gradual transition over the next six years of various national markets to one common market. The markets concerned are divided into three groups, namely, wheat, coarse grains, sugar and dairy produce; beef, pigmeat, poultry and eggs; fruit, vegetables and wine. Reference is also made to the institutional machinery needed to implement the policy.

356 **Recueil des travaux de la conférence consultative sur les aspects sociaux de la politique agricole commune, Rome, du 28 septembre au 4 octobre 1961**
Comm EEC, 1962. 106p (cat 8037)

Although certain principles concerning social policy in the agricultural sector were touched upon in the 1960 proposals (*see* 355), the Commission announced that it would convene a consultative conference whose object would be to help define policy by looking more closely at the various social problems likely to arise from the implementation of the common agricultural policy. This publication contains the texts of the main contributions made at the conference, held in Rome from 28 September to 4 October 1961, attended by representatives from Community farmer and employee organizations in the presence of observers from member governments. Speeches delivered at the opening and closing sessions and during the plenary session are reproduced along with summaries of the conclusions reached by each of the four working parties established to look more closely at the social problems of family farms and of agricultural wage-earners, occupational mobility and migration, vocational training and cultural development in the rural environment. (*See also* 357.)

357 **Programme d'action de la Communauté en matière de politique sociale dans l'agriculture**
V/VI/COM(63)353 final. 19 Sept 1963. 53p

Although the Commission identified social policy as one of the four main aspects of a common agricultural policy and established a number of general principles and objectives in its first major pronouncement on agricultural policy (*see* 355), it left further definition of social policy until a later date. This document represents the Commission's considered views on the subject, taking into account the recommendations of the consultative conference held in Rome from 28 September to 4 October 1961 (*see* 356), and the advice of two advisory committees established to assist the Commission. A number of preparatory chapters providing background information on the social situation in agriculture and the development of social policy so far precede the main section of the document which consists of an action programme whose implementation is designed to achieve social parity for those working in agriculture. Divided into short-term measures to be completed by 31 December 1965, and medium-term measures to be completed by 31 December 1970, the action programme contains proposals relating to such aspects of social policy as employment, vocational training, wages, conditions of work, social security, health and hygiene.

358 **Rapport de la Commission au Conseil sur l'éxecution des règlements de la politique agricole commune et sur les enseignements à en retirer**
VI/COM(63)424 final. 6 Nov 1963. 142p

A review of the first year of operation of the package of measures adopted by the Council of Ministers on 14 January 1962 on the progressive implementation during a transitional period extending from 1 July 1962 to 31 December 1969 of a common market for certain agricultural products. The Commission considers in turn each of the six product areas, namely, cereals, pigmeat, eggs, poultry, fruit and vegetables, and wine, which were the subject of Council Regulations (*JO* 30, 20 Apr 1962, pp 933–990). A separate annex provides statistical tables and graphs. Together with Regulation 25 on the financing of the common agricultural policy (*JO* 30, 20 Apr 1962, pp 991–993), Regulation 26 on the application of certain rules of competition (*JO* 30, 20 Apr 1962, pp 993–994), four Council Decisions on the implementation of a common market in farm produce (*JO* 30, 20 Apr 1962, pp 995–1005) and two Council Resolutions which laid down time limits within which the Commission was to submit proposals for dairy produce, beef and sugar (*JO* 30, 20 Apr 1962, p 1006), they usher in the first phase of the implementation of the common agricultural policy. These pieces of legislation were also published separately in *Regulations and decisions in the field of agriculture adopted by the Council on 14 January 1962* (cat 8064), published by the Commission in 1962. They also form the subject of a small booklet entitled *A farm policy for Europe* (cat 8040), also published by the Commision in 1962.

Rapport de la Commission au Conseil sur les mesures d'aides dans l'agriculture
VI/COM(63)423 final. 8 Nov 1963. 222p

An interim report on, and inventory of, aids and support granted by member states to farming, compiled by the Commission to assist application of certain rules of competition to the production of, and trade in, agricultural products, as envisaged in Council Regulation 26 of 14 January 1962 (*JO* 30, 20 Apr 1962, pp 993–994). The Commission assesses the effects of the various forms of aid granted by member states and makes appropriate recommendations. Annex 1 consists of an inventory of aids in operation in member states in the fields of pigmeat, milk products and rice. Annex 2 lists aid measures of a general character favouring production and marketing of agricultural products. (*See also* 366.)

Mémorandum de la Commission au Conseil sur les prix et la politique des prix des produits agricoles dans la CEE
VI/S/0207/64 final. 3 Mar 1964. 197p

A memorandum on prices and pricing policy presented to the Council as background to the proposal for harmonizing cereal prices in one single operation (VI/COM(64)175), rather than by progressive alignment during the transitional period as provided for in Council Regulation 19 of 4 April 1962 (*JO* 30, 20 Apr 1962, pp 933–945). The Commission traces the evolution of prices in member states since 1950 and describes the current situation before considering the consequences of the establishment of a common pricing system on agriculture, foreign trade and consumers. A number of annexes contain statistics on prices, factual information on social security in the agricultural sector and estimates of the production price of cereals for 1964/65. As a result of an invitation from the Council, the Commission submitted on 14 October 1964 a paper on the implications of the establishment of a common price level for cereals (VI/S/02777/64). Discussion of proposals for accelerating price unification led to the adoption on 13 June 1967 of Council Regulation (EEC) No 120/67 introducing a common level of cereal prices from 1 July 1967 (*JO* 117, 19 June 1967, pp 2269–2283). This Regulation was ultimately replaced by Council Regulation (EEC) No 2727/75 of 29 October 1975 (*OJ* L281, 1 Nov 1975, pp 1–16).

361 Coordination des politiques forestières nationales
VI/S/0322/64 final. 6 Apr 1964. 49p

A four-part report, drafted in association with the forestry departments of the member countries, on the coordination of forestry policy. The document opens with a brief description of the pattern of forestry in the EEC, its density, composition, timber production and the nature of the wood market. In Part 2 the Commission considers the appropriateness of establishing a common policy for forestry, with particular reference to the contribution of the Forestry Conference held in Brussels in June 1959. In Part 3 the Commission draws attention to the problems concerning forestry policy, grouped into technical problems arising from application of the Treaty of Rome, timber production problems and problems connected with structural policy. In Part 4 the Commission draws a number of conclusions with reference to a possible Community work programme on the subject. (*See also* 397.)

362 Rapport d'ensemble de la Commission au Conseil sur le financement de la politique agricole commune
VI/SEC(65)1009 final. 5 Apr 1965. 37p

A general review of arrangements made for financing the common agricultural policy, submitted to the Council in accordance with Regulation 25 of 14 January 1962 establishing a European Agricultural Guidance and Guarantee Fund, Article 4 of which stipulates that the Council shall, on the basis of a report from the Commission, review the operation of the Fund during its first three years before taking decisions on how the policy shall be financed beyond 1 July 1965 (*JO* 30, 20 Apr 1962, pp 991–993). The report analyses the performance of the Fund, which, as a result of Council Regulation (EEC) No 17/64 of 5 February 1964, acquired separate Guidance and Guarantee Sections (*JO* 34, 27 Feb 1964, pp 586–594), and its achievements over the past three years. Separate sections look in turn at the way in which the Fund's transactions have been developed, the nature of its expenditure, eligibility for assistance and the distribution of revenue. The report concludes with numerous annexes providing mainly statistical information relating to the operation of the Fund, several of which list, with appropriate references, the various documents produced and regulations adopted on this matter. (*See also* 364.)

363 Programmes d'action en matière de politique commune de formation professionnelle en général et dans l'agriculture
V/SEC(65)1355 final. 5 May 1965. 69p

See 509.

364 Financement de la politique agricole commune—ressources propres de la Communauté—renforcement des pouvoirs du Parlement européen
COM(65)320 final. 22 July 1965. 16p

On 31 March 1965 the Commission laid before the Council a series of proposals for financing the common agricultural policy, which included provision for a larger proportion of funds to come from the EEC's own resources and a consequent increase in the powers of the European Parliament. As a consequence of failure to reach agreement on these proposals at the Council meeting of 28 to 30 June 1965, and the subsequent withdrawal of France from Community participation, the Commission prepared this document containing new suggestions concerning EAGGF revenue and the pace at which the Fund should take over expenditure until 1970. The Commission deals in turn with the free movement of both industrial and agricultural products, the financing of the common agricultural policy and independent revenue. The Commission reserves its opinion on the question of widening the budgetary powers of the European Parliament. The document was published as a Supplement to the *Bulletin of the European Economic Community* 5-1965. After the Luxembourg Compromise of 18 January 1966 brought a solution to the crisis caused by the effective withdrawal of France from Community affairs, the Council was able to resume its discussions and on 26 July 1966 adopted Council Regulation (EEC) No 130/66 which introduced arrangements for financing the common agricultural policy in two distinct phases, the first extending from 1 July 1965 to 30 June 1967, and the second from 1 July 1967 to the end of the transitional period (*JO* 165, 21 Sept 1966, pp 2965–2970). (*See also* 373.)

5 **Rapport de la Commission au Conseil sur l'évolution prévisible de la production et des possibilités d'écoulement de certains produits agricoles importants**
COM(66)82 final. 4 Mar 1966. 84p

A report on the probable development of agricultural production and the possible outlets for some important agricultural products prepared by the Commission to assist the Council in its attempts to maintain a degree of equilibrium between production and demand. Separate sections deal with milk, beef and veal, sugar, rice, oilseeds and olive oil.

6 **Rapport et inventaire sur les aides en agriculture**
SEC(66)920. 23 Mar 1966. 97p

An inventory of state aids relating to production, marketing and investment in various groups of agricultural products, compiled by the Commission as a factual base for use in the application of the rules of competition provided for in the Treaty of Rome, and more particularly, in Regulation 26 of 14 January 1962 (*JO* 30, 20 Apr 1962, pp 993–994), to the agricultural sector. Aids are divided into three categories; those that are compatible with the common market; those that may distort competition but only in the long-term, and other aids which may affect competition more directly and on which the Commission is not yet in a position to take a general view. The inventory lists the measures that have been notified by member states in accordance with Article 93 of the EEC Treaty with comments from the Commission. The Commission was able to formulate guiding principles for state aids on the basis of the information gathered (*see* 367).

7 **Critères pour l'établissement d'une politique commune d'aides en agriculture**
COM(66)60 final. 23 Mar 1966. 35p

Using information contained in an associated document (*see* 366), the Commission reviews in this document the application of the EEC Treaty rules concerning state aids in the agricultural sector (Articles 92–94), identifies certain principles of action and formulates specific proposals.

368 Problèmes relatifs au financement de la politique agricole commune
COM(67)256 final. 14 June 1967. 23p

This document from the Commission contains proposals designed to speed up the reimbursement of expenditure incurred by member states in support of agricultural markets and to amend present arrangements to take account of the beginning of the single market stage for numerous products.

369 Mémorandum sur la réforme de l'agriculture dans la Communauté économique européenne
COM(68)1000. 18 Dec 1968. 6 vols, 73p, 56p, 28p, 203p, 54p, 191p

EP Report: *Doc de séance* 209/68. 14 Feb 1969. H. A. Lücker. 10p
EP Debate: *Annexe JO* No 111, 20 Feb 1969, pp 4–32 & 36–54
EP Resolution: *JO* C29, 6 Mar 1969, pp 6–7

EP Report: *Doc de séance* 227/68. 10 Mar 1969. H. A. Lücker. 32p
EP Debate: *Annexe JO* No 113, 12/13 Mar 1969, pp 61–93 & 118–156
EP Resolution: *JO* C41, 1 Apr 1969, pp 22–27
ESC Opinion: *JO* C19, 13 Feb 1970, pp 11–22

A key Commission blueprint of major political significance, commonly known as the 'Mansholt Plan' after Sicco Mansholt, member of the Commission responsible for its compilation, which represents a coherent and far-reaching programme for the reform of Community agriculture over a ten year period. Part A consists of the general memorandum, in which the Commission begins by describing how Community agriculture has evolved since 1957. It highlights the economic weaknesses inherent in the present situation, and the serious social problems that must be overcome if agriculture is not to continue to lag behind other sectors of the economy. A central feature of the memorandum is the 'Agriculture 1980' programme in which the Commission outlines the fundamental change of emphasis that is required if Community agriculture is to be modernized and rejuvenated. The Commission emphasizes that markets and price policy must be supplemented by measures concerning the structure of agricultural production and marketing if farm incomes are to rise. The cornerstone and most radical element of the programme are the sections of the document in which the Commission tables measures that are needed to change the shape of farming in the Community. Separate sections outline the way in which the Commission proposes to reduce the size of the agricultural population by means of retraining programmes, capital disembursements and other means and to increase the size and profitability of agricultural units. The memorandum also contains proposals relating to the reduction of the total area of land under agricultural use and to improvements in the structure of marketing. The report concludes with tentative estimates of the cost of this fundamental upheaval. Both Part A outlined above and Part B, which consists of some 22 statistical annexes, were published as a Supplement to the *Bulletin of the European Communities*

1-1969. Part C consists of a series of proposals for medium-term measures to restore equilibrium between production and consumption in a number of markets, and Part E of proposals for agricultural price levels for the coming year. Parts D and F are described in more detail in the following two entries.

> **Rapport sur la situation de l'agriculture et des marchés agricoles**
> COM(68)1000. 18 Dec 1968. Partie D. 203p

An analysis of the present state of agriculture in the Community and of the market for various agricultural products, prepared as part of a comprehensive review of agricultural policy in the Community (*see* 369). Divided into three main sections, the report first makes a general appraisal of economic trends in agriculture, with particular reference to such main indicators as production, consumption, prices, productivity, trade and income. The main body of the report is devoted to an analysis of the evolution of the market in 12 separate sectors, in each of which the Commission refers to the supply position, the state of the world market and prices. A third section is concerned with the level of protection in trade with third countries, financial assistance for various agricultural products and the effects of taxation on pricing policy.

1 **Rapport concernant les politiques nationales de structure agricole dans la Communauté**
COM(68)1000. 18 Dec 1968. Partie F. 191p

The first report to the Council on agricultural structures, submitted by the Commission in accordance with Article 2 of a Council Decision adopted on 4 December 1962 on the coordination of policies on the structure of agriculture (*JO* 136, 17 Dec 1962, pp 2892–2895). The report begins with a review of the situation as regards agricultural structure in the member states and a report on the general lines of their structure policies. This is followed by a detailed comparison of national structure policies and an evaluation of the degree of agreement between them. The report was submitted as part of a wide-ranging dossier on agricultural reform (*see* 369).

2 **La situation de l'agriculture dans la C.E.E.**

1969	COM(69)550. 11 June 1969. 222p
1970	COM(71)131 final. 8 Feb 1971. 328p
1971	COM(71)670 final. 18 June 1971. 246p
1972	COM(72)900 final. 12 Sept 1972. 2 vols, 113p, 196p
1973	COM(73)1850 final. 16 Nov 1973. 4 vols, 35p, 206p, 271p, 37p
1974	COM(74)2000 final. 27 Nov 1974. 3 vols, 40p, 277p, 414p
1975	COM(75)601 final. 10 Dec 1975. 3 vols, 64p, 284p, 377p

A series of substantial annual reports presented by the Commission to the Council in conjunction with the annual price proposals, in which the Commission presents a general survey of the agricultural situation in the Community in the year under review. Each report opens with a general appraisal of the agricultural situation in the Community. This is followed by detailed studies on trade in agricultural products, on individual agricultural markets, on agricultural structures and incomes and on the financial aspects of the common agricultural policy. A third part consists of a sizable series of statistical tables based mainly on data supplied by the Statistical Office of the European Communities and brought up-to-date by the Directorate-General for Agriculture. Preparation of the report in this form was discontinued with the 1975 report and replaced by a more specialized report concentrating upon the situation in different agricultural markets (*see* 389). The general survey of agricultural conditions now takes the form of an annual publication called *The agricultural situation in the Community*.

373 Financement de la politique agricole commune
COM(69)702. 16 July 1969. 22p

EP Report: *Doc de séance* 179/69. 9 Dec 1969. M. Cointat. 33p
EP Debate: *Annexe JO* No 120, 10 Dec 1969, pp 123–151
EP Resolution: *JO* C2, 8 Jan 1970, pp 25–31
ESC Opinion: *JO* C12, 30 Jan 1970, pp 9–10
　　　　　　 JO C59, 22 May 1970, pp 8–10

One of a package of proposals submitted to the Council by the Commission on the question of financing the common agricultural policy and the use of own resources to cover this expenditure (*see* 6). This document, together with a separate proposal tabled at the same time (COM(69)701), deal specifically with the agricultural policy aspects of the matter. As a consequence of subsequent consideration of these proposals, the Council was able to adopt Regulation (EEC) No 729/70 of 21 April 1970, which became the definitive text for financing the policy in so far as it provided for the replacement, from 1 January 1971, of national contributions by funds from the Community budget (*JO* L94, 28 Apr 1970, pp 13–18). Many of the important documents associated with the development of a system of financing agricultural policy from the Community budget are reproduced, with commentary, in a volume published by the European Parliament in 1972 called *The European Communities' own resources and the budgetary powers of the European Parliament* (cat 5801). (*See also* 364.)

374 L'équilibre des marchés agricoles
COM(69)1200. 19 Nov 1969. 30p

EP Report: *Doc de séance* 215/69. 3 Feb 1970. H. A. Lücker. 16p
EP Debate: *Annexe JO* No 121, 3 Feb 1970, pp 181–228
EP Resolution: *JO* C25, 28 Feb 1970, pp 57–60

A memorandum in which the Commission impresses upon the Council the need for measures to eliminate growing surpluses of farm products and to restore structural balance between production and sales. The Commission points to the need for measures in the field of price and market policy to bring about equilibrium in such markets as grain, sugar and milk products, and the early adoption of measures concerning structural reform as outlined in the Mansholt Plan (*see* 369). The Commission also considers the financial implications of its proposals.

375 Réforme de l'agriculture
COM(70)500. 29 Apr 1970. 135p

EP Report: *Doc de séance* 253/70. 8 Feb 1971. H. Richarts. 72p
EP Debate: *Annexe JO* No 133, 10/11 Feb 1971, pp 111–169 & 172–189
EP Resolution: *JO* C19, 1 Mar 1971, pp 26–31
ESC Opinion: *JO* C60, 14 June 1971, pp 7–16

EP Report: *Doc de séance* 176/71. 15 Nov 1971. H. Richarts. 120p
EP Debate: *Annexe JO* No 143, 16 & 18 Nov 1971, pp 65–113 & 170–174
EP Resolution: *JO* C124, 17 Dec 1971, pp 22–52
ESC Opinion: *JO* C131, 13 Dec 1972, pp 1–7

A first dossier of specific proposals designed to give effect to the principles expounded in the Mansholt Plan (*see* 369), modified and re-submitted in 1971 (COM(71)600 final) in the light of comments received from other Community institutions and particularly as a result of the joint socio-structural programmes envisaged in the Council Resolution of 25 May 1971 (*JO* C52, 27 May 1971, pp 1–7). On 17 April 1972 the Council adopted Directive 72/159/EEC on the modernization of farms (*JO* L96, 23 Apr 1972, pp 1–8), Directive 72/160/EEC concerning measures to encourage the cessation of farming (*JO* L96, 23 Apr 1972, pp 9–14) and Directive 72/161/EEC concerning the provision of socio-economic guidance for, and the acquisition of, occupational skills by persons engaged in agriculture (*JO* L96, 23 Apr 1972, pp 15–20), which together effectively ushered in a new phase by giving the common agricultural policy a socio-structural aspect. In 1973 the implementation of these measures was the subject of a brief report to the Council (SEC(73)2888). They were later supplemented by Council Directive 75/268/EEC of 28 April 1975 on mountain and hill farming and farming in certain less favoured areas (*OJ* L128, 19 May 1975, pp 1–7). Application of these Directives was the subject of a report to the Council in 1976 (*see* 388).

Communication et projet de résolution du Conseil concernant la nouvelle orientation de la politique agricole commune
COM(71)100 final. 15 Feb 1971. 10p

EP Report: *Doc de séance* 10/71. 16 Mar 1971. T. Brouwer. 6p
EP Debate: *Annexe JO* No 136, 18/19 Mar 1971, pp 4–47
EP Resolution: *JO* C30, 31 Mar 1971, pp 5–6

A memorandum and draft Council Resolution in which the Commission defines new guidelines for the common agricultural policy and reiterates arguments made in 1968 (*see* 369) that a policy for structural improvement must go hand in hand with market and price policy if the fundamental problems of Community agriculture, particularly the disparity of income within the sector, are to be overcome. The document consists of a brief introductory memorandum and a draft Council Resolution outlining the measures relating to prices and structural policy that are needed. As a result of this initiative, the Council was able to adopt on 25 May 1971 a significant Resolution in which the Council recognized the need for a more balanced concept of agricultural policy for the future (*JO* C52, 27 May 1971, pp 1–7).

Actions communautaires de politique régionale dans les régions agricoles prioritaires de la Communauté

COM(71)500 final. 26 May 1971. 29p

See 460.

378 **Rapport spécial de la Commission au Conseil sur les conséquences de la situation actuelle sur la politique agricole commune**
SEC(71)3407 final. 27 Sept 1971. 10p

A special report presented by the Commission at the request of the Council on the disruptive effects of the current monetary crisis on the operation of the common agricultural policy. As a consequence of the floating of certain currencies, the Council authorized the payment of monetary compensatory amounts by Regulation (EEC) No 974/71 of 12 May 1971 (*JO* L106, 12 May 1971, pp 1–2), a Regulation which was itself modified by Council Regulation (EEC) No 557/76 of 15 March 1976 which introduced the concept of 'representative rates' or green currencies, differing from official parities with the unit of account and closer to market rates, as a solution to the problems raised by the period of monetary instability (*OJ* L67, 15 Mar 1976, pp 1–3). The report was published in Supplement 6/71 to the *Bulletin of the European Communities*.

379 **Farm Accountancy Data Network for the EEC**

Results 1968–1970	SEC(72)2800. 26 Sept 1972. 30p
Results 1971–1972	COM(75)335 final. 7 July 1975. 330p
Results 1973	COM(75)683 final. 23 Dec 1975. 383p
Results 1974	COM(76)432 final. 27 Sept 1976. 332p
Results 1975	COM(77)548 final. 7 Nov 1977. 318p
Results 1976	COM(78)603 final. 16 Nov 1978. 359p

A set of mainly statistical reports from the Commission which present the survey results obtained by the Farm Accountancy Data Network (FADN). Established as a permanent mechanism for detailed observation of the state of Community agriculture by Council Regulation (EEC) No 79/65 of 15 June 1965 (*JO* 109, 23 June 1965, pp 1859–1865), the FADN is designed to provide the necessary economic data for the annual determination of agricultural incomes and a business analysis of agricultural holdings in the Community, the results of which are used by the Commission to prepare an annual report on the situation in agriculture (*see* 372). Each report contains a methodological commentary on the conduct of the survey during the period under review and observations on the principal results. The bulk of the report is devoted to substantial statistical appendices containing the main survey results from a sample size increasing from 10 000 agricultural units in 1968 to a planned 28 000 ten years later. The results themselves, providing detailed information on the differences and changes in farm incomes by type of farm, size of farm and geographical location as well as additional information on such topics as labour, working capital, gross production and output, all provide valuable comparable data upon which to base the operation and management of the common agricultural policy. A publication called *The Farm Accountancy Data Network for the European Economic Community* (cat 8396) contains the texts of relevant Regulations and describes the main characteristics of the FADN.

The agricultural cooperatives in the enlarged Community
Doc X/346/73. n.d. 49p

A brief status report on agricultural cooperatives in each member state, written by member organizations of the General Committee for Agricultural Cooperation in the EEC countries (COGECA), founded in 1959 to represent the interests of agricultural cooperatives, particularly vis-à-vis Community institutions.

Agricultural incomes in the enlarged Community: present situation and course of development
SEC(73)900. 7 Mar 1973. 92p

A working document in which the Commission collates statistical data and other information from a variety of national and Community sources as a basis for a better understanding of the complex question of agricultural incomes in the Community. Separate chapters analyse certain essential aspects of agricultural revenue at the Community, regional and individual farm level. A fourth chapter considers the incomes of farmers other than from farming. The report concludes with a series of substantial statistical appendices. (*See also* 390.)

Financial report on the European Agricultural Guidance and Guarantee Fund

1971	SEC(73)1259 final. 6 Apr 1973. 90p
1972	SEC(74)786 final. 8 Mar 1974. 105p
1973	SEC(74)5246 final. 13 Jan 1975. 104p
1974	COM(75)396 final. 24 July 1975. 112p
1975	COM(76)553 final. 25 Oct 1976. 141p
1976	COM(77)591 final. 21 Nov 1977. 128p
1977	COM(78)594 final. 24 Nov 1978. 63p
	COM(78)633 final. 24 Nov 1978. 99p
1978	COM(79)579 final. 29 Oct 1979. 75p

An annual financial report on the administration of the European Agricultural Guidance and Guarantee Fund, on the state of its resources and the nature of its expenditure, submitted by the Commission in compliance with Article 10 of Council Regulation (EEC) No 729/70 of 21 April 1970 on the financing of the common agricultural policy (JO L94, 28 Apr 1970, pp 13–18). Separate chapters, supported by numerous statistical tables, deal with the Guarantee Section, which finances expenditure arising from the common agricultural market and prices policy, and with the Guidance Section, which finances the agricultural structure policy. Additional chapters relate to the financing of Community food aid for products subject to common market organization and the checks undertaken to verify expenditure and prevent irregularities. In 1978 the Commission published a useful guide to the Fund and its operations under the title *EAGGF—importance and functioning* (cat CD-22-77-790-EN-C).

Improvement of the common agricultural policy
COM(73)1850 final. 31 Oct 1973. 37p

EP Report: *Working doc 337/73*. 6 Feb 1974. J. Scott Hopkins. 35p

EP Debate: *Annex OJ* No 171, 13/14 Feb 1974, pp 143–199 & 205–212
EP Resolution: *OJ* C23, 8 Mar 1974, pp 41–43
ESC Opinion: *OJ* C115, 28 Sept 1974, pp 22–32

A general document in which the Commission takes stock of the progress made in agricultural policy over the past ten years and makes suggestions as to how the common agricultural policy might be improved during the period up to 1978. After a series of introductory remarks, the Commission makes a critical appraisal of market and price policy, in which it highlights several general improvements that need to be made and proposes a series of measures for specific agricultural markets. Further brief sections deal with structural policy, the relationship of agricultural policy with other Community policies and external commercial relations. The Council later asked the Commission to prepare by 1 March 1975 a full-scale review of the common agricultural policy, with particular reference to the objectives set out in Article 39 of the EEC Treaty (*see* 386). The original memorandum was published as Supplement 17/73 to the *Bulletin of the European Communities* and also as a special issue of the *Newsletter on the common agricultural policy*, published in November 1973.

384 **Competition policy as an element of European agricultural policy**
Doc X/469/74. June 1974. 21p

Based on an address given by Dr K. O. Nass, Head of Division in the Directorate-General for Agriculture, this document contains a discussion of the rules of competition as they apply to agriculture. The document describes the provisions made in the common agricultural policy for free competition and the distortions that can apply. In particular, the document looks at state aids as they apply to agriculture, restrictive practices and the abuse of economic power and market structures. The document was published in the *Newsletter on the common agricultural policy* 6-1974.

385 **Memorandum from the European Commission to the Council of Ministers on the changed conditions of competition in certain sectors of agriculture resulting from the new situation on the energy market**
SEC(74)2200 final. 12 June 1974. 103p

A memorandum submitted by the Commission, at the Council's request, on the changed conditions of competition in certain sectors of agriculture as a result of the new situation in the energy market. In Chapter 1 the Commission describes the present situation and its repercussions on agriculture. In Chapter 2 the Commission outlines the measures it considers to be necessary. A series of annexes provide factual and other supportive evidence.

386 **Stocktaking of the common agricultural policy**
COM(75)100. 26 Feb 1975. 58p

EP Report: *Working doc* 115/75. 16 June 1975. J. Scott Hopkins. 55p
EP Debate: *Annex OJ* No 192, 17 June 1975, pp 30–101
EP Resolution: *OJ* C157, 14 July 1975, pp 17–22

A major appraisal of agricultural policy in the Community prepared by the

Commission in response to a request from the Council for a 'full-scale review of the common agricultural policy, after an examination of all the data at its disposal and with special reference to the objectives set forth in Article 39 of the EEC Treaty'. (*See also* 383.) In the introduction the Commission refers to the data used in the preparation of the report, including the *Progress report on the common agricultural policy* published by the Economic and Social Committee in 1975 and the major documents tabled by the Commission in 1960 (*see* 355), 1968 (*see* 369) and 1973 (*see* 383). The main body of the report is in three parts. In Part 1 the Commission appraises past developments in Community agricultural policy. In Part 2 the Commission evaluates the effectiveness of the instruments of the common agricultural policy in relation to the stated aims of the EEC Treaty, such as the extension of the common market to agriculture, the increase of productivity and the provision of a fair standard of living. In Part 3 the Commission summarizes the main problems that arise concerning market equilibrium, productivity and farm incomes, unity of the market and of expenditure. The Commission also makes a number of suggestions for future improvements. The document was published as Supplement 2/75 to the *Bulletin of the European Communities* and also appeared in an issue of the *Newsletter on the common agricultural policy* for January 1976.

Communication from the Commission to the Council and the European Parliament on action taken to simplify the agricultural legislation
COM(75)532 final. 27 Oct 1975. 21p

A communication from the Commission on the simplification of Community rules for agriculture, tabled in response to criticism concerning agricultural legislation and the difficulties involved in its implementation. The Commission informs the Council of action currently in hand in this area. Annexes contain the Commission's conclusions on the simplification of legislation in each sector and a draft Council Resolution relating to measures designed to simplify agricultural legislation. The Council subsequently adopted a Resolution supporting measures in this area on 23 November 1976 (*OJ* C287, 4 Dec 1976, pp 1–2).

Report on the application of the Council directives on agricultural reform of 17 April 1972
COM(76)87 final. 10 Mar 1976. 69p

EP Report: *Working doc* 301/76. 4 Oct 1976. C. Laban. 16p
EP Debate: *Annex OJ* No 209, 16 Nov 1976, pp 17–34
EP Resolution: *OJ* C293, 13 Dec 1976, pp 9–11

The first annual report from the Commission on the application in member states of the Council Directives on structural reform (*see* 375). Although the original intention was to provide the Council with sufficient data for an evaluation of the effectiveness of the measures adopted and an assessment of the need for change, delays in the application of the Directive prevented the Commission from collating anything but partial results for the purpose of this report. Consequently, as stated in the introduction, the principal aim of this first report is 'to describe how the member states have interpreted the Community concept in their implementing provisions, how they have adapted their existing systems in order to execute common measures, and the methods and criteria employed by the Commission to ascertain whether the implementing provisions adopted by Member States lead to the effective realization of the aims of the common measures'. Part 1 consists of a short summary of structural policy in member states and of the objectives and essence of the Council Directives on agricultural reform. In Part 2 the Commission records progress in the implementation of each of the Directives in member states. Parts 3 and 4 provide some tentative results of the application of these measures and offer some preliminary conclusions. The document concludes with a tabular presentation of the progress achieved so far. A second report was prepared in 1977 (*see* 392).

389 Situation of the agricultural markets

1976   COM(77)50 final. 11 Feb 1977. 2 vols, 171p, 260p
1977   COM(77)490 final. 10 Dec 1977. 2 vols, 158p, 205p
1978   COM(79)50 final. 31 Jan 1979. 2 vols, 165p, 177p

A series of annual reports which, unlike earlier reports (*see* 372), concentrates upon the situation in each of the different agricultural markets in the year under review and the outlook for the coming two years. The first volume consists of a series of detailed sectoral reports on the position in individual agricultural product markets; the second volume contains substantial statistical tables. A summary of the document appears in the annual publication called *The agricultural situation in the Community*.

390 Agricultural incomes in the Community

COM(77)60 final. 11 Feb 1977. 91p

A document in which the Commission presents to the Council the very latest figures on agricultural incomes provided by the Farm Accountancy Data Network (*see* 379) and the Statistical Office's Expert Group on the Sectoral Income Index. The report traces the development of agricultural incomes in 1975 according to the FADN data, and estimates the level of agricultural incomes in member states in 1976 on the basis of the results obtained by the Expert Group on the Sectoral Income Index. A series of annexes include FADN tables and graphs and a report from the Expert Group. A similar report was produced in 1978 (*see* 396).

391 Mediterranean agricultural problems

COM(77)140 final. 1 Apr 1977. 18p

EP Report: *Working doc 467/77.* 11 Jan 1978. G. Ligios. 49p
EP Debate: *Annex OJ* No 225, 19 Jan 1978, pp 163–183
EP Resolution: *OJ* C36, 13 Feb 1978, pp 36–37

In view of the applications for Community membership made by Greece, Portugal and Spain, the Commission appointed an inter-departmental working party to study the measures that need to be taken to rejuvenate agriculture in the depressed and low-growth Mediterranean regions. This communication from the Commission is based on the more detailed work of the working party; its aim is to review the problems experienced in the region and to make suggestions for preliminary measures. The document opens with a brief analysis of the current agricultural situation and the major problems besetting the agricultural economy in this area. On the basis of this assessment, the Commission then proceeds to outline the main features of a policy to deal with the problems highlighted, with particular emphasis on structural problems and the problems of market organization. Annex 1 lists the measures to be proposed or considered; Annex 2 lists those measures already proposed but not adopted and Annex 3 lists those measures already adopted. (*See also* 393, 394 & 613.)

Second report on the application of the Council directives on agricultural reform of 17 April 1972 (Part I, and Part II)
COM(77)650 final. 30 Nov 1977. 104p

The first report on the application of the Council Directives on structural reform was mainly restricted to a review of the ways in which member states had given effect to the Directives and of the immediate problems that had been experienced with their initial implementation (*see* 388). In this second report, the Commission is able to draw conclusions for the future development of the socio-structural policy from experience gained in the application of these Directives over a five year period. In Part 1 the Commission recalls the purpose and objectives of the measures, describes the instruments and their impact upon the economic and social situation in agriculture. On the basis of this review, the Commission then makes a number of suggestions for modifications and improvements. Part 2 consists of a more detailed analysis of how the socio-structural Directives are applied.

Guidelines concerning the development of the Mediterranean regions of the Community, together with certain measures relating to agriculture
COM(77)526 final. 9 Dec 1977. 2 vols, 32p, 63p

EP Report: *Working doc* 34/78. 10 Apr 1978. G. Ligios. 57p
EP Debate: *Annex OJ* No 229, 13 Apr 1978, pp 190–213
EP Resolution: *OJ* C108, 8 May 1978, pp 49–53

The Mediterranean regions of the Community seriously lag behind other Community areas in terms of economic development. Since agriculture still plays a predominant role in the area, this communication from the Commission concentrates upon measures for the improvement of the agricultural economy of the region. In the first volume the Commission establishes general guidelines and outlines a number of measures concerning the organization of common markets in oil, fresh and processed fruit and vegetables, wine, peas and beans and other measures concerning structural policy. In the second volume the Commission makes a series of specific proposals, the financial implications of which are considered in an accompanying document (*see* 394). (*See also* 391 & 613.)

Financial consequences of the proposals for measures to assist Mediterranean agriculture
COM(77)674 final. 9 Dec 1977. 19p

EP Report: *Working doc* 34/78. 10 Apr 1978. G. Ligios. 57p
EP Debate: *Annex OJ* No 229, 13 Apr 1978, pp 190–213
EP Resolution: *OJ* C108, 8 May 1978, pp 49–53

In this communication to the Council, the Commission considers the financial implications of the proposals for measures to assist Mediterranean agriculture made in an associated document (*see* 393). Introductory remarks set the context by summarizing the problems experienced by Mediterranean regions, describing the objectives of the proposed policy and the means to be adopted to achieve these aims. In the following two sections, the Commission first describes in more detail the specific proposals themselves before considering their financial implications and their cost to the Community budget.

395 Economic effects of the agri-monetary system
COM(78)20 final. 10 Feb 1978. 153p

A brief report supported by voluminous annexes on the effects of the agri-monetary system, described as 'that which results from the conjunction of the agricultural unit of account (AUA), of the representative rates (green rates) and of the monetary compensatory amounts (MCA), including the differential amounts applicable to colza and rape seed'. The Commission considers the effects of the green rates and MCAs on the working of the common agricultural policy, with particular regard to production and consumption, the allocation of resources, trade and their economic and financial cost. Substantial annexes include a chronological table of events concerning MCAs and a considerable number of statistical tables.

396 Agricultural incomes in the Community
COM(78)46 final. 9 Mar 1978. 133p

A statistical report, similar to that produced in 1977 (*see* 390), in which the Commission makes available to the Council the latest data on agricultural incomes in the Community. Derived from the work of the FADN (*see* 379) and of the Statistical Office's Expert Group on the Sectoral Income Index, the report contains a detailed analysis of the main changes in farm incomes during the course of 1976 and provisional estimates for 1977.

397 Forestry policy in the European Community
COM(78)621 final. 1 Dec 1978. 83p

EP Report: *Working doc* 184/79. 10 May 1979. F. Albertini. 42p
EP Debate: *Annex OJ* No 243, 10 May 1979, p 230 (no debate)
EP Resolution: *OJ* C140, 5 June 1979, pp 134–140
ESC Opinion: *OJ* C227, 10 Sept 1979, pp 10–12

The Commission's first major initiative on forestry policy, prepared in response to a request for a definition of general objectives in the forestry sector made in the Special Committee on Agriculture. The communication opens with introductory remarks on the contribution forestry has made to the well-being of the Community and the need for new initiatives to bring a greater sense of common purpose to national forestry policy. Reference is also made to the specific forestry measures already taken or under consideration in the context of other Community policies. The Commission then proceeds to look in closer detail at various aspects of forestry policy, beginning with an analysis of the structure and ownership of forests in the Community and the implications for forestry policy. This is followed by separate chapters which reflect the three main functions that forests fulfil, namely, the production of wood, the conservation of the environment and public recreation, in which the Commission suggests how defined objectives can be achieved. The document concludes with a description of the main instruments of forestry policy in member countries. Appended to the communication is a draft proposal for a Council Resolution on the objectives and principles of forestry policy (*OJ* C301, 15 Dec 1978, pp 8–11), and a draft proposal for a Council Decision setting up a Permanent Forest Committee. The report and proposals were subsequently published along with the Resolution of the European Parliament and the Opinion of the Economic and Social Committee in Supplement 3/79 to the *Bulletin of the European Communities*.

FISHERIES

8 Rapport sur la situation du secteur de la pêche dans les Etats membres de la CEE et les principes de base pour une politique commune
COM(66)250. 22 June 1966. 472p

EP Report: *Doc de séance* 174/67. 15 Jan 1968. H. Kriedemann. 12p
EP Debate: *Débs* 98, 25 Jan 1968, pp 211–223
EP Resolution: *JO* C10, 14 Feb 1968, pp 57–59

A comprehensive report on the situation in the fishing industry in member countries and on the principles to guide the evolution of a common policy in this sector. The Commission deals in the main with three aspects of a common fisheries policy, namely, structure policy, whose aim is to provide equal access to Community fish resources for all Community fishermen and to guide production in the light of market trends; market policy, the purpose of which is to establish a competitive framework within the industry and to stabilize supply; social policy, the intention of which is to improve working conditions in the industry. The Commission later submitted specific proposals on the basis of this analysis (*see* 399).

9 Politique commune de la pêche
COM(68)288 final. 29 May 1968. 74p

EP Report: *Doc de séance* 133/68. 30 Sept 1968. H. Kriedemann. 50p
EP Debate: *Annexe JO* No 107, 24 Oct 1968, pp 3–35
EP Resolution: *JO* C116, 8 Nov 1968, pp 3–20
ESC Opinion: *JO* C76, 17 June 1969, pp 11–19

As a follow-up to the comprehensive report on a common fisheries policy submitted by the Commission to the Council in 1966 (*see* 398), this document consists of three specific proposals for Regulations to establish a common structure policy for fisheries (*JO* C91, 13 Sept 1968, pp 1–5), to set up a common organization of the market in fishery products (*JO* C91, 13 Sept 1968, pp 5–18) and to suspend Common Customs Tariff charges applicable to certain fish (*JO* C91, 13 Sept 1968, p 19). As a consequence of these proposals, amended in 1970 (COM(70)605 final), the Council was able to adopt two important pieces of legislation on fisheries policy in 1970.

Council Regulation (EEC) No 2141/70 of 20 October 1970 introduced a common policy on the structure of the fishing industry (JO L236, 27 Oct 1970, pp 1–4) and Council Regulation (EEC) No 2142/70 of 20 October 1970 established a common organization of the market in fishery products (JO L236, 27 Oct 1970, pp 5–20). (*See also* 401.)

400 Report by the Commission to the Council on Community fisheries policy with reference to the problems raised by the Danish delegation's memorandum of 20 March 1973
SEC(73)2946 final. 18 Sept 1973. 6p

A report prepared by the Commission in acknowledgement of the need for measures to safeguard the interests of fishermen in Greenland and the Faroe Islands, two islands whose economies depend entirely on fishing. Problems given consideration include the conservation of stocks, fishing limits and structural measures to help local inhabitants.

401 Report from the Commission to the Council on the results obtained through the operation of the intervention system, and on the measures taken by producers' organizations, within the framework of the common fisheries policy
SEC(74)2669 final. 12 July 1974. 56p

Article 12 of Council Regulation (EEC) No 2142/70 of 20 October 1970 on the common organization of the market in fisheries products lays down that the Commission shall submit a report on the results of the operation of the intervention scheme introduced and the measures taken by producers' organizations (JO L236, 27 Oct 1970, pp 5–20). The report falls into three main parts. The first concerns the most important Community provisions relating to state intervention and producers' organizations. The second consists of a survey of the present situation in the Community and individual member countries, and the third of a series of conclusions. On 19 January 1976 Council Regulation (EEC) No 2141/70 of 20 October 1970 on a common structural policy for fisheries (JO L236, 27 Oct 1970, pp 1–4) and Council Regulation (EEC) No 2142/70 of the same day (JO L236, 27 Oct 1970, pp 5–20) were replaced by Council Regulation (EEC) No 100/76 on the common organization of the market in fishery products (OJ L20, 28 Jan 1976, pp 1–18) and Council Regulation (EEC) No 101/76 laying down structural policy for the fishery sector (OJ L20, 28 Jan 1976, pp 19–22). (*See also* 399.)

402 Problems which the introduction of economic zones of 200 miles poses for the Community in the sea fishing sector
COM(76)59 final. 18 Feb 1976. 10p

A communication in which the Commission suggests guidelines for safeguarding Community interests in the event of fishing zones being extended to 200 miles. Submitted for the guidance of the Council in advance of the forthcoming session of the United Nations Conference on the Law of the Sea, the communication suggests lines of action for consideration, with regard to the management and protection of fishing resources in Community waters. The Commission makes proposals for conservation of fish stocks which include a Community quota scheme and offers guidelines for the conduct of negotiations to be opened with non-member countries on fishing rights and the position that the Community should take in the United Nations Conference on the Law of the Sea. In response to a call from the European Council, the Council of the European Communities adopted on 27 July 1976 a declaration of its intention to extend Community fishing limits to 200 miles and to govern fishing within that zone according to the provisions of a common fisheries policy.

Third United Nations Conference on the Law of the Sea
COM(76)270 final. 2 June 1976. 75p

A detailed account of the proceedings of the Fourth Session of the Conference, held in New York from 15 March to 7 May 1976, and detailed guidelines for the Fifth Session, upon which the Council is requested to express an opinion so that a common position can be adopted during its proceedings. The report on the Fourth Session includes sections on the main questions discussed, including the exclusive economic zone, the continental shelf, protection of the marine environment and marine scientific research. (*See also* 405.)

Future external fisheries policy: an internal fisheries system
COM(76)500 final. 23 Sept 1976. 237p

EP Report: *Working doc* 474/76. 13 Dec 1976. N. A. Kofoed. 38p
EP Debate: *Annex OJ* No 212, 9 Feb 1977, pp 122–152
EP Resolution: *OJ* C57, 7 Mar 1977, pp 44–50

A series of proposals, explanatory memoranda and statistical appendices from the Commission concerning the internal and external consequences of extending fishing limits to 200 miles. The communication opens with a brief explanatory memorandum and a proposal for a Council Resolution formally extending member states' fishing zones to 200 miles as from 1 January 1977 and providing for the conservation, management and exploitation of the resources within these zones according to the rules of a common fisheries policy, also to be adopted by 1 January 1977. The second part of the communication consists of a memorandum in which the Commission makes recommendations for the conduct of negotiations with non-member countries who wish to gain access to Community fishing grounds and from whom reciprocal rights are desired. The memorandum also deals with the future role of the Community with regard to international cooperation concerning the conservation of resources and concludes with a recommendation for a Council Directive authorizing the Commission to negotiate fishing agreements with non-member countries. Substantial and detailed statistical appendices analyse catch sizes and species in the North Atlantic area from 1964 to 1976 and the total catch size, by principal species and country, in Community and non-Community waters. The Commission also analyses fishing in Community waters by third countries, and fishing in certain third country waters by country from 1964 to 1974. The third memorandum contained in the communication is concerned with the management and conservation of fish stocks. A number of objectives are defined and measures proposed to conserve, replenish and exploit resources. The memorandum concludes with a statistical annex containing summary tables showing the state of the main fish stocks fished in the North Atlantic and Baltic Seas by member country, and maps showing the distribution of the main species in the north of the future Community zone. The communication was closely followed by a separate proposal for a Community system for the conservation and management of fisheries resources (COM(76)535 final). On 3 November 1976 the Council adopted a Resolution, according to which member states agreed to extend the limits of their fishing zones to 200 miles as from 1 January 1977. However, member countries were unable to reach agreement on other measures in the Commission's communication, with the consequence that interim arrangements, described in the *Bulletin of the European Communities* 12-1976, pp 17–18, had to be adopted.

405 **Communication from the Commission to the Council on the Third United Nations Conference on the Law of the Sea**
COM(77)139 final. 14 Apr 1977. 41p

EP Report: *Working doc* 82/77. 9 May 1977. M. Bangemann. 56p
EP Debate: *Annex OJ* No 217, 13 May 1977, pp 251–261
EP Resolution: *OJ* C133, 6 June 1977, pp 50–52

A document in which the Commission assesses the progress made in the Fifth Session of the Third United Nations Conference on the Law of the Sea, held in New York from 2 August to 17 September 1976, and proposes guidelines for the next session. After an introductory section in which the Commission makes an overall appraisal of the Fifth Session and of preparations for the next session, separate chapters are devoted to the topics dealt with by each of the three main committees into which the work of the Conference was divided. These chapters deal in turn with the regime for the international sea-bed, the economic zone and the continental shelf and protection of the marine environment. In each chapter the Commission reviews progress achieved during the Fifth Session, highlights the major outstanding issues and reviews proposed guidelines for the next session. The Commission also devotes some attention to the procedures for the settlement of disputes. (*See also* 403.)

406 **Communication from the Commission to the Council concerning the future fisheries policy**
COM(77)164 final. 12 May 1977. 7p

An examination of certain fundamental issues concerning fisheries policy, lack of agreement upon which has so far prevented progress on the implementation of measures submitted by the Commission in September and October 1976 (*see* 404). The Commission highlights problems concerning the conservation and management of fisheries resources and relations with non-member countries. It underlines the basic considerations to be taken into account and the various measures that are necessary for an effective fisheries policy following the extension of fishing zones to 200 miles.

407 **Communication from the Commission to the Council on measures**

applicable in 1978 regarding the management and exploitation of fisheries resources
COM(77)635 final. 28 Nov 1977. 24p

EP Report: *Working doc* 543/77. 14 Feb 1978. J. Corrie. 18p
EP Debate: *Annex OJ* No 226, 15 Feb 1978, pp 121–138 & 151–161
EP Resolution: *OJ* C63, 13 Mar 1978, pp 31–33

A commentary on a statistical study of fishing resources lost to member states in the waters of non-member countries in the North Atlantic as a result of changes in jurisdiction and other factors, such as the need for conservation. The purpose of the document is to provide the Council with information to be taken into account when determining the measures to be applied in 1978 for the management and exploitation of Community fisheries resources. The substantial statistical report upon which the commentary is based is annexed to the document.

Community fishing policy
SEC(78)195. 16 Jan 1978. 10p

A series of statistical tables presenting member states' overall catch possibilities, species by species, for 1978 as compared with their average catches for 1973 to 1976. The tables also indicate the percentage of the total Community catch proposed for each member country in 1978 and taken by each member country in the period 1973 to 1976. An associated document of the same title (SEC(78)196) consists of further statistical tables prepared in conjunction with proposals submitted to the Council in January 1978 (*see* 409).

Communication from the Commission to the Council concerning the development of the common fisheries policy
COM(78)661 final. 21 Nov 1978. 8p

During the course of 1978, the Commission made a number of unsuccessful attempts to break the deadlock on arrangements for the allocation, conservation and management of fishery resources within the framework of a common fisheries policy. In this fresh attempt to find a compromise solution, the Commission takes stock of the present position and identifies the main issues upon which political decisions are necessary before progress can be achieved. The Commission begins by recalling the various proposals made during the year, ranging from the comprehensive series of draft measures prepared for Council meetings in January 1978 (COM(78)4 final – COM(78)8 final), to the amended proposals concerning quotas and technical conservation measures submitted in September (COM(78)490 final), to the fresh series of proposals designed to regulate fishing activities in 1979 forwarded in November (COM(78)635 final & COM(78)622 final). The Commission then considers provisions made in such proposals and suggests guidelines whose acceptance would overcome the main causes of disagreement. However, negotiations in the Council failed to produce agreement and further interim measures for 1979 were made necessary.

CHAPTER 9

Transport

Descriptive essay

Together with agriculture and foreign trade, transport is one of the three policy areas in which the Treaty of Rome requires the adoption of a common policy. Articles 74–84 provide a general framework within which the common policy is to be evolved by Community institutions and the procedure for its implementation. Article 74 establishes the separateness of the common policy by declaring that the objectives of the Treaty, as they relate to transport, will be pursued by member states within the context of a common transport policy. Article 75 establishes an institutional procedure and refers to the need for priority measures to do with common rules for international transport, and the operation of transport services in member states by non-resident undertakings before the end of the transitional period. Most of the remaining Articles are concerned with the elimination of discriminatory practices, including the application of state aid. Article 83 provides for the creation of an advisory committee of experts to advise the Commission, and Article 84 confines the applicability of these provisions to transport by road, rail and inland waterway, although it leaves the Council to decide 'whether, to what extent and by what procedure appropriate provisions may be laid down for sea and air transport'.

This clear Treaty mandate for a common policy lends transport documentation its particular characteristics. The fact that the Treaty specifically provides for the adoption of a common policy for transport and embodies certain guiding principles and rules, largely explains the comparative dearth of major policy blueprints and the abundance of documents of a more practical or technical nature. Once the Commission had set down in the Schaus memorandum its views on the Treaty provisions (see 412), and then elaborated the ways in which it intended to implement them (see 413), the Commission tabled no further substantial policy documents of a general nature until 1973, when the goals set for the enlarged Community at the Paris summit caused a major rethink of the role of transport policy and its contribution to Community objectives (see 433). The Commission did take stock of the situation in 1967 (see 416) and again in 1971 (see 424), but these initiatives were more of an attempt to stimulate practical implementation of already established guidelines than truly innovative in terms of the development of an overall strategy.

The Treaty of Rome provides the Commission with a framework within which to operate, but it does not define the substance of policy in any detail. As a consequence the Commission prepares, from time-to-time, general communications in which it outlines its views on the development of strategy for particular aspects of policy, such as goods transport (*see* 437), investment in transport infrastructure (*see* 414) and infrastructure costing (*see* 421 & 439), supported by a constant stream of draft proposals for legislation to give effect to their provisions, and to the objectives of the EEC Treaty. What most characterizes transport documentation is the sheer number of specific proposals for legislation submitted by the Commission to the Council, many of which are tabled in accordance with the provision of overall action programmes which highlight areas in which priority measures are needed and which give notice of the Commission's legislative intentions. The 1962 action programme (*see* 413) led to the submission of a number of specific measures in 1963 and 1964; the measures adopted by the Council as a result of the 1967 action programme (*see* 416) are considered to be the first significant, if limited, step towards the actual implementation of a common transport policy. Again, most of the activities of the Commission since 1973 have been designed to achieve the objectives established in the 1973 programme (*see* 433).

Although the Commission has invested considerable effort in the preparation of individual proposals for legislation in the transport field, only spasmodic and piecemeal progress has been made in the introduction of a common transport policy. At the end of 1978, for instance, no less than 41 Commission proposals were still awaiting Council decision, some dating back to 1967. Documents of this nature are outside the scope of this bibliographical guide. However, many of them are listed in the *Bibliography on transport*, published as *Documentation bulletin* B/13.

A number of pieces of secondary legislation that have been adopted by the Council require the Commission to submit annual reports on their implementation. The Commission is, for instance, required to produce an annual report on the application of a Regulation on social legislation relating to transport (*see* 425), and another on the accounting system for expenditure on transport infrastructure (*see* 435). Such reports often contain useful summarized statistical data which facilitate comparisons between countries. Additional statistical information may be obtained from the series of annual publications published by the Statistical Office of the European Communities under the title *Statistiques des transports*. Since 1975 this publication has been called *Annual statistics transport and communications, tourism*, a title which reflects its expansion to include chapters on posts and telecommunications, and tourism. Short-term data is published in the *Monthly tables on transport*, also produced by the Statistical Office of the European Communities.

Bibliographical record

Recommandations de la Commission en vue du développement de l'infrastructure des transports dans le cadre de la Communauté
VII/COM(60)76 final. 21 June 1960. 21p

Recognizing that a coherent common transport policy implies the development of transport infrastructures within a Community rather than a national framework, the Commission makes suggestions in this document for improvements in national transport networks, with a view to their effect upon communication within the

Community as a whole. The document opens with general remarks and recommendations from the Commission addressed to the six member governments. The remainder of the document is given over to a country-by-country enumeration of specific projects concerning rail, road and inland waterway transport, whose completion would be of general Community benefit.

411 **Applicabilité aux transports des règles de concurrence énoncées dans le traité instituant la Communauté économique européenne et interpretation et application du Traité en ce qui concerne la navigation maritime et aérienne**
Doc VII/S/05230 final. 12 Nov 1960. 25p

A memorandum from the Commission to the Council on the interpretation and application of the Treaty of Rome as it concerns sea and air transport. Article 84 of the EEC Treaty leaves to the discretion of the Council decisions relating to the applicability of Treaty provisions to these two modes of transport. In this document the Commission argues the case for their consideration within the scope of an overall concept of transport policy, a point of view which was reiterated many times by both the Commission and the European Parliament before a decisive initiative was taken in 1972 (*see* 428).

412 **Mémorandum de la Commission sur l'orientation à donner à la politique commune des transports**
VII/COM(61)50 final. 10 Apr 1961. 2 vols, 128p, 138p

EP Report: *Doc de séance* 106/61. 11 Dec 1961. P.J. Kapteyn. 96p
           Doc de séance 18/62. 2 May 1962. E. Müller-Hermann. 43p
EP Debate: *Débs* No 57, 8 May 1962, pp 16–49
EP Resolution: *JO* 40, 26 May 1962, pp 1256–1257

Intended as a basis for a wide-ranging exchange of views with member governments and Community institutions in advance of the submission of formal proposals to implement Treaty provisions for transport policy, this document contains the Commission's initial views on the general lines of approach to be adopted and the procedures to be followed. Popularly referred to as the 'Schaus Memorandum' after Lambert Schaus, member of the Commission responsible for transport policy, the document is divided into three parts. Part 1 deals with the economic basis for the common policy, in which the Commission analyses the Treaty provisions for transport, not only as outlined in the specific Title for transport, but also as outlined in the general Treaty rules on such matters as competition and the right of establishment. In Part 2 the Commission highlights the main features of a common policy for transport, so designed as to achieve three general objectives, namely, the elimination of obstacles which transport may place in the way of the establishment of the common market, the integration of transport services at the Community level and the general organization of the transport system in the Community. The Commission also identifies a number of guiding principles that must be adhered to if these objectives are to be realized. Part 3 contains an outline of the provisions necessary for the implementation of the policy; it also deals with the procedures and time-table for the application of the measures proposed. A number of annexes contain information and statistical data on national transport systems. After studying the memorandum, the Council asked the Commission to submit a comprehensive action programme before the end of May 1962 (*see* 413).

Programme d'action en matière de politique commune des transports
VII/COM(62)88 final. 23 May 1962. 2 vols, 124p 34p

EP Report: *Doc de séance* 132/62. 30 Jan 1963. J. Brunhes. 28p
EP Debate: *Débs* No 61, 7 Feb 1962, pp 125–135 & 138–145
EP Resolution: *JO* 33, 4 Mar 1963, pp 451–452

Prepared as a result of an invitation from the Council of Ministers to follow up its general policy statement (*see* 412) with a time-tabled programme for coordinated action, this document is intended to serve as a basis for subsequent specific proposals. More detailed than the 1961 memorandum but compatible with its general principles, this action programme is divided into seven chapters each of which contains a package of measures. The chapters are concerned with access to the market, transport rates, harmonization of the tax, social and technical fields, coordination of investment, approximation of operating conditions and structures as between the different types of transport, the application of special Treaty provisions, particularly relating to discrimination, aids and agreements, and studies on transport costs. A separate annex lays down a precise time-table of decisions to be taken. In 1963 the Commission submitted the first package of formal proposals in accordance with the programme (VII/COM(63)165 – VII/COM(63)169). These proposals, published in a Supplement to the *Bulletin of the European Economic Community* 6-1963, were concerned with the organization of the market, integration at Community level and harmonization of competitive conditions.

Exposé de la politique commune des transports dans les domaines des investissements d'infrastructure et proposition de décision du Conseil relative à l'action de la Communauté dans le domaine des investissements d'infrastructure de transport
VII/COM(64)97 final. 8 Apr 1964. 26p

EP Report: *Doc de séance* 7/65. 17 Mar 1965. H. S. Seifriz. 27p
EP Debate: *Débs* No 77, 23 Mar 1965, pp 108–115
EP Resolution: *JO* 62, 12 Apr 1965, pp 902–904
ESC Opinion: *JO* 63, 13 Apr 1965, pp 948–951

A communication in which the Commission defines the aims of, and underlines the need for, action relating to investment in transport infrastructure because of its long-term importance to the successful implementation of a common transport policy and its contribution to general economic policy. The Commission identifies the problems to be overcome and discusses the methods to be used. Separate sections deal with the objectives of the action proposed, its place in the overall transport policy framework, the means of action and the first projected measures. The memorandum was published as a Supplement to the *Bulletin of the European Economic Community* 6-1964. After consideration of the memorandum and its appended draft Council Decision, the Council of Ministers was able on 28 February 1966 to adopt Decision 66/161/EEC introducing a procedure for information and consultation on investment projects (*JO* 42, 8 Mar 1966, pp 583–584). (*See also* 441.)

415 Options de la politique tarifaire dans les transports
Comm EEC, 1965. 206p (cat 8146)

The report of a group of independent experts under the chairmanship of Professor Maurice Allais, invited by the Commission to study certain problems relating to tariff systems for transport services and charging policy for the use of infrastructures. The terms of reference required the committee to inform the Commission of the problems of establishing and implementing a tariff policy, to list and describe the ways of ensuring a rational transport rates and charges policy, and to outline the nature and timing of the measures that would be needed to implement these schemes. The report, published as number one in the series *Etudes—Série transports*, is divided into three main sections. Part 1 is concerned with the theory of optimum resource allocation and its application to transport; Part 2 is concerned with the criteria and options available in transport policy and Part 3 consists of a critical analysis of the various systems. Several years later, Mr René Malcor prepared a report on behalf of the Commission on the problems posed by the practical application of a tariff system for the use of road infrastructures. The report was published in 1970 in a volume called *Les problèmes posés par l'application pratique d'une tarification pour l'utilisation des infrastructures routières* (cat 8255), issued as number two in the series *Etudes—Série transports*.

416 La politique commune des transports à la suite de la résolution du Conseil du 20 octobre 1966
SEC(67)346 final. 10 Feb 1967. 46p

A communication prepared in response to a request made by the Council of Ministers in its Resolution of 20 October 1966 for fresh measures relating to the organization of the transport market, in which the Commission examines how far it has been successful in translating the general lines of policy elaborated in the 1961 and 1962 initiatives (*see* 412 & 413) into practical reality, and tables specific proposals designed to speed up progress. The Commission first gives a detailed account of the measures placed before the Council of Ministers during the first two stages of the transitional period. This is followed by a section in which the Commission highlights those differences of opinion concerning earlier Commission proposals referred to in the Council Resolution and examines means for their solution. The Commission then proceeds to outline the various measures it proposes as solutions to these differences together with a practical programme to be implemented in two phases up to the end of 1973. In an annex the Commission reports progress in infrastructure cost studies (*see also* 417). The communication was published as a Supplement to the *Bulletin of the European Economic Community* 3-1967. On the basis of this memorandum, and one from the Italian delegation, the Council of Ministers decided on 14 December 1967 to adopt Decision 67/790/EEC (*JO* 322, 30 Dec 1967, pp 4–5), whose implementation, largely completed by early 1969, was a significant if limited step towards the implementation of a common transport policy.

417 Projet de rapport sur l'étude prévue par l'article 3 de la décision du

Conseil 65/279/CEE du 13 mai 1965
SEC(69)700 final. 12 Mar 1969. 450p

The report of a pilot study to determine and verify the conditions surrounding the application of the various possible ways of fixing rates for the use of infrastructures, carried out in accordance with Article 3 of Council Decision 65/270/EEC of 13 May 1965 (JO 88, 24 May 1965, pp 1473–1499). This Decision laid down implementing arrangements for the conduct of an exhaustive survey of the infrastructure expenditure incurred by member states in 1966, first proposed by the Commission in 1963 and adopted by the Council in Decision 64/389/EEC of 22 June 1964 (JO 102, 29 June 1964, pp 1598–1599). As a result of the delay in the preparation of this and the main reports (*see* 418 & 419), a progress report on the studies was annexed to a communication submitted to the Council of Ministers in 1967 (*see* 416).

418 Rapport de la Commission au Conseil sur les résultats de l'enquête sur les coûts des infrastructures servant aux transports par chemin de fer, par route et par voie navigable
SEC(69)2169 final. 16 June 1969. 230p

A report on the results of the survey of infrastructure costs carried out by the Commission in 1966 in accordance with Council Decision 64/389/EEC of 22 June 1964 (JO 102, 29 June 1964, pp 1598–1599). The object of the exercise was to determine the total costs of land transport infrastructures in the Community and the costs to be apportioned between the different categories of user. The report includes a statement of expenditure on infrastructure in each member country and a study of how the costs were covered. (*See also* 419.)

419 Rapport sur les résultats des recensements et sondages effectués en 1966 sur l'utilisation des infrastructures de transport dans le cadre de l'enquête sur les coûts des infrastructures
SEC(69)3450 final. 30 Sept 1969. 230p

A report on the results of the censuses and sample surveys carried out in 1966 on the use of transport infrastructures in connection with the survey of infrastructure costs (*see* 418).

420 Les transports maritimes des pays de la Communauté 1955, 1960 et 1967: étude statistique
Doc 396/70. May 1970. 144p

A statistical study recording the growth of goods transport by sea during the period from 1955 to 1967, undertaken at the request of the European Parliament and compiled from national data made available to the Commission. An updating study for the period 1967 to 1969, published by the Commission in an English language version in 1971 under the title *The sea transport of the countries of the Community 1968 and 1969: statistical study* (cat 17453), includes data on the position in the three new member countries.

421 Mémorandum sur la tarification de l'usage des infrastructures dans le

cadre de la politique commune des transports
COM(71)268 final. 24 Mar 1971. 105p

EP Report: *Working doc* 195/73. 5 Nov 1973. N. Kollwelter. 63p
EP Debate: *Annex OJ* No 168, 16 Nov 1973, pp 238–244
EP Resolution: *OJ* C108, 10 Dec 1973, pp 67–71
ESC Opinion: *OJ* C123, 27 Nov 1972, pp 11–29

A memorandum and proposals from the Commission concerning the introduction of a standard system of charges for the use of transport infrastructures. The Commission first explains why a common system for the allocation of infrastructure costs is essential if the common transport policy is to ensure the optimum use of resources and eliminate distortion of competitive conditions between the three modes of transport. The Commission also recalls, with useful reference to relevant documents and legislation, the various initiatives that have been taken since 1961 to resolve this long-standing problem. The Commission then moves on to define the objectives of a common tariff system on the basis of which it makes a critical appraisal of a number of alternatives and explains why the Commission favours a balanced budget solution based on social marginal costs. The report then explains in some detail the ways in which the Commission envisages the scheme being implemented for the three modes of transport. A draft Council Decision on charging for the use of transport infrastructures was appended to the document (*JO* C62, 22 June 1971, pp 15–17). In December 1971 the Council decided that before it could take a decision on this proposal, member states should carry out, and the Commission coordinate, detailed studies of the likely impact of the proposals on rail, road and inland waterway transport in member states (*see* 439).

422 **Rapport de la Commission au Conseil sur l'exécution des travaux décidés par le Conseil le 27 janvier 1970 en relation avec la proposition de première directive du Conseil concernant l'aménagement des systèmes nationaux de taxes sur les vehicules utilitaires**
SEC(71)2911 final. 28 July 1971. 325p

A report from the Commission to the Council on the likely impact of the application of the proposed first Council Directive on the adjustment of national systems of commercial vehicle taxation, submitted by the Commission on 17 July 1968 (*JO* C95, 21 Sept 1968, pp 41–44). When considering this proposal at its meeting on 26 and 27 January 1970, the Council decided that each member state should prepare calculations from which the likely consequences of the proposed Directive could be assessed. The report contains the results of this exercise on a country-by-country basis, and a series of observations and comparisons drawn from these national reports.

423 **Communication de la Commission au Conseil sur l'organisation commune du marché des transports**
SEC(71)3190 final. 14 Sept 1971. 12p

A discussion document from the Commission, the purpose of which is to stimulate discussion with the Council on the reasons for slow progress in certain areas of transport policy and the ways in which the situation may be remedied. The

Commission takes stock of the activities of Community institutions in this field and indicates where specific progress needs to be achieved. In an annex to the document the Commission enumerates the measures already tabled.

Développement de la politique commune des transports
SEC(71)3923 final. 5 Nov 1971. 21p

Following up a number of points made earlier in the year (*see* 423), this package of proposals from the Commission contains suggestions for the development of a full-scale common transport policy over the next five years. The Commission briefly recalls the general objectives of the common transport policy before presenting a selection of priority measures to be adopted according to a defined time-table and as part of an overall plan for the introduction of a genuine common policy. The actions to be taken are grouped under three headings, the coordination of transport infrastructure investment, infrastructure charging and the organization of the market. The document was published as Supplement 8/71 to the *Bulletin of the European Communities*.

Rapport de la Commission au Conseil concernant l'application du règlement (CEE) No 543/69 du Conseil, du 25 mars 1969, relatif à l'harmonisation de certaines dispositions en matière sociale dans le domaine du transports par route
1 Oct 1969 – 30 Sept 1970   SEC(71)4515 final. 20 Dec 1971. 16p
1 Oct 1970 – 30 Sept 1971   SEC(73)1688 final. 8 May 1973. 21p
1 Oct 1971 – 31 Dec 1972   SEC(74)1599 final. 28 May 1974. 30p
1 Jan 1973 – 31 Dec 1973   COM(75)616 final. 5 Dec 1975. 49p
1 Jan 1974 – 31 Dec 1974   COM(77)170 final. 13 May 1977. 12p

An annual report presented to the Council on the application by member states of Council Regulation (EEC) No 543/69 of 25 Mar 1969 on the harmonization of certain social legislation relating to road transport (*JO* L77, 29 Mar 1969, pp 49–60). Each report summarizes information received from member states on the nature and operation of their administrative machinery for checking implementation, including data on the number and nature of infringements and charges brought. In 1976 the Commission made proposals for the modification of the Regulation on the basis of five years experience in its application (COM(76) 85 final). (*See also* 436.)

Aperçu des conditions de travail dans la navigation intérieure dans les pays de la Communauté: rapport de synthèse
Doc V/VII/17/72. n.d. 42p

A review of working conditions prevalent aboard shipping on inland waterways, compiled by the Commission from the results of a questionnaire survey, and from other information received from member states and other relevant professional organizations. The report contains comparative data on such topics as age and health regulations, working hours and rest periods.

Rapport de la Commission au Conseil sur les dispositions adoptées par les états membres pour l'exécution du règlement (CEE) No 1174/68 du

Conseil du 30 juillet 1968 relatif à l'instauration d'un système de tarifs à fourchettes applicables aux transports de marchandises par route entre les états membres
SEC(72)1149 final. 24 Mar 1972. 47p

A report from the Commission concerning the application in member states of Council Regulation (EEC) No 1174/68 of 30 July 1968 on the introduction of a system of bracket tariffs for the carriage of goods by road between member states (*JO* L194, 6 Aug 1968, pp 1–5).

428 **Projet de décision (CEE) du Conseil relatif aux premiers éléments d'une action commune en matière de transport aérien**
COM(72)695 final. 21 June 1972. 9p

EP Report: *Doc de séance* 195/72. 10 Jan 1973. L. Noe'. 45p
Doc de séance 328/72. 14 Mar 1973. L. Noe'. 9p
EP Debate: *Annex OJ* No 157, 17 Jan 1973, pp 78–91
EP Resolution: *OJ* C19, 12 Apr 1973, pp 51–55
ESC Opinion: *OJ* C100, 22 Nov 1973, pp 1–5

A limited proposal from the Commission designed to give impetus to the moves to bring air transport within the scope of the common transport policy. The proposal, published in the *Journal officiel des Communautés européennes* C110, 18 Oct 1972, p 6, goes no further than to provide for the examination of possible ways of initiating joint measures and asks the Council to study what should be done to initiate a common air transport policy.

429 **Aide-mémoire de la Commission sur les transports comme moyens d'action de la politique régionale et de l'aménagement du territoire sur le plan de la Communauté**
SEC(72)3827 final. 31 Oct 1972. 16p

See 464.

430 **Coordination of investments in transport infrastructures: analysis— recommendations—procedures**
Comm EC, 1973. 87p (cat 8423)

A study on the coordination of investments in transport infrastructures, compiled at the request of the Commission by a group of eminent academics from European universities and published as number three in the *Studies—Transport series*. The terms of reference require the group to submit a report 'comprising an investigation at methodological and operational level, of the problems of coordination on investment in transport infrastructure, in the context of the general philosophy of the common transport policy and taking into account more particularly (i) the need to guarantee the provision of services at least costs for the collectivity, as well as the use of the most efficient techniques of transport; (ii) the need to guarantee equal treatment between the various modes of transport; (iii) the setting of a pricing system for the use of infrastructure which guarantees budgetary balance'. After an introductory chapter the group, consisting of K. M. Gwilliam, S. Petriccione, F. Voigt and J. A.

Zighera, consider methodological problems and particularly the relationship between investment appraisal and user pricing principles. The group then discuss the framework for demand forecasting and the ways in which cost-benefit analysis can be more appropriately applied. The final chapter describes the administrative procedures to be applied.

Report on the implementation of Council Regulation (EEC) No 1191/69 of 26 June 1969, relating to the action by Member States concerning the obligations inherent in the concept of a public service in transport by rail, road and inland waterway
SEC(73)519 final. 16 Feb 1973. 17p

A report on the current situation in each member state as regards the implementation of Council Regulation (EEC) No 1191/69 of 26 June 1969 (*JO* L156, 28 June 1969, pp 1–7). The report contains a country-by-country review and synthesis of data in which the Commission makes observations and draws some tentative conclusions. (*See also* 434.)

Development of the common transport policy
COM(73)850 final. 30 May 1973. 22p

EP Report: *Working doc* 215/74. 16 Sept 1974. K. H. Mursch. 164p
EP Debate: *Annex OJ* No 181, 25 Sept 1974, pp 71–92
EP Resolution: *OJ* C127, 18 Oct 1974, pp 24–28

A working paper in which the Commission seeks to give fresh impetus to the common transport policy, and to define more clearly its role in the context of an enlarged Community given new vigour by the positive expressions of political will made at the Paris summit meeting. The Commission considers the measures that are needed to complete the common organization of the transport market and the harmonization of competitive conditions and makes proposals for their implementation. The document concludes with remarks relating to the extension of Community action into the sea and air transport fields.

Communication from the Commission to the Council on the development of the common transport policy
COM(73)1725. 24 Oct 1973. 38p

EP Report: *Working doc* 215/74. 16 Sept 1974. K. H. Mursch. 164p
EP Debate: *Annex OJ* No 181, 25 Sept 1974, pp 71–92
EP Resolution: *OJ* C127, 18 Oct 1974, pp 24–28
ESC Opinion: *OJ* C126, 17 Oct 1974, pp 26–32
            OJ C286, 15 Dec 1975, pp 1–5

A major policy initiative from the Commission in which it attempts to stimulate renewed commitment to the development of a common policy for transport, closely linked with other common policies, in the pursuit of the objectives of the enlarged Community as defined at the Paris summit meeting. In Part 1 the Commission analyses the changes that have taken place in the transport sector, and the ways in which the scope of transport policy needs to be extended beyond the objectives defined in the EEC Treaty if it is to contribute to the achievement of goals set at the Paris summit. Particular prominence is given to the need to strengthen links between transport policy and social, industrial, environmental, energy and other policies. Part 2 of the memorandum consists of a programme of action to be undertaken during the three year period 1974 to 1976, divided into measures that will be the subject of Commission initiatives, measures already placed before the Council and measures that need to be studied by the Commission before decisions are taken. The memorandum was published as Supplement 16/73 to the *Bulletin of the European Communities*. This memorandum became the basis for the Commission's work programme in the field of transport in the following years, although there was little progress in the Council on the definition of an overall concept of transport policy.

434 **Second report on the implementation of Council Regulation (EEC) No 1191/69 of 26 June 1969, relating to the action by Member States concerning the obligations inherent in the concept of a public service in transport by rail, road and inland waterway and of Council Regulation (EEC) No 1192/69 of 26 June 1969 relating to the harmonization of the accounts of railway undertakings**
SEC(74)2219 final. 18 June 1974. 35p

A second report on the implementation of Council Regulation (EEC) No 1191/69 of 26 June 1969 (*JO* L156, 28 June 1969, pp 1–7), drawn up by the Commission as a result of the call for amplification of information contained in the first report (*see* 431), and for further consideration of how the implementing measures taken by member states may be harmonized. The report opens with a summary of the de facto situation as it appears in member states in relation to both Regulation (EEC) No 1191/69 and also Council Regulation (EEC) No 1192/69 of 26 June 1969 on the harmonization of the accounts of railway undertakings (*JO* L156, 28 June 1969, pp 8–20). The Commission then turns to the chief problems which the application of these Regulations appear to raise at the present time, and makes certain observations and draws a number of conclusions upon which the Council is invited to express an opinion. (*See also* 444.)

435 **Report from the Commission to the Council on the results obtained from the accounting system for expenditure relating to rail, road and inland waterway transport infrastructures**
1st SEC(74)5285 final. 13 Jan 1975. 101p
2nd COM(75)312 final. 27 June 1975. 64p
3rd COM(76)53 final. 23 Feb 1976. 51p
4th COM(77)26 final. 18 Feb 1977. 62p
5th COM(78)48 final. 14 Feb 1978. 71p
6th COM(79)95 final. 6 Mar 1979. 77p

An annual statistical report on transport infrastructure expenditure and use, submitted by the Commission in accordance with Council Regulation (EEC) No 1108/70 of 4 June 1970 introducing an accounting system for transport infrastructure expenditure (*JO* L130, 15 June 1970, pp 4–14). Part 1 contains tabular results of the expenditure of each member state on road, rail and inland waterway transport infrastructures. Part 2 provides data on the volume of traffic using road, rail and inland waterway infrastructures in each member state. An annex includes unofficial figures for new member countries and a summary and preliminary analysis of the data.

36 Report relative to Article 13(2) of Regulation (EEC) No 543/69 of 25 March 1969 on the harmonization of certain social legislation relating to road transport
SEC(75)1637 final. 13 May 1975. 30p

The first two-yearly report on the situation regarding the fields covered by Council Regulation (EEC) No 543/69 of 25 March 1969 (JO L77, 29 Mar 1969, pp 49–60), presented to the Council in accordance with Article 13(2) of that Regulation. Covering the period from 1 October 1969 to 30 September 1971, the report is divided into two main parts. In Part 1 the Commission reviews the laws, regulations and administrative provisions concerning minimum age of drivers, driving periods, rest periods in force in member countries on 30 September 1971. Part 2 consists of comments and observations from member governments, professional and trade union organizations and conclusions from the Commission. (*See also* 425.)

37 Communication from the Commission to the Council on the operation of the markets in surface goods transport within the Community (road, rail and inland waterway)
COM(75)490 final. 1 Oct 1975. 92p

A communication in which the Commission sketches the main features of the current situation regarding inland transport markets in the Community, as a background against which the Council can consider eight specific proposals for Regulations annexed to the document, and designed to facilitate the gradual establishment of a Community goods transport market based on free enterprise (*OJ* C1, 5 Jan 1976, pp 28–31). The Commission studies the operation of inland freight transport markets with particular reference to the coordination of investments, charging for the use of infrastructures and harmonization of the conditions of competition. The Commission then discusses its long-term concept of the organization of the transport market, and elaborates upon the specific measures to be taken during the transitional period mentioned in the 1973 memorandum (*see* 433).

38 Report on the present situation of the goods transport markets in the Community
COM(75)491 final. 1 Oct 1975. 73p

An attempt to set the context within which specific proposals can follow later, this descriptive report from the Commission is in two main parts. In the first the Commission describes the main features of the national goods transport markets in the enlarged Community, in the light of the laws and regulations in force in member states, the development of goods transport and trends in transport rates. In the second part the Commission considers how far the operation of the transport market has contributed to Treaty objectives. Separate sections deal in turn with how the organization of the transport markets contributes to the development of the common market, the competitive situation of the market, integration of the transport sector, the common organization of transport markets in the context of the advance towards general policy objectives, and the effectiveness of state intervention in the common organization of the transport markets. An annex contains a description of the legal and regulatory situation in member countries and at the Community level.

439 Commission's interim report to the Council of Ministers on charging for the use of transport infrastructures
COM(75)493 final. 3 Oct 1975. 66p

A progress report, the purpose of which is to keep the Council informed of developments concerning the implementation of a common system of charging for the use of transport infrastructures. The Commission reports on studies that have been put in hand in response to the request from the Council that such studies should assess the potential impact of the implementation of the Commission's 1971 proposals (*see* 421). The Commission highlights those directions in which progress can be achieved and refers to outstanding problems. An annex contains the text of the 1971 proposal, the object of which was to identify all the costs arising from the use of road, rail and inland waterway infrastructures, to find out precisely who carried these costs and subsequently to recover the costs from the users responsible, amended in the light of the comments made by the European Parliament and the Economic and Social Committee.

440 The analysis of economic costs and expenses in road and rail transport
Comm EC, 1976. 36p (cat 8725)

A memorandum prepared by Professor Ralph Turvey and published as number four in the *Studies—Transport series*, whose purpose is to compare and contrast the cost concept which is relevant to the economic analysis of transport with that of the traditional cost analysis. Chapter 1 relates to the nature of economic cost; Chapter 2 consists of a critical examination of traditional expense analysis; Chapter 3 considers the implications of applying the concept of economic cost.

441 Communication from the Commission to the Council on action in the field of transport infrastructure
COM(76)336 final. 30 June 1976. 26p

EP Report: *Working doc 377/76*. 8 Nov 1976. K. Nyborg. 9p
　　　　　Working doc 185/77. 4 July 1977. K. Nyborg. 30p
EP Debate: *Annex OJ* No 209, 18 Nov 1976, pp 216–219
EP Resolution: *OJ* C293, 13 Dec 1976, p 57

Although it was recognized in the 1973 blueprint (*see* 433) that the establishment of a Community transport system would require measures in the infrastructure sector, the initial package of measures related mainly to the organization of the transport market. This memorandum seeks to give new impetus to progress in infrastructure policy by defining more clearly the main guidelines of policy. The Commission explains why new initiatives are necessary, establishes certain guiding principles and considers their practical implementation. Two specific proposals annexed to the document seek to improve and extend the consultation procedure established in 1966 (*see* 414) and to provide financial help for projects in the infrastructure field (*OJ* C207, 2 Sept 1976, pp 7–10). On 20 February 1978 the Council adopted Decision 78/174/EEC instituting a consultation procedure and setting up a committee in the field of transport infrastructure (*OJ* L54, 25 Feb 1978, pp 16–17).

Communication from the Commission to the Council on the Community's relations with non-member countries in shipping matters
COM(76)341 final. 30 June 1976. 19p

EP Report: *Working doc* 5/77. 23 Mar 1977. H. Seefeld. 44p
EP Debate: *Annex OJ* No 216, 20 Apr 1977, pp 155–161
EP Resolution: *OJ* C118, 16 May 1977, pp 41–43

A document prepared in response to the problems increasingly experienced by the Commission in its dealings with non-member countries in shipping matters. The Commission first emphasizes the importance of shipping to the Community's internal and external trade, then proceeds to outline the nature of the difficulties and problems being encountered in external maritime trade, with particular reference to flag discrimination, the disruptive effect of subsidies and dumping practices. A number of broad lines of action to meet these problems are suggested, considered under the headings of bilateral agreements, multilateral agreements and counter measures against flag discrimination.

Report of an enquiry into the current situation in the major Community sea-ports drawn up by the Port Working Group
Comm EC, 1977. 200p (cat CB-22-77-863-EN-C)

The report of a working group composed of representatives from the major European port authorities under the chairmanship of a representative from the Commission, charged with compiling a detailed report on the institutional and administrative structure of ports in the Communities. The terms of reference instruct the group '(a) to establish for the purpose of its work, definitions of the terms used in the area of port authorities; (b) on the basis of the results of this work to describe the existing situation ("fact-finding") especially insofar as it concerns the organizational structure of ports; the division of responsibility between public and private bodies concerned in port authority; operational conditions of each organization, whether public or private; financial and taxation matters of each organization, whether public or private; statistics currently provided by port authorities'. In Part 1 the working group describes the background to the report, the group's composition, its terms of reference and work programme. It also includes the questionnaire distributed to port authorities. Part 2 consists of an overall summary of the main results of the survey, with chapters on ports structure, internal organization, external relations, dues and charges, division of responsibility and powers, financial and associated questions, employment and statistics. Part 3 consists of summaries of the situation in each member state.

First biennial report on the economic and financial situation of railway undertakings (Article 14 of Decision 75/327/EEC)

COM(77)295 final. 29 June 1977. 90p

Article 14 of Council Decision 75/327/EEC of 20 May 1975 on the improvement of the situation of railway undertakings and the harmonization of rules governing financial relations between such undertakings and states declares that 'every two years, the Commission shall submit to the Council a report on the implementation by Member States of this Decision and of Regulations (EEC) No 1191/69, (EEC) No 1192/69 and (EEC) No 1107/70'. The intention was for such reports to provide a clear picture of the situation of railway undertakings and thus to make it possible to discern the measures to be taken to achieve progressive improvements and financial equilibrium. (*See also* 434.)

445 Priority business for a Council working programme to 1980
COM(77)596 final. 24 Nov 1977. 10p

EP Report: *Working doc* 512/78. 5 Jan 1979. H. Seefeld. 83p
EP Debate: *Annex OJ* No 238, 15 Jan 1979, pp 13–26
EP Resolution: *OJ* C39, 12 Feb 1979, pp 16–18

A programme of priority actions in the field of transport policy, drawn up by the Commission to assist the Council in deciding its work programme for the period 1977 to 1980. Viewed essentially as a means of implementing the agreed aims of the 1973 blueprint (*see* 433), the document lists a whole range of priority measures for action during this three year period and explains why they are relevant and urgent. The document concludes with a draft Council Resolution adopting the programme and a time-table of decisions to be taken by the Council in each of the three years concerned. As yet the Council has not adopted the programme.

446 Report on the application of the Council directive of 17th February 1975 concerning the establishment of common rules for certain combined rail/road carriage of goods between Member States
COM(77)676 final. 15 Dec 1977. 24p

A report to the Council on the application of Council Directive 75/130/EEC of 17 February 1975, Article 7 of which lays down that the Commission shall make a report on its implementation before the end of December 1977 (*OJ* L48, 22 Feb 1975, pp 31–32). Based on views obtained from professional organizations in member states, the document contains the Commission's opinions on the measures taken by member states to apply the Directive and on the need for continued action at national and Community level.

447 Report by the Commission to the Council on the progress made in the preparation of a programme of cooperation among railway undertakings
COM(77)694 final. 20 Dec 1977. 29p

A progress report on the preparation of a work programme to promote cooperation among railway undertakings, devised by the Commission in the context of Council Decision 75/327/EEC of 20 May 1975 on the improvement of the situation of railway undertakings and the harmonization of rules governing financial relations between such undertakings and states (*OJ* L152, 12 June 1975, pp 3–7). After introductory remarks, the Commission reviews earlier Community measures to promote cooperation among railway undertakings before outlining new Commission initiatives. The Commission then presents a resumé and assessment of the general questions incorporated in the short-term programme drafted by the Group of Nine Railways of the Community on the strengthening of international cooperation. The Commission also suggests a series of supplementary measures to be taken in a number of defined fields before concluding with comments on the respective responsibilities of the railways, member states and the Community.

CHAPTER 10

Regional policy

Descriptive essay

No single chapter or title of the Treaty of Rome pertains specifically to regional policy. However, the architects of the Treaty did give implicit recognition to the need for balanced economic development within the Community and the elimination of disparities between regions. In the Preamble to the Treaty, for instance, the signatories refer to their desire 'to strengthen the unity of their economies and to ensure their harmonious development by reducing the differences existing between the various regions and the backwardness of the less favoured regions'. These sentiments are echoed in Article 2 which established the task of the Community to be 'to promote throughout the Community a harmonious development of economic activities, a continuous and balanced expansion, an increase in stability, an accelerated raising of the standard of living and closer relations between the states belonging to it'. Furthermore, there are a number of explicit references in specific Articles to Community regions, usually providing for exceptions to general rules in order to give special assistance to backward areas. However, it cannot be said that these references, even in association with the regional implications of provisions for common policies in such fields as agriculture and transport, together add up to a clear mandate for an overall Community regional policy.

As a consequence, progress during the 1960s towards the definition of a coherent regional policy was both gradual and disjointed. Tangible assistance to Community regions was mainly channelled through other Community financial instruments, notably the Guidance Section of the European Guidance and Guarantee Fund (*see* Chapter 8), the loan and guarantee operations of the European Investment Bank, the retraining and resettlement opportunities offered by the European Social Fund (*see* Chapter 12) and the provisions made in Article 56 of the Treaty of Paris concerning reconversion in the coal and steel industries.

That is not to say, of course, that efforts were not made during the 1960s to initiate a positive Community regional policy. Documents listed in this chapter reveal that the Commission was by no means inactive in this matter. In 1961 the Commission organized an international exchange of information and views on regional policy (*see* 451) which subsequently led to the formation of three specialized working parties whose reports (*see* 452–454) were of assistance to the Commission in the preparation of its first major policy statement on an overall regional policy in 1965 (*see* 455). This was followed in 1969 by another major policy initiative and important proposals for giving regional policy an institutional and financial focus (*see* 457).

However, it may be said that genuine Community regional policy dates from October 1972 when the Heads of State or Government meeting in Paris in the first summit conference of the enlarged Community, declared their political will to 'give top priority to correcting the structural and regional imbalances in the Community' and invited the Commission to prepare as soon as possible a report on regional problems in the enlarged Community. Member states also committed themselves to coordinating their regional policies and invited Community institutions to set up a European Regional Development Fund by 31 December 1973. In fulfilment of this mandate, the Commission prepared and submitted to the Council a seminal document on regional policy in May 1973, which became the blueprint upon which subsequent specific proposals were based (*see* 466). Adoption of these proposals, albeit late and after much wrangling within the Council, saw the introduction in 1975 of a genuine, if modestly funded, Community regional policy.

Financial assistance for regional development is channelled through the European Regional Development Fund, established by Council Regulation (EEC) No 724/75 of 18 March 1975 for the purpose of making available to member governments investment grants to cover a percentage of the cost of suitable industrial development and infrastructure projects in the Community's problem areas (*OJ* L73, 21 Mar 1975, pp 1–7). Valuable information on the impact of the Fund on regional development is provided in the annual reports presented by the Commission to the Council and the European Parliament on the Fund's management (*see* 468). Additional information of a general nature appears in the *General report on the activities of the European Communities* and in the *Bulletin of the European Communities*. Lists of projects, for which assistance has been granted from the Fund, are published periodically in the 'C' series of the *Official journal of the European Communities* on a country-by-country basis. It should also be noted that towards the end of the period under review, the Commission undertook a fundamental appraisal of regional policy and of Fund operations (*see* 469).

The second main instrument of regional policy is the Regional Policy Committee created by Council Decision 75/185/EEC of 18 March 1975 (*OJ* L73, 21 Mar 1975, pp 47–48) and composed of senior civil servants from member countries serviced by the Commission. The task of the Committee, in the words of the Decision, is one of 'examining, at the request of the Council or of the Commission, or on its own initiative, problems relating to regional development, progress made or to be made towards solving them and regional policy measures needed to further the achievement of the Community's regional objectives'. A report from the Regional Policy Committee, containing a summary of its activities during the first two years of its existence, some initial conclusions based on this experience and some indications of its work programme for the immediate future, was published in the *Official journal of the European Communities* C210, 2 Sept 1977, pp 1–5.

Illustrative of the important coordinating role attaching to the Regional Policy Committee is its work concerning regional development programmes. Article 6 of the Council Regulation establishing the European Regional Development Fund stipulates that 'investments may benefit from the Fund's assistance only if they fall within the framework of a regional development programme, the implementation of which is likely to contribute to the correction of the main regional imbalances within the Community which are likely to prejudice the attainment of economic and monetary union'. Such programmes, 'which constitute the reference framework for assessing ERDF projects', were to be submitted by the end of 1977 according to a common outline to be produced by the Regional Policy Committee before 31 December 1975. This outline was subsequently prepared and published in the *Official journal of the European Communities* C69, 24 Mar 1976, pp 2–5 and used by member governments as guidance for the compilation of national regional development programmes, summaries of which were published by the Committee in 1979 in a volume called *The regional development programmes* (cat CB-NS-79-017-EN-C. ISBN 92-825-1221-5), issued as number 17 in the *Studies—Regional policy series*. Further volumes in the same series reproduce the complete programmes for France (cat CN-NS-78-013-EN-C. ISBN 92-025-0796-3); Denmark (cat CB-NS-78-012-EN-C. ISBN 92-825-0617-7); Luxembourg (cat CB-NS-78-011-EN-C. ISBN 92-825-0614-2); United Kingdom (cat CB-NS-78-010-EN-C. ISBN 92-825-0491-3); the Netherlands (cat CB-NS-78-008-EN-C. ISBN 92-825-9525-1); Ireland (cat CB-NS-78-007-FR-C. ISBN 92-825-0659-2); and Greenland (cat CB-NS-77-002-EN-C).

It will be apparent from a number of the documents represented in this chapter that another Community aim in the field of regional policy has been to coordinate the principles upon which national governments grant state aids to encourage and promote economic activity in particular regions. Article 92 of the EEC Treaty declares that 'save as otherwise provided in this Treaty, any aid granted by a Member State of through State resources in any form whatsoever which distorts or threatens to distort competition by favouring certain undertakings or the production of certain goods shall, in so far as it affects trade between Member States, be incompatible with the common market'. In order to ensure that regional aids and subsidies do not distort competition, the Commission proposed and the Council accepted in 1971 a common set of principles and rules to govern regional aid schemes in the most industrialized regions (*see* 461 & 465), later revised and extended to all regions in 1975 (*see* 467) and further refined in 1978 (*see* 470).

An essential management tool for the prosecution of an active Community regional policy is a body of statistical data whose presentation, according to common standards and definitions, facilitates the clear and accurate assessment of regional disparities within the Community. Recognizing the need for sound management data to assist the Community decision-making process, the Statistical Office of the European Communities has invested considerable time and effort in the preparation of comparable statistics. A notable feature of this work has been the preparation of a Nomenclature of Statistical Territorial Units (NUTS), which has been used to define Community regions in the compilations of regional statistics published by the Statistical Office.

The most wide-ranging of the regional statistics published by the Statistical Office is *Regional statistics: main regional indicators 1970–1977*, published for the first time in 1978 as a statistical analysis and commentary on the principal regional economic and social indicators for the period 1970 to 1977. The social statistics presented in this publication are analysed in more depth in a separate annual publication called *Regional statistics: population, employment, living standards*, whose title reflects its three main areas of concern. Other tables in the general compendium of regional indicators mentioned above are supplemented by another annual publication

Regional statistics: Community's financial participation in investments, which gives details of investment grants from the EAGGF, ERDF and loans from the EIB and from the ECSC under the terms of the Treaty of Paris. Another publication, called *Regional accounts: economic aggregates*, presents the results of the work on regional accounting carried out by the statistical offices of member states on the initiative of the Statistical Office of the European Communities.

Bibliographical record

Politiques régionales des états-membres de la CEE : étude préliminaire
Doc II/5387/59. Nov 1959. 42p

A preliminary study of the regional policies and instruments pursued in member states, prepared by the Commission as a first step towards achieving the general objectives established in the EEC Treaty, Article 2 of which talks about promoting a harmonious development of economic activities' and 'a continuous and balanced expansion'.

Note sur le problème du développement régional dans la Communauté économique européenne
Doc II/5107/60. n.d. 14p

An early and rather general discussion of regional policy in the Community context. Divided into five sections, the paper first debates the regional dimensions in economic development before using a number of criteria to illustrate the Community's lack of homogeneity. Further discussion of the general conditions required for harmonious regional development precedes a brief analysis of the likely effect of the common market on regional economic development, with particular reference to the customs union and the institutional provisions of the EEC Treaty. The document concludes with a summary of its contents.

Essai de délimitation régionale de la Communauté économique européenne
Doc II/747/2/61. 30 Jan 1961. 173p

The report of a working party of experts on regional policy, charged by the Commission with the task of compiling as complete and accurate a picture of the regions of the Community as available data would permit. Conceived as an essential preliminary to work on regional policy proper, the report first identifies and then describes in turn the various regions and their characteristics in each member country. A separate annex contains a useful collation of statistical data. The report was published as an annex to volume two of *Documents de la conférence sur les économies régionales, Bruxelles 6–8 décembre 1961* (see 451).

Documents de la conférence sur les économies régionales, Bruxelles 6–8 décembre 1961
Comm EEC, 1963. 2 vols, 457p, 241p (cat 8048)

A record of the proceedings of the conference of experts and high-ranking officials called by the Commission to Brussels in December 1961. The conference represented the Commission's first major initiative in the field of regional policy, intended as an opportunity for officials to establish closer relations and to exchange experience, to highlight the Community dimension of regional policy and to assist the Commission in formulating general principles and objectives. Volume 1 contains the inaugural speeches together with 20 reports presented to the two working groups into which the conference was divided. Group A, under the chairmanship of Sicco Mansholt, studied the problem of the peripheral agricultural and frontier regions; Group B examined the techniques of regional development. Volume 2 contains the reports and concluding speeches presented to the final plenary session, and a number of annexes which include a paper on regional delimitation prepared by experts from member countries, and statistical data on the regions of each member country.

452 Rapport sur les objectifs et les méthodes de la politique régionale dans la Communauté européenne
Doc II/720/5/64. n.d. 113p

A report from one of the three working parties established by the Commission to examine certain problems thrown into relief by the Conference on Regional Economies (*see* 451). This working party, under the chairmanship of Dr W. Langer, was given the task of studying the objectives and methods of regional policy. After a discussion of general principles, the working party looks more closely at the elements of the regional economy, particularly the role of infrastructures and the contribution of agriculture and industry. The working party then distinguishes between a number of types of region and examines the broad lines of regional policy that are applicable to them. Further chapters are concerned with the elaboration of a regional policy and with the various means for its implementation, including financial and fiscal incentives and infrastructure programmes. The report, together with a series of annexes containing contributions from individual members of the working party on the policy followed by each member state, and a note from the European Investment Bank in favour of regional development, was published by the Commission in 1965, together with reports from two other working parties (*see* 453 & 454), in a volume called *Rapports de groupes d'experts sur la politique régionale dans la Communauté économique européenne* (cat 8154).

453 L'adaption des régions d'ancienne industrialisation
Doc II/1962/2/64. n.d. 183p

The report prepared by the second of three working parties established by the Commission to give further consideration to matters brought to its attention during the Conference on Regional Economies in 1961 (*see* 451). Chaired by F. Persoons, the task of the working party was to examine the problems of areas where long-established industries were in decline. In the first part of the report, the working party analyses the difficulties these regions experience in adapting to changed economic circumstances. The working party then moves on to look more closely at the possibilities for change and the problems attendant upon major adjustment to changed economic circumstances. A third section consists of a series of conclusions and suggestions for future action. Together with a number of annexes, the report was published by the Commission in 1965 in a volume called *Rapports de groupes d'experts sur la politique régionale dans la Communauté économique européenne* (cat 8154).

Rapport sur moyens de la politique régionale dans les états-membres de la C.E.E.
Doc II/1045/4/64. 20 May 1964. 97p

A report from the third working party established by the Commission as a consequence of the Conference on Regional Economies (*see* 451). Charged with an investigation of the instruments of regional policy this working party, under the chairmanship of F. Bloch-Laine, produced a three-part report. In the first part, the working party considers incentives and advantages to be granted in the area of infrastructure. The second part is concerned with financial advantages, and the third part with the adaptation of administrative organization and the problems of regional development. The report was published by the Commission in 1965 in a volume entitled *Rapports de groupes d'experts sur la politique régionale dans la Communauté économique européenne* (cat 8154).

Première communication de la Commission sur la politique régionale dans la Communauté économique européenne
II/SEC(65)1170 final. 11 May 1965. 104p

EP Report: *Doc de séance* 58/66. 23 May 1966. G. Bersani. 78p
EP Debate: *Débs* No 86, 27 June 1966, pp 23–41 & 43–54
EP Resolution: *JO* 130, 19 July 1966, pp 2427–2429

The Commission's first major presentation of an overall concept of regional policy, based on conclusions reached by the three working groups set up to consider regional problems (*see* 452–454) and other preparatory studies. The first section is concerned with the aims and methods of regional policy in the Community. It defines the basic considerations concerning regional policy objectives and makes suggestions concerning the role and nature of regional programmes. In the second section, the Commission considers the principal instruments of regional policy available to both member governments and Community institutions. It gives attention to the various ways in which member governments can promote regional policy through, for instance, financial assistance. The Commission also examines the means at the disposal of the Community, both in respect of the ways in which such policies as the common agricultural policy, common transport policy and energy policy can contribute to the correction of regional imbalances, and in respect of the financial instruments which the Community can bring to bear through the European Investment Bank, ECSC loans and grants from the Social Fund and the European Agricultural Guidance and Guarantee Fund. The Commission then considers a number of procedural matters, before concluding with a series of recommendations in which it outlines an action programme designed to realize the objectives of a Community regional policy. The findings of the three working parties referred to above are summarized in a series of annexes. The memorandum and its annexes were subsequently published as *Community topics*, 24.

456 **Problèmes de la politique régionale**
In Doc 788/II/1966 final. 25 Mar 1966. 127p

See 63.

457 **Proposition de décision du Conseil relative à l'organisation de moyens d'action de la Communauté en matière de développement régional et note sur la politique régionale dans la Communauté**
COM(69)950. 15 Oct 1969. 271p

EP Report: *Doc de séance* 29/70. 11 May 1970. K. Mitterdorfer. 53p
EP Debate: *Annexe JO* No 125, 12 May 1970, pp 23–58
EP Resolution: *JO* C65, 5 June 1970, pp 22–29
ESC Opinion: *JO* C108, 26 Aug 1970, pp 12–19

This major Commission blueprint consists of two separate documents and two annexes. The first document is a discussion paper in which the Commission outlines its general approach to regional policy. In successive chapters it examines the nature of the regional problems facing the Community, the objectives of regional policy and the ways in which it can be put into operation. Two substantial annexes collate much of the statistical data upon which the Commission's philosophy is based. In Annex 1 the Commission examines the measures taken in each member country to solve its own regional problems; in Annex 2 the Commission uses the rather inadequate statistical data to present an overall Community perspective of regional development. The memorandum serves as a background to the second and more specific document, which takes the form of a draft proposal to the Council for measures to implement a practical regional policy. The draft proposal recommends the compilation of regional development plans, their examination in a Standing Regional Development Committee and the creation of a Regional Development Rebate Fund to facilitate their implementation (*JO* C152, 28 Nov 1969, pp 6–9). The two documents were published as Supplement 12/69 to the *Bulletin of the European Communities* and in a separate publication issued by the Commission in 1969, the English language version of which was called *A regional policy for the Community* (cat 5058).

458 **Rapport sur les moyens financiers pour le développement régional**
SEC(70)4377 final. 5 Dec 1970. 24p

Prepared by the Commission as a further contribution to the debate on its 1969 proposals (*see* 457), this document describes the financial resources presently available for the amelioration of regional problems and illustrates their inadequacy as instruments of regional development.

459 **L'évolution régionale dans la Communauté : bilan analytique**
Comm EC, 1971. 316p (cat 8369)

A publication in which the Commission updates and expands the preliminary assessment of regional development in the Community contained in the annexes to the 1969 memorandum (*see* 457). Main sections deal with population trends, including its increase, movement and regional distribution, employment in agriculture, industry and services and with regional product and income. The report concludes with a substantial statistical annex. The report was published in an English language version under the title *Regional development in the Community: analytical survey*. The analysis of regional structures and policies contained in this volume was extended to the new member countries in three supplementary documents prepared in 1972, *Structures et politiques économiques régionales du Danemark* (doc XVI/33/72), *Structures et politiques économiques régionales de l'Irelande* (doc XVI/22/72) and *Structures et politiques économiques régionales du Royaume-Uni* (doc XVI/23/72).

Actions communautaires de politique régionale dans les régions agricoles prioritaires de la Communauté
COM(71)500 final. 26 May 1971. 29p

EP Report: *Doc de séance* 264/71. 9 Mar 1972. K. Mitterdorfer. 41p
EP Debate: *Annexe JO* No 148, 16 Mar 1972, pp 98–100
EP Resolution: *JO* C36, 12 Apr 1972, pp 28–30
ESC Opinion: *JO* C21, 3 Mar 1972, pp 14–25

Taking the form of a brief background memorandum and two draft Council Regulations, this document from the Commission seeks to begin practical implementation of the 1969 initiative (*see* 457) by tackling the problems facing regions in which the structural transformation of agriculture has resulted in a surplus of manpower. The two specific proposals are concerned with the use of the Guidance Section of the European Agricultural Guidance and Guarantee Fund to finance development projects in priority agricultural regions and with the functioning of the European Interest Rebate Fund (*JO* C90, 11 Sept 1971, pp 14–24). Two years later the Commission proposed another Regulation on finance from the Guidance Section of the European Agricultural Guidance and Guarantee Fund for development projects in priority areas (COM(73)1750), published in the *Official journal of the European Communities* C106, 6 Dec 1973, pp 23–26.

Régimes généraux d'aides à finalité régionale
SEC(71)2336 final. 23 June 1971. 15p

This document broadly defines the principles which the Commission will apply from 1 January 1972 to regional aid arrangements in the central regions of member states in pursuit of its aim to coordinate national aids. In Part 1 the Commission establishes the principles of coordination to apply to regional aid schemes. Part 2 consists of a statement from the Commission confirming that from 1 January 1972 it will apply these principles in accordance with the powers vested in it by Article 92 of the EEC Treaty. Together with its annex on methods of implementation the document was published in the *Journal officiel des Communautés européennes* C111, 4 Nov 1971, pp 7–13. Representatives of member states meeting in the Council adopted these principles on 20 October 1971 by way of a Resolution on the matter (*JO* C111, 4 Nov 1971, pp 1–6). (*See also* 465.)

Politique régionale et union économique et monétaire: les déséquilibres géographiques face à la réalisation des équilibres économiques fondamentaux

Doc XVI/137/71. 19 Oct 1971. 54p

An examination of the implications of the movement towards economic and monetary union (*see* 46–60) for regional policy. Part 1 looks at geographical and monetary imbalances, and Part 2 considers the implications of economic and monetary union for the adjustment of regional structures.

463 **Communication en vue des décisions du Conseil concernant la politique régionale de la Communauté**
COM(72)530 final. 31 May 1972. 9p

EP Report: *Doc de séance* 123/72. 20 Sept 1972. K. Mitterdorfer. 20p
EP Debate: *Annexe JO* No 153, 20 Sept 1972, pp 7–14
EP Resolution: *JO* C103, 5 Oct 1972, p 6
ESC Opinion: *JO* C131, 13 Dec 1972, pp 7–12

In its Resolution of 21 March 1972 on economic and monetary union, the Council invited the Commission to present its views on regional policy (*see* 53). In this response the Commission reviews the present situation and confirms that its policy statement tabled in 1969 (*see* 457), and the related but more specific proposals submitted in 1971 (*see* 460) remain the basis for a solution of regional problems within the Community. A draft Resolution of the Council concerning the instruments of regional policy is appended (*JO* C94, 9 Sept 1972, p 7).

464 **Aide-mémoire de la Commission sur les transports comme moyens d'action de la politique régionale et de l'aménagement du territoire sur le plan de la Communauté**
SEC(72)3827 final. 31 Oct 1972. 16p

A document in which the Commission draws attention to the role and importance of transport as an instrument of regional policy. General comment on the significance of transport policy in the regional context is followed by more specific consideration of various aspects of the common transport policy.

465 **Implementation of the principles of coordination of regional aid in 1972**
SEC(73)1462 final. 17 Apr 1973. 12p

EP Report: *Working doc* 264/73. 10 Dec 1973. H. K. Artzinger. 26p
EP Debate: *Annex OJ* No 170, 15 Jan 1974, pp 14–59
EP Resolution: *OJ* C11, 7 Feb 1974, pp 8–9

A report on the implementation in 1972 of the principles of coordination of regional aid adopted by the Council in its Resolution of 20 October 1971 (*see* 461). The Commission takes stock of the work accomplished during the year, under four main headings, namely, administrative measures taken by member states, the supervision procedure, limitation of the capacity of certain types of aid and the effects of regional aid on different sectors of industry.

466 **Report on the regional problems in the enlarged Community**
COM(73)550 final. 3 May 1973. 289p

EP Report: *Working doc* 120/73. 4 July 1973. F. L. Delmotte. 33p
EP Debate: *Annex OJ* No 164, 5 July 1973, pp 174–205
EP Resolution: *OJ* C62, 31 July 1973, pp 33–35

A major blueprint for regional policy prepared by the Commission in response to an invitation from the Heads of State or Government meeting in Paris on the eve of the Community's enlargement, when it was agreed to give a high priority in the forthcoming Community programme to the correction of regional imbalances. The Commission makes an overall assessment of regional problems in the enlarged Community and outlines general guidelines for the regulation of future action. Individual sections deal with the present position regarding Community regional policy; the moral, environmental and economic case for a regional policy; regional disequilibria; guidelines for a Community regional policy; the mechanism of a Regional Development Fund and the coordination of national regional policies. A substantial annex of more than 300 pages of textual analysis, statistical tables, graphs and maps is presented in support of the memorandum. Chapter 1 updates the study of regional development completed in 1971 (*see* 459) and extends it to include the regions of the three new member countries. As in 1971 special attention is devoted to demographic considerations, employment and production. Chapter 2 concerns the degree and character of the principal forms of disequilibria in regions, and Chapter 3 considers the aims and instruments of regional policies in member states. The report, popularly known as the 'Thomson Report' after George Thomson, member of the Commission responsible for regional policy, was published, without its annex, as Supplement 8/73 to the *Bulletin of the European Communities*. Specific proposals designed to implement the report's recommendations followed later in the year; these included a proposal for a Council Regulation establishing a Regional Development Fund (COM(73)1170 final) and a draft Council Decision on the creation of a Regional Policy Committee (COM(73)1171 final), both published in the *Official journal of the European Communities* C86, 16 Oct 1973, pp 7–14. However, it was not until 1975, after much discussion and hard bargaining in Council, that the first effective instruments of regional policy were created. On 18 March 1975 the Council adopted Regulation (EEC) No 724/75 establishing a European Regional Development Fund for a three year trial period with a total allocation of 1300 million units of account (*OJ* L73, 21 Mar 1975, pp 1–7) and Decision 75/185/EEC establishing a Regional Policy Committee to facilitate the coordination of regional policy in member states (*OJ* L73, 21 Mar 1975, pp 47–48). (*See also* 468 & 469.)

General regional aid systems
COM(75)77 final. 26 Feb 1975. 6p

Following a communication amending and supplementing the principles of coordination adopted in 1971 (*see* 461) to take account of conditions prevailing in the enlarged Community (COM(73)1110) and in the light of guidelines established in November 1973 (SEC(73)4469 final), this document from the Commission establishes new principles of coordination to apply in all Community regions for three years from 1 January 1975. Hitherto principles of coordination had applied only to the central regions of the Community. (*See also* 470.)

468 European Regional Development Fund: annual report

1975   COM(76)307 final. 23 June 1976. 56p
1976   COM(77)260 final. 17 June 1977. 66p
1977   COM(78)310 final. 4 July 1978. 82p
1978   COM(79)349 final. 9 July 1979. 83p

An annual report submitted by the Commission to the Council and to the European Parliament in compliance with Council Regulation (EEC) No 724/75 of 18 March 1975 establishing a European Regional Development Fund, which requires the presentation each year of a report on the implementation of the Regulation in the previous year and on the financial management of the Fund's operations (*OJ* L73, 21 Mar 1975, pp 1–7). Each report begins with an assessment of the current economic situation and the outlook for the future before moving on to describe the Fund's activities during the year under review. Annexes contain relevant statistical data. The first report was published as Supplement 7/76 to the *Bulletin of the European Communities*. Subsequent reports have been published separately by the Commission.

469 Guidelines for Community regional policy
COM(77)195 final. 7 June 1977. 60p

EP Report: *Working doc* 307/77. 10 Oct 1977. L. Noe'. 48p
EP Debate: *Annex OJ* No 221, 13 Oct 1977, pp 147–169
EP Resolution: *OJ* C266, 7 Nov 1977, pp 35–43
ESC Opinion: *OJ* C292, 3 Dec 1977, pp 5–11
             OJ C84, 8 Apr 1978, pp 2–3

Council Regulation (EEC) No 724/75 of 18 March 1975 establishing a European Regional Development Fund, provides for the Commission to submit proposals in 1977 for the future development of regional policy and of the Fund beyond its initial three year trial period (*OJ* L73, 21 Mar 1975, pp 1–7). Consequently, the Commission undertakes in this document a fundamental review of regional policy and makes proposals for its future development. In the first part of the document, the Commission defines the economic and social background against which to consider regional policy, with particular regard to those trends that should have an influence on the future shape of regional policy. In the second and third parts of the paper, the Commission deals with the aims of regional policy and with the means of achieving these objectives. Finally, the Commission makes an assessment of the future outlook for regional policy in the Community. This brief but fundamental review is followed by specific proposals for legislation to give effect to the sentiments expressed by the Commission. The document was published as Supplement 2/77 to the *Bulletin of the European Communities*. At its meeting on 26 and 27 June 1978 the Council was able to adopt a Resolution based on the guidelines established in the Commission's memorandum (*OJ* C36, 9 Feb 1979, pp 10–11). The Council also agreed in principle to amend the Regulation governing the European Regional Development Fund, but was unable to complete formal adoption during 1978.

470 Regional aid systems: principles of coordination
COM(78)636 final. 21 Dec 1978. 24p

A document in which the Commission informs the Council of the principles of coordination it will apply from 1 January 1979 to regional aid systems already in force or to be established in the regions of the Community. The Commission describes the five principal aspects of coordination, namely, differentiated ceilings of aid intensity, transparency, regional specificity, the sectoral repercussions of regional aid and supervision. An annex outlines methods for implementing the principles. The whole document was published in the *Official journal of the European Communities* C31, 3 Feb 1979, pp 9–15. (*See also* 467.)

CHAPTER 11

Environment and consumer protection

Descriptive essay

Concern for the environment is of relatively recent origin in modern industrial society. Since the late 1960s there has been increasing awareness that economic progress and prosperity is not an end in itself, and that the quality of human life deserves greater consideration than in the past. This marked shift in social values is reflected in the efforts made by the European Communities to institute a policy to improve the environment and to prevent its further degradation. Although the founding Treaties make no specific provision for an environmental policy as such, member states have pledged their political will to achieve progress in this matter, a commitment expressed no more positively than at the Paris summit conference in October 1972, the final declaration of which declares that 'special attention will be paid to non-material values and wealth and to protection of the environment so that progress shall serve mankind'.

It will be clear from the documents listed in this chapter that the Commission of the European Communities has directed its main effort towards the development and implementation of an environmental action programme, designed to give the Community a coherent policy for the sound management of natural resources and for the improvement of living conditions. Although the Commission tabled its first thoughts on environmental policy in 1971 (*see* 471), and followed this in 1972 with a document in which it sketched the broad lines of an action programme (*see* 472), the crucial impetus came from the Paris summit conference, at which Heads of State or Government agreed to place greater emphasis than hitherto on improvements in the quality of life in the Communities and specifically requested Community institutions to draw up an action programme before 31 July 1973. The resultant Commission initiative became the blueprint for the action programme on the environment adopted by the Council on 22 November 1973 (*see* 473). Later the Commission expressed its views on the need for a second action programme (*see* 476), and subsequently made proposals to that end, which were adopted by the Council on 17 May 1977 in the form of a second programme to last until 1981 (*see* 478).

In its efforts to give practical substance to the environmental action programme, the Commission has submitted numerous specific proposals for legislation. A document published in 1978, for instance, lists no fewer than 43 proposals adopted by the Council and a further 24 still on the table. Particular attention has been devoted to means of combating pollution of the air and water. Quality objectives have been set for the various uses of water, and regulatory norms proposed for the emission of pollutants into air and water. In addition, the Commission has made proposals on a wide variety of related matters, including the protection of the natural environment and its flora and fauna, the reduction of noise levels, the disposal of waste and improvements in the urban and working environment.

Clearly such specific proposals fall outside the scope of this bibliographical guide. However, it is possible to keep track of their progress through the Community's legislative processes by referring to the periodic status reports on the implementation of the action programme (*see* 474). Of considerable value in this respect is the publication *State of the environment*, a detailed review of Community environmental policy whose publication was provided for in the first environmental action programme as a means of drawing public attention to environmental problems. The first report, published in 1977 (cat 1070) consists of an overall review of Community activities and achievements during the past three years, with particular emphasis on the implementation of the action programme. The second volume, published in 1978 (cat CB-24-78-152-EN-C. ISBN 92-825-0936-2) is more selective in its description of progress achieved but is again a very useful guide to the documentation of environmental protection. It lists, for instance, proposals adopted or being discussed by the Council as at 31 March 1978 and Community reports, publications and other documents on environmental matters.

In order to set appropriate quality objectives, emission norms, pollutant controls, qualitative and quantitative standards, Community institutions must first have at their disposal a substantial body of scientific and technical data on, for instance, the harmful effects of certain pesticides on the ecological system. Consequently, in order to give the action programme essential scientific and technical support, the Commission proposed and the Council adopted a multi-annual environmental research and development programme in 1973. A second programme followed in 1976 to cover the period 1976 to 1980 (*see* 477). Specific proposals for specialized research and development programmes are not included in this guide, neither are details of the various projects granted assistance under the terms of such research programmes. However, reports on the results obtained from this work may be traced through the pages of *Euro abstracts*, Section 1 of which includes a place for environmental protection in the chapter on the life sciences.

Just as environmental policy dates largely from the period introduced by the Paris summit with its greater emphasis on the quality of life, so too does the policy for consumer protection have a similar origin. In response to the sentiments expressed at the Paris summit, the Commission compiled a programme for consumer information and protection designed particularly to improve health and safety standards, to eliminate unfair commercial practices and to provide greater protection for European consumers (*see* 480). Information on the proposals submitted by the Commission in application of the action programme subsequently adopted by the Council, on such subjects as doorstep selling, the labelling of foodstuffs and consumer credit, may be obtained from the annual report on *Consumer protection and information policy* compiled by the Commission (*see* 482) and from the pages of the *General report on the activities of the European Communities*.

Bibliographical record

ENVIRONMENT

471 Première communication de la Commission sur la politique de la Communauté en matière d'environnement
SEC(71)2616 final. 22 July 1971. 171p

EP Report: *Doc de séance* 9/72. 14 Apr 1972. H. E. Jahn. 128p
EP Debate: *Annexe JO* No 149, 18 Apr 1972, pp 31–53
EP Resolution: *JO* C46, 9 May 1972, pp 10–13

The first major initiative on environment policy in which the Commission seeks to define in outline the general features of a common policy for the protection and improvement of the environment. Intended primarily as a discussion document, it begins with a general review of the problems to be faced and the contribution the Communities can make in the field of environmental protection. The Commission then moves on to outline a nine-point action programme designed to give effect to Community objectives. Due consideration is given to the ways and means for carrying out the programme, with regard to the legal instruments and financial resources at the disposal of Community institutions. Finally, the Commission identifies and describes fields in which priority measures are needed. The document concludes with a series of annexes, the first of which outlines the areas in which each of the three Communities is active in environmental matters. Other annexes include a list of the principal international organizations concerned with environmental problems and a first schedule of research on air and water pollution.

472 Communication de la Commission au Conseil sur un programme des Communautés européennes en matière d'environnement
SEC(72)666 final. 22 Mar 1972. 69p

EP Report: *Doc de séance* 74/72. 3 July 1972. H. E. Jahn. 102p
EP Debate: *Annexe JO* No 152, 6 July 1972, pp 218–228 & 231–249
EP Resolution: *JO* C82, 26 July 1972, pp 42–45
ESC Opinion: *JO* C123, 27 Nov 1972, pp 29–32
OJ C25, 28 Apr 1973, pp 5–6

A communication in which the Commission makes proposals for the implementation of a programme to protect and improve the environment, drafted in accordance with intentions expressed in the Commission's earlier discussion document on the topic (*see* 471) and in the light of comments subsequently received. The communication has two main sections. In the first part the Commission recalls the environmental problems caused or faced by modern industrial society and the contribution the European Communities can make to their solution. The Commission outlines the nature and importance of environmental issues, reviews the provisions of each of the three founding Treaties as they relate to environmental matters and reaffirms the principal objectives of Community environment policy, as enumerated in the Commission's first communication. The second part constitutes the environmental action programme proper. Divided into five main sections, the programme consists of concrete proposals designed to reduce pollution and nuisances and to safeguard the natural environment; to establish a mechanism for informing the Commission of member states' legislative intentions as regards the environment; to establish a common attitude to environmental matters considered within the framework of other international organizations; to improve the working environment inside factories and to improve the flow of information on environmental matters. Appended to the communication are three draft instruments whose adoption would contribute to the realization of the action programme. They consist of a draft Council Resolution on a programme to reduce pollution and nuisances and to safeguard the natural environment (COM(72)333); a draft Agreement on a procedure for informing the Commission of impending action on the environment in member states (COM(72)334), which the Council adopted on 5 March 1973 (*OJ* C9, 15 Mar 1973, pp 1–3), and a draft Council Recommendation to member state signatories of the Berne Convention establishing the International Commission for the Protection of the Rhine against Pollution (COM(72)335). The communication and its associated proposals appeared as Supplement 5/72 to the *Bulletin of the European Communities* and also received publication in the *Journal officiel des Communautés européennes* C52, 26 May 1972, pp 1–40.

Programme of environmental action of the European Communities
COM(73)530 final. 10 Apr 1973. 142p

EP Report: *Working doc* 106/73. 27 June 1973. H. E. Jahn. 58p
EP Debate: *Annex OJ* No 164, 3 July 1973, pp 57–78
EP Resolution: *OJ* C62, 31 July 1973, pp 16–19
ESC Opinion: *OJ* C88, 22 Oct 1973, pp 1–2

A package of four separate documents which together constitute a draft Community action programme on the environment, submitted by the Commission in compliance with the request made by Heads of Government or State at their summit meeting in Paris on 19 and 20 October 1972 that such a programme, together with a precise time-table, be drawn up before 31 July 1973. Part A is a draft Council Resolution on a Community environmental action programme. In Part B the Commission defines the objectives and principles of an environment policy and describes in general terms the work to be accomplished during the next two years. Part C consists of a detailed description of the many practical proposals designed to protect and improve the environment and at the same time, to contribute to the elevation of living standards and the attainment of full employment. The specific measures themselves fall into three groups, those whose intention is to reduce pollution and nuisances, those whose aim is to improve the environment and those designed to foster a common attitude towards matters considered within the context of other international organizations. Annexes provide a glossary of environmental protection terminology and a table giving the correlation between the projects listed in the Community's environmental programme and the on-going or proposed joint research. Part D is a proposal for a Decision on information on environmental matters. All four parts were published as Supplement 3/73 to the *Bulletin of the European Communities*. The Council adopted the programme by way of a Declaration on 22 November 1973, in which it confirmed that the aim was to 'improve the setting and quality of life and the surroundings and living conditions of the peoples of the Community' (*OJ* C112, 20 Dec 1973, pp 1–53). (*See also* 474.)

474 **Communication from the Commission to the Council concerning the state of progress of the European Community's environment programme ...**
as at 1 June 1974   SEC(74)2297. 21 June 1974. 13p
as at 15 October 1974   SEC(74)3889. 28 Oct 1974. 14p
as at 1 May 1975   SEC(75)1774. 5 May 1975. 22p
as at 15 November 1976   COM(76)639 final. 2 Dec 1976. 32p
as at 1 January 1978   SEC(78)1337. 23 Mar 1978. 20p

On 22 November 1973 the Council adopted a Declaration embodying the environmental action programme proposed by the Commission in 1973 (*see* 473). In this series of reports, the Commission reports to the Council on progress made during the period under review towards the achievement of the objectives established in the programme. Later reports relate to the programme as extended as a result of a Commission initiative in 1976 (*see* 478).

475 **Implementation of Title II 'action to improve the environment', of the programme of action of the European Communities on protection of the environment**
SEC(74)4195 final. 4 Nov 1974. 11p

Following proposals from the Italian government for further action on matters covered in Title II Part II of the action programme adopted in 1973 (*see* 473), the Commission reviews in this document what it is doing and intends to do with regard to various aspects of water supply problems, the progressive depletion of Community and world stocks of raw materials and the protection of the natural environment. The survey concludes with a time-table for the Commission's work in each of these fields.

476 **Initial reflections on the second action programme of the European Communities on the environment**
COM(75)289 final. 17 June 1975. 9p

A document in which the Commission sets out its preliminary views on the complexion of the second environment action programme which it intends to submit to the Council early in 1976. The Commission devotes short sections to the three elements around which the new programme should be constructed, namely, the continuation of measures already undertaken during the first programme, emphasis upon the preventative nature of environment policy and a balanced approach to ecological and economic necessities.

477 **Proposal for a multiannual environmental research and development programme of the European Economic Community (indirect action) 1976–1980**
COM(75)353 final. 15 July 1975. 30p

EP Report: *Working doc* 328/75. 3 Nov 1975. H. E. Jahn. 28p
EP Debate: *Annex OJ* No 196, 14 Nov 1975, pp 309–317

EP Resolution: *OJ* C280, 8 Dec 1975, pp 59–60
ESC Opinion: *OJ* C35, 16 Feb 1976, pp 29–31

Detailed proposals for a second common research and development programme to run from 1976 to 1980, the intention of which is to provide the environmental action programme (*see* 473) with essential scientific and technical support. The Commission begins by tracing the development of environmental research activities in the European Communities, with particular emphasis upon the first environmental research programme adopted by the Council on 14 May 1973 in Decision 73/126/EEC (*OJ* L153, 9 June 1973, pp 11–12) and on 18 June 1973 in Decision 73/174/EEC (*OJ* L189, 11 July 1973, pp 30–31) and Decision 73/180/EEC (*OJ* L189, 11 July 1973, pp 43–44). The Commission then enumerates the objectives of this second programme and identifies two basic means for its implementation, common action funded partly or wholly by the Community budget and concerted action, financed essentially from national sources but carried out according to a jointly agreed programme. The main body of the document is devoted to a description of the various topics to be undertaken within each of the four research areas into which the programme is divided, namely, criteria research, environmental information management, the reduction and prevention of pollution and nuisances, and the improvement of the environment. The Council adopted the programme in Decision 76/311/EEC of 15 March 1976 (*OJ* L74, 20 Mar 1976, pp 36–37). In 1978, in accordance with the provisions of this Decision, the Commission submitted proposals for a revision of the programme to take account of current research requirements (COM(78)307 final).

Continuation and implementation of a European Community policy and action programme on the environment
COM(76)80 final. 24 Mar 1976. 97p

EP Report: *Working doc* 215/76. 7 July 1976. H. E. Jahn. 75p
EP Debate: *Annex OJ* No 205, 8 July 1976, pp 221–229
EP Resolution: *OJ* C178, 2 Aug 1976, pp 44–48
ESC Opinion: *OJ* C281, 27 Nov 1976, pp 21–29

A proposal from the Commission for a second action programme on the environment to run from 1977 to 1981, and designed to carry on and expand the work undertaken as a result of the first such programme (*see* 473). The document begins with a draft Council Resolution on the continuation and implementation of an action programme. The Commission then outlines the main features of the draft programme itself in five main chapters. In the first the Commission reiterates the objectives and the principles of a Community environmental action programme. The following four chapters outline in some detail the contents of the programme itself. The programme was adopted by the Council on 17 May 1977 in a Resolution on the subject (*OJ* C139, 13 June 1977, pp 1–46). The Commission's proposals were published as Supplement 6/76 to the *Bulletin of the European Communities* and also appeared in the *Official journal of the European Communities* C115, 24 May 1976, pp 1–40.

The place and role of a preventive policy for the environment in a

balanced development of economic activities within the whole of the Community
COM(78)601 final. 15 Nov 1978. 17p

A brief document in which the Commission draws the Council's attention to the relationship between environmental policy and socio-economic development and invites further consideration of preventive measures to combat pollution and nuisances at source. In an annex the Commission enumerates proposals adopted or being discussed by the Council. The document closes with a brief paper on waste management policy.

CONSUMER PROTECTION

480 **A preliminary Community programme for consumer information and protection**
COM(73)2108. 5 Dec 1973. 28p

EP Report: *Working doc 64/74.* 8 May 1974. G. Bersani. 23p
EP Debate: *Annex OJ* No 176, 13 May 1974, pp 22–23
EP Resolution: *OJ* C62, 30 May 1974, pp 8–9

The first attempt to initiate a coordinated consumer policy in the European Communities, prepared by the Commission in response to the concern expressed at the Paris summit for social and environmental issues to be given more emphasis, for greater attention to the quality of life and to the human side of Community developments. The document opens with a review of the economic background against which consumerism has evolved. The Commission follows this with comments on the legal base for Community consumer action and on the work already accomplished on a piece-meal basis in such fields as prices, competition and consumer information. In the third main chapter, the Commission outlines a number of basic objectives for a consumer information and protection programme and sets out a conspectus of consumer needs under four headings, consumer protection, assistance, information and representation. The ways of implementing consumer policy and a number of priorities for action within the next three years are also considered. After brief reference to collaboration with other international organizations, the document concludes with an annex listing a selection of measures with a consumer interest adopted by the Council or submitted to it and a draft Council Resolution adopting the programme. The document was subsequently modified in 1974 (SEC(74)1939 final) and a programme finally adopted by the Council when on 14 April 1975 it agreed a Resolution centred upon measures relating to five fundamental rights, the right to health and safety, the right to protection of economic interests, the right to redress, the right to information and education and the right to representation (*OJ* C92, 25 Apr 1975, pp 1–16).

481 **European consumers: their interests, aspirations and knowledge on consumer affairs**
Doc X/309/76. May 1976. 175p

A picture of the European consumer, his attitudes and behaviour, derived from a sample survey of some 9500 individuals in the nine member states, conducted in October and November 1975. Part 1 contains the main results of the survey, with information on attitudes towards advertising and the media, consumer organizations, public authorities, political parties and the European Communities. Part 2 consists of an analysis of the significance of the results. The report was published by the Commission under the title *The European consumer—his preoccupations—his aspirations—his information* (cat 8811).

Consumer protection and information policy: first report 1977
Comm EC, 1977. 99p (cat CB-23-77-364-EN-C)

Published in compliance with the provisions of the preliminary programme for consumer information and protection (*see* 480), this report constitutes a general summary and description of the work of the Community institutions, and of the measures taken by member states in the field of consumer interests during the period 1 January 1973 to 31 December 1976. Developments are assessed according to the priority areas established in the action programme. Separate chapters provide accounts of the achievements of the Consumers' Consultative Committee, the European Parliament, the Economic and Social Committee and of relations with other international organizations. The report concludes with a number of annexes which include the text of the Council Resolution on the 1975 action programme and a list of those Directives adopted in the interests of consumers between 1 June 1974 and 31 December 1976. Other useful publications issued by the Commission on consumer protection include the *Proceedings of the symposium of consumer organizations on 2 and 3 December 1976* (cat CB-23-77-922-EN-C. ISBN 92-825-0286-4) and *The consumer organizations and the public authorities* (cat CG-22-76-140-EN-C), a directory published in 1977.

CHAPTER 12

Social affairs

Descriptive essay

The Treaty of Rome makes no specific provision for a common social policy, although there are a number of references to matters of social concern. The Preamble to the Treaty affirms the essential objective of the signatories to be 'the constant improvement of the living and working conditions of their peoples'. Article 2 confirms one of the Community's aims to be 'an accelerated raising of the standard of living' and Article 3, enumerating means for the achievement of these aims, refers to freedom of movement and the creation of a European Social Fund 'in order to improve employment opportunities for workers and to contribute to the raising of their standard of living'.

The main provisions for social policy are contained in Articles 117–128. In Article 117 the member states agree upon the need 'to promote improved working conditions and an improved standard of living for workers' and affirm their belief that 'such a development will ensue not only from the functioning of the common market, which will favour the harmonisation of social systems, but also from the procedures provided for in this Treaty and from the approximation of provisions laid down by law, regulation or administrative action'. Article 118 gives the Commission responsibility for promoting close cooperation between member states 'by making studies, delivering opinions and arranging consultations' in the social field, particularly in matters relating to employment, labour law and working conditions, vocational training, social security, occupational safety and hygiene and industrial relations. Other Articles identify specific obligations, including the principle of equal pay for equal work (Article 119), paid holidays (Article 120) vocational training (Article 128) and the creation of a European Social Fund (Article 123–127).

Considered with the social aspects of other policies, such as agriculture and transport, these provisions do not provide the Community institutions with an adequate legal base or a clear mandate for social action other than in a limited number of defined areas. The underlying assumption was that social benefits would accrue quite naturally from economic progress. Consequently, the documentation of the 1960s is characterized by a dearth of major policy documents treating social policy as a legitimate goal in its own right. More typical of this period are those documents which adopt a sectoral approach, seeking to attain specific Treaty objectives and to develop the social aspects of such policies as those for agriculture and transport. Indeed, in 1968 (*see* 490) and again in 1970 (*see* 493), the Commission prepared reports concerned with the coordination of the social aspects of other policy areas.

The belief that economic progress would of itself bring social benefits was not a view to which the Commission subscribed. As early as 1962 in its Action Programme for the Second Stage (*see* 3), the Commission had urged for social policy to receive more than a subordinate role, and again in 1966 it argued for the clear identification of economic expansion with social progress (*see* 488). However, in view of the lack of a clear Treaty remit and the absence of effective instruments for the pursuit of social objectives the Commission could do little, without the positive support of member states.

Documents dating from the 1970s show a marked and significant change of attitude from those that went before. They treat social policy as an end in itself and emphasize the need for positive social action to become an essential component in Community development. The political will to give new emphasis to social policy was given first expression at The Hague summit conference in December 1969, in response to which the Commission produced the first wide-ranging discussion document on social goals (*see* 494). This emphasis upon greater responsiveness to social needs was confirmed and given greater prominence at the Paris summit conference, in response to which the Commission prepared guidelines for a social action programme (*see* 495) and subsequently a programme itself, complete with lists of priorities and a time-table of work (*see* 497). In early 1974 the Council adopted a Resolution on social policy which embodied a programme of nearly 40 separate proposals and which became the basis for the work of Community institutions in the social field during the following years.

Progress in the implementation of this Social Action Programme, and indeed in the development of all aspects of social policy, may be followed through the pages of the *Report on the development of the social situation in the Communities*, published every April since 1958 in accordance with Article 122 of the Treaty of Rome. Each report reviews the achievements and events of the past year in all fields of social concern in which the Commission is active. The substantial statistical annex published at the end of each report up to 1976 was superseded in 1977 by a separate publication from the Statistical Office of the European Communities called *Social indicators for the European Community 1960–1975*. Useful information on the development of social policy may also be obtained from the annual *General report on the activities of the European Communities* and the monthly *Bulletin of the European Communities*, both of which have regular chapters on social policy.

EUROPEAN SOCIAL FUND

The principal instrument of Community social policy is the European Social Fund, established according to Articles 123 to 127 of the Treaty of Rome 'in order to improve employment opportunities for workers in the common market and to contribute thereby to raising the standard of living' by providing from the Community budget half the cost of industrial training, retraining and settlement schemes designed with the object of rendering 'the employment of workers easier and of increasing their geographical and occupational mobility within the Community' (Article 123).

Documents relating to the Social Fund, listed in this chapter, are concerned with its management and with attempts to broaden its scope to give it more flexibility to deal with increasing problems of unemployment, particularly as they relate to specific categories of people. After an abortive attempt at reform in 1965 (*see* 486), the Fund was successfully reorganized in 1971 with the purpose of turning it into a dynamic instrument of Community social and employment policy (*see* 492). Detailed information on the work of this reconstituted Fund, and the impact it has made on employment problems in the Community may be derived from the series of annual reports published since 1973 (*see* 496). After a further review of the Fund's *modus operandi* in 1977 (*see* 500) new operating rules were adopted and its purview extended to cover a number of defined categories of people (*see* 502).

VOCATIONAL TRAINING

During the 1960s European economies were buoyant and manpower was in demand. During this period the Social Fund was used alongside other instruments of policy to create conditions in which Community industry could make best use of the available labour force. Above all this meant removing the obstacles to the free movement of labour (*see* Chapter 4) and related measures to promote occupational and geographical mobility among the labour force. To this end, the Commission worked for better coordination between national employment services whose responsibility it was to fill existing vacancies (*see* 513), made provision for the exchange of young workers (*see* 125) and placed considerable emphasis upon improving the match between labour demand and the skills existing within the available labour force. Finance from the European Social Fund was made available for training, retraining and settlement and in compliance with Article 128 of the Treaty of Rome, general principles for implementing a common vocational training policy were established (*see* 506), and work programmes established in 1965 (*see* 509) and in 1972 (*see* 519).

A new focus for vocational training activities within the Community was established in 1975 when the European Centre for the Development of Vocational Training (CEDEFOP) was established in West Berlin (*see* 524), information on the activities of which may be gathered from *Vocational training*, a quarterly information bulletin now published by the Centre. Separate supplements published between 1976 and 1978 were devoted to descriptions of the provisions made for vocational training in each of the nine member states.

In the closely related field of vocational guidance, the Commission has published annual reports on the activities of member states in application of Commission Recommendation 66/484/EEC of 18 July 1966 in which the Commission invited member states not only to step up their national efforts but regularly to exchange information and experience on problems relating to vocational guidance for young persons and adults (*JO* 154, 24 Aug 1966, pp 2815–2819). Five reports covering the period 1964 to 1974 have so far been published, the latest being *Report on vocational guidance activities in the Community* (cat 8739), published in 1976 covering the years 1971 to 1974. Each report reviews developments in member states with particular reference to the legal and administrative framework in each member state, the organization of vocational guidance and improvements in methods and techniques.

SOCIAL SECURITY

Another major contribution to the more efficient exploitation of the Community's common pool of manpower and to the removal of obstacles to the movement of labour has been the work of the Commission in the field of social security. The provisions of the Treaty of Rome concerning social security have two distinct aspects. On the one hand, Article 51 provides for the adoption of 'such measures in the field of social security as are necessary to provide freedom of movement for workers'. On the other hand, there is provision within the overall context of Community social policy for the 'harmonization of social systems' (Article 117), and for the Commission to promote close cooperation between member states as regards social security (Article 118).

The Commission first turned its attention to the removal of social security impediments to labour movement by formulating rules to ensure that workers who move from one country to another receive equal treatment without loss of entitlement to benefits possibly accumulated. Two basic Regulations on the social security of migrant workers took effect on 1 January 1959, progress in the implementation of which is recorded in the annual reports prepared by the Administrative Commission of the European Communities on Social Security for Migrant Workers, set up to supervise their implementation. Subsequent initiatives refined and broadened the scope of the scheme to include such groups as frontier workers, seasonal workers and seafarers and ultimately led to its complete revision.

In order to inform migrant workers of their rights and to draw attention to their duties, the Administrative Commission has produced a series of booklets for each member state called *Social security for migrant workers*, in which are summarized the main provisions of Community Regulations and main features of the social security system operating in the country under review. *A practical handbook of social security for employed persons and their families moving within the Community* (cat CB-28-79-035-EN-C) provides up-to-date information on the provisions of the various legal instruments on social security. The work of the Administrative Commission is described in *Dix années d'activité de la Commission Administrative pour la Sécurité Sociale des Travailleurs Migrants et d'application des règlements communautaires*, published by the Commission in 1968 and in *Le rôle de la Commission Administrative pour la Sécurité Sociale des Travailleurs Migrants dans l'application et l'amélioration des règlements communautaires 1958–1973*, published by the Commission in 1973.

As for the harmonization of social security systems, the first requirement was a detailed and up-to-date comparative picture of social security systems currently in force in member states. To this end a number of studies of various aspects of social security were commissioned from independent experts, some of which were subsequently published in the series *Etudes—Série politique sociale* (*see* 548–550). During the preparatory period, the Commission also convened a European Conference on Social Security in order to consult with government and independent experts on the matter (*see* 551). It was during this period that the Commission also began publication of *Comparative tables of the social security systems in the Member States of the European Communities*, the tenth edition of which was published in 1978, and which presents in tabular form the basic features of the social security systems in force in each member state.

EMPLOYMENT

It will be clear from the documents listed in this chapter that the Community has experienced acute unemployment problems as the European economy has, in common with other industrialized economies, suffered the consequences of recession. Although the documents listed in the chapter reflect the fact that the most severe difficulties have been experienced during the 1970s, the Commission has always kept a watching brief over employment trends in the Community. This is well illustrated by the commentaries on the labour market that have regularly appeared in the annual *Report on the development of the social situation in the Communities* and in the more general survey of social conditions published in the *General report on the activities of the European Communities*. In addition the Commission has prepared a specialized report called *Les problèmes de main-d'oeuvre dans la Communauté*, whose publication began with the volume for 1964 but was seemingly discontinued after the volume for 1971.

Many of the documents on employment problems listed in this chapter were prepared by the Commission for discussion in the context of the Tripartite Conference, held annually since 1975 between representatives from member governments, the Commission and employers' and labour organizations, or of the Standing Committee on Employment, consisting of Ministers of Labour, representatives of employers' and workers' organizations and Commission representatives. Particular attention has been given to the employment prospects and problems of specific groups of people, such as women (*see* 514, 523 & 539), young people (*see* 518, 529, 539, 540 & 544) and the handicapped (*see* 512).

Quantitative information on the size of the employment problem may be drawn from a number of statistical serials issued by the Statistical Office of the European Communities. In addition to general statistical publications on the economic and social situation in the Community referred to in the introduction to Chapter 3, there are a number of more specialized titles. The annual publication *Employment and unemployment* is a compendium of annual data covering a seven year period on population, employment, the labour market and industrial relations in member countries. Each volume, including the first published in 1977 under the title *Population and employment*, also contains a retrospective section containing historical data back to 1950. Additional information on employment and unemployment is available from the *Labour force sample survey* carried out at two-yearly intervals since 1973, the results of which are also published by the Statistical Office. Data on population rates and changes appear in the annual *Demographic statistics*.

LIVING AND WORKING CONDITIONS

In addition to measures to enhance employment prospects within the member countries of the European Communities, the Commission has devoted attention to the conditions of employment. The documents listed in this chapter reveal the Commission's interest in workers' rights in the face of redundancy (*see* 568), the insolvency of employers (*see* 578), mergers (*see* 578) and employee participation (*see* 576). Two specific areas of concern are equal rights for men and women workers (*see* 565 & 573) and safety and health at work (*see* 574, 584 & 585). In this latter area, the Commission has been able to build on the valuable experience gained by the High Authority in the regulation of industrial safety in the coal and steel industries. Information on the work of the Steel Industry Safety and Health Commission, established in 1964 by the High Authority to promote the exchange of practical experience and research for the benefit of all concerned in the industry, may be drawn from the *Report of the Steel Industry Safety and Health Commission*, the ninth report of which for 1977 was published in 1978 (cat CA-24-78-693-EN-C. ISBN 92-825-0458-1). Information on the work of its sister Commission in the coalmining industry may be derived from the *Report of the Mines Safety and Health Commission*, the 15th report of which for 1977 was published in 1979 (cat CB-24-78-677-EN-C. ISBN 92-825-0930-3).

Other than in the case of equal pay (*see* 565), the contribution of the Commission as regards wage conditions and structures has been mainly in the compilation and analysis of data. Wage bargaining remains very much on a national, not to say, local basis. Following the precedent set by the High Authority, which monitored wage levels and working conditions in the ECSC industries, the Commission has undertaken a number of major fact-finding exercises. The Statistical Office has published, for instance, the results of the periodic surveys of labour costs undertaken in the Community, that for 1975 being the latest to be published in a four-volume set under the title *Labour costs in industry*. The Statistical Office also regularly publishes *Hourly earnings: hours of work*, which contains harmonized data on workers' hourly wages, on labour costs and weekly hours worked. In addition, the Statistical Office published in 1977 *Working conditions in the Community*, containing information on part-time, shift and night work and related topics drawn from a survey carried out as part of the 1975 labour force sample survey, the results of which have also been published by the Statistical Office.

Bibliographical record

Recueil des travaux de la conférence consultative sur les aspects sociaux de la politique agricole commune, Rome, du 28 septembre au 4 octobre 1961
Comm EEC, 1962. 106p (cat 8037)

See 356.

Progrès technique et Marché commun: perspectives économiques et sociales de l'application des nouvelles techniques, Bruxelles, Palais des Congrès, 5–19 décembre 1960
Comm EEC, Comm ECSC, Comm EAEC, 1962. 2 vols, 354p, 736p (cat 8018)

A two volume collection of the documentation generated by the conference held under the auspices of the three Community executives in Brussels from 5 to 10 December 1960, with the aim of reviewing the economic and social problems posed by current technological developments in Community countries. Attended by invited representatives from government organizations, academic institutions and both sides of industry, the conference conducted its business through a number of working groups. These two volumes contain the speeches delivered at both the opening and closing plenary sessions, together with the reports and conclusions from each of the working groups into which the conference was divided.

485 **Programme d'action de la Communauté en matière de politique sociale dans l'agriculture**
V/VI/COM(63)353 final. 19 Sept 1963. 53p

See 357.

486 **Propositions de règlements du Conseil visant à accroitre l'efficacité des interventions du Fond social européen**
V/COM(65)28 final. 27 Jan 1965. 66p

EP Report:*Doc de séance* 53/65. 14 June 1965. I. Elsner: 25p
EP Debate: *Débs* No 79, 17 June 1965, pp 119–138
EP Resolution: *JO* 119, 3 July 1965, pp 2006–2016
ESC Opinion: *JO* 134, 23 July 1965, pp 2235–2246

A set of proposals in which the Commission argues the case for modifications to the rules governing the operation of the Social Fund, as defined in Regulation 9 of 25 August 1960 (*JO* 56, 31 Aug 1960, pp 1189–1198), modified by Regulation (EEC) No 47/63 of 31 May 1963 to take account of changed economic conditions and the accelerating process of integration in the Community (*JO* 86, 10 June 1963, pp 1605–1608). In an explanatory memorandum, the Commission explains that the proposals are designed to increase the effectiveness of the European Social Fund by associating it more closely with efforts to maintain high levels of employment, more balanced regional development and improved living conditions for migrant workers. The provisions and likely repercussions of each of the two draft Regulations are examined article by article. Although the need for a more flexible instrument was reiterated in 1962 (*see* 3) and in 1964 (*see* 4), the Council was unable to reach agreement on the basis of these proposals for the reform of the European Social Fund.

487 **Aspects sociaux du problème charbonnier**
HA doc 2366/66. n.d. 10p

See 165.

488 **Lignes directrices des travaux de la Commission dans le secteur des affaires sociales**
SEC(66)3487 final. 30 Nov 1966. 29p

EP Report: *Doc de séance* 138/67. 15 Nov 1967. H. B. Gerlach. 16p
EP Debate: *Débs* No 96, 1 Dec 1967, pp 198–207
EP Resolution: *JO* 307, 18 Dec 1967, pp 31–32

A series of guidelines designed to provide a coherent framework for future specific measures the Commission intends to initiate in the social sector. An introductory section recognizes the early emphasis placed upon the achievement of specific social goals set in the EEC Treaty, such as equal pay and paid holidays. However, the Commission also urges the need for social policy to develop a wider dimension by the clear identification of economic expansion with social progress and the consideration of social factors when shaping other aspects of Community policy. The work to be accomplished with regard to working and living conditions, employment and vocational training is also reviewed. The document concludes with a brief review of the social aspects of other policies, particularly transport and agriculture, and a comment on social statistics. The document was published as a Supplement to the *Bulletin of the European Economic Community* 2-1967.

Exposé sur la politique sociale de la Communauté
SEC(67)5014 final. 18 Dec 1967. 18p

A useful resumé of the achievements of social policy over the past ten years and prospects for the future, presented by Mr Levi Sandri on the occasion of the first Council meeting of Ministers of Social Affairs, after the merger of the three Community executives. General lines of development since 1958 are described, with particular reference to those areas where tangible progress has been achieved, notably, free circulation of workers, social security for migrant workers and the European Social Fund. Reference is made to the Commission's general intentions in the social domain and emphasis given to the need for social policy to counteract social disequilibria likely to follow in the wake of economic change.

Rapport intérimaire sur les corrélations entre la politique sociale et les autres politiques de la Communauté
SEC(68)1932 final 12 July 1968. 27p

EP Report: *Doc de séance* 213/68. 12 Mar 1969. W. Behrendt. 15p
Doc de séance 58/69. 17 June 1969. W. Behrendt. 22p
EP Debate: *Annexe JO* No 116, 1 July 1969, pp 71–88
EP Resolution: *JO* C97, 28 July 1969, pp 31–33

An interim report on the relationship between the Community's social policy and its other policies, submitted by the Commission in reply to a request from the Council. Recognizing the need to ensure consistency between the social aspects of various Community policies, the Commission first looks at the social dimension of policies in such fields as agriculture and transport. The Commission briefly outlines the social implications of general economic policy in both the short and medium-term, and outlines the problems that will determine the direction of social policy in the years ahead. (*See also* 493.)

Aspects sociaux de la politique charbonnière (dans le cadre d'une politique énergetique communautaire)
COM(69)148. 26 Feb 1969. 8p

See 172.

Avis de la Commission au Conseil sur la réforme du Fonds social européen (article 126 du Traité CEE)
COM(69)347 final. 4 May 1969. 50p

EP Report: *Doc de séance* 170/69. 4 Dec 1969. A. Lulling. 27p
   Doc de séance 43/70. 13 May 1970. A. Lulling. 4p
EP Debate: *Annexe JO* No 120, 9 Dec 1969, pp 42–62
EP Resolution: *JO* C2, 8 Jan 1970, pp 7–10
ESC Opinion: *JO* C26, 4 Mar 1970, pp 6–13

A document on the reform of the European Social Fund, prepared by the Commission in accordance with provisions made in Article 126 of the Treaty of Rome for a thorough reappraisal of the Fund's operations at the end of the transitional period. The document, published in the *Journal officiel des Communautés européennes* C131, 13 Oct 1969, pp 4–20, explains how, in the opinion of the Commission, the Fund needs to be transformed into a much more dynamic instrument of policy, flexible enough to make a real impact upon employment problems in the Community. Divided into five main chapters and a number of annexes, the document first establishes the need for a European Social Fund before turning to the Commission's plans to remove existing constraints on the Fund's operating conditions so as to allow it to respond positively to the growing needs of an economy in the process of rapid economic, structural and technological change. The Commission outlines the ways in which it envisages a Fund freed of existing legal and administrative constraints will work and examines the financial implications consequent upon a reform which will significantly broaden the Fund's spheres of interest. Annex 1 consists of a brief resumé of current arrangements for assistance from the Fund. Annexes 2 and 3 record the opinion of Community and other organizations on the reform of the Fund. After taking cognizance of the opinion of Community institutions, the Council adopted Decision 71/66/EEC of 1 February 1971 concerning general principles to govern the new European Social Fund (*JO* L28, 4 Feb 1971, pp 15–17). A number of implementing Regulations followed in November 1971 (*JO* L249, 10 Nov 1971, pp 54–61) and in April 1972 (*JO* L101, 28 Apr 1972, pp 3–4). The new Fund became operational on 1 May 1972 and a memorandum on the presentation of applications for assistance was published in September 1972 (*JO* C96, 20 Sept 1972, pp 1–7).

493 Deuxième rapport de la Commission au Conseil sur les corrélations entre la politique sociale et les autres politiques de la Communauté
SEC(70)510 final. 17 Mar 1970. 33p

EP Report: *Doc de séance* 77/70. 1 Sept 1970. W. Behrendt. 17p
EP Debate: *Annexe JO* No 129, 6 Oct 1970, pp 16–38
EP Resolution: *JO* C129, 26 Oct 1970, pp 10–12

A second report on the correlation between social policy and other Community policies, providing an overall picture of social policy pursued within the context of sectoral policy. As in the first such report (*see* 490), the Commission gives particular attention to the social aspects of common policies for agriculture and transport, and the social implications of general economic policy, industrial and regional policies. During the course of its meeting on 27 July 1971, the Council adopted a work programme concerning the implementation of Article 118 of the Treaty of Rome, which gives the Commission 'the task of promoting close cooperation between Member States in the social field' (*JO* C23, 8 Mar 1972, pp 20–24).

Orientations préliminaires pour un programme de politique sociale communautaire
SEC(71)600 final. 17 Mar 1971. 89p

EP Report: *Doc de séance* 35/72. 5 June 1972. H. Vredeling. 48p
EP Debate: *Annexe JO* No 151, 13 June 1972, pp 29–67
EP Resolution: *JO* C70, 1 July 1972, pp 12–14

In response to the call for a 'closely concerted social policy' made by Heads of Government or State at The Hague summit conference in December 1969, and to the new prospects opened up by the decision to move towards economic and monetary union, the Commission felt that a wide-ranging debate with Community institutions and both sides of industry was an essential preliminary to the formulation of a social policy programme. Consequently, this document takes the form more of a discussion paper than a set of formal proposals. After a brief, general survey the Commission analyses trends in the present situation, with particular regard to employment and vocational training, incomes and wealth, working and living conditions. The 'major aims of society' are the subject of a separate chapter, that is, full and better employment, greater social justice and a better quality of life, to which economic and monetary union will be expected to contribute. In the final chapter the Commission identifies seven areas for priority action during the first stage of economic and monetary union. The document was given full publication as Supplement 2/71 to the *Bulletin of the European Communities*.

Guidelines for a social action programme
COM(73)520 final. 18 Apr 1973. 16p

The Commission's first considered response to the new emphasis on social progress and the quality of life, announced at the Paris summit conference in October 1972, and to the specific request from Heads of Government or State that a social action programme be drawn up before 1 January 1974. This preliminary report is intended as a basis for discussion with Community institutions and both sides of industry, in the light of which formal proposals will be drafted and submitted to the Council during the autumn. In its general remarks the Commission makes it clear that its philosophy is to consider social policy as an end in itself. Three main objectives are advanced, namely, full and better employment, improved living and working conditions and participation of the social partners in the economic and social decisions of the Community. Under each of these headings the Commission tables a series of wide-ranging and detailed proposals. The memorandum was published as Supplement 4/73 to the *Bulletin of the European Communities*. (*See also* 497.)

Annual report on the activities of the new European Social Fund
Financial year 1972 SEC(73)3536 final. 9 Oct 1973. 35p
Financial year 1973 SEC(74)2400 final. 3 July 1974. 79p
Financial year 1974 COM(75)355 final. 23 July 1975. 109p
Financial year 1975 COM(76)388 final. 28 July 1976. 61p
Financial year 1976 COM(77)398 final. 28 July 1977. 96p
Financial year 1977 COM(78)476 final. 6 Oct 1978. 2 vols, 129p, 85p
Financial year 1978 COM(79)346 final. 29 June 1979. 114p

An annual report on the activities of the new European Social Fund, provided for in implementing Regulation (EEC) No 858/72 of 24 April 1972 (*JO* L101, 28 Apr 1972, pp 3–4). Each report consists of a detailed review of the operations undertaken during the year in question, an account of the administrative, financial and budgetary aspects of the Fund's activities and a survey of the range and type of operations undertaken. The report highlights the main problems encountered and methods for their solution. Each report concludes with an appraisal of prospects for the year ahead, the texts of any relevant documents produced during the year, and financial and other data on the Fund's activities.

497 Social Action Programme
COM(73)1600 final. 24 Oct 1973. 46p

EP Report: *Working doc* 256/73. 6 Dec 1973. L. Girardin. 40p
EP Debate: *Annex OJ* No 169, 10 Dec 1973, pp 9–59
EP Resolution: *OJ* C2, 9 Jan 1974, pp 11–19
ESC Opinion: *OJ* C37, 1 Apr 1974, pp 30–46
CC ECSC Opinion: *OJ* C115, 28 Dec 1973, pp 3–4

A response to the original Paris summit mandate for a Social Action Programme by 1 January 1974 and the subsequent discussion document on the subject (*see* 495), this Commission initiative identifies a number of priorities for social action and establishes a time-table of work for the period 1974 to 1976. A brief introductory chapter introduces the subject and places the proposed actions in their general context, grouped under headings that correspond to the three main objectives identified in the earlier discussion document, namely, full and better employment, improvement of living and working conditions and industrial democracy. A number of annexes provide more information on each specific proposal. Annex 1 lists a group of seven priority actions upon which proposals will be placed before the Council before the end of 1973. Annex 2 contains details of actions to be taken during the period 1974 to 1976, with comments on the purpose of the action, a brief description of the present situation and the means to be employed. Annex 3 provides similar details of other supporting actions upon which proposals will follow later. Annex 4 lists those actions for which proposals are already being discussed in the Council, and Annex 5 estimates the cost of the Social Action Programme in 1974. The document, which also includes a draft Council Resolution on the matter, was published as Supplement 2/74 to the *Bulletin of the European Communities*. On 21 January 1974 the Council formally adopted the Action Programme by way of a Resolution on the topic (*OJ* C13, 12 Feb 1974, pp 1–4). Useful information on progress achieved in the implementation of this work programme by the end of March 1977 was given in an answer to Written Question 37/77 in the European Parliament (*OJ* C200, 22 Aug 1977, pp 1–4).

498 Action programme in favour of migrant workers and their families
COM(74)2250. 18 Dec 1974. 27p

EP Report: *Working doc* 160/75. 7 July 1975. W. Albers. 66p
EP Debate: *Annex OJ* No 194, 24 Sept 1975, pp 177–201
EP Resolution: *OJ* C239, 20 Oct 1975, pp 34–36
ESC Opinion: *OJ* C12, 17 Jan 1976, pp 4–32

A document which contains the Commission's first action programme on behalf of migrant workers and their families. The programme contains proposals for measures to assist migrant workers from within the Community and from non-member countries, and to improve the coordination of national policies towards migrant workers from non-member countries. Drafted by the Commission within the framework of the Social Action Programme (see 497), the document begins with an introductory chapter in which the Commission discusses the phenomenon of migration, its socio-economic consequences for both Community and third countries, and the nature of the measures needed to correct the present imbalances caused by migration. The specific social and educational measures to improve the conditions of migrant workers and their families, emphasized in the Council Resolution on the Social Action Programme, form the subject of the second chapter. The Commission makes proposals for measures to improve the living and working conditions of migrant workers, considered under such aspects as free movement of workers, social security, vocational training, social services, housing, education, health and statistics. Further chapters are concerned with civic and political rights, from the exercise of which migrant workers are often excluded, and the problem of illegal migration. The document, which concludes with a chapter on the need for greater coordination of the policies of member states on migration, was published as Supplement 3/76 to the Bulletin of the European Communities. On 9 February 1976 the Council adopted a Resolution on the Action Programme (OJ C34, 14 Feb 1976, pp 2–3), with a view to the implementation of which the Commission submitted in 1976 a proposal for a Council Directive on the approximation of laws of member states on measures to combat illegal migration and illegal employment (OJ C277, 23 Nov 1976, pp 2–3). (See also 594.)

Men and women of Europe: comparative attitudes to a number of problems of our society

Doc X/608/75. Dec 1975. 215p

A report which contains the main results of a questionnaire survey of some 9500 men and women over the age of 15, conducted in the nine member states on the occasion of International Women's Year. Part 1 contains the main findings of the comparative survey of attitudes to such subjects as women's status, opportunities for men and women, jobs, politics and the European Communities. Part 2 offers a number of explanations for the attitudes expressed.

Review of the rules governing the tasks and operations of the European Social Fund

COM(77)90 final. 29 Mar 1977. 78p

EP Report: Working doc 84/77. 11 May 1977. R. Adams. 30p
EP Debate: Annex OJ No 217, 12 May 1977, pp 203–230
EP Resolution: OJ C133, 6 June 1977, pp 39–40

Council Decision 71/66/EEC of 1 February 1971 on the reform of the European Social Fund provided for a Council review of the Decision not later than five years after its entry into force (JO L28, 4 Feb 1971, pp 15–17). These Commission proposals, submitted in accordance with this provision, are designed to meet criticism of the Fund's administrative procedures and to adjust the nature of the Fund's interventions to take greater account than in the past of the needs of the employment situation. Divided into two main sections, Part 1 outlines the present structure of the Fund as defined in 1971 and the modifications envisaged. In Part 2 the Commission concentrates on an analysis of the proposals, which place greater emphasis on assistance to regions with chronic unemployment problems and greater administrative efficiency. The Council formally adopted new operating rules for the Fund on 20 December 1977 when it agreed Regulation (EEC) No 2893/77 (*OJ* L337, 27 Dec 1977, pp 1–4), and other legislative measures which included Decision 77/803/EEC on action by the Fund for migrant workers (*OJ* L337, 27 Dec 1977, pp 12–13), and Decision 77/804/EEC on action by the Fund for women (*OJ* L337, 27 Dec 1977, p 14).

501 **Report of the study group on the new characteristics of socio-economic development: 'blueprint for Europe'**
Doc II/570/7/76. Dec 1977. 60p

See 39.

502 **Guidelines for the management of the European Social Fund during 1979–1981, and transitional guidelines for 1978**
COM(78)178 final. 2 May 1978. 15p

Submitted to the Council in accordance with Council Regulation (EEC) No 2396/71 of 8 November 1971 (*JO* L249, 10 Nov 1971, pp 54–57), this document consists of a series of guidelines for the management of the European Social Fund and for application to requests for aid up to the end of 1981. Published in the *Official journal of the European Communities* C116, 19 May 1978, pp 2–10 and to be re-examined every year when guidelines for the next three years will be set, these new instructions are intended to concentrate subsidies in areas more appropriate to the current economic and social situation in the Community. On 27 June 1978 the Council took Decision 78/742/EEC on the submission to the Commission of applications for assistance and claims for payment from the European Social Fund (*OJ* L248, 11 Sept 1978, pp 1–124).

503 **The economic implications of demographic change in the European Community: 1975–1995**
Doc II/528/77. June 1978. 2 vols, 120p, 85p

See 43.

504 **Social aspects of the iron and steel policy**
COM(78)570 final. 31 Oct 1978. 25p

See 208.

EMPLOYMENT

505 **L'évolution de l'emploi dans les Etats membres (1954–1958)**
Comm EEC, 1961. 280p (cat 8010)

A general study of employment trends in member countries during the period 1954 to 1958, prepared in response to the Commission's desire for policy decisions to be based on as comprehensive and precise a picture of the labour market and its attendant problems as possible. Considered by the Commission as a departure point for further, more analytical work on the maintenance of a balanced labour market, the report provides essential background information against which to view current difficulties. The Commission first discerns a number of general threads in the evolution of employment in the Community, before looking in more detail at the situation in each individual member country. The report concludes with substantial statistical annexes. In 1960 the Commission made provision for the preparation of an annual study of manpower problems in the Community, the fifth of which for 1964 and subsequent reports up to 1971 were given full publication by the Commission under the title *Les problèmes de main-d'oeuvre dans la Communauté*. Each report provides information on the trend in the labour market by country, branch of activity and region and quantified forecasts of future developments.

Principes généraux pour la mise en oeuvre d'une politique commune de formation professionnelle
COM(61)101 final. 26 June 1961. 46p

EP Report: *Doc de séance* 5/62. 21 Mar 1962. A. Sabatini. 20p
EP Debate: *Débs* No 56, 29/30 Mar 1962, pp 84–112 & 114–122
EP Resolution: *JO* 31, 26 Apr 1962, pp 1034–1038

Article 128 of the EEC Treaty states that 'the Council shall, acting on a proposal from the Commission and after consulting the Economic and Social Committee, lay down general principles for implementing a common vocational training policy capable of contributing to the harmonious development both of the national economies and of the common market'. The Commission submitted this document with a view to implementing the article. It consists of a short introductory note in which the Commission interprets the legal scope of the article and gives consideration to its economic, social and practical implications. This is followed by a draft Council Decision embodying ten general principles for the implementation of a common policy on vocational training, each of which is the subject of brief comment in a third and final section. The document was published as a Supplement to the *Bulletin of the European Economic Community* 12-1961. On 2 April 1963 the Council adopted Decision 63/266/EEC implementing a modified version of these principles (*JO* 63, 20 Apt 1963, pp 1338–1341). The constitution and rules governing the Advisory Committee on Vocational Training envisaged in the fourth principle were published in the *Journal officiel des Communautés européennes* 190, 30 Dec 1963, pp 3090–3091. (*See also* 509.)

Bilan annuel des activités de compensation et de placement dans la Communauté économique européenne (1.10.1961 – 30.9.1962)
V/COM(63)111 final. 28 Mar 1963. 42p

A report on the activities during late 1961 and most of 1962 of the Coordinating Office established with the purpose of coordinating the clearance of vacancies and job applications in the Community. The document opens with introductory remarks on the creation, function and role of the Coordinating Office and with an appraisal of the main characteristics of the labour market during the period under review. This is followed by a country-by-country analysis of the position concerning vacancies and applications and a chapter on the need for accelerated development of training schemes in member countries. (*See also* 513.)

508 **L'évolution et les caractéristiques de l'emploi dans la sidérurgie de la Communauté**
HA doc 3196/64. 26 May 1964. 22p

See 190.

509 **Programmes d'action en matière de politique commune de formation professionnelle en général et dans l'agriculture**
V/SEC(65)1355 final. 5 May 1965. 69p

EP Report: *Doc de séance* 2/66. 1 Mar 1966. A. Sabatini. 8p
          Doc de séance 3/66. 1 Mar 1966. A. Sabatini. 7p
EP Debate: *Débs* No 84, 11 Mar 1966, pp 189–201
EP Resolution: *JO* 53, 24 Mar 1966, pp 784–785

A first action programme for a common policy on vocational training, drafted by the Commission on the basis of the statement of principles adopted by the Council in 1963 (*see* 506). The first part of the document is devoted to the general programme in which the Commission explains the background before describing the objectives to be attained and the procedures to be followed for their achievement. A similar format is followed in the second part of the document relating to a programme of vocational training in the agricultural sector. A new work programme was submitted by the Commission in 1972 in the light of fresh guidelines adopted by the Council in 1971 (*see* 519).

510 **Documents du colloque sur la formation professionnelle, Bruxelles, 16–20 novembre 1964**
Comm EEC, 1966. 436p (cat 8170)

A compendium of major papers presented at the international conference called by the Commission to Brussels in November 1964 to discuss matters relating to vocational training. Composed of invited experts from member governments, employer and employee organizations and other interested parties, the aim of the conference was to establish contacts, to discuss matters of mutual concern and to draw lessons for incorporating into the framework of a common policy for vocational training. The publication contains the papers presented to the two working parties into which the conference was divided, together with the opening and closing addresses. The position in the coal and steel industries was studied in *La formation professionnelle dans les industries de la CECA* (cat 3686), published by the High Authority in 1965.

511 **La situation de la main-d'oeuvre dans les charbonnages de la Communauté**

HA doc 2160/66. 24 Mar 1966. 14p

See also 168.

Problèmes de la politique de l'emploi et de la formation professionnelle
In doc 788/11/1966 final. 25 Mar 1966. 127p

See 63.

Les services de main-d'oeuvre des Etats membres de la Communauté: exposé de synthèse
Comm EEC, 1967. 134p (cat 8193)

Published as number 16 in the series *Etudes—Série politique sociale*, this volume consists of a synthesis of the main results of a fact-finding comparative study of the organization and methods of national employment services in the Community, carried out for the Commission by an expert in each member country. Predominantly descriptive in nature, separate chapters are devoted to such aspects of these services as their basic philosophy, their methods of operation, their organization and structure, financing and personnel. In the final chapter some conclusions are drawn from the data and comments expressed on prospects for the future. The Commission endeavoured to keep the survey up-to-date by publishing an annual report called *Exposé annuel sur les activités des services de main-d'oeuvre des Etats membres de la Communauté*. However, only three reports were published, in 1968 (cat 1037), 1969 (cat 1042) and 1971 (cat 1046).

L'emploi des femmes et ses problèmes dans les états membres de la Communauté économique européenne
Comm EC, 1970. 237p (cat 8333)

A report prepared on behalf of the Commission by Mrs E. Sullerot, a Paris sociologist, on the employment of women and the problems it raises in the member states of the Community. In this analysis of the structure and coordination of female employment in Europe, Mrs Sullerot looks first at the number of working women and the variation in employment rates by country and by region. She examines the level of participation of women in economic activities, the age structure of women at work and their position in the working world.

Rapport de synthèse sur la situation du marché de l'emploi en 1971/72
SEC(71)4201 final. 25 Nov 1971. 36p

A summary report reviewing the main changes that have occurred in the employment market during the year 1971 and outlining the anticipated course of developments in 1972. In Chapter 1 the Commission describes in brief the main characteristics of the current economic situation and its consequences; Chapter 2 consists of an appraisal of the employment market in each member country in 1971. Other chapters record the measures taken by member states and make some evaluation of the prospects for 1972.

Mémorandum du gouvernement italien sur la politique de l'emploi dans la Communauté

SEC(72)1283 final. 12 Apr 1972. 46p

A document in which the Commission sets out its first thoughts on the contents of a memorandum on employment policy submitted by the Italian government during the Council session of 24 June 1971. In reflection of that memorandum's three principal themes, the Commission report contains sections on the problems posed by regional disequilibria, priority measures for manpower and the need to harmonize social security arrangements in member states.

517 **Rapport de synthèse sur la situation du marché de l'emploi en 1971–72**
SEC(72)1736 final. 19 May 1972. 27p

A summary report recapitulating on the main changes in the employment market since November 1971. The report outlines the measures taken during that time and the expected trend in the coming months. Chapter 1 consists of an appraisal of the general economic situation during the period November 1971 to March 1972 and its consequences. Chapter 2 traces the changes that have taken place in the employment market since November 1971. The employment policy measures taken by member states during this period form the subject of the next chapter; prospects for the months ahead are considered in the fourth chapter.

518 **Conclusions et suggestions de la Commission concernant l'emploi et le chômage des jeunes**
SEC(72)2251 final. 3 July 1972. 14p

A report on youth employment and unemployment drawn up by the Commission using data from reports on the situation in each member country prepared by national delegations. Drafted as part of the Commission's efforts to look more closely at employment problems in respect of particular groups of workers, the report draws certain conclusions and makes recommendations on a number of aspects of the problem, including improved information on employment prospects, access to jobs, various forms of aid and the transition from school to working life.

519 **Premières mesures en vue de la mise en oeuvre d'une politique commune de formation professionnelle**
SEC(72)3450 final. 25 Oct 1972. 51p

EP Report: *Working doc* 83/73. 5 June 1973. F. Pisoni. 16p
EP Debate: *Annex OJ* No 163, 5 June 1973, pp 62–68
EP Resolution: *OJ* C49, 28 June 1973, pp 16–17

A new work programme for the implementation of a common policy for vocational training, prepared by the Commission in the light of new Council guidelines for Community action in this field (*JO* C81, 12 Aug 1971, pp 5–11) and designed to supplement and further develop the original work programme agreed on 5 May 1965 in the light of recent economic, social, technical and educational developments (*see* 509). In Chapter 1 the Commission outlines the basis of the work programme and Chapter 2 summarizes the priorities that have been established. Chapter 3 constitutes the main body of the report, in which the Commission describes the three main sections which make up the programme. These concern the evolution of vocational training policies, structure and organization; the adaptation of training methods and the solution of training problems concerning certain categories of people, certain sectors and regions. Within each section a number of specific projects are enumerated, more details of which are provided in an annex which describes their aims and work methods. The document concludes with comments on the programme from the Advisory Committee for Vocational Training. (*See also* 524.)

Memorandum from the Commission to the Council on measures to be taken in application of point 16 of the Hague Communiqué
COM(73)635 final. 27 Apr 1973. 16p

EP Report: *Working doc* 41/74. 3 May 1974. H. Seefeld. 51p
           Working doc 41/74/Annex. 10 June 1974. A. Terrenoire. 19p
EP Debate: *Annex OJ* No 177, 11 June 1974, pp 61–88
EP Resolution: *OJ* C76, 3 July 1974, pp 16–23
ESC Opinion: *OJ* C97, 16 Aug 1974, pp 30–37

A memorandum in which the Commission presents its views and proposals on concrete measures to be taken in application of point 16 of the Hague communiqué, which states that 'all the creative activities and the actions conducive to European growth decided upon here will be assured of a greater future if the younger generation is closely associated with them. The Governments have endorsed this need and the Communities will make provision for it' (*Bull EC*, 1-1970, p 16). The document consists of a brief introductory memorandum explaining the background to the two annexed recommendations for Council Decisions setting up a Committee for Youth Questions and a Youth Advisory Committee.

The Community employment policy: first report of the working party of experts
SEC(73)2592 final. 6 July 1973. 158p

A report drawn up by Dr Albert De Smaele on behalf of an independent group of experts on the objectives and means of employment policy and its relationship to economic and monetary union. Divided into four main parts, the report considers the socio-economic implications of economic and monetary union and the motives and objectives of a Community employment policy. It also describes the outline of a Community employment policy and includes papers presented by each of the individual experts.

Community action programme 'employment of handicapped persons in an open market economy'
SEC(73)4006 final. 26 Nov 1973. 10p

EP Report: *Working doc* 353/73. 11 Feb 1974. C. Durand. 10p
EP Debate: *Annex OJ* No 171, 12 Feb 1974, pp 64–70
EP Resolution: *OJ* C23, 8 Mar 1974, p 17
ESC Opinion: *OJ* C97, 16 Aug 1974, pp 38–40

This action programme for the employment of handicapped persons in an open market economy represents the Commission's first major expression of the long-term aim to make normal work accessible to the largest possible number of handicapped persons. The document outlines the basic aims of the programme, its spheres of activity and its contents. It discusses the methods for implementing the programme during the period up to the end of 1977, and describes the nature of the proposals for Community assistance for rehabilitation activities and the adaptation of structures for rehabilitation and vocational training. On 27 June 1974 the Council adopted a Resolution establishing a first Community action programme for the vocational training of handicapped persons (*OJ* C80, 9 July 1974, pp 30–32). On the same day the Council also adopted Decision 74/328/EEC on action by the European Social Fund on behalf of handicapped persons (*OJ* L185, 9 July 1974, pp 22–23), extended on 25 July 1977 by Council Decision 77/476/EEC (*OJ* L196, 3 Aug 1977, p 14).

523 Women and employment in the United Kingdom, Ireland and Denmark
Doc V/649/75. Mar 1974. 240p

A wide-ranging document consisting of three separate reports on women's employment in the United Kingdom, Ireland and Denmark, prepared by R. B. Cornu on behalf of the Commission. The report on the United Kingdom begins with an introductory outline of the pattern of women's employment in the United Kingdom, with reference to the national, regional, industrial and occupational patterns that may be discerned. Further chapters deal with women's wages and earnings and with factors affecting women's employment, treated under such headings as demography, education, training, conditions of employment, equal opportunity of access and facilities for working mothers. The report concludes with a summary and bibliography. The national report for Ireland summarizes the economic and social situation as it affects the employment of women in that country and is divided into two main parts. The first is concerned with the distribution of employment and the second with the factors affecting women's employment. The report concludes with a summary and bibliography. The national report for Denmark follows a similar pattern, with chapters on women in the labour force, factors affecting women in employment and a summary and conclusions. The three reports are supported by considerable numbers of statistical tables. Similar reports on the employment and training levels of women in each of the original six member states were conducted in 1966 (*see* 514).

524 Establishment of a European Vocational Training Centre
COM(74)352 final. 27 Mar 1974. 14p

EP Report: *Working doc* 231/74. 17 Sept 1974. F. Pisoni. 24p
EP Debate: *Annex OJ* No 181, 25 Sept 1974, pp 59–71
EP Resolution: *OJ* C127, 18 Oct 1974, pp 20–23
ESC Opinion: *OJ* C125, 16 Oct 1974, pp 41–47

In its Social Action Programme adopted on 21 January 1974, the Council expressed its political will 'to implement a common vocational training policy, with a view to attaining progressively the principal objectives thereof, especially approximation of training standards, in particular by setting up a European Vocational Training Centre' and noted the Commission's intention to submit proposals before 1 April

1974 (*OJ* C13, 12 Feb 1974, pp 1–4). As a consequence of proposals made in this document, as amended in a later submission (COM(74)1932 final) and published in the *Official journal of the European Communities* C72, 27 June 1974, pp 17–20, the Council adopted Regulation (EEC) No 337/75 of 10 February 1975 establishing a European Centre for the Development of Vocational Training (*OJ* L39, 13 Feb 1975, pp 1–4). The Centre was officially opened in West Berlin on 9 March 1977, with a mandate to support the Commission in carrying out operational tasks relating to training, to act as a forum and framework within which interested parties could exchange experience and look for solutions to common problems. Among the publications recently issued by the Centre, often referred to as CEDEFOP after its French title, are *Youth unemployment and vocational training in the European Community*, published in 1977 and *Youth unemployment and vocational training: occupational choice and motivation of young people, their vocational training and employment prospects: survey of member states*, published in 1978. The annual statement of accounts and expenditure of CEDEFOP is published in the 'C' series of the *Official journal of the European Communities*.

Employment and the energy situation: a report on the repercussions of the energy crisis on the employment situation of the Community
SEC(74)1358 final. 2 May 1974. 45p

A report from the Commission on the threat to employment of the impact of oil price increases on the balance of payments of member states, on domestic inflation and on the pattern of internal demand. The Commission makes an assessment of the present situation and identifies the actions which the Commission feels should be taken by the Community, national governments and both sides of industry in the next two years or so. Policies to protect and promote employment are advanced, and the impact of the energy crisis on the overall employment situation in each member country and on different sectors of the national economies is treated in a series of annexes.

Conference in the social field 'Prospects of a European social policy'
SEC(74)4943. 6 Dec 1974. 16p

A working paper prepared by Dr Hillary, member of the Commission, for the Tripartite Conference, in which he outlines an overall strategy for the control of employment trends in the present crisis. The causes of the present problems in the labour market are diagnosed and a number of themes upon which future policy must be concentrated are identified.

Equality of treatment between men and women workers (access to employment, to vocational training, to promotion, and as regards working conditions)
COM(75)36 final. 12 Feb 1975. 52p

See 573.

Work in the field of employment
COM(75)125 final. 16 Apr 1975. 25p

The continuing deterioration in the employment situation in the Community is a cause of considerable concern and brings greater urgency to the need for the coherent and coordinated approach to employment problems envisaged in the Social Action Programme (*see* 497). This document, which consists of two communications from the Commission and a proposal for a research programme, provides a detailed account of the work undertaken or planned by the Commission in the field of employment policy. The first communication is concerned with the coordination of employment policy. The Commission calls for close cooperation between national administrations and the Commission and outlines a short-term work programme for coordination, which the Council is asked to endorse. The second communication deals with the development of employment forecasts, adopted by the Council as a priority objective in the Social Action Programme. It begins with an explanation of why such forecasts are necessary and the nature of their limitations; it refers to existing forecasts available in member states and provides a brief appraisal of the work accomplished by the Commission during the past year and its future plans. The third document takes the form of proposals for a research and action programme designed to provide better knowledge of the Community employment market.

529 **Measures to reduce youth unemployment**
SEC(75)1706. 6 May 1975. 24p

A document in which the Commission recognizes that the disproportionately high increase in youth unemployment over the past 12 months is a cause for particular concern and for remedial action. The Commission looks at ways of preparing young people for the world of work and in particular at the educational system, the vocational training system and the vocational guidance system. It considers matters relating to the provision of jobs, including job creation and work sharing, and then at the opportunities for Community action.

530 **Repercussions on employment of the steel programme**
SEC(75)3156 final. 26 Sept 1975. 15p

See 201.

531 **Commission communication to the Council on programme of employment statistics**
COM(75)485 final. 9 Oct 1975. 18p

A report on the statistical information at present available on employment in the Community and a programme for its improvement, submitted in compliance with a request from the Council that the Commission prepare a plan to improve statistical information on the position and trends in the Community labour market. The Commission begins by describing the variety of purposes for which it needs employment statistics, both in connection with the Social Action Programme and with other Community policies with a bearing on employment problems, such as regional policy, industrial policy and education policy. The Commission then moves on to draw attention to the limitations of existing statistics for its requirements, before making proposals for the development of a system of employment statistics which will give a more complete picture of the state of the labour market in Community countries and of current trends in employment. In an annex to the document, the Commission lists and briefly describes the main sources of statistical information available at present at Community level. On 9 February 1976 the Council adopted Regulation (EEC) No 311/76 on the compilation of statistics on foreign workers (*OJ* L39, 14 Feb 1976, p 1).

Tripartite Conference: economic and social situation in the Community and outlook
COM(75)540/2. 5 Nov 1975. 20p

A general appraisal of the economic and social situation in the Community and its medium-term outlook, prepared by the Commission for Ministers of Social and Economic Affairs and representatives of unions and employers meeting with the Commission in the Tripartite Conference. The document begins with a brief summary of the main features of the existing economic situation and a plea from the Commission that the problems caused by the severe recession be tackled in the spirit of Community solidarity and cooperation. The Commission then goes on to refer to a series of short-term measures, relating to such matters as public expenditure, unemployment and working hours, which can alleviate the worst consequences of the present recession. The Commission also considers medium-term problems, with particular reference to the connection between foreign trade and employment.

The preparation of young people for work and for transition from education to working life
Bull EC Supp 12/76

See 592.

A Community strategy for full employment and stability
SEC(76)1400. 31 Mar 1976. 24p

EP Report: *Working doc* 160/76. 15 June 1976. E. Glinne. 19p
EP Debate: *Annex OJ* No 204, 17 June 1976, pp 159–175
EP Resolution: *OJ* C159, 12 July 1976, pp 30–32

EP Report: *Working doc* 168/76. 15 June 1976. H. K. Artzinger. 7p
EP Debate: *Annex OJ* No 204, 17 June 1976, pp 159–175
EP Resolution: *OJ* C159, 12 July 1976, pp 28–29

A document intended by the Commission to serve as the basis for consultations with the social partners in preparation for the 1976 Tripartite Conference. The document opens with an assessment of the present situation, the reasons for the recession and the lessons to be drawn from it. The Commission then proceeds to look in closer detail at the ways in which full employment may be obtained without undermining stability. Separate sections deal with such aspects of the strategy as investment policy, incomes, prices and monetary policies.

Employment trends to 1980 in the member states of the Community
V/628–1/75. 10 May 1976. 25p

An analysis of trends in the structure of employment in the Community countries with quantitative forecasts of the likely pattern of employment in the different branches or sectors by 1980. Based on the work of a group of national experts on medium-term employment prospects, the report is divided into two parts. As the introduction indicates, the first part is concerned with the overall balance of the Community's labour market, the major characteristics of the labour market in each country and also the trends in the composition of the national labour forces. The second part is concerned with past trends in the size and pattern of employment within the major branches of activity in the member states and with the likely situation in 1980.

536 Restoring full employment and stability in the Community
SEC(76)2003 final. 26 May 1976. 10p

EP Report: *Working doc* 160/76. 15 June 1976. E. Glinne. 19p
EP Debate: *Annex OJ* No 204, 17 June 1976, pp 159–175
EP Resolution: *OJ* C159, 12 July 1976, pp 30–32

A document prepared by the Commission for consideration by the Tripartite Conference as a basis for discussion with the social partners on an earlier document on the same subject (*see* 534). The Commission first looks at the common problems facing the member states in restoring full employment and stability. It then warns of the dangers for the Community in a continuation of current trends before, in the main part of the document, outlining the principal measures which the Commission thinks must be implemented if the problems are to be solved and these dangers averted. In its conclusions the Commission sets targets for attainment and enumerates a number of immediate actions that need to be taken if the Community strategy for full employment and stability is to be successful.

537 Outlook for employment in the European Community to 1980
Doc V/409/76. July 1976. 72p

The report on the first phase of work of a group of experts invited by the Commission to identify the main trends affecting employment in the medium-term, to determine areas in need of priority action and, if necessary, to draw up specific guidelines or recommendations. Chapter 1 is concerned with the present employment situation in the Community and with its prospects. Chapter 2 presents a general view of the main problems arising from the present and forecast employment situation. Chapter 3 is concerned with the various types of action that might help to create these conditions.

538 Growth, stability and employment: stock-taking and prospects
COM(77)250 final. 23 May 1977. 16p

A paper prepared by the Commission for the Tripartite Conference held on 27 June 1977 in order to take stock of progress achieved since the last conference in June 1976 and to assess prospects for the future. After a general appraisal of developments in economic and social fields since the last conference, the Commission highlights the main internal and external problems inherent in the present situation and their consequences. The Commission then moves on to give its assessment of the ways in which the Community should react to these difficulties, with particular emphasis upon the need for a concerted effort to beat such evils as unemployment and inflation, for coherent measures dealing with incomes, prices and related policies and the more effective use of Community financial instruments. Finally, the Commission identifies a number of unresolved questions around which further debate should take place.

Report to the European Council on Community action in the field of the labour market (particularly on behalf of training and employment of young people and women)
COM(77)301 final. 15 June 1977. 5p

Following its meeting on 25 March 1977, the Council 'agreed that action should be taken at Community level, in particular to encourage the adoption of measures intended to contribute to the solution of certain specific labour market problems, more especially by improving the training and job opportunities for young persons and women'. In this brief report to the Council, the Commission sets out ways in which such a contribution might be made. It reviews the Community measures already in hand and suggests additional initiatives which would complement and add to existing Community activities.

Communication from the Commission to the Council on youth employment
COM(77)476 final. 17 Oct 1977. 51p

Growing concern at the increase in unemployment among young people caused the European Council, meeting in June 1977, to call upon the Commission to continue its work on this problem and to request that the Council of Ministers of Social Affairs 'meet in early Autumn to consider, in the light of this work and the results of national measures, what common action might be necessary'. This communication from the Commission was drawn up for that Council meeting. Introductory remarks on the background to the paper are followed by a chapter in which the Commission presents the facts of the present situation as regards youth unemployment in the Community and the prospects for the future. Also included is a diagnosis of the causes of youth unemployment as revealed by the Commission's analysis. The following chapter reviews and draws conclusions from the measures taken by member states and at the Community level, with particular reference to the European Social Fund and the contribution that can be made by vocational preparation for work and education. In Chapter 4 the Commission suggests ways in which the Community can make a greater impact upon this problem. In particular, the document envisages the use of Community financial aid to facilitate the creation of jobs and increased Community aid to post-school training for young people. The Commission also makes suggestions for measures of a wider scope and indicates that it will submit specific proposals in the light of discussion on the guidelines and suggestions put forward in this document. The communication concludes with a detailed review of, and commentary on, the measures taken by member states to promote the employment and training of young persons. The whole document, together with extracts from the press releases issued by the Council and the Standing Committee on Employment after initial examination of the communication, were published as Supplement 4/77 to the *Bulletin of the European Communities*.

541 Analysis of vocational preparation in the member states of the European Community
Comm EC, 1978. 58p (cat CB-25-78-186-EN-C)

Concern at the continued growth of youth unemployment led the Commission to adopt on 6 July 1977 a Recommendation to member states on vocational preparation for young people who are unemployed or threatened by unemployment (*OJ* L180, 20 July 1977, pp 18–23). The term 'vocational preparation' is used 'to designate those activities that aim to assure for young people a satisfactory transition from school to work by providing them with the minimum knowledge and skills necessary for working life'. This report, prepared by Olav Magnusson for the Commission, assesses present needs and existing provision of vocational preparation for young people in the Communities. Chapter 1 consists of a short survey of youth unemployment problems, with special emphasis upon the factors influencing youth unemployment. In Chapter 2 the author assesses the magnitude of the problem in terms of numbers and training needs in the various member states. In Chapter 3 Magnusson presents a survey of present provision for vocational preparation in each member state and compares these programmes with the measures proposed in the Commission's Recommendation. The contribution of vocational preparation to the alleviation of youth unemployment and the improvement of employment prospects is the subject of Chapter 4. The text of the Commission Recommendation is appended.

542 Work-sharing
SEC(78)740. 20 Feb 1978. 13p

EP Report: *Working doc* 179/78. 3 July 1978. W. Albers. 5p
EP Debate: *Annex OJ* No 232, 7 July 1978, pp 262–265
EP Resolution: *OJ* C182, 31 July 1978, p 66

At the end of the 1977 Tripartite Conference, it was agreed that there should be an investigation of the possibilities for redistributing the volume of work available in the economy in such a way as to increase employment opportunities. This document represents the Commission's contribution to the meeting which the Standing Committee on Employment intends to devote to work-sharing in March 1978. The Commission first outlines the economic and social background, defines the forms and methods of work-sharing and offers some general comments upon the subject. The Commission then moves on to look, in three separate sections, at the possibilities for Community action in this field. The first concerns a Community initiative to reduce the annual amount of work performed by each worker. The Commission then enumerates those areas where specific Community action will be explored, namely, restrictions on overtime work, shift working and an extension of the right to training. Finally, the Commission identifies areas in which further study is necessary, namely, the influence of social security on work sharing, temporary work, part-time work and equal treatment for men and women. (*See also* 543.)

543 Work-sharing—objectives and effects

SEC(78)740/2. 24 Feb 1978. 31p

An analytical working document prepared and used by the Commission in its consultations with its social partners, prior to drafting its contribution to the meeting of the Standing Committee on Employment on work-sharing (*see* 542). Issued as an annex to that document, this paper attempts to evaluate work-sharing as a strategy in the battle against unemployment. In preliminary chapters the Commission explains why work-sharing needs to be considered as an option, explores the possible forms of work-sharing and describes the current working-time patterns in member countries. The Commission then attempts to evaluate the potential effects of work-sharing and distils certain principles for action. Finally, the Commission offers an initial assessment of specific measures that might be implemented, namely, shortening the working week, the extension of annual holidays, the expansion of part-time employment, changes in retirement age and the extension of schooling and training.

Proposals for Community aids to promote the employment of young people
COM(78)89 final. 10 Apr 1978. 22p

EP Report: *Working doc* 88/78. 2 May 1978. P. Lezzi. 12p
　　　　　Working doc 88/78/Annex. 9 May 1978. J.-M. Caro. 12p
EP Debate: *Annex OJ* No 230, 9 May 1978, pp 37–56
EP Resolution: *OJ* C131, 5 June 1978, pp 22–24
ESC Opinion: *OJ* C283, 27 Nov 1978, pp 29–32

In its general communication on youth employment problems submitted to the Council in October 1977 (*see* 540), the Commission gave notice of its intention to submit firm proposals. This document contains a general memorandum on the state of work in the field of youth employment and a proposal for a Regulation to combat youth unemployment by introducing a new form of aid from the European Social Fund. The general memorandum recapitulates on the problems of youth employment and describes the measures taken by the Community. The proposal for a Council Regulation (*OJ* C100, 25 Apr 1978, pp 4–5) was adopted by the Council on 18 December 1978 in Council Regulation (EEC) No 3039/78 (*OJ* L361, 23 Dec 1978, pp 3–4).

Working paper on the role of the tertiary (including public) sectors in the achievement of growth, stability and full employment
SEC(78)1526 final. 14 Apr 1978. 27p

EP Report: *Working doc* 179/78. 3 July 1978. W. Albers. 5p
EP Debate: *Annex OJ* No 232, 7 July 1978, pp 262–265
EP Resolution: *OJ* C182, 31 July 1978, p 66

A brief working document prepared for a meeting of the Standing Committee on Employment on the future development of the tertiary sector, a concept the document uses to describe 'those economic activities whose purpose is neither to exploit national resources nor to manufacture goods, but to provide services. This includes commerce, banks and insurance, other market services and non-market services (principally education, health, defence and administration)'. The Commission outlines the problems concerning employment in this heterogeneous sector, analyses trends in the sector and suggests a series of subjects for preliminary discussion in the Standing Committee. The more substantial report upon which this summary document is based is annexed to it for information.

546 Tripartite Conference of 9 November 1978
COM(78)512 final. 10 Oct 1978. 34p

A general assessment of the economic and social situation in the Community and description of the broad strategy and action necessary to bring about a significant improvement in employment levels, prepared by the Commission for the 1978 Tripartite Conference. In Chapter 1 the Commission paints a brief picture of the present economic and social situation and its consequences for employment. Chapter 2 is concerned with the overall strategy the Commission considers necessary to bring about a recovery in the employment situation. Chapter 3 describes the action that must be taken to implement this strategy. A series of annexes contain the conclusions of the Standing Committee on Employment, and the Economic and Social Committee on a number of matters identified for further discussion at the 1977 Tripartite Conference.

SOCIAL WELFARE

547 Synthèse des rapports établis en 1960 sur la situation actuelle du service social des travailleurs migrants dans les six pays membres de la C.E.E.
Doc V/5664/1/60. n.d. 68p

A summary of the reports drawn up by national experts on the position of migrant workers and their families vis-à-vis the social services in each member country in 1960. The report looks at the characteristics of migratory movements, at the problems caused by migration for social service departments and at the provision made in countries of immigration and emigration for migrant workers.

548 Etude sur la physionomie actuelle de la sécurité sociale dans les pays de la CEE
Comm EEC, 1962. 130p (cat 8058)

A review prepared at the invitation of the Commission by a group of independent experts, in which they present a synoptic report on the situation regarding social security in each member state as at 1 January 1962. Published as number three in the series *Etudes—Série politique sociale*, the report deals in Chapter 1 with the development of social security in member states and the relationship between social security and the law. Chapters 2 and 3 examine the scope of social security schemes as they apply to various categories of recipient and their organization. The following three chapters are concerned with the various categories of benefit, financial and economic aspects and finally with social security and international relations. A series of conclusions draw out the main differences between national systems and the points on which they agree.

Etude comparée des prestations de sécurité sociale dans les pays de la CEE
Comm EEC, 1962. 145p (cat 8059)

A report prepared by the ILO at the Commission's request and published as number four in the series *Etudes—Série politique sociale*, on the relative value of social benefits within each member country and between individual countries. Separate chapters are concerned with the real value of various categories of benefit, including sickness, maternity, invalidity, old age, death, accident and unemployment benefits.

Financement de la sécurité sociale dans les pays de la CEE
Comm EEC, 1962. 164p (cat 8060)

Prepared for the Commission by the ILO and published as number five in the series *Etudes—Série politique sociale*, this report examines the various methods and sources of financing the allocation of resources, transfers between contingencies and between schemes and the flexibility of schemes in relation to the cover provided. After an introductory chapter on the scope and methods used in the investigation, the report outlines the legal provisions governing financial administration and traces the developments in contribution rates and ceilings between 1949 and 1961. Further chapters provide statistics on schemes applicable to wage-earners and highlight the divergences between various types of firm and branches of industry with regard to contributions and the cost of certain social benefits. The report then looks more closely at financial arrangements in agriculture, and concludes with a number of chapters which provide figures on the costs of social security as a whole and on the financial operations of general schemes for wage-earners.

Conférence européenne sur la sécurité sociale
Comm EEC, Comm EAEC, HA ECSC, 1964. 2 vols, 759p, 348p (cat 8096)

The proceedings of the European Conference on Social Security organized on the initiative of the three Community executives in Brussels from 10 to 15 December 1962 and attended by representatives of employers' and workers' organizations, together with observers and delegates from other Community institutions, member governments and other interested parties. The first of the two volumes of published proceedings contains the texts of the speeches delivered at the opening and closing plenary sessions together with the reports on the main conference topics from the three working committees into which the conference was divided, namely, the extension of the scope of social security, the financing of social security and the possibilities for harmonizing social security benefits. It also contains the texts of the reports from special working parties invited to examine problems peculiar to certain sectors, mining, transport, agriculture and nuclear energy. The second volume contains a range of written communications and documents prepared for the conference.

Suites données à 'la recommandation de la Commission aux états membres concernant l'activité des services sociaux à l'égard des travailleurs se déplacant dans la Communauté'
Doc 6936/1/V/64. n.d. 138p

On 23 July 1962 the Commission issued a Recommendation to member states on the question of social services for workers moving from one Community country to another (*JO* 75, 16 Aug 1962, pp 2118–2122). This document contains the official reports from member states on the action they have taken during the period August 1962 to December 1964 in response to this attempt to tackle some of the human problems arising from internal migration within the Community. Statistical data include figures on the movements of the working population in the Six and on the sums of money allocated to assistance for migrant workers.

553 Les régimes complémentaires de sécurité sociale dans les pays de la CEE
Comm EEC, 1966. 98p (cat 8185)

A study of supplementary social security schemes in force in member countries, conceived as one of a series of reviews designed to build up a complete picture of the social security position in the European Community, published as number 15 in the series *Etudes—Série politique sociale*. Part 1 establishes the importance and the general characteristics of supplementary social security schemes in the different member states. Part 2 is devoted to a more detailed examination of supplementary pension schemes in member countries, and the following part with supplementary benefits for other risks, particularly unemployment. The study is completed by a series of conclusions, appendices on supplementary social security schemes in agriculture and the building trade and a bibliography.

554 La sécurité sociale des pays membres de la Communauté et les travailleurs migrants des pays tiers
HA doc 4657/66. n.d. 90p

A detailed comparative analysis of the social security rights accorded to migrant workers coming from third countries in the laws of member states of the European Communities. The document consists of an introductory chapter followed by separate chapters on the position in each member country except Italy; it concludes with a number of statistical appendices. The report also outlines the provisions of the various bilateral and multilateral agreements on the subject.

555 Rapport sur la comparaison du système britannique de sécurité sociale avec les systèmes des pays de la Communauté
Doc 15.408/XVII/68. n.d. 83p

A report prepared by the Commission with the help of the National Coal Board in the United Kingdom, comparing Community and British social security schemes as at 1 January 1967. Part 1 consists of a description of the general and mineworkers' schemes in operation in the United Kingdom and in Community countries. Part 2 consists of a comparative analysis of the application of these schemes and their results.

556 Les incidences économiques de la sécurité sociale
Comm EC, 1970. 203p (cat 8275)

A first study at Community level of the impact of the various elements of social security policy on the economy as a whole, conducted at the request of the

Commission by a committee of independent experts under the direction of Professor A. Coppini and published as number 21 in the series *Etudes—Série politique sociale*. The study begins with a brief review of working methods, the aims and limitations of the report and a preliminary description of demographic aspects and the scale of social security transfers. Further chapters deal with such topics as the primary redistribution of incomes through social security, the transfer of social charges, the effects of social security on consumption, manpower supply and demand and on price structure.

L'évolution financière de la sécurité sociale dans les Etats membres de la Communauté 1965–1970–1975
Comm EC, 1971. 55p (cat 8375)

A summary of the survey of trends in the financing of social security arrangements in member states from 1965 to 1975, conducted by a group of independent experts with assistance from the Commission. Seen as an important step towards the preparation of a European Social Budget (*see* 558), this synthesis of more detailed national reports prepared by members of the working group, describes the way in which social security expenditure and financing has developed in member states and compares both with national revenue and gross national product. Further monographs on social security were also published by the Commission in 1971 under the titles *Indicateurs de sécurité sociale* (cat 8292) and *Les études économiques et financières sur la sécurité sociale: rapport de synthèse* (cat 8359).

Programme de travail pour l'élaboration du budget social européen
SEC(72)2832 final. 12 Sept 1972. 34p

On 26 November 1970 the Council decided to establish a European Social Budget and invited the Commission to submit a work programme for its realization (*JO* C23, 8 Mar 1972, p 22). This response from the Commission serves two basic purposes. It contributes to the clearer definition of the budget's essential features by looking at such elements as its content, framework, the period to be covered and structure. The Commission also proposes a work programme for its achievement which includes comments on the methods to be employed and calendar of work and decisions to be taken by the Council. (*See also* 559.)

First European Social Budget (1970–1975)
SEC(74)4500 final. 27 Nov 1974. 70p

A first attempt to provide the Community with a valid instrument for forecasting social expenditure, a quantitative source of information on past and future trends in social expenditure, prepared by the Commission in response to the mandate granted by the Council at its meeting on 9 November 1972, the complete text of which is reproduced in this document. Drawn up in collaboration with government experts, the Social Budget is not a true budget in the accepted public finance sense. Rather it provides estimates of expenditure and receipts for several sectors of social policy, particularly social security, for the period 1973 to 1975, based on existing social accounts data for the period 1970 to 1972. The intention is to foster closer understanding of the social policies of member states, to bring out the characteristics of national policies on social protection and to make appropriate comparisons. After preliminary observations on the partial nature of the exercise, on methodology and presentation, further chapters, liberally provided with statistical tables, report on the main findings. (*See also* 560.)

560 European Social Budget
COM(75)647 final. 15 Dec 1975. 6p

EP Report: *Working doc* 38/76. 6 Apr 1976. K. Albertsen. 8p
EP Debate: *Annex OJ* No 202, 6 Apr 1976, pp 42–67
EP Resolution: *OJ* C100, 3 May 1976, p 18

A brief document in which the Commission continues work on the development of a European Social Budget, intended to be a comprehensive source of comparative data on past and future trends in social expenditure and an effective aid to decision-making. Recognizing the first Social Budget (*see* 559) as no more than an initial attempt, the Commission defines a number of objectives for the future and establishes a series of guidelines for the second Budget, intended to cover the period from 1976 to 1980, with further budgets to follow at two-yearly intervals. (*See also* 561.)

561 First European Social Budget (revised) 1970–1975
COM(76)201 final. 12 May 1976. 64p

EP Report: *Working doc* 397/76. 8 Nov 1976. K. Albertsen. 13p
EP Debate: *Annex OJ* No 209, 18 Nov 1976, pp 169–180
EP Resolution: *OJ* C293, 13 Dec 1976, pp 44–46

A review of the first European Social Budget, the aim of which is to take account of the economic and legislative changes that have taken place since the forecasts for 1975 were made in 1973 (*see* 559). Projections for 1975 are brought in line with the new economic order, dominated by the energy crisis and high raw material prices unforeseen in 1973. After preliminary remarks about the basic features of the first Budget, the Commission explains the new projections, outlines the main findings of an examination of trends in social expenditure and receipts over the years 1970, 1972 and 1975 and compares the level of social expenditure with that of the national income or gross national product.

562 Dynamization of social security benefits
COM(76)719 final. 11 Jan 1977. 2 vols, 25p, 100p

One of the objectives of the Social Action Programme was 'progressively to introduce machinery for adapting social security benefits to increase prosperity in the various Member States' (*see* 497). It is the purpose of this communication to draw the attention of the Council to current problems concerning this matter. Part 1 consists of a synthesis of the data collected by the Commission on the present situation in member states as regards the systematic adjustment of social security benefits. Parts 2 and 3 present the Commission's initial thoughts on the topic and then a summary of the views of government experts and representatives of both sides of industry. In the final section of the document, the Commission draws conclusions from the work accomplished and the consultations held so far. A separate volume contains a number of appendices. The first records in some detail the current situation in each of the member states; the second provides a further account of the views of government experts as reflected in the summary records of meetings held with the Commission.

Second European Social Budget (1976–1980)
COM(78)318 final. 12 July 1978. 2 vols, 219p, 383p

As previously stated by the Commission (*see* 559 & 561), the purpose of the Social Budget is to assist policy-making at both national and Community level by providing medium-term data upon which member governments can assess their own social progress as compared with that of Community partners. Based primarily upon social protection accounts, health and social security data, the report provides projections for 1980 as well as statistics for 1970 and 1975. Divided into two separate parts, the document first presents the basic results with comments on the functions of social benefits and social protection and the economic environment. The second part consists of a series of national reports describing legislative changes in member states and details of the methodology used in the exercise. The document was published by the Commission in 1978 in a volume of the same name (cat CB-25-78-704-EN-C).

LIVING AND WORKING CONDITIONS

Evolution quantitative et qualitative de la construction résidentielle dans les pays de la C.E.E. depuis 1945
Doc III/D/2474/61. n.d. 55p

A review of progress in housing construction in each member country since 1945, a period when war damage, population growth and internal migration caused rapid development of the construction industry. The report contains statistical data from national and international sources on the number of dwellings built in each member country and qualitative information on the type of housing constructed in this period.

Rapport de la Commission au Conseil sur l'état d'application de l'article 119 CEE au ...

30 June 1962	V/COM(62)321 final. 17 Dec 1962. 18p
30 June 1963	V/COM(64)11 final. 22 Jan 1964. 31p
31 Dec 1964	V/COM(65)270 final. 7 July 1965. 78p
31 Dec 1966	SEC(67)3204 final. 31 July 1967. 134p
31 Dec 1968	SEC(70)2338 final. 18 June 1970. 151p
31 Dec 1972	SEC(73)3000 final. 18 July 1973. 45p
31 Dec 1973	SEC(74)2721 final. 17 July 1974. 52p
12 Feb 1978	COM(78)711 final. 16 Jan 1979. 145p

Article 119 of the EEC Treaty declares that 'each Member State shall during the first stage ensure and subsequently maintain the application of the principle that men and women should receive equal pay for equal work'. In 1960 the Commission addressed a Recommendation to member states on the implementation of this Article (*Bull EEC*, 6/7-1960, pp 46–47). In a Resolution adopted on 30 December 1961, representatives of member governments gave the principle more definition and established a time-table for reducing the differences in pay between men and women (*Bull EEC*, 1-1962, pp 7–9). In this series of periodic reports, the Commission makes use of information received by way of questionnaire returns from member governments, employers, and workers' organizations to survey the application of the principle in each member country. Each report assesses the situation pertaining in individual member states and describes recent legislative measures and collective agreements adopted in application of the principle. In view of continuing discrepancies in the application of the principle in member states, the Commission decided to make a formal proposal for a Directive harmonizing legislation on the matter (COM(73)1927 final), modified in 1974 (COM(74)1010 final), which was adopted in Council Directive 75/117/EEC of 10 February 1975 (*OJ* L45, 19 Feb 1975, pp 19–20).

566 Projet de recommandation de la Commission aux états membres concernant le logement des travailleurs qui se déplacent à l'intérieur de la Communauté
V/COM(64)255 final. 8 July 1964. 15p

A document in which the Commission recommends to member states a number of measures which can contribute to the solution of complex problems concerning the housing of migrant workers. The Commission considers it to be a particularly opportune moment to examine this matter, coinciding as it does with the entry into force of Council Regulation (EEC) No 38/64 of 25 March 1964 on the free circulation of workers (*JO* 62, 17 Apr 1964, pp 965–980). The document consists of an explanatory memorandum giving background information and recommendations for action designed to achieve a number of enumerated objectives. The Recommendation, finally adopted on 7 July 1965, lists a number of measures designed to improve the plight of workers who move from one Community country to another (*JO* 137, 27 July 1965, pp 2293–2298).

567 Contribution à l'étude des modes de représentation des intérêts des travailleurs dans le cadre des sociétés anonymes européennes
Comm EC, 1970. 64p (cat 8278)

See 107.

568 Dispositions en faveur des travailleurs en cas de licenciement dans le droit des pays membres des Communautés européennes
SEC(72)1516 final. 3 May 1972. 39p

A synthesis of the legal provisions made in the labour law of member states to protect workers in the event of redundancy. The comparison highlights a number of notable discrepancies as regards the measures that have been taken to protect workers against the adverse effects of collective dismissal. The Commission subsequently submitted firm proposals for harmonizing legislation on this matter

(COM(72)1400), which it amended later in the light of comments from the European Parliament and Economic and Social Committee (COM(73)1980). On 17 December 1974 the Council approved Directive 75/129/EEC, the purpose of which was to protect workers in the event of mass dismissals (*OJ* L48, 22 Feb 1975, pp 29–30).

9 **Agricultural incomes in the enlarged Community: present situation and course of development**
SEC(73)900. 7 Mar 1973. 92p

See 381.

0 **The creation of a European Foundation for the Improvement of Living and Working Conditions**
COM(73)2026 final. 5 Dec 1973. 24p

EP Report: *Working doc* 93/74. 22 May 1974. E. Jahn. 23p
EP Debate: *Annex OJ* No 177, 12 June 1974, pp 141–152
EP Resolution: *OJ* C76, 3 July 1974, pp 33–36

EP Report: *Working doc* 94/74. 22 May 1974. L. Marras. 13p
EP Debate: *Annex OJ* No 177, 12 June 1974, pp 141–152
EP Resolution: *OJ* C76, 3 July 1974, pp 36–37

A brief communication in which the Commission outlines the tasks, structure and organization of the European Foundation for the Improvement of Living and Working Conditions, whose formal creation is proposed in an attached draft Council Regulation (*OJ* C35, 28 Mar 1974, pp 5–8). Support for such an institution had been expressed at the Paris summit, as a consequence of which the Commission decided, in its draft Social Action Programme (*see* 497), to replace its earlier suggestions for a European Institute for the Environment (*see* 471 & 472) with expanded proposals for a single institute to study both living and working conditions. On 26 May 1975 the Council formally adopted Regulation (EEC) No 1365/75 establishing the Institute (*OJ* L139, 30 May 1975, pp 1–4).

1 **Machinery for adjusting wages and salaries to the cost of living**
SEC(74)4268. 14 Nov 1974. 40p

A working paper presented to the Council by the Commission as part of its study programme on the effects of inflation on incomes. The report is divided into three main sections. The first consists of a descriptive summary of the existing situation in member states, with regard to the index-linking of salaries. For the purpose of this analysis, member states are grouped into those that have a well-established system of salary indexing (Belgium, Luxembourg, Denmark and Italy); those that at present have various reasonably well developed systems for linking wages to prices (Netherlands, France, United Kingdom and Ireland) and those countries where index-linking plays no part in wages policy (West Germany). In the second section the Commission looks more closely at the various schemes for protecting the purchasing power of wages and identifies a number of technical problems concerning their implementation. The final section summarizes the main arguments generally used for and against indexing wages to the cost of living. The document concludes with a number of statistical annexes.

572 Programme of pilot schemes and studies to combat poverty drawn up in accordance with the Resolution of the Council of 21 January 1974 concerning a social action programme
SEC(74)5225 final. 8 Jan 1975. 31p

Initial guidelines for the introduction of a poverty action programme, submitted in accordance with the Council Resolution of 21 January 1974 on the Social Action Programme in which the Council expressed its political will to 'implement, in cooperation with the Member States, specific measures to combat poverty by drawing up pilot schemes' (*see* 497). Selected as one of the nine priority measures upon which the Commission undertook to submit proposals during 1974, the document falls into three parts. Part 1 consists of introductory material on the background to the proposals and acknowledgement of the benefit the Commission derived in the formulation of its proposals from a consultative document drawn up by a working party representing a wide range of public and private interests and discussed at a seminar in Brussels in June 1974. In Part 2 the Commission outlines the main features of the scheme. The objective is declared to be 'to stimulate schemes to combat poverty in the Member States by selecting a limited number of projects to be part-financed by the Community, which can identify the main causes of poverty and indicate effective action for its alleviation'. The Commission proposes various guidelines and criteria for the selection of schemes, gives details of provisions for aid and for cooperation with member states and outlines a method for classifying schemes. Part 3 contains a preliminary list of schemes and studies drawn up during the course of consultations, more detailed information on which appears in an accompanying annex. The document was followed in April 1975 by a draft proposal for a Council Decision on the subject (COM(75)172 final), upon which the Council adopted Decision 75/458/EEC of 22 July 1975 (*OJ* L199, 30 July 1975, pp 34–35). (*See also* 577.)

573 Equality of treatment between men and women workers (access to employment, to vocational training, to promotion, and as regards working conditions)
COM(75)36 final. 12 Feb 1975. 52p

EP Report: *Working doc* 24/75. 7 Apr 1975. Lady Elles. 14p
EP Debate: *Annex OJ* No 190, 29 Apr 1975, pp 52–68
EP Resolution: *OJ* C111, 20 May 1975, pp 14–17
ESC Opinion: *OJ* C286, 15 Dec 1975, pp 8–19

The problems facing women in employment are the subject of this communication from the Commission. Drawn up after consultations with groups of experts nominated by member states and representatives of the social partners, the communication and draft Directive are presented in accordance with the priority objectives established in the Social Action Programme adopted by the Council on 21 January 1974 (*see* 497). The communication begins with a short analysis of the problems facing working women in the Community in which the Commission offers some general guidelines for action. In further chapters the Commission looks in turn at more specific problem areas, namely, employment, recruiting conditions and promotion; vocational guidance, training and retraining; working conditions; child care facilities and support for workers with family responsibilities, and social security. In the final chapter the Commission sets out the action envisaged by the Commission at Community level during the coming year, with reference to the use of the European Social Fund for projects in the field of women's employment and improvements in information about women's work. The draft Directive requests member states to eliminate within one year of adoption all legal and administrative measures which discriminate against women at work on the basis of sex, marital or family status (*OJ* C124, 4 June 1975, pp 2–4). The Council subsequently adopted the proposal in Council Directive 76/207/EEC of 9 February 1976 on the implementation of the principle of equal treatment for men and women (access to employment, working conditions, vocational training) (*OJ* L39, 14 Feb 1976, pp 40–42).

Guidelines for a Community programme for safety, hygiene and health protection at work
COM(75)138 final. 8 Apr 1975. 15p

EP Report: *Working doc* 211/75. 31 Aug 1975. C. Meintz. 16p
EP Debate: *Annex OJ* No 194, 24 Sept 1975, pp 201–205
EP Resolution: *OJ* C239, 20 Oct 1975, pp 36–38

A set of general guidelines on the development of an action programme on safety, hygiene and safety at work, prepared by the Commission in response to the call made in the Social Action Programme for such a programme (*see* 497) and to the growing number of industrial accidents and diseases. The Commission identifies eight broad objectives and describes the action necessary for their attainment. The eight objectives are concerned with joint action to ensure that technical regulations for accident prevention are continuously updated, the coordination of research, the improvement of statistics and information on prevention methods, and the promotion of safety at enterprise level and in certain specific sectors and groups. (*See also* 585.)

Rehabilitation of handicapped persons – elimination of architectural barriers to their mobility
COM(75)432 final. 25 July 1975. 26p

On 27 June 1974 the Council adopted a Resolution establishing an initial action programme for the vocational rehabilitation of handicapped persons which underlined that the general aim must be to help the handicapped become capable of leading normal lives fully integrated into society (*OJ* C80, 9 July 1974, pp 30–32). This communication from the Commission is concerned with the work of a group of independent experts invited by the Commission to work out a framework of minimum standards regarding accessibility to and mobility within houses for wheelchair users. The bulk of the document is taken up with a summary of the group's findings, and a series of proposals for pilot schemes and studies designed to improve the mobility of the physically handicapped by the elimination of architectural barriers.

576 Employee participation and company structure in the European Community

COM(75)570 final. 12 Nov 1975. 188p

A contribution from the Commission to the debate on the role of employees in relation to the decision-making structures of companies in the European Community, this memorandum is divided into two main parts. Part 1 begins with comments upon the need and justification for Community legislation in this controversial area. It explains that the purpose of the document is 'first to give an account of the principal positions and trends, political and legal, which are discernible in the Community'. The second function is to 'focus attention on what appears to be the fundamental questions which must be answered, and the possible answers to those questions, if the current debate is to be brought to a useful conclusion for the time being at the European level'. The Commission then presents a brief summary of Community programmes and proposals to date, before describing in much more detail the problems facing the Community as regards company structure and the ways in which employees are able to influence the decisions of companies for which they work. This part of the document concludes with a summary of the common features and trends in company structure and employee participation, disclosed by the preceding analysis, and emphasizes the need for a flexible approach to the problem. Part 2 consists of a country by country survey of the present situation in each member country. The document concludes with a short appendix on employee participation in companies which are members of a group and another on the proposed functions of a European Works Council. The communication was published as Supplement 8/75 to the *Bulletin of the European Communities*.

577 Pilot schemes and studies to combat poverty

SEC(75)3835 final. 27 Nov 1975. 64p

Council Decision 75/458/EEC of 22 July 1975 authorized the Commission to promote or to provide financial assistance for pilot schemes which test and develop new methods of helping persons beset by or threatened by poverty, and pilot studies to improve understanding of the nature, causes, scope and mechanics of poverty in the Community (*OJ* L199, 30 July 1975, pp 34–35). This document contains details of the 21 pilot schemes proposed by the governments of member states and two cross national studies proposed by the Commission for which the Commission has approved financial support. (*See also* 572 & 580.)

578 Comparative survey of the protection of employees in the event of the insolvency of their employer in the Member States of the European Communities

Doc V/305/1/76 final. n.d. 26p

A comparative analysis of provisions made in the laws of member states to protect employees in the event of their employer's bankruptcy, drawn up for the Commission by Professor Gerhard Schnorr on the basis of contributions from academic experts, employees' and employers' organizations and government experts. In view of the inadequate levels of protection under existing bankruptcy law, the Commission later made a formal proposal to harmonize and reinforce the protection accorded to employees in the event of their employer's insolvency (COM(78)141 final), later published in the *Official journal of the European Communities* C135, 9 June 1978, pp 2–4. This proposal follows an earlier proposal to ensure that employees suffer no detriment in the event of the transfer of ownership and control of companies (COM(74)351 final), finally adopted by the Council on 14 February 1977 in Directive 77/187/EEC (OJ L61, 5 Mar 1977, pp 26–28).

Reform of the organization of work (humanisation of work)
COM(76)253 final. 3 June 1976. 26p

In its Resolution on the Social Action Programme, the Council called for 'an action programme for workers aimed at the humanisation of their living and working conditions' with particular reference to improvements in safety and health at work, the gradual elimination of physical and psychological stress at work and a reform of the organization of work (*see* 497). The purpose of this communication is to inform the Council of action taken by the Commission with regard to the last of these priorities and its proposals for future action. The Commission defines the broad concept of 'humanisation of work' in such a way as to include 'all those changes in the design of the work process within the enterprise and in relations between workers or within the structure of management, calculated to improve working conditions by reducing such negative factors as isolation and boredom and making work more meaningful and satisfying'. The Commission begins by recalling the main contributions it has made so far to the evolution of a common strategy, then refers to relevant developments concerning the approximation of laws. A number of guidelines for future policy and action are defined, and a work programme proposed for the European Foundation for the Improvement of Living and Working Conditions. The document concludes with an annex which consists of a background paper on improvements in the quality of life, reflecting the discussions held between the Commission and its social partners.

Report from the Commission to the Council on the European programme of pilot schemes to combat poverty 1976
COM(76)718 final. 13 Jan 1977. 89p

A condition under which assistance was approved in 1975 for pilot schemes and studies to combat poverty was that each project leader should submit a progress report to the Commission (*see* 577). This document summarizes these project reports. In Part 1 the Commission outlines the history of the programme from its inclusion in the Council Resolution of 21 January 1974 on the Social Action Programme (*see* 497). Part 2 explains the aims of the programme and contains summaries of the project reports; in Part 3 the Commission looks to the future and presents the case for continuing the projects and suggests a modest expansion of the programme. Council Decision 77/779/EEC of 12 December 1977 extended the programme for a further three years (OJ L322, 17 Dec 1977, pp 28–29). (*See also* 582.)

Agricultural incomes in the Community

COM(77)60 final. 11 Feb 1977. 91p

See 390.

582 The perception of poverty in Europe
Doc V/171/77. Mar 1977. 120p

A report of a public opinion survey on the perception of poverty, carried out in member states as one of the pilot schemes to combat poverty (*see* 580). Conducted by questionnaire during May and June 1976, the survey reports upon people's attitudes towards income, the conditions of life and poverty.

583 Communication from the Commission concerning the European Trade Union Institute
COM(77)275 final. 24 June 1977. 16p

In its Resolution on the Social Action Programme, the Council expressed its political will to 'help the trade union organizations participating in the work of the Community to set up services for training and information in European affairs and to create a European Trade Union Institute' (*see* 497). The Executive Committee of the European Trade Union Confederation subsequently set up an ad hoc group to prepare a draft Statute for such an Institute. In this brief communication the Commission comments on the structure and activities of the Institute as proposed in the draft Statute, the text of which is reproduced in an annex to the document. The Commission also makes brief comments on financial arrangements for the Institute.

584 Progress report on the Advisory Committee on Safety, Hygiene and Health at work
1st   COM(77)400 final. 29 July 1977. 53p
2nd   COM(78)522 final. 20 Oct 1978. 36p

Reports on the work of the Advisory Committee on Safety, Hygiene and Health at Work, a body established as a consequence of Council Decision 74/325/EEC of 27 June 1974 with the 'task of assisting the Commission in the preparation and implementation of activities in the fields of safety, hygiene and health protection at work' (*OJ* L185, 9 July 1974, pp 15–17). Each report begins with background information on the membership of the Committee, its rules of procedure, structure and operation. The main body of the report consists of a description of the activities of the Committee and its working parties during the period under review. After brief conclusions and comments upon future plans, a series of annexes contain the texts of relevant documents.

585 Draft Resolution of the Council of the European Communities on a Community action programme on safety and health at work
COM(77)657 final. 12 Dec 1977. 27p

In this document the Commission outlines its proposals for an action programme on safety and health at work and invites the Council to adopt the programme in the form of a Resolution on the subject. In an introductory section the Commission recalls the reasons why the Community must initiate and develop a preventive policy in this area and makes reference to the guidelines established in 1975 (*see* 574). The Commission then proceeds to identify and describe the main aims of the programme, with particular reference to the need to improve working conditions in terms of increased safety, to improve the state of knowledge in order to identify and assess the risks and perfect prevention and control methods, and to improve human attitudes in order to promote and develop health and safety consciousness. Then the Commission describes the initiatives that must be taken in order to attain these objectives. Six concrete initiatives are singled out for particular emphasis. The Council adopted the programme by means of a Resolution on the matter on 29 June 1978 (*OJ* C165, 11 July 1978, pp 1–13).

Agricultural incomes in the Community
COM(78)46 final. 9 Mar 1978. 133p

See 396.

The attitude of the working population to retirement: results and analysis of a survey carried out in the countries of the European Community
Doc V/457/78. May 1978. 52p

A summary of the results of the sample survey of Europeans' attitudes to retirement, carried out in late 1977 at the request of the Directorate-General for Employment and Social Affairs. The objective was to establish whether there was any consensus of opinion among the European public on the topic, and to measure how feelings towards retirement change as it approaches. A total of 8936 people aged 15 and over were questioned by professional interviewers about their intentions in the context of existing retirement legislation, their reaction to early retirement and their views on a lowering of the retirement age.

CHAPTER 13

Education and culture

Descriptive essay

The documents listed in this chapter reveal that a European education policy is of recent origin. The EEC Treaty makes few explicit references to education; it refers to the mutual recognition of diplomas in the context of the free movement of persons (Article 57) and to the vocational training of workers in the context of Community social policy (Article 118), but makes no provision for a common education policy. Consequently, it was not until the early 1970s, in a climate of opinion determined by the concern for social values expressed at the Paris summit conference in October 1972, that decisive progress was made.

The accession of the three new member states in January 1973 gave the Commission the opportunity to reorganize its internal structure and to create a new Directorate-General for Research, Science and Education under the control of Commissioner Ralf Dahrendorf. The new priority given to education was consolidated during 1973 by the early preparation of a working programme for research and education (see 589) and the publication of an important piece of preparatory work compiled by Henri Janne, former Minister of Education in Belgium, on behalf of the Commission (see 588). The impetus was maintained in 1974 when the Commission submitted a comprehensive memorandum on education policy, after consideration of which the Council agreed priority areas for cooperation and set up an Education Committee with instructions to draw up an action programme for education (see 590). This task was duly completed and approved by the Council at its meeting in December 1975.

Other documents listed in this chapter are in the main concerned with the implementation of the major elements of the education action programme approved by the Council. In recognition of the general problems raised by application of the principle of the free movement of labour, the action programme makes provision for improved educational facilities for Community and non-Community migrants and their children. In 1977 the Commission published a study of the educational problems associated with migrant children, in which it also makes reference to the Council Directive adopted in July 1977 requiring member countries to provide certain facilities to cater for the needs of migrants (see 594). In order to 'improve mutual understanding of the various educational systems in the Community and to ensure continuous comparison of policies, experience and ideas in Member States', the action programme also lists a number of ways, including study visits, exchanges and meetings, in which closer links can be forged between national systems. In particular, the action programme supports increased cooperation in the field of higher education (*see* 599 & 600) and the compilation of up-to-date education documentation and statistics. The programme also advocates equal education opportunities for all (*see* 601) and the teaching of foreign languages (*see* 598). Particular attention is devoted to the need for measures to prepare young people for work (*see* 592).

A considerable amount of work has been undertaken by the Commission of the European Communities in the higher education sector, particularly with regard to the promotion of European Studies as a curriculum subject. The University Information Division acts as a focal point for promotional activities which include the organization of international seminars, the provision of research funds and the maintenance of several hundred European Documentation Centres in institutions of higher education whose teaching and research programmes would benefit from the free availability of extensive collections of Community publications and documents. The role played by University Information as a clearing house for information on matters relating to higher education in general and European Studies in particular, is illustrated by its range of publications. These include *European university news*, a bi-monthly information bulletin which contains short news items on current research projects, forthcoming conferences and meetings, interesting developments in European Studies and book reviews. The Division is also responsible for *University studies on European integration*, a register of current academic research, and for the preparation of practical guides to assist students who wish to pursue courses of higher education in another Community country. Of particular merit is *Higher education in the European Community: a handbook for students* (cat CG-28-79-762-EN-C. ISBN 92-825-1307-6), the second edition of which was published in 1979. This handbook describes the main features of the higher education system in each member country, including information on such practical matters as applications procedures and fees, and lists the main sources from which more detailed information may be obtained. It also contains a section on the European University Institute, established in Florence in 1976, more detailed information on which may be obtained from its annual *Report on activities*.

Bibliographical record

8 **For a Community policy on education**
Bull EC Supp 10/73

In July 1972 the Commission invited Henri Janne, Professor at the Free University of Brussels and former Belgian Minister of Education, to consult with eminent colleagues and to prepare a report which could serve as the basis for future work on education policy in the European Communities. This subsequent report was submitted to the Commission on 27 February 1973. As Ralf Dahrendorf, member of the Commission responsible for education policy, states in the preface to this published version of the report, it 'does not simply indicate the directions which a future Community education policy might take but goes beyond this to state ways and means in which the Community might achieve these aims'. The report opens with an introductory chapter in which Professor Janne describes his brief, lists the experts consulted and makes preliminary remarks on the links between education policy and other fields covered by the Treaty of Rome, with particular reference to cultural policy and scientific policy. The main body of the report consists of a summary of the views of the many experts consulted during the investigation. The chapter begins with an analysis of the state of education in Western Europe and brief discussion of the implications of the cultural revolution and the problem of values. The report then moves on to discuss the extent and the type of powers to be assumed by Community institutions in education, and the introduction of a European dimension into the teaching process. Specific aims of a Community education policy are defined, including language teaching, professional mobility, exchanges and cooperation, permanent education and new educational technologies. The third chapter consists of a synthesis of the results of the consultations, in which Professor Janne draws broad conclusions from the investigation. The Commission later made considerable use of the report in the preparation of its first major initiative on education in early 1974 (*see* 590).

589 Working programme in the field of research, science and education
SEC(73)2000/2. 23 May 1973. 33p

A personal statement by Ralf Dahrendorf, member of the Commission responsible for the new Directorate-General set up in the wake of the Paris summit to coordinate science, research and education policy in the European Communities. The document consists of three parts dealing with education and training, science, research and development and scientific and technical information. The chapter on education, training and cultural matters outlines the nature of Treaty provisions in this field and summarizes the measures taken so far. Dahrendorf then proceeds to define a number of short and medium-term objectives for education policy and considers the organization and financing of means for their achievement. The document was the forerunner of a significant Commission initiative on the matter (*see* 590).

590 Education in the European Community
COM(74)253 final/2. 14 Mar 1974. 40p

EP Report: *Working doc* 52/74. 22 Apr 1974. K. P. Schulz. 8p
EP Debate: *Annex OJ* No 175, 23 Apr 1974, pp 39–57
EP Resolution: *OJ* C55, 13 May 1974, pp 22–24

The Commission's first major initiative on education policy, submitted after due consideration of the Janne Report (*see* 588). The communication begins with an introductory chapter in which the Commission recalls developments in the field of education policy since The Hague summit conference in December 1969. In the following chapter, the Commission outlines its views on the general objectives of a Community education policy, its scope and the ways in which it could contribute to the solution of educational problems arising from the application of the principles embodied in the founding treaties. Two such problems, mobility in education and the education of the children of migrant workers, are considered in subsequent chapters. The Commission also examines ways in which education can be given a European dimension by the promotion of foreign language teaching, the study of Europe, collaboration between institutions of higher education and further development of the idea of European Schools. The communication concludes with a brief consideration of cooperation with other international bodies in this field. Attached to the communication are a draft Council Resolution on cooperation in the field of education and a draft Council Decision establishing a European Committee for Educational Cooperation (*OJ* C58, 18 May 1974, pp 20–22). The whole document was published as Supplement 3/74 to the *Bulletin of the European Communities*. The Ministers of Education meeting in the Council subsequently adopted a Resolution on education policy on 6 June 1974, in which they defined a number of priority areas for future action and established an Education Committee composed of representatives from member states and the Commission (*OJ* C98, 20 Aug 1974, p 2). The Education Committee later submitted to the Ministers of Education a draft Resolution consisting of an action programme in the field of education, which was adopted by Ministers meeting in Council on 10 December 1975 and formally adopted in a Resolution on 9 February 1976 (*OJ* C38, 19 Feb 1976, pp 1–5). In addition to defining a number of priority areas for action, the Resolution granted permanent status to the Education Committee. (*See also* 591 & 597–601.)

Papers requested from the Commission by the Education Committee
Doc XII/748/74. 15 Nov 1974. 67p

A series of notes prepared by the Commission at the invitation of the Education Committee on each of the seven priority themes established by Ministers of Education in their Resolution of 6 June 1974 (*see* 590). Devoting one chapter to each theme, the Commission indicates the most significant developments at international level, refers to the activities of the Community and of Commission services, and suggests lines of action for future cooperation in these fields. The document concludes with two annexes. The first concerns the activities of international organizations in the field of the education of migrants. The second consists of a communication from the Commission to the Standing Conference of European Ministers of Education conference on the education of migrants, outlining Community action in this field.

The preparation of young people for work and for transition from education to working life
Bull EC Supp 12/76

A report prepared by the Education Committee under the terms of the action programme adopted on 9 February 1976 (*see* 590), and in response to a request from the Council and Ministers of Education for special priority to be given to the problems facing young people in their transition from education to working life. The report, drawn up with the assistance of three experts appointed by the Commission and of liaison officers designated by each Ministry of Education, consists of the main conclusions drawn by the Education Committee from its analysis of the situation in each member state. It includes sections in which it makes suggestions for measures to be taken by member states and at the Community level. The report and its conclusions are based on a background analysis of the situation, which is appended to it, and upon nine country statements. A Resolution on the measures to be taken at national and Community level was formally adopted by the Council on 13 December 1976 (*OJ* C308, 30 Dec 1976, pp 1—3), the text of which is also published in this Supplement to the *Bulletin of the European Communities*. As a consequence of the Resolution, a number of pilot projects were prepared for implementation in the period 1978 to 1980. The reports from member states upon which the Education Committee relied for much of its information were circulated separately (SEC(76)4080 final).

593 Community action in the cultural sector
SEC(76)217. 21 Jan 1976. 35p

EP Report: *Working doc* 542/75. 2 Mar 1976. J. B. Broeksz. 1p
EP Debate: *Annex OJ* No 200, 8 Mar 1976, pp 6—14
EP Resolution: *OJ* C79, 5 Apr 1976, p 6

A working document prepared by Guido Brunner, member of the Commission, on Community action in the cultural sector. Taking account of the guidelines established by the European Parliament in its Resolution of 13 May 1974 (*OJ* C62, 30 May 1974, pp 5—7), the document looks at the application of the EEC Treaty in respect of cultural matters and at cultural preparation for European Union. An annex lists the titles of those studies which independent experts have been invited to prepare as an essential preliminary to any action in this matter. Studies completed for the Commission include *The mobility of cultural workers in the Community* (Doc XII/835/75) by H. M. J. M. Haase; *The tax arrangements applicable to cultural foundations and patronage in the Member States of the European Economic Community* (Doc XII/670/75) by I. Claeys Boùùaert; *Copyright in the European Community* (Doc XII/125/76) by Dr A. Dietz; *Protection of the work of artist-craftsmen* (Doc XII/905/76) by W. Duchemin; *Means of combating the theft of and illegal traffic in works of art in the nine countries* (Doc XII/757/76) by J. Chatelain; *Performers' rights in the European Economic Community* (Doc XII/52/78) by F. Gotzen; *Right to work and employment problems of workers in the performing arts and musicians in the European Economic Community* (Doc XII/97/78) by M.-M. Krust. (*See also* 596.)

594 The children of migrant workers
Comm EC, 1977. 53p (cat CB-NQ-77-001-EN-C)

A study of educational problems as they relate to the children of migrant workers in the European Communities. The report, published as number one in the *Studies— Education series*, defines the main linguistic, cultural and social problems encountered by these children at various levels of education. It describes the facilities for educational and vocational guidance available to migrant children in member countries and the provisions made for teacher training. The study concludes with a review of recent activities undertaken by the European Communities, with particular reference to the action programme on migrant workers adopted by the Council (*see* 498) and to the action programme in the field of education adopted on 9 February 1976 (*see* 590). The chapter also refers to Council Directive 77/486/EEC of 25 July 1977 on the education of the children of migrant workers (*OJ* L199, 6 Aug 1977, pp 32—33).

Education in the European Community 1976–1977
Doc XII/263/77. n.d. 33p

A document which summarizes the most significant action arising from the meetings of the Ministers of Education in the Council during 1975 and 1976. The document also outlines recent developments involving interaction between education and other sectors of Community policy, particularly vocational training but also regional development and environmental policy. A final section concerns cooperation between the Community and other international organizations active in the field of education. The texts of the Resolutions adopted by the Ministers of Education after their meetings are annexed.

Community action in the cultural sector
COM(77)560 final. 2 Dec 1977. 52p

EP Report: *Working doc 325/78*. 9 Oct 1978. G. Amadei. 10p
EP Debate: *Annex OJ* No 238, 17/18 Jan 1979, pp 158–161 & 167–179
EP Resolution: *OJ* C39, 12 Feb 1979, pp 50–51
ESC Opinion: *OJ* C128, 21 May 1979, pp 19–30

Following a preliminary paper on the subject (*see* 593), this memorandum from the Commission describes the present state of progress in, and future plans for, the cultural sector, defined in the introduction as 'the socio-economic whole formed by persons and undertakings dedicated to the production and distribution of cultural goods and services'. An introductory section refers back to the expressions of support for action in this area that have come from elsewhere in the Community, to the cooperative action undertaken with other inter-governmental organizations and to the scope of the envisaged action. The first of two main sections deals with the application of the EEC Treaty in the cultural sector. As the introductory statement suggests 'most Community action in the cultural sector is nothing more than the application of the EEC Treaty to this sector'. Consequently, the section contains paragraphs on the freedom to trade in cultural goods, freedom of movement and establishment for cultural workers, harmonization of taxation in the cultural sector and other legislation. The second section looks at other action which might be taken over and above the application of the Treaty of Rome. This includes the preservation of the architectural heritage, the development of cultural exchanges, cooperation between cultural institutes and the promotion of socio-cultural activities at the European level. The document concludes with a draft Council Resolution on the matter (*OJ* C34, 10 Feb 1978, p 2). The whole document was published as Supplement 6/77 to the *Bulletin of the European Communities*.

Educational activities with a European content: the study of the European Community in schools
COM(78)97 final. 9 Mar 1978. 19p

Measures to strengthen the European dimension in schools were envisaged in the action programme on education adopted in 1976 (*see* 590). This communication contains proposals to give effect to one aspect of this policy, namely, the study of the European Community itself. The Commission takes a look at existing teaching programmes and practice before outlining a suggested approach to teaching about the European Community. The Commission then proceeds to examine in more detail the organizational aspects of the projected programme and its implications for resource allocation. Financial implications are considered in an annex to the document.

598 Education action programme at Community level: the teaching of languages in the Community
COM(78)222 final. 14 June 1978. 37p

A nine-point plan, prepared in pursuit of goals established in the education action programme (*see* 590), the purpose of which is to strengthen and improve the teaching of foreign languages within the Community and to promote greater educational mobility for pupils up to the age of 18 years. The nine points outlined in the memorandum cover such aspects of the subject as the training of foreign language teachers, the mobility of pupils and the teaching of foreign languages to various groups of pupils, including the less able children and adults. The document concludes with a number of annexes, the first of which contains proposals for the development of a foreign language teaching assistant scheme. The second annex looks more closely at mobility and the exchange of pupils and the third at schools which teach through the medium of more than one language. Finally, there is an annex in which the financial and staffing implications of the plan are examined.

˙599 Admission to institutions of higher education of students from other member states
COM(78)468 final. 22 Sept 1978. 15p

Following discussions with representatives from institutions of higher education as provided for in the education action programme (*see* 590), the Commission prepared this communication in which it sets out specific proposals concerning the development of a common policy on the admission of students from other member states to higher education institutions. Separate paragraphs deal with various aspects of the proposals, including numerical limitations, admissions criteria, financial conditions, linguistic requirements and administrative procedures. A summary indication of present practice in member states and of the present scale of intra-Community student movement form the subject of an annex.

600 Education action programme at Community level: a European Community scholarships scheme for students
COM(78)469 final. 22 Sept 1978. 5p

A review of the position regarding scholarships for students and proposal for a Community scholarships scheme, prepared in the context of the education action programme, paragraph 14 of which calls for a report 'to establish whether and to what extent the national schemes for scholarships ... should be extended to increase mobility in the Community' (*see* 590).

601 Education action programme at Community level: equal opportunities in education and training for girls (second level education)
COM(78)499 final. 3 Oct 1978. 14p

A communication on the position of girls in second level education, prepared by the Commission within the framework of the action programme for education (*see* 590) and in the wider context of action to achieve equality of treatment between men and women workers. It 'summarises the extent, type and character of inequalities arising in the second level education of girls, proposes areas of common concern on which cooperative action should be prepared'. The communication leans heavily on a report prepared for the Commission by Dr Eileen Byrne, published under the title *Equality of education and training for girls (10–18 years)* (cat CB-NQ-78-009-EN-C. ISBN 92-825-0975-3) in 1978 as number nine in the *Studies—Education series*.

CHAPTER 14

External relations

Descriptive essay

The relations of the Community with third countries constitute an important area of Community activity and one in which notable achievements have been made. The Treaty of Rome gives the Community a significant role to play in the conduct of external economic policy with regard to non-member countries. In particular, it singles out the colonies and other countries and territories enjoying special relationships with member countries and makes provision, in Articles 131 to 136, for their association 'in order to increase trade and to promote jointly economic and social development'. As befits the world's largest trading bloc and in conformity with Articles 110 to 116, the Community has developed a vigorous commercial policy with other non-member countries all over the world. In addition, the international relations of the Community include active participation in the work of other international organizations (Articles 228 to 231), and the conduct of negotiations with countries seeking membership of the Community (Article 237). Aspects of the Community's relations with developing countries are dealt with in the next chapter on development cooperation.

It will be noted from the documents listed in this chapter and the next on the closely related topic of development cooperation that the Community has substantial competence to conduct external policy in the economic field. It is just as well to remember however, that despite the fact that the Treaty gives the Community no specific authority in the field of foreign policy, including defence, the political impact of the Community on international relations has nevertheless been considerable. Some of the documents listed in this and the following chapter reveal, for instance, just how closely the Community has been involved as a single unit in the work of other international organizations, particularly GATT and UNCTAD, and been able to speak with a single voice in the North-South and Euro-Arab dialogues and in such a forum as the Conference on Security and Cooperation in Europe. Furthermore, as a result of the Davignon report on cooperation in foreign policy approved by the Ministers of Foreign Affairs in October 1970 (*Bull EC* 11-1970, pp 9–14), and a second report in July 1973 (*Bull EC* 9-1973, pp 14–21), a number of measures have been taken to coordinate diplomatic activity in areas of international affairs which affect the interests of the Community. Not the least of these has been the regular meeting of Heads of Government or State in the European Council, supported by quarterly meetings of the Ministers of Foreign Affairs, and monthly meetings in the Political Committee of senior officials from the ministries of Foreign Affairs.

COMMERCIAL POLICY

Of course, if the Community is to play its full part in world affairs and attain Treaty objectives, then it must have relations with countries other than those with whom it has historical ties. Such relations are vital in view of the fact that the Community is not rich in raw materials and is consequently highly dependent upon supplies from third countries, particularly in the developing world, and the markets they provide. In point of fact, agreements have been signed and consultations taken place with most countries in the world as part of an external policy whose aim is 'to contribute, in the common interest, to the harmonious development of world trade, the progressive abolition of restrictions on international trade and the lowering of customs barriers' (Article 110).

In its trade relations with the outside world, the Community adopts a single common position through the Common Customs Tariff, an essential feature of the customs union described in Chapter 4, and the provisions of the common commercial policy delineated in Articles 110 to 116. In accordance with the terms of these clauses, member states agree to surrender to Community institutions certain responsibilities in the field of commercial relations. Article 113 declares that 'the common commercial policy shall be based on uniform principles, particularly in regard to changes in tariff rates, the conclusion of tariff and trade agreements, the achievement of uniformity in measures of liberalisation, export policy and measures to protect trade such as those to be taken in case of dumping or subsidies'. Provision is made for agreements with third countries to be conducted by the Commission, in consultation with a special committee appointed by the Council, according to a mandate determined by the Council.

Ever since its formation, the Community has been involved in negotiations with third countries which have led to the conclusion of many agreements. Such agreements fall into a number of different categories. There are association agreements which include financial and technical cooperation as well as commercial arrangements, preferential trade agreements involving reciprocal tariff concessions, commercial agreements which emphasize trade cooperation rather than reductions in customs duties and tariffs and economic cooperation agreements which envisage a higher degree of cooperation between contracting partners.

As responsibility for the conduct of negotiations and the conclusion of such agreements has passed from national governments to Community institutions, a great deal of documentation has been generated over the years in the establishment and maintenance of relations with third countries. However, just as Community legislation enacted in the development of common policies is excluded from this bibliographical guide, so too is its equivalent in the field of international relations, the bilateral or multilateral agreement and associated documentation, with the notable exception of a limited number of documents concerned with the great set-piece events that took place at Yaoundé and Lomé.

However, there are a number of Community publications which make these agreements more accessible. Notable among these is the *Collection of the agreements concluded by the European Communities*, a five-volume compendium of the texts of bilateral and multilateral agreements concluded with non-member countries and still in force on 31 December 1975. The intention is to maintain its currency by means of annual volumes, that for 1976 having been published in 1979. Then there are a number of loose-leaf *Collected acts*, published by the Secretariat of the Council of the European Communities, each volume of which brings together not only the texts of agreements signed with individual countries but also the main acts pertaining to these agreements and other acts adopted by the Community with regard to the countries concerned. Volumes have been published for association agreements with Cyprus, EASTAF (Tanzania, Uganda and Kenya), Greece, Turkey, Tunisia, Morocco and Malta. A similar collection of legislative acts has been published for the overseas countries and territories and French overseas departments which have not become independent. Bibliographical information on the documents associated with such agreements is provided in the supplements to the *Documentation bulletin* that have been published on Community relations with groups of countries such as the Mediterranean states (B/14) and the state-trading countries (B/20). Finally, it should be noted that *Europe information: external relations 6/78* consists of a useful list of the main trade and association agreements concluded with third countries.

Essential for the management of the common commercial policy are detailed statistics on imports and exports between member states and between the Community and third countries. Recognizing the need for a common basis for comparable statistics on intra and extra-Community trade, the Statistical Office of the European Communities has devised a common classification scheme called the Nomenclature of Goods for the External Trade Statistics of the Community and Statistics of Trade between Member States (NIMEXE). Applied since 1966 NIMEXE is revised annually by a special committee and then published in its new version in the *Official journal of the European Communities*. Detailed statistical data on the external trade of the Community are published annually in a 13 volume series called *Foreign trade: analytical tables NIMEXE*, which provide detailed figures on imports and exports by commodity broken down by origin and destination, expressed according to the NIMEXE nomenclature. Short-term intra and extra-Community trade statistics are available from the *Monthly external trade bulletin*. Each year a four volume set of *Tariff statistics* is also published by the Statistical Office of the European Communities.

ASSOCIATION POLICY

The policy of association provided for in the Treaty of Rome, renewed and extended by subsequent conventions, constitutes a cornerstone of Community external policy. In the Preamble to the Treaty, the founder members confirm 'the solidarity which binds Europe and the overseas countries' and refer to a desire 'to ensure the development of their prosperity, in accordance with the principles of the Charter of the United Nations'. Moreover, Part IV of the Treaty, Articles 131–136, provides a framework within which those overseas countries and territories enjoying special relationships with member countries can be associated with the Community. Article 131 states that 'the purpose of association shall be to promote the economic and social development of the countries and territories and to establish close economic relations between them and the Community as a whole'. Other Articles lay down the essential features and the terms of association, which are elaborated in greater detail in an Implementing Convention annexed to the Treaty.

During the period covered by this bibliographical guide, there have been three contractual agreements in addition to the original Treaty provisions for association which expired at the end of 1962. The first Yaoundé Convention (*JO* 93, 11 June 1964, pp 1430–1506) ran from 1 June 1964 to 1 June 1969 and was replaced from 1 January 1971 by a second Yaoundé Convention (*JO* L282, 28 Dec 1970, pp 2–30) which expired on 31 January 1975. After a short interim period, the Lomé Convention (*OJ* L25, 1 Jan 1976, pp 1–143) came into force on 1 April 1976 and was due to run until 31 March 1980. Of these agreements the Lomé Convention is undoubtedly the jewel in the Community showcase. Concluded in 1975 with no less than 46 African, Caribbean and Pacific countries (now grown to 58), the Lomé Convention is a much more broad-based and ambitious model than previous agreements, with such innovative features as Stabex, the system to help stabilize the export earnings of ACP states (*see* 636 & 638). Founded on the twin pillars of commercial cooperation and financial aid, each of these association agreements has been implemented by the progressive construction of an edifice of detailed legislation concerned with customs duties, tariff rates, trade preferences and quota restrictions and a multitude of other regulatory mechanisms governing relations between the Community and a host of developing countries, including administrative and procedural rules for the allocation and use of Community aid. The amount of consequent documentation has been multiplied enormously by virtue of the fact that a fresh body of legislation is generated each time a five-year convention is replaced by a new regime. This legislative and often technical documentation, whose purpose is to give practical effect to the provisions of the various association conventions, falls outside the scope of this bibliographical guide. However, it should be noted that the Secretariat of the Council of the European Communities has assembled a number of extremely useful loose-leaf volumes in which the main legislative texts relating to various conventions of association, first published in the *Official journal of the European Communities*, are brought together and kept up-to-date on a regular basis. For example, a two volume compilation called *Convention ACP–EEC of Lomé : Collected Acts* includes, in addition to the text of the convention itself, acts adopted pursuant to that convention, and acts adopted by the EEC with regard to ACP countries in such fields as trade cooperation, industrial cooperation and financial cooperation.

Although this chapter does not reflect the immense amount of work involved in the practical implementation of the terms of the association agreements and the complex negotiations for their renewal, it does include a number of important documents concerning these association agreements. The chapter contains reference to a number of descriptive studies carried out during the early years when there was an urgent need for basic information on the economic, social and political structure of associated states (*see* 629 & 630). Supplementary factual information on these countries may be obtained from the *Statistical yearbook of the AASM* and from a more recent Eurostat publication *ACP: statistical yearbook*, published for the first time in 1978, in which a selection of basic economic and social indicators are published. Reference is also made to a number of key policy statements prepared by the Commission during negotiations for the renewal of association agreements. The first such document was prepared in 1961 shortly before the expiry of the Treaty arrangements for the association of overseas countries and territories (*see* 631) and which ultimately led to the conclusion in July 1963 of the first Yaoundé

Convention. The Commission similarly outlined its general attitude to negotiations to replace the second Yaoundé Convention (*see* 633), and in 1978 set out its position in anticipation of discussions for a renewal of the Lomé Convention (*see* 639).

As already noted, the association agreements concluded at Yaoundé and Lomé are founded on two essential elements, trade cooperation and financial assistance. Their impact on trade relations may be discerned from a number of statistical publications issued by the Statistical Office of the European Communities. Regular analyses of the structure and trends of ACP trade with both the Community and other countries appear in *ACP: yearbook of foreign trade statistics*. Short-term data on trade flows appear in *EC trade with the ACP states and the South Mediterranean states*, a quarterly publication issued on a regular basis since 1979. In November 1978 a three volume analysis of ACP–EEC trade was published in draft form by the Statistical Office. This exhaustive study of the structure of ACP trade and its relationship with the Community was subsequently given full publication in 1979 under the title *Analysis of trade between the European Community and the ACP states* (cat CA-25-78-364-EN-C. ISBN 92-825-1128-6). Two statistical surveys published much earlier as numbers one and two in the series *Etudes: Série aide et développement* also have lasting interest. They are *Les échanges commerciaux des pays en voie de développement avec les pays développés et notamment avec la CEE 1953–1966* (cat 8224) published in 1967 and *Les échanges commerciaux entre la CEE et les Etats africains et malgache associés 1958–1966/67* (cat 8254), published in 1969.

Financial assistance is channelled to associated countries through the European Development Fund (EDF) established by the Implementing Convention annexed to the Treaty of Rome, with second and third Funds established under the Yaoundé Conventions and a fourth under the Lomé Convention. Although this chapter contains reference to some of the annual reports submitted by the Commission both to the Council and to association institutions on the administration and implementation of financial aid (*see* 632 & 637), and to efforts made by the Commission to ensure free and fair access to contracts (*see* 635), it makes no reference to the mass of administrative documentation concerned with the processing of tenders and the distribution of funds. However, invitations to tender for EDF projects are regularly published in the *Official journal* (the 'S' series since 1978 and the 'C' series before that), as are official notifications of the outcome of these invitations. The annual balance sheets and accounts of the Fund are also published in the *Official journal* 'C' series. Among the information booklets published by the Commission, one called *The European Development Fund from the introduction of the project to its completion* (cat 8383) is particularly useful. An earlier publication *Les critères d'appréciation des projets soumis au Fonds européen de développement* (cat 8149) issued in 1965 as number three in the series *Etudes—Série développement de l'outre-mer*, is concerned with the criteria to be applied in the evaluation of investment projects.

Each of the association agreements concluded at Yaoundé and Lomé with developing countries has provided for the creation of institutional machinery to supervise the implementation of convention provisions. The Yaoundé Conventions established two main institutions, an Association Council composed of members of the Commission and Council on the one hand, and members of the governments of associated states on the other, and a Parliamentary Conference consisting of members of the European Parliament and parliamentarians from each associated state. The terminology attaching to these institutions changed when the Lomé Convention created an ACP–EEC Council of Ministers and an ACP–EEC Consultative Assembly. Information on the activities of the Council of Ministers, which like its predecessor meets at least annually, may be obtained from the *Annual report* prepared and published by the institution and presented to the Consultative Assembly. The ACP–EEC Council of Ministers has also published a three volume *Compilation of texts* which reproduces the texts of ACP–EEC Council acts and Community acts on the implementation of the convention and on matters relating to ACP states. Volume 1 covers 1 April 1976 to 31 July 1976; volume 2 covers 1 August 1976 to 31 August 1977 and volume 3 covers 1 September 1977 to 30 September 1978. Two further volumes provide supplementary texts on industrial cooperation. The minutes and resolutions adopted by the Consultative Assembly and its predecessor, the Parliamentary Conference, at its annual session are published in the 'C' series of the *Official journal*. Somewhat fuller and less formal reports of Assembly proceedings are published as separate booklets in the *European Parliament information* series.

Bibliographical record

COMMERCIAL POLICY

Premier mémorandum de la Commission au Conseil relatif à la procédure du développement d'une politique commerciale commune
COM(61)48. 24 Mar 1961. 18p

Article 111 of the Treaty of Rome declares that 'Member States shall coordinate their trade relations with third countries so as to bring about, by the end of the transitional period, the conditions needed for implementing a common policy in the field of external trade'. In this first overall policy document, the Commission first sketches the present procedure for bringing commercial policy into line. In the second part the Commission makes practical proposals for developing the common commercial policy, as a result of which the Council, at its meeting in July 1961, adopted a Decision on mutual consultation prior to negotiations for bilateral trade agreements (*JO* 71, 4 Nov 1961, pp 1273–1274) and another introducing uniformity in the duration of bilateral trade agreements, none of which should extend beyond the end of the transitional period (*JO* 71, 4 Nov 1961, pp 1274–1275). (*See also* 604.)

Les appareils commerciaux des pays de la C.E.E.
Doc III/D/6021/61. Dec 1961. 3 vols, 44p, 129p, 102p

A substantial working document in which the Commission presents a synoptic review of the commercial instruments of member states, and the problems being experienced as the Community passes into the second stage of its transitional period. Volume 1 consists of a general overview of the situation in the Community as a whole. Volume 2 consists of six separate chapters, each one of which is devoted to an analysis of the situation in one member state. Volume 3 contains methodological information and statistical data.

604 **Deuxième mémorandum de la Commission au Conseil relatif à un programme d'action en matière de politique commerciale commune, établi en vertu des dispositions de l'article III CEE**
I/COM(62)10 final. 21 Mar 1962. 20p

A second general memorandum on the development of a common commercial policy (*see also* 602). In the first part the Commission lays down general principles for a common commercial policy; it defines the objectives of a common policy, identifies the conditions necessary for its realization and establishes the principles upon which future action should be based. The second part of the document consists of a draft action programme, on the basis of which the Council took a Decision on 25 September 1962 adopting an action programme (*JO* 90, 5 Oct 1962, pp 2353–2357).

605 **Négociations à la suite du Trade Expansion Act: autorisation de négociations tarifaires dans le cadre du G.A.T.T.**
I/COM(63)115. 26 Mar 1963. 7p

Article 229 of the Treaty of Rome states that 'it shall be for the Commission to ensure the maintenance of all appropriate relations with the organs of the United Nations, of its specialised agencies and of the General Agreement on Tariffs and Trade'. In this brief memorandum the Commission presents its proposals for the conduct of tariff negotiations in the GATT framework following the American Trade Expansion Act. GATT came into force on 1 January 1948 with the aim of liberalizing world trade by dismantling trade barriers, in the context of which the Commission conducts negotiations on behalf of the Community as a whole, in consultation with a special committee appointed by the Council to assist in this task. The Final Act of the subsequent Kennedy Round of negotiations was signed on 30 June 1967 and the Community emerged with the lowest customs tariffs of any of the major trading powers (*JO* L305, 19 Dec 1968, pp 1–176). (*See also* 614.)

606 **Note d'information de la Commission au Conseil sur le programme d'action de la Communauté en matière de législation douanière**
III/COM(63)261 final. 31 July 1963. 12p

The establishment of the customs union by the end of the transitional period involves action not only to dismantle tariff barriers but also to harmonize national customs laws. In order to instil a greater sense of urgency into this work, the Commission drew up an action programme to provide a uniform basis for this considerable and necessarily lengthy operation. The document lists the measures necessary to ensure that duties in the Common Customs Tariff have a uniform impact and that there are identical customs instruments in member states.

607 **Déclaration de la Commission au Conseil concernant un programme d'uniformisation de la politique commerciale**
I/COM(64)51 final. 26 Feb 1964. 8p

A document in which the Commission lists the matters concerning the systematic unification of commercial policy before the end of the transitional period upon which it intends to submit proposals. The Commission stresses the need for certain decisions to be taken if commercial policy is to be unified by the end of the transitional period and outlines the areas in which firm proposals will be made.

Accélération de la mise en place d'une politique commerciale à l'égard des pays à commerce d'état
I/COM(64)53 final. 26 Feb 1964. 10p

A document in which the Commission first reviews the measures taken by the Council as regards commercial policy towards state-trading countries, before drawing attention to the need to speed up the evolution of a common policy regarding such countries. The document concludes with a draft Council Resolution and Decision on the matter.

Octroi de préférences tarifaires par les pays industrialisés aux produits semi-finis et finis de l'ensemble des pays en voie de développement
SEC(66)3585 final. 22 Nov 1966. 30p

A document in which the Commission gives its reasons as to why the Community, in the face of opposition from some industrialized countries, should reaffirm its support for the principle of granting tariff preferences to developing countries to assist their industrialization through reductions in customs duties, an idea first put forward during a meeting of GATT ministers in May 1963. The Commission also makes proposals in the document concerning the nature of a system of preferences for manufactured and semi-manufactured products.

Rapport de la Commission au Conseil du rapport sur l'examen des accords relatifs aux relations commerciales et des traités de commerce et de navigation conclus par les Etats membres
SEC(69)1175 final. 28 Mar 1969. 196p

A report to the Council on the state of commercial relations between member and third countries as at 31 December 1967. The Commission analyses 128 friendship, commercial and navigation treaties and 196 commercial agreements. In the first part the Commission examines the nature and economic import of the treaties and agreements; in the second part it assesses their significance in terms of the establishment of the common commercial policy. A series of substantial annexes provide more specific detail about the agreements and treaties concluded.

Préférences généralisées en faveur des produits manufacturés et semi-manufacturés des pays en voie de développement
SEC(69)3637 final. 8 Oct 1969. 20p

During the Second Session of UNCTAD held in New Delhi from 1 February to 29 March 1968, it was agreed to introduce at an early date a non-discriminatory system of generalized preferences for finished and semi-finished products exported by developing countries. This document consists of a broad statement of the Commission's position on the possibility of establishing such a system. On 17 March 1971 the Commission submitted a memorandum on the implementation of a Community scheme (SEC(71)1000 final), shortly after which the Council agreed to 1 July 1971 as the date for its introduction. Concrete proposals were then tabled by the Commission (COM(71)610) and the necessary Council Decisions were taken in June 1971 for the scheme to take effect from 1 July 1971 (*JO* L142, 28 June 1972, pp 1–99). (*See also* 616.)

612 Conséquences pour la Communauté de la situation actuelle dans les domaines monétaires et commerciaux
SEC(71)3274 final. 15 Sept 1971. 33p

See 83.

613 Les relations entre la Communauté et les pays du bassin meditérranéen
SEC(72)3111 final. 27 Sept 1972. 28p

A document in which the Commission makes proposals for the establishment of an overall approach to relations with Mediterranean countries. Until now relations have been based on separate agreements with individual countries, notably the association agreements with Greece and Turkey. In this document the Commission explores the ways and means of formulating and implementing an overall policy with regard to Community relations with Mediterranean countries. The Commission examines the definition of a global approach, the nature of agreements to be concluded and at the means for implementing such a policy. Since 1975 the Community has concluded a number of preferential trade agreements with Mediterranean countries, based on the common approach referred to in this document, and confirmed by Heads of Government or State at the Paris summit in October 1972. Agreements have been concluded with Israel in 1975, with the Maghreb countries (Algeria, Morocco and Tunisia) in 1976 and with the Mashrek countries (Jordan, Syria, Egypt and the Lebanon) in 1977. (*See also* 391, 393 & 394.)

614 Development of an overall approach to trade in view of the coming multilateral negotiations in GATT
COM(73)556. 4 Apr 1973. 17p

EP Report: *Working doc* 118/73. 2 July 1973. C. de la Malène. 18p
EP Debate: *Annex OJ* No 164, 4 July 1973, pp 88–107
EP Resolution: *OJ* C62, 31 July 1973, pp 22–23

In October 1972 the Heads of State or Government meeting at the Paris summit expressed their readiness to enter into new multilateral trade negotiations within the GATT framework, and invited Community institutions to define by 31 July 1973 an overall concept to guide the Community in its forthcoming discussions. This preparatory document sets out the Commission's views on the approach to be adopted by the Community. An explanatory memorandum, in which the Commission draws attention to the beneficial effect the Community has had on the expansion and liberalization of world trade, precedes a definition of the Community's basic objectives for the forthcoming conference. Other chapters deal with the fields to be covered by the negotiations and with the broad lines to be followed in order to achieve Community objectives. These chapters relate specifically to industrial customs tariffs, non-tariff barriers, agriculture, the developing countries and the safeguard clauses. The document was published as Supplement 2/73 to the *Bulletin of the European Communities*. This Tokyo Round of multilateral trade negotiations was officially launched in September 1973 (*see* 617).

Communication on problems arising from cooperation agreements
COM(73)1275 final. 3 Oct 1973. 21p

EP Report: *Working doc* 359/73. 11 Feb 1974. J. E. Jahn. 14p
EP Debate: *Annex OJ* No 171, 11 Feb 1974, pp 14–23
EP Resolution: *OJ* C23, 8 Mar 1974, p 9

Since the mid sixties an increasing number of agreements for economic, scientific and technical cooperation have been concluded between member states and East European countries. In this document the Commission considers the implications of this trend, which still remains the domain of member governments, for the common commercial policy and makes proposals for an alignment of policy in this area. In Part 1 the Commission describes the change in economic relations with state-trading countries which has led to the conclusion of cooperation agreements. Following an earlier document in which it highlighted the problems arising from such agreements (SEC(70)4500 final), the Commission then considers the implications of the proliferation of cooperation agreements for the common commercial policy. In Part 2 the Commission considers possible solutions to the problems raised. Since East European countries refuse to negotiate with the Community as a single unit, the Commission's proposals centre on a draft Decision designed to coordinate bilateral agreements, the text of which is reproduced as an annex to the document. In the final part the Commission outlines other areas in which work needs to be undertaken. On 22 July 1974 the Council adopted Decision 74/393/EEC instituting a consultation procedure for cooperation agreements whereby member states intending to conclude such agreements inform the Commission and other member states of the broad lines of their intentions, so as to make it possible to ensure that such action does not conflict with the aims of the common commercial policy (*OJ* L208, 30 July 1974, pp 23–24).

The future development of the European Community's generalised tariff preferences
COM(75)17 final. 3 Feb 1975. 7p

EP Report: *Working doc* 285/75. 10 Oct 1975. W. Dondelinger. 34p
EP Debate: *Annex OJ* No 195, 16 Oct 1975, pp 230–246
EP Resolution: *OJ* C257, 10 Nov 1975, pp 30–31

In July 1971 the Community instituted a system whereby imports of agricultural products, finished and semi-finished industrial products from developing countries were given preferential treatment in the form of tariff concessions (*see* 611). In this document the Commission uses the experience gained during the past four years to reflect on the way in which the system should develop in the future. The Commission begins by reviewing the effectiveness of the Generalized System of Preferences (GSP) as an instrument of development cooperation policy and the ways in which this effectiveness could be improved. The Commission then reviews the long-term prospects for the GSP in the light of its stated objectives to 'increase the export earnings of the developing countries, to promote their industrialisation and to accelerate their rates of economic growth', before considering means of developing the scheme up to 1980. Detailed information on the application of the scheme is also available in an annual volume published by the Commission called *Practical guide to the use of the European Communities' Scheme of Generalized Tariff Preferences*, the latest volume of which was published in May 1979 (CB-28-79-172-EN-C. ISBN 92-825-0994-X).

617 GATT multilateral negotiations
COM(78)275 final. 16 June 1978. 18p

EP Report: *Working doc* 86/78. 8 May 1978. P.-B. Cousté. 63p
EP Debate: *Annex OJ* No 231, 15 June 1978, pp 206–210 & 218–249
EP Resolution: *OJ* C163, 10 July 1978, pp 57–60

The Tokyo Round of tariff negotiations conducted within the GATT framework was launched in 1973 and entered its negotiating phase in 1975. This document from the Commission offers to the Council a number of guidelines to assist it during the coming decision-making phase. The Commission deals in turn with the main points that need to be settled, for each of which the Commission outlines guiding principles. Negotiations were concluded successfully during 1979. (*See also* 614.)

ENLARGEMENT

618 Rapport au Parlement européen sur l'état des négociations avec le Royaume-Uni
Comm EEC, 1963. 102p (cat 8082)

In 1961 the United Kingdom, Denmark, Ireland and Norway made applications to join the European Communities in accordance with the provisions of the Treaty of Rome, Article 237 of which declares that 'any European state may apply to become a member of the Community', and similar provisions in the ECSC Treaty (Article 98) and the EAEC Treaty (Article 205). This report on the state of negotiations with the United Kingdom was prepared by the Commission at the invitation of the European Parliament shortly after President De Gaulle's famous press conference on 14 January 1963, at which he effectively vetoed the applications. After introductory remarks about the British application and the bases upon which negotiations had been conducted, the main body of the report is concerned with major problems raised by the British application. Such issues as the level of the Common Customs Tariff, Commonwealth trade, agriculture and relations with the European Free Trade Association are the subject of separate chapters in which the Commission describes the results already obtained and the problems still outstanding. The document concludes with the Commission's general assessment of the state of negotiations at the point where they broke down at the end of January 1963.

619 Avis de la Commission au Conseil concernant les demandes d'adhésion du Royaume-Uni, de l'Irelande, du Danemark et de la Norvège, en vertu des articles 237 du traité CEE, 205 du traité CEEA et 98 du traité CECA
COM(67)750. 29 Sept 1967. 108p

A preliminary opinion from the Commission, to be developed further as negotiations progress, on the applications for membership received from the United Kingdom, Ireland, Denmark and Norway, submitted to the Council in accordance with Article 237 of the EEC Treaty, Article 205 of the EAEC Treaty and Article 98 of the ECSC Treaty. The document opens with an assessment of the general problems raised by the applications, with particular regard to the working of Community institutions in an enlarged Community, and the arrangements to be made for the transition of applicant countries into full membership. The Commission then proceeds to highlight a number of problematic areas where difficulties must be overcome if enlargement is not to disrupt continued Community development. Special attention is devoted to the customs union, agricultural policy, economic and financial policy and other problems relating to economic union. The Commission also refers to problems peculiar to the European Coal and Steel Community and to the European Atomic Energy Community. The general effect of enlargement on relations with non-member countries is also the subject of some discussion, as are the implications of enlargement for the functioning of the main Community institutions. At its meeting on 18 and 19 December 1967, the Council failed to agree to open negotiations with the applicant countries. As a consequence, much of 1968 was devoted to an examination of interim arrangements that might be made between the European Communities and applicant countries (*see* 620). The Commission's opinion was published separately in 1967 in a volume of the same title (cat 8220).

Avis de la Commission au Conseil concernant certains problèmes consécutifs aux demandes d'adhésion du Royaume-Uni, de l'Irelande, du Danemark et de la Norvège
COM(68)210. 2 Apr 1968. 16p

Following the failure of the Council to agree at its meeting in December 1967 to open negotiations with the applicant countries, attention switched in 1968 to the discussion of transitional arrangements that would facilitate the eventual accession of the United Kingdom, Ireland, Denmark and Norway to the European Communities. This document contains the Commission's views on the various suggestions made by member states and the broad lines of an agreement which could be concluded with applicant countries in preparation for their accession at a later date. The Commission concentrates upon three aspects of the proposed transitional arrangements, namely, commercial arrangements, with particular reference to the problems raised by the establishment of preferential trade, procedures for consultation and cooperation in economic and monetary matters and cooperation in scientific and technological matters. The document was published as a Supplement to the *Bulletin of the European Communities* 4-1968.

Avis de la Commission au Conseil concernant les demandes d'adhésion du Royaume-Uni, de l'Irelande, du Danemark et de la Norvège en vertu des articles 237 du traité CEE, 205 du traité CEEA et 98 du traité CECA
COM(69)1000. 3 Oct 1969. 44p

After discussions during 1968 and 1969 on the possibility of concluding arrangements with applicant countries, the Council asked the Commission to bring its 1967 opinion up-to-date (*see* 619). Section 1 of this subsequent document consists of an analysis of the various problems associated with enlargement, including economic problems relating to agriculture, financial affairs and practical problems concerning the actual entry of applicant countries into full Community membership. In Section 2 the Commission considers enlargement from the point of view of the Community's future development. The functioning of Community institutions in an enlarged Community forms the subject of Section 3. Finally, the document concludes with remarks on a procedure to be adopted for the conduct of negotiations. The document was published as a Supplement to the *Bulletin of the European Communities* 9/10-1969. Negotiations were opened with the applicant countries during 1969 and concluded successfully in 1972 with the signing of the Treaty of Accession. The United Kingdom, Denmark and Ireland joined the Communities on 1 January 1973 according to transitional arrangements to apply during the period 1973 to 1977. Norway failed to ratify the Treaty as a result of a negative referendum result. *The enlarged Community: outcome of the negotiations with the applicant states*, published as Supplement 1/72 to the *Bulletin of the European Communities*, contains a useful account of the conduct of the negotiations and description of the provisions of the final package.

622 **Avis de la Commission au Conseil concernant les relations de la Communauté élargie avec les Etats membres et associés de l'AELE non candidats à l'adhésion**
Bull EC Supp 3/71

A document in which the Commission gives its views on the position to be adopted by the Community with regard to those members of the European Free Trade Association (EFTA) who have not applied for membership of the European Communities but wish to establish special relations with the organization. The Commission outlines the stated position of each of the countries concerned, namely, Sweden, Switzerland, Austria, Finland, Iceland, and Portugal, on the basis of which the Commission draws some conclusions and makes its observations.

623 **Opinion on Greek application for membership**
COM(76)30 final. 29 Jan 1976. 46p

EP Report: *Working doc* 670/78. 9 Mar 1979. G. Amadei. 20p
EP Debate: *Annex OJ* No 241, 13 Mar 1979, pp 27-44
EP Resolution: *OJ* C93, 9 Apr 1979, pp 32-34
ESC Opinion: *OJ* C105, 26 Apr 1979, pp 50-51

A document in which the Commission, in accordance with Article 237 of the EEC Treaty, Article 98 of the ECSC Treaty and Article 205 of the EAEC Treaty, submits its opinion on the Greek application for membership of the European Communities. In Part 1 the Commission considers general questions and the wider issues raised by the Greek application, made in June 1975. Part 2 begins with brief observations on the Greek economy and on the state of the association agreement concluded with Greece in 1962. The Commission then proceeds to discuss the main problems raised by the Greek application and the matters that have to be studied and resolved, with regard to such areas as the customs union, agriculture, regional policy and social policy. The document concludes with statistical tables concerning the main indicators for the Greek economy. The document was published as Supplement 2/76 to the *Bulletin of the European Communities*. Following the Commission's favourable opinion, negotiations were opened with Greece in July 1976 and were concluded successfully with the signing of the instruments of accession on 28 May 1979, after the ratification of which Greece will become the tenth member state on 1 January 1981 (*OJ* L291, 19 Nov 1979, pp 1–192).

4 General considerations on the problem of enlargement
COM(78)120 final. 24 Apr 1978. 20p

EP Report: *Working doc* 479/78. 6 Dec 1978. J.-F. Pintat. 7p
EP Debate: *Annex OJ* No 238, 17 Jan 1978, pp 138–158
EP Resolution: *OJ* C39, 12 Feb 1979, pp 47–49
ESC Opinion: *OJ* C247, 1 Oct 1979, pp 24–43

A paper in which the Commission sets out its views on the main political, institutional and socio-economic problems raised by the membership applications received from Greece in July 1975 (*see* 623), Portugal in March 1977 and Spain in July 1977 and the special measures that will have to be taken if enlargement is not to disrupt the continued development of the Communities. In particular the Commission considers the consequences of the less developed state of the economies of the three applicant countries for Community policy in such fields as agriculture, industry, energy, social affairs and regional affairs. The Commission also considers the effects of enlargement on the Community's role in the wider world and touches upon the question of arrangements for a transitional period. The document concludes with remarks on the impact of enlargement on the Community's institutional structure. The document was published as Supplement 1/78 to the *Bulletin of the European Communities*. Two associated documents contain more detailed analyses of the economic and institutional implications of enlargement (*see* 625 & 626).

5 The transitional period and the institutional implications of enlargement
COM(78)190 final. 24 Apr 1978. 22p

The transitional arrangements needed to ensure the smooth entry of applicant countries into full membership, with the least amount of disruption to Community operations, is the subject of this Commission memorandum. In Part 1 the Commission outlines a strategy for the assimilation of the three applicant countries taking into account their lower level of development. The negotiating period, the interim period between the signature and entry into force of the act of accession and the transitional period proper are each considered in turn. Part 3 is concerned with the adjustments that will have to be made to the Treaty as a consequence of an increase in the number of member states, with particular attention being paid to the decision-making process in Community institutions. Submitted to the Council with two associated documents (*see* 624 & 626), the memorandum was given full publication in Supplement 2/78 to the *Bulletin of the European Communities*.

6 Economic and sectoral aspects: Commission analyses supplementing its views on enlargement

COM(78)200 final. 27 Apr 1978. 2 vols, 231p, 125p

One of three related communications from the Commission on the implications of enlargement (*see* 624 & 625). In the first part of the document the Commission concentrates upon the general economic problems that applicant countries will face and pose when joining the Communities. The Commission describes the general characteristics of each applicant country's economy and the structure of its industry, on the basis of which it identifies common features likely to pose problems for the enlarged Community. The Commission then looks more closely at those economic problems connected with enlargement, both of a general nature and also specific to industry, agriculture and the regions. Finally in this section the Commission studies the financial aspects of enlargement, with reference to the scale of financial flows between the Community and applicant countries, the nature and operation of Community instruments and the financial implications for the Community budget. The second main part of the document consists of a series of chapters, each of which evaluates the implications of enlargement on one Community sector. Separate chapters are concerned with enlargement as it affects industry and energy, social affairs, regional affairs, agriculture and fisheries and external relations. The first part of the document was published as Supplement 3/78 to the *Bulletin of the European Communities*.

627 Commission opinion to the Council on Portugal's application for accession
COM(78)220 final. 19 May 1978. 68p

The opinion of the Commission on Portugal's application to accede to the European Communities, submitted to the Council in accordance with Article 237 of the EEC Treaty, 98 of the ECSC Treaty and 205 of the EAEC Treaty. Based on the specific application to Portugal of the general considerations contained in a series of documents submitted earlier in the year (*see* 624–626), this document contains a discussion of the economic difficulties that must be overcome if Portugal is to become a full member of the European Communities. The Commission also emphasizes the political considerations that lead it to support the application. The document was published as Supplement 5/78 to the *Bulletin of the European Communities*. Following this favourable opinion from the Commission, negotiations were opened with Portugal in October 1978.

628 Commission's opinion to the Council concerning Spain's application for accession
COM(78)630 final. 30 Nov 1978. 2 vols, 70p, 57p

This document contains the Commission's opinion on Spain's application for membership of the European Communities, submitted in accordance with Article 237 of the EEC Treaty, 98 of the ECSC Treaty and 205 of the EAEC Treaty. Intended to be read in the light of the Commission's earlier and more general communication on the subject of enlargement (*see* 624) and two associated documents (*see* 625 & 626), the document is divided into two main parts. In the first the Commission offers general remarks on its attitude to the application. The Commission compares the economic situation in Spain with that in the

Community, on the basis of which it looks more closely at areas such as industry, agriculture and regional affairs, where problems remain to be overcome. Specific considerations concerning the accession of Spain are the subject of the second part. The Commission highlights the difficulties to be overcome in such sectors as the customs union, industry, energy and transport. The document concludes with a separate annex containing a substantial number of statistical tables, graphs and maps illustrating in figures the main characteristics of Spain's economic position. Negotiations opened with Spain in February 1979.

ASSOCIATION POLICY

Document de travail sur la situation et la structure politiques administratives et économiques des Pays et Territoires d'Outre-Mer associés à la Communauté
Comm EEC, 1958. 54p

A descriptive study of the situation in, and political, administrative, economic and social structure of associated states, prepared by the Commission for the information of members of the European Parliament. As such, it constitutes the first assessment of the overall position and principal problems in the overseas dependencies of the original six member states granted associate status according to the provisions of Articles 131–136 of the Treaty of Rome and an Implementing Convention annexed to the Treaty. Part 1 contains basic geographical, climatic and demographic data on each of the associated states, followed in Part 2 by a description of their institutional, political and administrative organization. Part 3 is concerned with various aspects of the economic structure of associated states, notably, their levels of production, transport systems, trade and investment performance.

Rapport sur la situation sociale dans les pays d'outre-mer associés à la Communauté économique européenne
Comm EEC, 1960. 245p (cat 8001)

A first overall picture of social conditions prevalent in associated countries, compiled by the Commission in response to a request from the European Parliament for information on the matter. The Commission reports on the conditions of work as they apply in associated countries, the standard of living of their inhabitants and problems experienced in such fields as education and vocational training, health and hygiene and housing.

Association des états d'outre-mer à la Communauté : considérations sur le futur régime d'association
VIII/COM(61)110 final. 12 July 1961. 43p

Article 136 of the Treaty of Rome declares that before the expiry of the five year Implementing Convention governing the association of countries and territories with the Community, the Council shall 'lay down provisions for a further period, on the basis of the experience acquired and of the principles set out in this Treaty'. In this document the Commission outlines the basic principles upon which a new convention should be formulated, bearing in mind in particular, the fact that the majority of associated countries gained their independence at the beginning of the 1960s. The Commission considers the shape of any new agreement from a number of points of view. It considers the juridical problems, questions relating to economic and trade relations, investment, technical cooperation, the right of establishment and the liberalization of capital movements. In the event 17 Associated African States and Madagascar (AASM) concluded a new five year association agreement with the Community on 20 July 1963 at Yaoundé in the Cameroon (*JO* 93, 11 June 1964, pp 1430–1506). This Yaoundé Convention, with its reciprocal rights and duties concerning free trade, its provisions for financial and technical aid and its institutional machinery for joint action, was replaced by a second five year Yaoundé Convention on 29 July 1969, enlarged in 1972 by the adherence of Mauritius (*JO* L282, 28 Dec 1970, pp 2–30).

632 Rapport de la Commission au Conseil d'Association sur la gestion de la coopération financière et technique

1972 SEC(73)2072 final. 15 Mar 1973. 88p

1973 SEC(74)2430 final. 2 July 1974. 113p

1974 COM(76)1 final. 15 Jan 1976. 77p

An annual report to the Association Council on the administration of financial and technical cooperation between the European Economic Community and the Associated African States, Madagascar and Mauritius (AASM) provided for in the second Yaoundé Convention (*JO* L282, 28 Dec 1970, pp 2–30). Each report contains an account of activities in this field during the year, including an analysis of the principal financing decisions taken, a description of the projects granted Community aid and comment on associated administrative matters.

633 Memorandum of the Commission to the Council on the future relations between the Community, the present AASM states and the countries in Africa, the Caribbean, the Indian and Pacific Oceans referred to in Protocol No 22 to the Act of Accession

COM(73)500 final. 4 Apr 1973. 62p

EP Report: *Working doc* 388/74. 9 Dec 1974. C. Flesch. 54p

EP Debate: *Annex OJ* No 184, 10 Dec 1974, pp 87–112

EP Resolution: *OJ* C5, 8 Jan 1975, pp 24–27

Protocol 22 of the Treaty of Accession invites 20 independent Commonwealth countries in Africa, the Caribbean and the Pacific to consider various means of regulating their relationship with the Community, an offer which included the opportunity to participate in the negotiations to replace both the second Yaoundé Convention concluded in 1969 with African and Malagasy Associated States (*JO* L282, 28 Dec 1970, pp 2–30) and the more limited Arusha Agreement reached in the same year with Kenya, Tanzania and Uganda (*JO* L282, 28 Dec 1970, pp 55–74), both of which expire on 31 January 1975. In this memorandum the Commission 'sets out ideas for the renewal and enlargement of the Association which it considers would enable the Association to emerge from the forthcoming negotiations not only enlarged but also enriched and strengthened'. Taking account of the lessons drawn from past experience and of the new guidelines laid down in Protocol 22, the Commission explains its views on the main characteristics of a new model for association. Separate sections are devoted to the Commission's proposals on the two essential aspects of an association agreement, namely, trade arrangements and financial and technical cooperation. The Commission also considers cooperation in other fields, notably, the right of establishment and provision of services, investment, external payments and capital movements. In addition, the Commission makes suggestions for adjusting and improving the institutional machinery as defined by the Yaoundé Convention and the Arusha Agreement. The memorandum was published as Supplement 1/73 to the *Bulletin of the European Communities.*

4 Relations between the European Economic Community and the Associated Overseas Countries and Territories (OCT)
COM(75)133 final. 3 Apr 1975. 95p

EP Report: *Working doc* 280/75. 7 Oct 1975. P. Deschamps. 10p
EP Debate: *Annex OJ* No 195, 16 Oct 1975, pp 214–215
EP Resolution: *OJ* C257, 10 Nov 1975, pp 257–258

A document in which the Commission makes proposals for a renewal of the Association of the Overseas Countries and Territories with the EEC due to expire, after a six month extension, on 30 June 1975. The document consists of an explanatory memorandum in which the Commission explains its proposals and its intention to offer terms no less favourable than those embodied in the new Lomé Convention with ACP states, a recommendation for a Council Regulation and a draft Agreement on trade with OCT in products within the ECSC province. On 29 June 1976 the Council took Decision 76/568/EEC on the Association of the OCT with the EEC (*OJ* L176, 1 July 1976, pp 8–97).

5 Commission communication to the Council on the arrangements made to ensure that contracts financed by the European Development Fund are placed on equal terms
COM(75)227 final. 28 May 1975. 95p

The rules governing the allocation of works and supply contracts financed from the European Development Fund insist that, in order to attract competitive quotations and ensure equal access to contracts, invitations to tender should be issued on an international basis. Following similar reports in 1966 (SEC(66)1415) and 1968 (SEC(68)3394), this document contains the Commission's assessment of how existing provisions to assure this objective are operating. In the first chapter the Commission recalls the principles that have been adopted for organizing invitation to tender procedures, and in the following chapter it analyses available statistical data regarding participation and the placement of contracts in order to construct an accurate picture of the performance of present procedures. More detailed information on tenders is available in a series of annual reports from the Commission informing the Council of the results of invitations to tender. The most recent reports are for 1974 (COM(75)140 final), 1975 (COM(76)167), 1976 (COM(77)179 final) and 1977 (COM(78)110 final).

636 International action on stabilization of export earnings
COM(75)294 final. 11 June 1975. 15p

In an earlier communication to the Council, the Commission underlined the importance of international action designed to stabilize the export earnings of developing countries (*see* 647). Taking the case one stage further, the Commission now submits to the Council an analysis of two aspects of a possible system, namely, its coverage and practical arrangements. The Commission explains that the general aim of the scheme would be to minimize the disruptive economic effects of sharp price and quantity fluctuations in the raw materials trade and suggests a number of criteria, supported by statistical tables, to determine which countries and which products should be covered by the scheme. Means of implementing the scheme and the possibility of additional financial help from the International Monetary Fund are also discussed. The memorandum was published as Supplement 6/75 to the *Bulletin of the European Communities*. (*See also* 638.)

637 Commission report to the ACP–EEC Council of Ministers on the administration of financial and technical cooperation in ... under the Lomé Convention
1976   COM(77)111 final. 31 Mar 1977. 53p
1977   COM(78)73 final. 3 Mar 1978. 44p

An annual report on the administration of financial and technical cooperation between the European Economic Community and the ACP states, drawn up by the Commission for presentation to the ACP–EEC Council of Ministers in accordance with Article 41 of the Lomé Convention (*OJ* L25, 30 Jan 1976, pp 2–143). The first report, covering the period from 1 April 1976 to 31 December 1976, contains introductory remarks on the main elements of the Lomé Convention and the general guidelines upon which financial and technical cooperation is based. Both reports review the performance of the administrative machinery and procedural rules established for the management of Community aid and programmes. Moreover, each report describes the way in which the Community aid provided for in the Lomé Convention has been spent during the period under review, with brief descriptions of the projects financed by the European Development Fund and the European Investment Bank, broken down by method of financing and by sector. The report concludes with statistical data on the administration of financial aid during the period under review.

638 Report on the operation during ... of the system for stabilizing export earnings set up by the Decision on the association of the OCT with the EEC
1975   COM(77)274 final. 21 June 1977. 5p
1976   COM(78)188 final. 11 May 1978. 13p

An annual report on the application of the system for stabilizing export earnings in overseas countries and territories, set up by Council Decision 76/568/EEC of 29 June 1976 (*OJ* L176, 1 July 1976, pp 8–97), presented to the Council in accordance with Article 29 of the Internal Agreement on the financing and administration of Community aid (*OJ* L25, 30 Jan 1976, pp 168–177). Each report deals with general developments during the period under review, the results of the application of the system and the economic effects of the transfers. Similar reports are concerned with the operation of the system as regards ACP states (COM(76)656 final). On 13 September 1978 the Commission submitted a brief report on the use of the funds transferred for 1975 and 1976 to the overseas countries and territories under the export earnings stabilization system (COM(78)446 final).

Commission memorandum on the future ACP–EEC negotiations for the renewal of the Lomé Convention
COM(78)47 final. 16 Feb 1978. 24p

The Lomé Convention stipulates that 18 months before its expiry 'the Contracting Parties shall enter into negotiations in order to examine what provisions shall subsequently govern relations between the Community and the Member States and the ACP States' (*OJ* L25, 30 Jan 1976, pp 2–143). This document contains the Commission's thoughts on the shape a new agreement should take. It offers guidelines for the negotiations on such topics as human rights, trade and industrial cooperation, financial and technical cooperation. Extensive and complex negotiations were opened and eventually concluded successfully with the signing of a new ACP–EEC Convention, usually referred to as Lomé II, on 31 October 1979 between the Community, its nine member states and 58 ACP partners. The full text of the Convention was published in a special number of the *Courier*, No 58, Nov 1979.

CHAPTER 15

Development cooperation

Descriptive essay

The Treaty of Rome contains no explicit mandate for an overall development cooperation policy. During the late 1950s Europe had pressing needs of her own and there was little interest in formulating a comprehensive, global policy towards the Third World. As mentioned in the previous chapter, initial emphasis was placed upon assistance to the countries and territories enjoying special relationships with member countries. However, during the 1970s, it was recognized that in addition to essentially regional agreements with a limited number of associated countries, the Community needed to develop a coherent global policy if it was to fulfil in full measure its obligations to the Third World. Consequently, in 1971 the Commission tabled its first overall policy document on development cooperation (*see* 640), quickly followed by an initial action programme (*see* 642). The Commission was given crucial support in its resolve to broaden Community policy by the Heads of State or Government at the Paris summit in 1972, the final declaration of which declares that 'the Community must respond more than ever before to the expectations of all the developing countries'. In 1974 the Commission submitted to the Council a seminal document in which it established guidelines and priorities for Community action on a global scale (*see* 643).

Other documents enumerated in this chapter reflect the nature of the international action taken by the Community in this field. Reference is made to the proposals submitted by the Commission in March 1975 for an action programme to assist non-associated countries (*see* 646), as a result of which a programme of financial and technical aid was established (*see* 651 & 661). The chapter also includes reference to the Commission proposal for a mechanism to allow the joint financing of development projects with non-governmental organizations (*see* 650), and reports on the subsequent implementation of the scheme (*see* 653 & 658). Efforts on the part of the Commission to promote the greater harmonization and coordination of national development cooperation policies are also included (*see* 645 & 652).

Food aid, whose aim is to assist countries hit by natural disasters and soaring raw material costs and to assist economic development, also figures prominently in Community policy. A number of documents concerned mainly with the definition of an overall food aid policy with the aim of establishing continuous programmes, are included (*see* 664, 665 & 666). Finally, two other aspects of development cooperation policy are reflected in the documents listed in this chapter. Firstly, the numerous documents concerned with the work of other inter-governmental organizations emphasize the international context within which development policy is conducted. Just how closely is the EEC involved in the work of other organizations is illustrated in a book called *The European Community, international organisations and multilateral agreements* (cat CB-23-77-017-EN-C) published by the Commission in 1977, which systematically lists and describes the exact nature of the relationship concluded between the Community and other inter-governmental organizations. Secondly, the documents on raw materials (*see* 664 & 647) underline the interdependence of Community and developing countries, a point further emphasized by Michael Noelke in his study of how intertwined are the interests of the Community and developing countries (*see* 660).

General information on the evolution of these and other aspects of development cooperation policy may be obtained from the *General report on the activities of the European Communities* and from the annual reports on development cooperation published by the Commission in response to a request made by the Council in its Resolution of 8 November 1976 on the coordination and harmonization of development cooperation policies, the text of which appears as an annex to the *24th review of the Council's work*. The first report was a retrospective review of events during the period from 1971 to 1976. Entitled *The development cooperation policies of the European Community from 1971 to 1976* (cat CG-22-77-184-EN-C), it deals amongst other things with trade, commodities, the transfer of financial resources, food aid and industrial and technological cooperation. The first of the regular annual series, called *Annual report on the development cooperation policies of the Community and its Member States 1977–1978* (cat CB-25-78-736-EN-C. ISBN 92-825-1024-7), published in 1979, examines the scope, the instruments and the implementation of Community policy during the period under review. The bi-monthly magazine *Courier* contains additional news and comment on all aspects of Community development cooperation policy.

Bibliographical record

Mémorandum de la Commission sur une politique communautaire de coopération au développement: document de synthèse
SEC(71)2700 final. 27 July 1971. 47p

EP Report: *Doc de séance* 63/72. 26 June 1972. H. Vredeling. 82p
EP Debate: *Annexe JO* No 152, 4 July 1972, pp 65–118
EP Resolution: *JO* C82, 26 July 1972, pp 18–21

A major policy initiative from the Commission, the general intention of which is to 'open a debate in depth within the Community institutions and in the Member States on the direction to be taken by a policy of cooperation and the means of implementing it'. Recognizing that the Community has global responsibilities over and above its more specific obligations to associated countries, the Commission sets out a general plan of campaign and means for implementing a common policy for cooperation in development. The reasons why such a policy is so necessary and appropriate at this juncture are explained in an introductory chapter. Further background information follows in the form of a description of the nature of existing cooperative action undertaken by member states with developing countries and of Community policy towards certain geographical regions and on such matters as trade, commercial policy and food aid. Chapter 3 is concerned with the definition of the principles upon which the policy is to be constructed and the guidelines which should determine its main characteristics. In the light of these considerations, Chapter 4 contains an outline of the various types of action to be implemented. The Commission makes it clear that more precise proposals will follow in due course (*see* 642). The memorandum was published as Supplement 5/71 to the *Bulletin of the European Communities* and also in a monograph whose English language version was called *Memorandum on a Community policy on development cooperation* (cat 8375), published by the Commission in 1972. This latter publication also contains associated documents (*see* 641) and a number of statistical studies.

641 Bilan de douze ans de coopération avec les pays en voie de développement
Doc VIII–1/200/71. n.d. 150p

A factual summary document prepared to assist the Commission in its preparation of a policy statement on development cooperation (*see* 640). As its introductory statement indicates, the purpose of this working document is 'to review the efforts made by the Member States and the Community on behalf of the developing countries since 1958, by giving an account of the national policies pursued by the Member States in this connection, followed by a record of the activities of the Community as such on behalf of these countries'. In Chapter 1 the Commission reviews the national policies of member states over the past 12 years towards developing countries, with regard to financial and technical assistance and other specific fields. In Chapter 2 the Commission traces the evolution of relations between the Community and the developing countries, with separate sub-sections on the association agreements, Mediterranean policy, commercial policy, food aid and other activities. The document was reproduced in a volume called *Memorandum on a Community policy on development cooperation* (cat 8375), published by the Commission in 1972.

642 Mémorandum de la Commission sur une politique communautaire de coopération au développement: programme pour une première série d'actions
SEC(72)320 final. 2 Feb 1972. 26p

EP Report: *Doc de séance* 63/72. 26 June 1972. H. Vredeling. 82p
EP Debate: *Annexe JO* No 152, 4 July 1972, pp 65–118
EP Resolution: *JO* C82, 26 July 1972, pp 18–21

In its memorandum on development cooperation, the Commission announced its intention to forward to the Council more concrete proposals at a later stage (*see* 640). This action programme contains an initial set of proposals divided into two broad groups. The first series of measures is designed to favour exports from the developing countries and involve commodity agreements, with particular reference to coffee, cocoa and sugar, trade promotion, the gradual abolition of excise duties on tropical products and the protection of registered designation of origin for foodstuffs. The second group of measures is intended to promote the economic development of developing countries. They include proposals to intensify and regularize public aid efforts and to relax financial conditions attached to aid, the gradual loosening of aid at Community level, the coordination of Community aid and technical assistance and the encouragement of better regional cooperation between developing countries. The action programme was reproduced in a volume whose English language version was called *Memorandum on a Community policy on development cooperation* (cat 8375), published by the Commission in 1972. It also appeared as Supplement 2/72 to the *Bulletin of the European Communities*. In the light of these proposals and particularly of the decisive impetus given to development aid by the Paris summit, the final declaration of which invites Community institutions 'to activate an overall policy of cooperation in development on a world scale' (*Bull EC* 10-1972, pp 14–23), the Council established a Cooperation and Development Group to 'define the principles and aims of a global and consistent cooperation and development policy on a world scale'. In response to the summit mandate, the Council adopted a series of Resolutions and Recommendations during April and July 1974 (*Bull EC* 7/8-1974, pp 14–16).

3 Development aid: 'fresco' of Community action tomorrow
COM(74)1728 final. 30 Oct 1974. 33p

EP Report: *Working doc* 42/75. 28 Apr 1975. G. Bersani. 41p
EP Debate: *Annex OJ* No 190, 30 Apr 1975, pp 77–93
EP Resolution: *OJ* C111, 20 May 1975, pp 22–24

Having submitted to the Council a memorandum on the form of Community development aid already agreed or under consideration (COM(74)800), the Commission now sketches in broad outline its ideas on how the problems arising in developing countries may be tackled in the longer term. Part 1 is concerned with general guidelines, the underlying philosophy of which may be, according to the introduction, summed up in the phrase 'to each according to his needs, by bringing all our means to bear'. The Commission analyses the types of development aid that are required, the methods of promoting development aid and its organization at Community level. Part 2 is devoted to an examination of a number of factors affecting the situation. The Commission draws attention to the fact that there are substantial differences between the various groups of developing countries and takes stock of the various instruments available at Community level, calling for their selective use and adjustment to the needs of particular countries. The document, including its statistical annex, was published as Supplement 8/74 to the *Bulletin of the European Communities*.

4 The Community's supplies of raw materials
COM(75)50. 5 Feb 1975. 31p

EP Report: *Working doc* 585/76. 7 Mar 1977. H. Schwörer. 38p
EP Debate: *Annex OJ* No 216, 19 Apr 1977, pp 78–89
EP Resolution: *OJ* C118, 16 May 1977, pp 26–28

A communication in which the Commission draws attention to Europe's high level of dependence on imported raw materials, its consequent vulnerability to economic dislocation and the need to implement a European supply policy within the

Community. Divided into three main sections the memorandum first pinpoints the main supply problems confronting the Community, classified under such headings as insufficient knowledge of the present and future outlook for each raw material; the prospects for relative or absolute shortages in the medium and long-term; insufficient diversification of sources of supply; the trend towards processing raw materials in their country of origin; the risk of temporary bottlenecks and price fluctuations. A further section consists of a product by product examination of the position as regards certain key groups of raw materials, with particular emphasis upon those whose supply is causing some concern. On the basis of this analysis of the present and future situation, the Commission makes proposals for the preparation of a common Community strategy, involving close consultation and cooperation between national authorities and means for financing the investment needed for exploration and guarantees against the political risks of investment in developing countries. (*See also* 647.)

645 The harmonization and coordination of development cooperation policies within the Community
COM(75)94 final. 5 Mar 1975. 10p

EP Report: *Working doc* 42/75. 28 Apr 1975. G. Bersani. 41p
EP Debate: *Annex OJ* No 190, 30 Apr 1975, pp 77–93
EP Resolution: *OJ* C111, 20 May 1975, pp 22–24

The fact that an overall policy for development cooperation must involve not only the evolution of a common Community policy but also the coordination and gradual alignment of national policies was recognized by the Council in its Resolution on the subject on 16 July 1974. This communication attempts 'to define the object of coordination, to outline a programme of priority issues to be tackled and to define the mechanisms and procedures to be implemented'. The text of the Council Resolution is appended to the communication.

646 Community financial and technical aid to non-associated developing countries 1976–1980
COM(75)95 final. 5 Mar 1975. 11p

EP Report: *Working doc* 133/75. 18 June 1975. K. Härzschel. 17p
EP Debate: *Annex OJ* No 192, 19 June 1975, pp 184–195
EP Resolution: *OJ* C157, 14 July 1975, pp 30–31

A document in which the Commission gives practical effect to general policy statements on financial and technical aid made in its 1974 blueprint on development aid (*see* 643). Proposals are made for the establishment of a five year medium-term programme of measures concerning financial and technical aid from budgetary resources, starting in 1976. The Commission outlines the priority objectives which should determine the application of Community aid and its geographical allocation according to the underlying principles expounded in the 1974 blueprint. The Commission also discusses the ways in which aid can be best channelled to non-associated developing countries, the amount of Community aid to be set aside for non-associated developing countries and the terms and conditions upon which it should be allocated. As the Council has not taken a decision on the programme as a whole, one year programmes have been entered in the Community budget. (*See also* 651).

Communication from the Commission to the Council on raw materials in relations with the developing countries which export raw materials
COM(75)226 final. 21 May 1975. 16p

The problems facing the developing countries which export raw materials are the concern of the Commission in this communication to the Council. In its introductory remarks the Commission emphasizes the need for a clear and constructive Community policy on the matter. It then proceeds to outline the considerations to be taken into account when planning an overall approach to the problem. The Commission then outlines broad lines of action to help developing countries better to resolve their problems in the raw materials sector. Separate sections are devoted to trade cooperation, industrial cooperation, the production of supplies, information and consultation, measures to limit excessive price fluctuations and the stabilization of export earnings. The document, which concludes with an annex summarizing points made in an earlier Commission memorandum (*see* 644), was published in Supplement 6/75 to the *Bulletin of the European Communities*.

Product agreements designed to limit excessive price fluctuations
COM(75)290 final. 11 June 1975. 22p

A communication in which the Commission concentrates its attention upon just one of the package of measures outlined in its communication on raw materials and the developing countries (*see* 647), namely, product agreements designed to limit excessive price fluctuations. The Commission first looks at the conditions which must be met if a product agreement is to have the greatest possible chances of success in stabilizing markets which are marked by frequent and substantial disparities between supply and demand, resulting in sharp price fluctuations. The Commission then analyses the main features of the various methods that have been used to achieve such stabilization, looking in turn at quotas, buffer stocks, long-term contracts, financial mechanisms, combined and other systems. The document ends with a summary of the conclusions reached by the Commission on this first overall examination of the problems of product by product agreements. It was published in Supplement 6/75 to the *Bulletin of the European Communities*.

Effects of developments in the international monetary situation on the working of the European Development Fund
COM(75)428 final. 25 July 1975. 13p

A document in which the Commission makes proposals for alleviating the serious problems in the administration of the European Development Fund caused by the current disruption in the international monetary market.

Relations between the European Communities and the Non-Governmental Organizations (NGOs) specializing in development cooperation
COM(75)504 final. 6 Oct 1975. 8p

A communication in which the Commission draws attention to the scope and immense value of the work undertaken by non-governmental organizations in the field of development cooperation in developing countries, stresses the complementary nature of NGOs and Community development projects and the mutual benefit that would be derived from carrying out joint development projects. To this end the communication outlines proposals for creating a mechanism whereby such cooperation can take place. It briefly describes the conditions and criteria for the selection of projects and arrangements for joint financing and urges the Council to approve that portion of the Commission's 1976 budget proposals earmarked for this purpose. In April 1976 the Council broadly approved the guidelines so allowing the 1976 Community budget to include, for the first time, an appropriation for co-financing projects in developing countries. In March 1976 the Commission submitted to the Council a memorandum on the procedures and general conditions for co-financing contracts with NGOs (SEC(76)1163). (*See also* 653.)

651 Financial and technical aid to non-associated developing countries
COM(76)89. 3 Mar 1976. 6p

Having established a number of principles concerning the provision of technical and financial aid to non-associated developing countries in two earlier documents (*see* 643 & 646), the Commission turns in this communication to the practicalities of expending the rather modest sum of 20 million units of account provided in the 1976 Community budget for that purpose. The Commission confirms its earlier sentiments on who should benefit from the aid and the criteria upon which aid should be based. In view of the limited amount of aid available, the Commission makes suggestions as to the priorities to be attached to the selection of projects. It also deals with such practical aspects as the procedures for selection and the terms upon which aid is to be granted. In 1977 a sum of 45 million units of account was entered in the Community budget and in 1978 70 million European units of account. (*See also* 661.)

652 Harmonization and coordination of development cooperation policies within the Community
COM(76)358 final. 7 July 1976. 12p

Taking account of reactions to and developing the ideas contained in an earlier communication on the same subject (*see* 645), the Commission seeks in this document to increase the effectiveness of the development cooperation policies pursued in member states by their closer coordination and alignment. The communication contains proposals whose aim is gradually to bring closer together member states' and Community policies in the field of development cooperation, with the final objective being to establish the principle of overall Community responsibility for development cooperation. At the same time the Commission puts forward proposals to improve the exchange of information between member states and the Community, giving particular prominence and support to a proposal from the German Government for the preparation of an annual report on the development cooperation policies pursued in member states and the Community.

The Commission concludes with practical arrangements and a time-table for the implementation of the proposed measures.

Report on relations with non-governmental organizations (NGOs) active in the field of development, with special reference to the co-financing of projects
COM(77)83 final. 18 Mar 1977. 46p

A report on the first full year of collaboration with NGOs in the co-financing of projects in developing countries, made possible by the appropriation in the 1976 budget for that purpose (*see* 650). The Commission recalls the procedures and conditions laid down for the co-financing of projects, analyses and makes comments upon the projects carried out so far. Detailed factual information on each of the projects is also provided in tabular form. The Commission also takes the opportunity to examine the trend of relations with NGOs in other important spheres, notably, development education and the coordination of relations with NGOs. The document concludes with a substantial number of tables providing factual information on projects already undertaken. (*See also* 658.)

Reciprocal implications of the Community's development cooperation policy and its other policies
SEC(77)2060 final. 14 June 1977. 16p

An initial discussion document in which the Commission discusses the ways in which the instruments of development cooperation policy interrelate with other Community policies. Particular attention is devoted to possible conflicts of interest between trade cooperation with developing countries and the Community's internal objectives, in the areas of employment, regional development and industrial restructuring.

Commission communication to the Council on the coordination of the actions of the Community and the Member States in emergency and humanitarian aid
COM(77)382 final. 28 July 1977. 6p

A communication in which the Commission outlines a mechanism for strengthening the coherence of Community and national aid in the event of natural disaster or similar event. The Commission considers means for improving the coordination of the immediate response to a disaster when speed is of the essence and during the second, short-term phase when there must be concerted efforts to restore the affected country to normality. The Commission also considers the administrative implications of its proposals for improved coordination and their practical operation. At its meeting on 28 November 1977 the Council gave its assent to the practical procedures for organizing this type of coordination.

Policies of the Member States of the Community as regards migration with respect to non-member countries and nationals of non-member countries resident on Community territory
Doc V/867/78. n.d. 40p

An investigation into the policies pursued by member states as regards the inflow of foreign labour, a particularly important topic now that the high economic growth that allowed foreign labour to be easily absorbed in considerable quantities during the 1960s has been replaced by a much less favourable economic climate. In Part 1 the Commission looks at the position adopted by member states and the steps they have taken with regard to labour from non-member countries and their international commitments and policy. Part 2 is concerned with the migration of labour between Community and non-Community countries.

657 Need for Community action to encourage European investment in developing countries and guidelines for such action
COM(78)23 final. 30 Jan 1978. 13p

A communication in which the Commission presses the Council to adopt guidelines for Community action to encourage European investment in developing countries. The Commission draws attention to the factors that have tended to discourage investment in developing countries and to the importance of increasing investment flows for the economies of both developing countries and Community countries. Having established the case for action at the Community level, the Commission then proceeds to describe the two Community instruments it envisages as a means of improving the investment climate in developing countries, namely, the agreements on basic rules for investment protection and the conclusion of specific protection agreements, guarantees and promotion measures for projects of particular economic interest.

658 Report on relations with non-governmental organizations (NGOs) active in the field of development, with special reference to the co-financing of projects (1977)
COM(78)75 final. 3 Mar 1978. 46p

A report on the collaboration between the Community and NGOs in the joint financing of development projects in developing countries, allowed for under item 945 of the 1977 Community budget. The report reviews the rules under which joint projects are funded and the use of the allocated budget in 1977. The report also deals with other important aspects of cooperation with NGOs, notably, the prospects for cooperation in educating European public opinion in development matters and the coordination of NGO–Community relations. The report concludes with a report of a meeting between Commission staff, representatives from member states and NGOs and a number of tables summarizing the projects undertaken during the year under review. A similar report was undertaken in 1977 (*see* 653).

659 Cooperation with developing countries in the field of energy
COM(78)355 final. 31 July 1978. 18p

See 307.

660 Dossier on Europe—Third World interdependence
Doc 481/X/78. 28 Aug 1978. 402p

A substantial report prepared by Michael Noelke, from the Development Division of Directorate-General X (Information), in which he uses official statistical sources to illustrate the interdependence between the Community and the Third World. Liberally provided with tables, graphs and diagrams of all kinds, the report makes use of a wealth of statistical and factual evidence to show, for instance, the extent of Community dependence on external sources for energy supplies and raw materials and for markets for its goods. Mr Noelke also analyses the balance of trade between Community countries and the Third World, the industrialization and the purchasing power of the Third World, as well as its access to public aid and to external financial markets. The study was later published under the title *Europe—Third World interdependence: facts and figures* (cat CB-NX-78-002-EN-C. ISBN 92-825-0919-2) as number two in the *Dossiers: general development series*.

General guidelines for financial and technical aid for non-associated developing countries in 1979
COM(78)472 final. 25 Sept 1978. 8p

A document in which the Commission presents its views on the general guidelines which should govern the Community's 1979 financial and technical aid programme to non-associated developing countries. The Commission first draws lessons from the experience gained since the inception of the policy in 1976. It then proceeds to establish general guidelines for use in determination of aid for 1979, with particular reference to the size of the amount to be kept in reserve for emergencies, the geographical allocation of the aid, the proportion of aid to be reserved for regional cooperation, the distribution of aid according to various economic sectors and the proportion to be allocated to projects jointly financed with other aid organizations. The document concludes with a statistical table showing disbursements up to the end of July 1978 according to the 1976 and 1977 programmes. (*See also* 651.)

Development cooperation and the observance of certain international standards governing working conditions
COM(78)492 final. 10 Nov 1978. 16p

A series of guidelines for promoting social progress in developing countries and for establishing a 'link between the advantages offered by the Community (particularly in the commercial field) and the observance of certain basic international standards governing working conditions'. Anxious to promote the social objectives of development and to deny unfair commercial advantage to those who maintain inhumane working conditions, the Commission takes four fundamental labour standards from the many covered by the conventions of the International Labour Organisation and uses them as the basis for a text on minimum labour standards. The Commission also considers the means of applying the text and the procedures and arrangements for its implementation in trade and in the field of technical and financial assistance.

FOOD AID

L'aide alimentaire de la C.E.E. aux pays en voie de développement: problèmes posés et possibilités réelles

Doc 7829-1/VI/61. July 1963. 2 vols, 78p, 303p

A detailed study of food aid from the EEC to developing countries carried out at the invitation of the Commission by a panel of experts consisting of Professors M. Cépede, A. Maugini and H. Wilbrandt. The purpose of the study was to gather all the information necessary to assess the possibilities of distributing EEC agricultural surpluses in the form of food aid, to establish the limits of such outlets and to place this specific form of aid in the general context of economic assistance to developing countries. After a summary, the report proper opens with a section concerned with the food needs of developing countries as far as they may be deduced from available data. The panel of experts look at the problems of nutrition, the food deficit in the countries investigated and at the choice of products to be made available in the form of food aid. The experts then turn to the question of disposing of surplus agricultural products to developing countries, with particular reference to the problems that must be overcome. A series of annexes contain a number of detailed regional surveys upon which the general report is based. Both report and annexes were published in a volume of the same title published in 1965 as number 14 in the series *Etudes—Série agriculture* (cat 8102).

664 Food crisis and the Community's responsibilities towards developing countries
COM(74)300 final. 6 Mar 1974. 8p

EP Report: *Working doc* 171/74. 9 July 1974. H. Seefeld. 32p
EP Debate: *Annex OJ* No 179, 12 July 1974, pp 290–307
EP Resolution: *OJ* C93, 7 Aug 1974, pp 88–90
ESC Opinion: *OJ* C125, 16 Oct 1974, pp 23–28

A brief document in which the Commission draws urgent attention to the seriousness of the food crisis facing developing countries in terms of both a general scarcity of basic foodstuffs and their high prices and the Community's responsibilities towards the victims of this crisis. The memorandum is divided into two parts. In the first the Commission examines the nature of the crisis, its symptoms, its short and long-term causes and its consequences for developing countries. In the second part the Commission considers the contribution the Community, as a large producer of foodstuffs, can play in assisting the poorer developing countries, with regard to the encouragement of greater market stability, the availability of food supplies and financial assistance. The Commission also establishes certain general principles for implementing a more ambitious food aid programme and makes quantitative proposals for a first three year food aid programme to replace existing national and Community action. More detailed information on food aid policy is contained in a supplementary memorandum submitted to the Council as part of the same document (*see* 665).

665 Memorandum on food aid policy of the European Economic Community
COM(74)300 final. 6 Mar 1974. 32p

EP Report: *Working doc* 171/74. 9 July 1974. H. Seefeld. 32p
EP Debate: *Annex OJ* No 179, 12 July 1974, pp 290–307
EP Resolution: *OJ* C93, 7 Aug 1974, pp 88–90

ESC Opinion: *OJ* C125, 16 Oct 1974, pp 23–28

Having stressed the urgent need for a coherent food aid policy at Community level in another memorandum contained in this document (*see* 664), the Commission now 'elaborates the reasons and suggests the general principles along which such a policy could be formulated and implemented'. The Commission first puts the case for adopting a coherent Community food aid policy, with reference to the rising food aid needs of developing countries, the role of food aid in economic development, the deficiencies of the present EEC system and the Community's capacity for expanding food aid. Part 2 outlines the salient features of the proposed policy. It describes the characteristics of the Community's proposed commitments, the principles of food aid use in recipient countries as well as distribution, procedural and management aspects. The document concludes with a proposal for a first indicative three year programme beginning with the 1974/75 season. At its meeting of 15 to 17 July 1974 the Council rejected the concept of a three-year programme. No action was taken until 9 June 1976 when the Council adopted the principle of medium-term planning (*see* 666).

3 year indicative food aid programme, 1977–1979
COM(76)425 final. 14 Sept 1976. 15p

EP Report: *Working doc* 407/76. 15 Nov 1976. J. B. Nielsen. 19p
EP Debate: *Annex OJ* No 209, 19 Nov 1976, pp 243–246
EP Resolution: *OJ* C293, 13 Dec 1976, pp 72–73

Consequent upon a Council Decision of 9 June 1976 to accept the concept of medium-term planning of food aid as originally suggested by the Commission in March 1974 (*see* 665), this document contains proposals for a programme running from 1977 to 1979. The Commission sketches the general features of the proposed scheme and indicates the size and nature of the programme for each of three main food products, namely cereals, skimmed milk powder and butter oil. A series of statistical and financial tables complete the document. However, as a result of a marked lack of enthusiasm for the implications of a medium-term food aid programme, the Commission subsequently withdrew the proposal and decided to continue to submit annual programmes.

Nutritional and developmental perspectives for dairy products in the third world
COM(77)540 final. 31 Oct 1977. 10p

EP Report: *Working doc* 492/77. 19 Jan 1978. H. Aigner. 45p
EP Debate: *Annex OJ* No 225, 20 Jan 1978, pp 236–241
EP Resolution: *OJ* C36, 13 Feb 1978, pp 54–56

A communication in which the Commission stresses the vital contribution dairy products can play in developing countries by alleviating chronic malnutrition and protein deficiency. The Commission reviews the efforts being made to modernize and develop dairy industries in developing countries and demonstrates the role food aid can play in stimulating dairy development. The Commission concludes with general recommendations for the adoption of a more rational approach to Community aid involving direct assistance to specific projects in recipient countries.

668 **Commission communication to the Council on the supply of food aid in the form of skimmed-milk powder and butter oil to India for the second phase of 'Operation Flood'**
COM(77)541 final. 31 Oct 1977. 17p

'Operation Flood' was launched by the Indian Government in 1970 with the purpose of promoting rural development, particularly in the dairy sector. Although its main aims were achieved by 1977 the Indian Government decided to launch a second phase for the years 1978 to 1985, for which it requested direct Community food aid. In this communication the Commission provides background information on the project and on the role food aid would play before outlining its views on what response should be given to the request. The document concludes with a number of draft instruments to give effect to the Commission's recommendations. At its meeting on 25 April 1978 the Council agreed to assist the scheme.

Inter-governmental Organizations

669 **Rapport sur la deuxième session de la Conférence des Nations Unies sur le Commerce et le Développement (La Nouvelle Delhi—1er février–29 mars 1968)**
SEC(68)2581 final. 30 July 1968. 123p

The Community and all member states individually took part in the United Nations Conference on Trade and Development (UNCTAD) which held its Second Session in New Delhi from 1 February to 29 March 1968. This report from the Commission delegation reviews the work of the Conference, with particular emphasis upon the Community contribution. It describes the decisions of the Conference, the problems with which it was concerned and the joint proposals submitted by the EEC states on commodities. A series of annexes contains the texts of resolutions adopted by the Conference, proposals presented by the six Community countries and declarations made in the name of the EEC.

670 **La troisième Conférence des Nations Unies sur le Commerce et le Développement**
SEC(72)800 final. 3 Mar 1972. 102p

EP Report: *Doc de séance* 278/71. 13 Mar 1972. P.-B. Cousté. 71p
EP Debate: *Annexe JO* No 148, 14 Mar 1972, pp 33–59
EP Resolution: *JO* C36, 12 Apr 1972, pp 23–26

A detailed memorandum prepared by the Commission in which it analyses the main problems that will be examined at the forthcoming third United Nations Conference on Trade and Development, held in Santiago, Chile from 13 April to 21 May 1972. Separate chapters deal with the main points on the conference agenda, including raw materials, manufactured goods, the promotion of exports from developing countries to member states and special measures in favour of least developed countries. (*See also* 671.)

Préparation de la 3ème Conférence des Nations-Unies sur le Commerce et le Développement
SEC(72)931 final. 8 Mar 1972. 11p

EP Report: *Doc de séance* 278/71. 13 Mar 1972. P.-B. Cousté. 71p
EP Debate: *Annexe JO* No 148, 14 Mar 1972, pp 33–59
EP Resolution: *JO* C36, 12 Apr 1972, pp 23–26

A memorandum in which the Commission outlines the stance it thinks the Community should take at the forthcoming third United Nations Conference on Trade and Development (UNCTAD), held in Santiago, Chile from 13 April to 21 May 1972. The Commission outlines the context within which the Conference will meet and its prospects for success. It then proceeds to give its opinion on the role the Community should play in the deliberations and the position it should adopt on each of the principal agenda items, which are examined in more detail in an associated document (*see* 670).

Second General Conference of the United Nations Industrial Development Organization (UNIDO) to be held in Lima from 12 to 26 March 1975: preparation of the Community contribution
COM(75)45 final. 12 Feb 1975. 51p

The aim of the Lima Conference was to formulate an international declaration on industrial development and cooperation and to draw up an action programme to assist developing countries to speed up the process of industrialization. This document was prepared by the Commission for the guidance of the Community and member states in their participation in the Conference. The document opens with background information on the aim and origination of the conference before moving on to an assessment of what is at stake and the role the Community should adopt. The document includes a chapter in which the Commission suggests a number of general guidelines for industrial cooperation to be included in the statement to be made by Community representatives at the Conference. The Commission then subjects to detailed scrutiny the Group of 77's draft Declaration and Plan of Action, the text of which is annexed to the document.

Seventh Special Session of the UN General Assembly and mid-term review and appraisal of the International Development Strategy for the Second UN Development Decade
COM(75)225 final. 4 June 1975. 62p

EP Report: *Working doc* 507/75. 6 Feb 1976. L. Krall. 54p
EP Debate: *Annex OJ* No 199, 11 Feb 1976, pp 130–157
EP Resolution: *OJ* C53, 8 Mar 1976, pp 17–18

The purpose of this communication is to provide the Council with all the necessary information to allow the Community to play an active and constructive role in the mid-term review and appraisal of the International Development Strategy for the Second UN Development Decade to be undertaken by the Seventh Special Session of the United Nations General Assembly. It also contains the Commission's recommendations for presenting a united front on the issues to be discussed. The document opens with a brief historical account of the evolution of the International Development Strategy and its antecedents. The Commision then proceeds to delineate general guidelines for a constructive Community contribution to the forthcoming review before devoting separate sections to each of the major topics upon which a positive Community contribution can be made, namely, raw materials, international trade, industrial cooperation and the transfer of technology, the transfer of financial resources and the international monetary system. A series of annexes includes an assessment of the progress made by developing countries during the first half of the Second Development Decade, and a review of the action taken by the Community to implement measures called for by the International Development Strategy during this period. The document was published as Supplement 6/75 to the *Bulletin of the European Communities*.

674 Commission communication to the Council on the future of the dialogue begun at the Paris Preparatory Meeting (7 to 16 April 1975)
COM(75)293 final. 11 June 1975. 12p

An outline of the approach the Commission thinks should be taken if the dialogue between industrialized and developing countries set in motion by the Paris Preparatory Meeting of the Conference on International Economic Cooperation (CIEC) in April 1975, but adjourned without agreement, is resumed. The Commission proposes that the Community should speak with one voice on such matters as raw materials, energy and development policy. A fresh preparatory meeting of CIEC, held in October 1975, was more successful (*Bull EC* 10-1975, pp 6–12) and resulted in the first Conference on International Economic Cooperation (*Bull EC* 12-1975, pp 11–17). (*See also* 323.)

675 Preparation for the U.N. Conference on Trade and Development (Meeting of the UNCTAD Trade and Development Board 8th–19th March, 1976)
COM(76)39 final. 4 Feb 1976. 23p

EP Report: *Working doc 333/76.* 11 Oct 1976. P. Deschamps. 70p
EP Debate: *Annex OJ* No 207, 12 Oct 1976, pp 24–38
EP Resolution: *OJ* C259, 4 Nov 1976, pp 13–14

A document prepared by the Commission for the guidance of Community representatives at the annual meeting of the Trade and Development Board to be held from 8 to 19 March 1976 with the object of considering the draft agenda for the forthcoming United Nations Conference on Trade and Development. The Commission first draws attention to those agenda items likely to be of major significance and then proceeds to define overall Community objectives and the tactics that might be employed at the Trade and Development Board. A substantial annex outlines the major features of existing Community positions on agenda items.

676 Preparation for the U.N. Conference on Trade and Development, Nairobi, 5th–28th May 1976
COM(76)139 final. 31 Mar 1976. 13p

EP Report: *Working doc 333/76.* 11 Oct 1976. P. Deschamps. 70p

EP Debate: *Annex OJ* No 207, 12 Oct 1976, pp 24–38
EP Resolution: *OJ* C259, 4 Nov 1976, pp 13–14

A document in which the Commission takes account of the outcome of the preparatory Trade and Development Board meeting in Geneva (*see* 675) and sets out 'the area and scope of decisions to be taken by the Community' at the fourth United Nations Conference on Trade and Development, to be held in Nairobi from 5 to 28 May 1976. Having first reflected on the results of the Trade and Development Board meeting, the Commission then submits a number of broad ideas on the major issues likely to come before the Conference and guidelines on the common objectives and strategy to be adopted by the Community at the Conference. Annexes contain details of the Conference procedures, time-table and agenda.

Forthcoming international meetings under UNCTAD in connection with the North–South dialogue—guidelines

COM(78)22 final. 25 Jan 1978. 17p

If the Community is to continue to play a leading role in the discussions concerning the North–South dialogue between industrialized and developing countries then it must prepare its position on a number of urgent matters. In this communication the Commission presents its ideas on the approach the Community should adopt on a number of key issues facing the international community in the near future. In particular, it outlines the position the Community should adopt on such matters as the Common Fund, the developing countries' debt problems and the problems of the least developed countries.

The Community and the preparation of a new international development strategy—guidelines

COM(78)421 final. 8 Sept 1978. 15p

A general discussion document in which the Commission reviews the achievements of the United Nations' Second Development Decade and the state of relations between industrialized and developing countries, on the basis of which it advances a number of general considerations upon which the Community might base its approach to the United Nations' new International Development Strategy for the 1980s. The communication opens with a critical assessment of the results achieved during the Second Development Decade and an appraisal of North–South relations at the end of the 1970s. The Commission then proceeds to sketch out the broad lines of the position the Community should take on the new strategy for the 1980s on the basis of experience of developments during the 1970s.

Preparation of the United Nations Conference on an international code of conduct on transfer of technology (Geneva, 16 October – 10 November 1978)

COM(78)447 final. 20 Sept 1978. 16p

A communication in which the Commission presents proposals for a common position to be adopted by the Community and member states at the United Nations conference, to be held under the auspices of UNCTAD, in Geneva, from 16 October to 10 November 1978 in order to negotiate an international code of conduct on transfer of technology. An introductory section traces the historical background to the conference, in which the Commission urges the Community to define a common position with regard to certain key problems and general tactics. The Commission then examines more closely certain problems concerning the compatibility of the proposed code with Community law and makes proposals for a Community position.

Indexes

The following pages contain three separate indexes: a Documents Index, a Subject Index and an Author/Title Index. Documents which form the subject of main entries and other Commission documents cited in the text are listed in numerical order in the Documents Index and alphabetically by subject in the Subject Index. Individual authors, the chairmen and members of expert working parties, and the rapporteurs of European Parliament committees are listed in the Author/Title Index, which also includes the titles of publications cited in the text but excludes the titles of documents.

Documents index

This index lists in numerical order those documents which form the subject of main entries and other Commission documents cited in the text. References are to entry numbers.

COM documents

COM(60)16 final,   1
VII/COM(60)76 final,   410
COM(60)105,   355
I/COM(61)48,   602
VII/COM(61)50 final,   412
V/COM(61)101 final,   506
VIII/COM(61)110 final,   631
I/COM(62)10 final,   604
VII/COM(62)88 final,   413
I/COM(62)276 final,   74
COM(62)300,   3
V/COM(62)321 final,   565
V/COM(63)14 final,   125
V/COM(63)111 final,   507
I/COM(63)115,   605
VII/COM(63)165,   413
VII/COM(63)166,   413
VII/COM(63)167,   413
VII/COM(63)168,   413
VII/COM(63)169,   413
II/COM(63)216 final,   20
III/COM(63)261 final,   606
II/COM(63)271 final,   61
V/VI/COM(63)353 final,   357
VI/COM(63)423 final,   359
VI/COM(63)424 final,   358
V/COM(64)11 final,   565
I/COM(64)51 final,   607

I/COM(64)53 final,   608
VII/COM(64)97 final,   414
VI/COM(64)175,   360
V/COM(64)255 final,   566
V/COM(65)28 final,   486
V/COM(65)270 final,   565
COM(65)320 final,   364
COM(66)27 final,   222
COM(66)60 final,   367
COM(66)82 final,   365
COM(66)170,   64
COM(66)170 annexes,   65
COM(66)250,   398
COM(67)256 final,   368
COM(67)750,   619
COM(68)138 final,   130
COM(68)148 final,   66
COM(68)160,   236
COM(67)210,   620
COM(68)288 final,   399
COM(68)600,   75
COM(68)800,   238
COM(68)801,   236
COM(68)1000,   369–371
COM(68)1040,   275
COM(69)148,   172
COM(69)150,   46
COM(69)200,   131

SEC documents

Directorate-General documents

High Authority documents

Euratom documents

Miscellaneous

Subject index

This index refers alphabetically by subject to those documents which form the subject of main entries and also other Commission documents cited in the text. References are to entry numbers.

Author/title index

This index lists individual authors, the chairmen and members of expert working parties, and the rapporteurs of European Parliament committees. It also includes the titles of publications cited but excludes the titles of documents; citations for the *Bulletin of the European Communities, General report on the activities of the European Communities* and *Official journal of the European Communities* are only given where the actual nature of these publications is described. References in italic type are to page numbers, and all other references are to entry numbers.